"This is a story of a bold vision and an even bolder set of leaders that ultimately established 3D design as we know it. More remarkable than the accolades, Emmy and Academy Awards this team has earned, is the story of how a small and passionate team transformed the world of gaming, entertainment, and digital experiences. Seb has penned a book with many lessons and inspirations for us all."

- **Scott Belsky**, Founder, Behance, Chief Strategy Officer & EVP, Design & Emerging Products, Adobe

"A page-turning allegory of deep humanity and intrigue for both right-brained and left-brained creators, artists, and entrepreneurs. A stunning account of the people who made Allegorithmic, from its deep technical roots in Clermont-Ferrand pondering fractal generation and free will, through an intimate first-hand view of the emerging 3D industry, and ultimately, the acquisition by Adobe."

- **Joshua St. John**, Director of Product Management, HP

"Within every success story lies a real passion and a visionary man. Sebastien Deguy is one the few people who master technology, creativity, and entrepreneurship. This book tells his story and how he created tools that are widely recognized in the video game, animation and VFX industries."

- **Xavier Bec,** Head of R&D, Illumination Studios Paris

"Similarly to "NVIDIAns", the individuals at Allegorithmic have always been putting customers first. Sébastien's unique combination of art and technology skills but also his capability to attract and keep talents around him and to lead them, helped turning a small French startup into the team driving Adobe's 3D future."

- **Guillaume Polaillon,** Product Line Manager at NVIDIA

"While working at Autodesk and Epic Games, I had the privilege of observing Sébastien and his team's rise to industry leadership, transforming Allegorithmic and later Adobe into critical players in 3D content creation. It's a story worth reading!"

- **Marc Petit,** 35 years in Computer Graphics, Ex Machina, TDI, Softimage, Discreet Logic (then Autodesk M&E), Fabric Engine and Epic Games, now supporting the community to create an open and fair foundation for the next iteration of the internet as it embraces real time 3D and gaming technologies

"Trusting your gut feelings, surrounding yourself with the right people, and relentlessly pursuing your beliefs are key themes in this book. Creating real value for customers and engaging them in the process demands time and effort but yields long-term rewards. Building a company is a journey, a way of life fueled by honest passion rather than a quick route to wealth. When faced with decisions like selling your company to a major player, trusting your instincts remains crucial. I highly recommend this book to anyone considering starting a tech company in the 3D space or those who have witnessed this industry's evolution firsthand, as I have."

- **Martin Enthed,** Innovation Manager at IKEA | Khronos Vice President | Keynote Speaker on 3D and Spatial Computing

"Sébastien had a vision that combined both of his passions for art and science, in service of solving a creative problem. With Allegorithmic over the years, Sébastien and his team stuck with that vision, it is still at the core of the Substance product today. For all the companies that are trying to harness the power of AI or any new tech – read this book and start with passion and a problem that you want to solve, don't start with just an exciting technology."

- **Rick Stringfellow,** Fellow, Head of Visual Content, Electronic Arts

"My profession and passion only exist thanks to all the extraordinary individuals who contributed to the story of Allegorithmic. In this book, Sébastien shares the incredible and deeply human adventure that led to the creation of industry defining products. Substance changed the life of many artists, me included."

- **Kelly Recco,** Material Artist, DON'T NOD Montréal

"Substance has long revolutionized material art, demonstrating the power of aligning principles, architecture, and community. Even now, it excites me more than any other software when I think about future pipelines. I firmly believe the best is yet to come as workflows fully harness the deterministic power of the engine and ecosystem."

- **Bradford Smith,** Senior Technical, Materials, & Environment Artist at Crystal Dynamics - previously at Epic Games, Naughty Dog, EA

Allegorithmic

Allegorithmic: The Company That Brought Substance to the World of 3D explores the journey of Allegorithmic, the software company behind Substance, a suite of tools that revolutionized texturing in computer graphics. This engaging narrative by Sébastien Deguy, the visionary founder and CEO of the company, chronicles the growth of Allegorithmic from its inception as a small startup to becoming a leader in digital content creation, pivotal in shaping the visual aesthetics of video games and films.

The book highlights key technological innovations and strategic decisions that propelled the company forward, offering a detailed look at the challenges and triumphs of developing cutting-edge software solutions while building a team attached to its strong values and passion for digital artists.

Key Features:

- Provides a detailed history of Allegorithmic, a company at the forefront of technological innovation in procedural textures and 3D content.
- Covers significant technical ground, discussing complex environments, procedural textures, and software development, while also delving into the creative aspects of these technologies.
- Spans the growth of a startup into a major player in the tech industry, providing insights into business strategies, team building, and international expansion.
- Reflects on the cultural shifts within the company and the broader industry, offering lessons on adapting to technological advancements and market demands.

Ideal for tech enthusiasts, artists, and entrepreneurs, this deep book provides a comprehensive overview of the creativity and perseverance required to influence and lead in the tech industry.

Sébastien Deguy is a prominent figure in the field of 3D Computer Graphics and Immersive technology. He founded Allegorithmic in 2003, building upon his doctoral thesis which he had completed at the turn of 2002. Under his leadership, Allegorithmic developed the Substance tool suite and became a market leader in the production workflows for various industries, including Video Games, Film, TV, Industrial Design, and Marketing. In January 2019, when Allegorithmic was acquired by Adobe, Deguy assumed the role of Vice President of 3D & Immersive at Adobe. His work has significantly influenced the development and application of 3D technology across multiple sectors, and he has been awarded a Scientific and Technical Achievement Award by the Academy in 2023 for his contribution to the art and science of movie making.

Allegorithmic

The Company That Brought Substance to the World of 3D

Sébastien Deguy

CRC Press
Taylor & Francis Group
Boca Raton London New York

CRC Press is an imprint of the
Taylor & Francis Group, an **informa** business

Design cover image: Andrew Calnen, based on art by Andrei Zelenco, using exclusively the FX-Maps function in Substance Designer.

First edition published 2025
by CRC Press
2385 NW Executive Center Drive, Suite 320, Boca Raton FL 33431

and by CRC Press
4 Park Square, Milton Park, Abingdon, Oxon, OX14 4RN

CRC Press is an imprint of Taylor & Francis Group, LLC

This document was typeset with the help of KOMA-Script and LaTeX using the kaobook class.

English translation (from French) by Valeria Gerontopoulous and Paul Gresty, additional editing by Paul Gresty.

ISBN: 978-1-032-87820-1 (hbk)
ISBN: 978-1-032-87818-8 (pbk)
ISBN: 978-1-003-53462-4 (ebk)

DOI: 10.1201/9781003534624

Typeset in TexGyrePagellaX-Regular font
by KnowledgeWorks Global Ltd.

Publisher's note: This book has been prepared from camera-ready copy provided by the authors.

To Laëtitia

To the whole Allegorithmic team

Table of Contents

Table of Illustrations

Part I

Preamble and Introduction

Preface: An accident

Memento

In the very early hours of a Sunday morning, my father got a phone call from his local hospital, asking him to come. I had received a significant head injury.

He found me lying on a stretcher, waiting for a brain MRI. I was awake, and spoke to him.

"What happened?" I asked.

"You were in a car accident."

"Was anybody hurt?"

"No, just you," he told me. "They're going to take a look at your head injury."

"It's always just me who gets hurt," I said, trying to make a joke to break the tension of the moment, and to put on a brave face. "I have terrible luck."

We stopped talking there. Three minutes passed. And then I spoke again.

"What happened?" I asked.

"Well... You were in a car accident," my father answered.

"Was anyone hurt?"

"No, just you. They're going to look at your injury soon."

I suppose it seemed an appropriate moment to make a joke. "It's always just me who gets hurt. I have terrible luck."

Silence between us, a little longer. And then, a few minutes later, I asked:

"What happened?"

Again, I asked the same questions. And I made the exact same joke.

And then again, three minutes later, joke and all.

And again, three minutes after that...

Introduction

Ictus

I have no memory of my accident in August 1995. I've pieced it together and related it in the Preface based on what I've since been told.

I later learned that following the accident I suffered from a 'post-traumatic transient amnesia,' a loss of memory resulting from a violent impact to the head and swelling of the brain.[1] This swelling, in the restricted space of the skull, disrupts or even blocks the 'circulation of information' between short-term memory and long-term memory, located in different areas of the brain. This blockage made it impossible for me to remember my father's answers to my questions, causing me to ask these identical questions again and again, a few minutes apart. I was unable to store the previous information established, as my short-term 'buffer' was full. . .

1: I relate here what I understood, without being a specialist.

It was a benign but disturbing condition which made me experience the same situation as Leonard, the main character in Christopher Nolan's film *Memento*. For about 24 hours, I ceaselessly repeated the same questions to my father and the hospital staff, and then to my neighbor in the next bed in the hospital, who I must have driven crazy. The injury also made me lose a chunk of my memories, for a period of around 6 months, at a guess. For instance, I learned a second time, and with the same joy, that I'd successfully obtained my diploma a few weeks before the accident.

The scariest moment was when the swelling began to decrease, and connections began to rebuild themselves little by little. This was when I realized, in a blurry, cottony way, without being quite certain, that I'd asked the same question a thousand times. . . and that I didn't yet know if I was on the way to recovery, or whether the accident would have any long-term after-effects.

But the biggest impact of this event was neither physical nor psychological. Rather, it was essentially meta-physical, even philosophical: when I learned about the endless, looping conversation I'd had with my father, I become aware that, in a given environment, when the same or sufficiently close stimuli were regularly provided, my brain produced exactly one response, systematically, without any exception to the rule: I always asked the same sequence of questions, always used the same words. I always made the same final joke.

This deterministic response, this predictability, was therefore the biggest shock for me. Are we, humans, globally predictable, incapable of free will, the playthings of our environment and our cerebral 'wiring,' as well as the movements of the elementary particles which compose and surround us? Was I, like everyone else? The visceral realization of this fact, deep within my core, was a profound shock, which would remain with me for the rest of my life.

Once I'd physically recovered, I become interested in this subject of randomness. Sometime later, I asked one of my university professors, the probabilistic mathematician Albert Benassi,[2] "Does random chance

2: See Chapter 1

actually exist?" To this he answered, "Ah, you finally asked me the right question. . . Welcome!"

This quest, to understand or even master chance, would lead me to create Allegorithmic. This is the adventure that I tell in this book—a recollection.

Memory

I've divided this book into seven main parts, which correspond to the seven main periods of the life of Allegorithmic, notably including pivots or major events, recounted as I remember them. Each part is then divided, classically, into chapters and subsections, with accompanying images where possible.

These images include, in some cases, full-page promotional ads for our products throughout the years. In other cases, I've integrated or cited examples of artwork created by some of the most outstanding artists using our tools, a testament to the incredible talent of our users and the growing impact over the years of our tools on this artistic form that is '3D.' Finally, at the end of each main part, I present the 'milestones' of each period, which provide information on the company in terms of its human, commercial, and financial development.

The text contains numerous notes in the margins, which provide details, images, and anecdotes around a fact described in the main text.[3]

3: I've always liked these 'books within books'; they bring a richness to the story which is a reflection of reality, I believe—a complexity potentially beyond that which the main text alone might provide.

I've added notes entitled 'In retrospect,' to certain passages, the aim of which is to provide a point of view some years after the events recounted, with a knowledge of the at times far-reaching consequences of those events. Some of these fragments of memory make me smile now, others are striking, *a posteriori*, because of their impact and their accuracy, even though at the moment they might have seemed inconsequential.

Substance

Before getting into the main text, it seems important to specify here that this book is anything but a management lesson or even a personal development manual. Rather, it is rich and all-encompassing—but it does not present a clear and perfectly developed thesis with well-organized takeaways, or any sort of clinical rhetorical effectiveness.

I've tried to write down what I feel has been important in the story of Allegorithmic, including elements of 'early indications,' this information so often drowned out by noise, or even the micro-decisions which can ultimately make an immense difference (the 'butterfly effect' so important to the chaos theory that constitutes the basis of some of the principles upon which the technology at the heart of our products is built), as well as the intangible connective tissue: all the invisible links established by our various teams; all the energy, good humor, generosity, everything given that extends beyond the required functions stipulated in an employment contract, which render everything coherent and cohesive. A company is an ecosystem in which all elements, even the smallest, have their place.

Without them, everything falls out of order, the spark of life fails to take hold, and the ecosystem dies.

Though I've been lucky enough to carry out this project and experience this adventure, I am certainly no guru and, although what I say here is a reflection of the truth, everybody knows that history smiles on those who write it. I am, of course, incredibly proud of what we accomplished: we demonstrated great talent, and we worked day and night (literally, at times), but there were also times when we were, quite simply, saved by luck.[4] Once again, please try not to infer too much wisdom from this journey.

This book is above all intended to record an adventure which is particularly dear to me, and which involved many people. It is intended to tell our epic story and to try to extract the *substance* from it.

4: Here I'll provide one of the rare equations that I like to give when someone asks me for the 'formula for success':

$$Success = Work \times Talent \times Luck$$

Each element multiplies another here because without work, nothing is created; without talent, nothing is good quality; without luck, everything is canceled out. All three elements are required in a non-zero quantity. This is all I can honestly say without falling into charlatanism. . .

Part II

1996–1998

Key Meetings | 1

1.1 Sébastien Rubens

The accident I discussed in the preamble of this memoir made me reconsider my path and my centers of interest. Inspired by films like *Tron* and *Wargames*, and by books by William Gibson and other science fiction writers exploring the subject of cyberspace, I'd been caught up in the wave of the internet, a wave that carried away everything in its path, in France and all over the wider world. Before the accident, I'd been thinking of focusing on this area, which was gaining more and more interest. Now, however, my questions around the subject of probability made me deeply reconsider my choice of specialization, and although I'd started a degree in computer science at *Université Blaise Pascal*, one of the universities in Clermont-Ferrand, I ultimately chose a different route; I turned away from computer science and focused on subjects closer to applied mathematics, and to my new area of consideration and interest: chance.

Shortly after this, at the beginning of 1997, while I was doing my master's degree, I met Sébastien Rubens, a DEA student[1] in computer science. He listened to me talk about my new interest in this branch of applied mathematics as well as my passion for computer graphics, which I hid from no one (see in particular Section 2.2), and he decided to introduce me to his internship director, Albert Benassi, a researcher in mathematics at the CNRS, who was working on an absolutely fascinating area: self-similar random processes, a general class of 'fractals' (see figure 1.1).

1: A *Diplôme d'Études Avancées*, or 'Advanced Studies Diploma,' is the last year of a graduate degree; unlike the DESS—the *Diplôme d'Etudes Supérieures Spécialisées*, or 'Specialized Superior Studies Diploma'—the DEA is more research-oriented, and is sort of an antechamber to the doctorate (see section 2.1).

DOI:10.1201/9781003534624-1

Figure 1.1: Fractals, like the Mandelbrot set here (top), are mathematical objects of infinite complexity, with 'never smooth' contours that always show the same aspect no matter how much we zoom in. A Romanesco cauliflower (bottom) is a naturally occurring fractal object. Any single branch of the cauliflower resembles, within a factor of scale, the entire cauliflower. A branch of this branch in turn resembles the 'parent' branch, and so on. The Romanesco cauliflower is therefore a self-similar object.

1.2 Albert Benassi

I met Albert (see figure 1.3) in his small office in the mathematics laboratory of *Université Blaise Pascal* (see figure 1.2), a cave stuffed with books and other scientific articles, the blackboard is covered with increasingly opaque formulas. Right away, I was literally overwhelmed by his passion and his ambition.

Figure 1.2: Exterior view of the Cézeaux campus building, home to the mathematics laboratory that Albert Benassi belonged to when I met him.

Figure 1.3: The meeting with Albert Benassi, which changed everything. He went on to become my thesis supervisor, and an initial investor in Allegorithmic. It was on Albert Benassi's work that I based my own research thesis, which was used in the procedural texture generation engine that I wrote my thesis on: TAON (see Chapter 3).

Albert was delighted to have the opportunity to discuss his work with a student who seemed interested, and rapidly wrote out some new equations and drawings on the blackboard, which lost me completely,[2] although this didn't deter my fascination in this rarely studied mixture of cutting-edge science and random mathematical objects (this randomness being the lifeblood of these processes, which could no longer be described with 'classic' mathematical tools) that managed to reproduce phenomena of unrivaled complexity and beauty, and its potential applications in the world of computer graphics—and its importance to my fundamental questions.

2: Albert tended to take shortcuts, expecting to have somebody with a similar level of understanding in front of him. During one of his DEA mathematics classes, I saw him begin his session with, "If I throw a coin to one side of the room, and another coin to the opposite side, you'd agree that the face they'd show would be independent of one another, wouldn't you? Very well, once this is understood, everything else follows from this. . . " He then launched into working on gigantic formulas to triple integrals, changing notations in the middle of his demonstration! He had a gift for losing his whole class. On this note, he would often tell me while I was writing my thesis with him that a good presentation is divided into three parts: everyone understands the first part; only specialists understand the second part; in the third, even the specialists realize that you are the only *real* expert on the subject.

Following this meeting that had so affected me, I rapidly decided to begin a master's internship under Albert's supervision. Albert, for his part, could count on a student who was interested in his research subjects, with the goal of programming these concepts and helping him to demonstrate their value, both fundamentally as well as applied. Researchers tend to be fond of students who are able to help them in their work, whether helping to develop theoretical aspects, working on details of the whole, or implementing (programming) intuitions and other models, in order to empirically demonstrate founding principles, or even simply by 'feeling out' the subject, and providing ideas for future research. The place of computer science in research, even mathematical research, was already significant at that time, and would of course expand much further over the coming years.

And so I began an internship that would change the trajectory of my studies and lead me, several years later, to create Allegorithmic, which would utilize the results of my research during this period.

1.3 Silicon Graphics, *Doom*, image processing, and procedural textures

During this internship, and for the first time, I worked on mathematical models coming from Albert's work, alongside Sébastien Rubens, who took me under his wing.

Sébastien was a demo-maker,[3] and was a member of Mentasm [2], a group dedicated to the Amiga. I'd always been fascinated by this universe, and had immense respect for the demo-makers that constituted it. Sebastien impressed me with his strength of character and his 'no bullshit' approach, and he taught me a lot—his passion for programming, and the work that he could create this way, was contagious.

Within the small IT laboratory provided by the *Université Blaise Pascal*, I confess we played a little *Doom*, connected by LAN[4] on legendary Silicon Graphics Indy machines (see figure 1.4)—but we also programmed algorithms to generate random processes and image analysis, following Albert's instructions and mathematical inspirations as well as we could.

At the end of my master's internship, in mid-May 1997, I defended the results of my work with Sébastien and Albert. As we left the room after my presentation, I said to Sébastien, not entirely seriously, "I think I'm finally starting to understand what I've been doing these last few months. . . "

My results for my bachelor's and master's degrees (both received with honors), as well as the work for my master's internships—two research-oriented internships[5]—resulted in me being accepted onto a DEA, as well as allowing me to receive an excellence grant, which largely financed this additional year of study.

3: He was nicknamed 'Gary Copper,' in reference to several hardware components from the Amiga. The 'demoscene'[1] was a cultural movement, whose members programmed 'demos,' real-time audio-visual computer projects which demonstrated expertise in programming, visual arts, and music. This was an incredible source of inspiration for me when I owned an Atari ST: it was perhaps one of the purest forms of activity at the interface of art and science, an interface that is very important to me. I was never a demo-maker myself, but I eagerly consumed every production I could get my hands on.

4: Things would come somewhat full circle some years later, when we worked with Dave Taylor, one of the programmers of Doom at id Software (see Chapter 13).

Figure 1.4: A Silicon Graphics Indy, which I used to program my first procedural textures. Image by Bilby, own work, CC BY 3.0, `https://commons.wikimedia.org/w/index.php?curid=10963214`

5: The work I did with Albert, but also another internship I'd done earlier in the year with the mathematician Gérard Fleury, that also had a focus on probability; my work was titled, *How to shuffle cards, or the study of various techniques of uniform distribution on a group of probabilities*. The work earned me a mention in the book, *Jeux mathématiques et mathématiques des jeux*, or "Mathematical games and the mathematics of games," by Jean-Paul Delahaye (see [3]).

DEA, Femis | 2

2.1 DEA

The DEA, (the *Diplôme d'Études Avancées*, or 'Advanced Studies Diploma,' a pre-PhD) at Blaise Pascal University had three sections dedicated to computer science. I joined the 'Imaging' section that focused on image synthesis (a little) and processing (a lot), including medical imaging.[1] I particularly liked this year as it was very focused on subjects at the interface between computer science, applied mathematics, and imaging, with the application of concepts studied which at times still remained to be discovered.

One of the main instructors was Jean-Pierre Réveillès, a professor at LLAIC1,[2] who taught us in particular discrete geometry, his domain of choice.

As part of a research internship that lasted several months, I decided to continue the work I'd started the year before with Albert Benassi. I felt a potential here, a theoretical power which fascinated and motivated me. Albert also insisted that I extend my research, and so I began working in areas that built upon the subject of my master's internship. I notably focused on texture generation so that I could get as close as possible to real-world textures. My goal was to test the power of expression of the mathematical model, and to run estimators[3] on simulations, and then on real-world textures, in order to gather useful information.

The DEA was the antechamber of the PhD thesis, and every year the various laboratories hosted by the university allocated a few thesis grants to top-ranking students[4] who wished to write a PhD thesis. This year I was head of my class in the DEA section, and so I was eligible for a grant from the Ministry of Research.

I did indeed want to begin a PhD thesis, to extend my work with Albert. We worked well together, and the wish to continue our adventure was mutual. Albert and I pushed for the allocation of the grant. Once this had been given, I began my PhD at LLAIC with Jean-Pierre and Albert as my supervisors. It wasn't possible for Albert alone to be my supervisor as he was only authorized to direct research in mathematics, and the CNRS he belonged to didn't extend to computer science[5]. Thus I prepared to become a doctoral student and, with Albert, began thinking of a plan of attack, and... a subject for my thesis (see Chapter 3).

1: And so I found myself studying how MRIs work, as well as other medical imaging acquisition techniques, Radon transforms and other advanced methods, the goal being to automatically detect a pathology in a patient via new image processing algorithms.

2: *Laboratoire de Logique, Algorithmique et Informatique*, or 'Laboratory of Logic, Algorithmics and Computer Science," at Clermont 1, Clermont-Ferrand's other university. Jean-Pierre is a well-known figure in the world of discrete geometry, the geometry of discrete numbers, which is particularly applicable to computer screens, where pixel position is represented by a combination of two discrete numbers: drawing in this 'discrete space' is essentially drawing on a matrix of such numbers. The 'Réveillès line' is the perfect example of this—it allows you to draw efficient, elegant pixel lines, thanks to an algorithm established by Jean-Pierre.

3: A mathematical estimator allows one to statistically determine, by analysis of a realization of this process, the value of one of its parameters.

4: At that time in France students could not start a PhD thesis without a grant; these were either attributed by the Ministry of Research and Higher Education, or financed by the industry, a CIFFRE grant.

5: Even though my work focused on the interface between applied mathematics, signal processing and computer science. I'll also draw a distinction between the French term that was applicable in this context, *Informatique*, and the English near-translation 'Computer Science' I'm using in this text. The sense of *Informatique* is too vague; I find 'Computer Science' much clearer.

2.2 Femis

But before throwing myself headlong into this project, I, earlier in the year and in parallel with my DEA, had made an attempt to follow a path that wasn't scientific...

DOI:10.1201/9781003534624-2

Figure 2.1: A few art video projects created while I was still a student torn between cinema and science. From top to bottom: "Read My Lips" Part 1[4] and Part 2[5], "Attack of the Giant Oyster"[6], "Flying Oyster Circus"[7] and "Oyster Invasion"[8], the last three were part of my 1997 short film "Oysters."

For many years, I'd been very active in several artistic projects and associations, and I produced a lot of creative works, ranging from writing to music, including the production of films and video art (see figure 2.1), live events and even coding 3D anaglyphs (see figure 2.2), as well as film reviews. I was an active part of associations such as 'Vidéofac,' 'Cinéfac,' 'Les Toiles de Clermont,' and a few others throughout my student years. These associations, where I met many more students from scientific fields than from artistic fields,[6] were of major importance to me, as I'd always been drawn equally to science and to the arts;[7] as my studies were focused on science, my participation in these associations nourished my passion for creation and the arts.

Among the figures who particularly inspired and influenced me was David-Olivier 'DOL' Lartigaud, a thesis student in art history, with an endless knowledge of all the areas I was passionate about (and on many areas in general). He possessed a unique talent and creativity, which, thanks to numerous, rich discussions, opened my eyes to the world around me. He was the first to make me understand the fundamental connection between art and science, and between the tools, the work, and the artist: true artists build their own tools. . . This strong link between concepts that are too often considered to oppose one another would remain with me throughout the following years, and would become the source of one of the driving forces of Allegorithmic. In this, David-Olivier played the role of a mentor to me, and I am grateful to him to this day.[8]

Fueled by all these projects and encounters, and attracted by my passion for cinema in particular and before definitively committing to a scientific career path, I issued myself a challenge in order to give myself one last opportunity to switch fields, and to principally invest myself in the arts: I decided to take the entrance exam to FEMIS.[9] The entrance exam lets you choose from several areas: directing, screenplay, and so on. I chose 'Directing,' which is more 'jack of all trades' than screenwriting, which is more focused on a specific area and which I see as less rewarding. The exam was split into two parts—a film analysis essay on the premises of the school in Paris, and a take-home assignment where we had to create a film project portfolio on one of three themes proposed by the school.

And so, in parallel with my science DEA, I, therefore, began the creation of this portfolio for FEMIS on the theme that I'd chosen: 'the fold.' I poured myself into this project, spending whole nights at work on it. The project was full of creative ideas, but was also—and this is particularly glaring even now, as I write these words some 24 years later—very immature. It was directionless, essentially going all over the place.

My result on film analysis was acceptable and would have allowed me to pass an important stage of the selection process. My grade for the portfolio was very poor, however, and so I was eliminated. I would not go to FEMIS, and would certainly never become a student of an artistic discipline. . .

But I had no time to feel sorry for myself: reassured by my prominent spot in my DAE section and with funding from the Ministry of Research in my pocket, I began my doctoral thesis, with Albert and Jean-Pierre, my two scientific mentors who greatly inspired me, on a subject that fascinated me.

6: It seems that the French system gives far too much weight to sciences, and that many people follow this route because they are capable and because it opens more doors, rather than because of genuine interest. . .

7: I mention this here as this dual interest would have a significant impact on Allegorithmic.

8: DOL is currently the head of the Art and Design Research Unit, *l'Unité de Recherche Numérique en Art et Design*, at ESAD Saint-Etienne/ENSBA Lyon

9: FEMIS, the *Fondation Européene pour les Métiers de l'Image et du Son*, is a *grande école* created in 1943 in Paris. It is the absolute reference of film schools for those who want to become directors or screenwriters. The entrance exam is very demanding.

In retrospect...

This dual passion for the arts and for science defines me, and, even if I were not made for artistic studies, I would return to the arts and cinema a few years later via a different, more technical door, at first thanks to my research work and then due to Allegorithmic (see Chapter 5). This interface between art and science is a central component of the Allegorithmic project, as its name attests (see Chapter 6).

Figure 2.2: An anaglyph image, taken from a 3D credits sequence that I made in 1998 for Vidéofac, using a tool that I'd made that could generate an anaglyph film from two video sources.

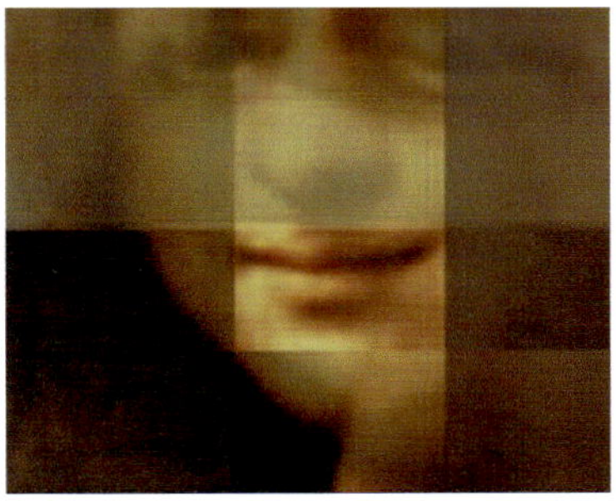

Figure 2.3: The Mona Lisa, folded, leaving the famous smile on display. The fold is the focus.

Part III

1998–2001

PhD Thesis | 3

3.1 Complex environments

Many people experience a PhD thesis as a marathon. Some marathon runners, just like some doctoral students, are physically and mentally ready for the challenge. Others are... less so. One thing is certain: for many, the struggle is greater than imagined, and the effort required is more significant than anticipated. I fell into this group and entered my PhD student years somewhat unprepared. I was naive, and even excited–I couldn't see what lay on the path before me.

Another generally accepted observation concerns the division of the work required:[1] in the first year, the student tries to find their subject; in the second, the student thinks they have found their subject and, realizing the immensity of what must still be accomplished,[2] and having fundamental doubts about their ability to produce interesting work ("Is this going to work at all?"), finally gets into the guts of the project,[3] far removed from the initial excitement around the work, and even further away from the end of the tunnel; in the third year, the student realizes that they never *really* had a good subject, and they now have to redo everything. In one year. Work worthy of a doctoral thesis, for which three years had initially been allotted, which must now be compressed into one. And knowing that the final 6 months are dedicated to drafting the thesis. Panic is never far away...

1: When I was preparing for my doctoral thesis, doctorates in the so-called 'hard sciences' generally took place over three years, in France.

2: ...and having 'wasted' a year already...

3: This period is psychologically very demanding, and requires great strength of character.

In all, the thesis is an ordeal. And, as with any ordeal, it is incredibly rich in learning experiences.

In the laboratory that hosted me (the LLAIC1), and another that I visited almost every day (the LaMP[4]), I frequently ran into other doctoral students and incredibly inspiring researchers, who would perhaps teach me more in three years than throughout the rest of my entire academic career. Here I think specifically of people like Frédéric Szczap, Roger Espel Llima, Yan Gérard, and Alain Daurat[5]—I shared a lab with Alain at the LLAIC1. Alongside them, I learned a lot about languages, logic, computer science, mathematics, and much more. I was overwhelmed by their knowledge, their intelligence and their kindness.[6]

4: The *Laboratoire de Météorologie Physique*, or 'Physical Meteorology Lab' of Université Blaise Pascal, that housed my thesis supervisor Albert Benassi as a professor, having previously been a member of the CNRS mathematics laboratory in Clermont-Ferrand. Both labs were located on the same campus, 'Cézeaux,' in Aubière, south of Clermont-Ferrand.

5: Alain sadly passed away a few years after my thesis defence, due to a sudden illness...

6: The permanent atmosphere of excellence and intelligence of the research laboratories provided fertile ground for ideas to grow. While writing a doctoral thesis is an ordeal, this period nonetheless remains one of the most exciting and inspiring times of my life.

I spent an immense amount of time managing Linux and UNIX systems (particularly those of the lab), as well as learning to write LaTeX,[7] and learning good practice in written French and English (non-breaking spaces! Capital letters with accents! etc.).

But I was also making progress on my research work.

7: I'm writing this book using LaTeX, which remains a pleasure for me as well as a guarantee of 'neatness of code.'

3.2 Estimators

As my thesis was primarily oriented toward image processing and computer vision, I implemented estimators of parameters of random

DOI:10.1201/9781003534624-3

processes. We were trying to demonstrate that certain complex natural processes could be described using the mathematical models developed by Albert Benassi and his team. The statistical estimators defined for these processes therefore had to make it possible to effectively characterize these natural phenomena. So, for instance, these statistical estimators needed to be able to distinguish a cumulonimbus cloud from a simple nimbus, by analyzing the data captures of these two phenomena, whether by photo or another technique.

Figure 3.1: Christophe Debain, in his research environment at Cemagref. Christophe was very present during my doctoral thesis, and would be one of the initial investors in Allegorithmic, a company I officially created in 2003.

I began programming these estimators, and Christophe Debain approached us with an original application for this work. Christophe was a young researcher from Cemagref, a national research laboratory dedicated to agriculture and the environment, one of whose branches was based on the same campus as our lab, a few dozen meters away from the LLAIC1[8] and the LaMP. His idea was that, by using a camera and a computer, these estimators could determine the quality of corn silage.[9] We adapted the algorithms I was developing for my thesis to this original purpose, and then I took a large number of photos of silage collected on small cardboard plates. And we ultimately obtained accurate results. The automatic estimator made it possible to classify different types of silage with a good level of accuracy.

Figure 3.2: Two images of corn silage. The quality of the cut of the plants directly influences their nutritional properties. The goal here was to was to automatically classify this silage in terms of cut quality, by using artificial vision and applying the estimators of Albert Benassi's mathematical model studied during the thesis. The estimators produced decent results.

3.3 Clouds

The counterpart of the statistical estimators was the model itself. To test the estimators on pure realizations of the model, and also to test their generative abilities, I programmed a synthesizer of complex environments, the aim of which was not to analyze images, but to produce them. One of its main objectives was to generate clouds, which were the major subject of study of the LaMP. Clouds were hard to generate using traditional mathematical tools, but we anticipated that we could, thanks to our mathematical model,[10] generate them with the right spectral properties, such as those observed when we carried out in-situ measurements when we were on a plane or using a drone passing through clouds. These measurements, which provided variations of water concentration, made it possible for us to obtain 'spectral signatures' for different types of clouds: might we be able to generate simulations, using our model, in the form of 1D, 2D, or 3D images—clouds that would respect these different spectral signatures, depending on the parameter values that we input?

We were very proud of our first results, which not only allowed us to successfully test and validate the statistical estimators of the parameters

8: The window of my thesis office looked out over Cemagref.

9: My first summer job when I was a teenager wanting a little pocket money was detasseling, or trimming, corn. Things had come full circle once again.

10: Which involved a representation of random processes via 'wavelets,' a relatively new tool at the time, and one that was very powerful and versatile.

of the model that we used, but also to show beautiful, visually satisfying results.[11]

11: They were not satisfying for everybody, however; when I proudly showed these synthesized images of clouds to the director of the laboratory, he looked them over for a while then said to me, "I guess you don't look at clouds very often."

3.4 Pretty bugs

And at this point, as would happen in any decent science fiction film, a 'major plot point' occurred: I made a coding mistake. And this mistake, though it broke the purity of Albert's mathematical model, allowed me to generate textures I found interesting... I presented the results of my software to Albert, and he was wary; investigating, we soon found the source of this surprise, the error in the program.

This error produced 'pretty bugs,' however, and Albert had the intelligence and inspiration not to ask me to correct it, but on the contrary pushed me to continue to explore this model which, while certainly imperfect, provided greater control and made it possible to acquire textures from rich and varied environments (see, for example, figure 3.3).

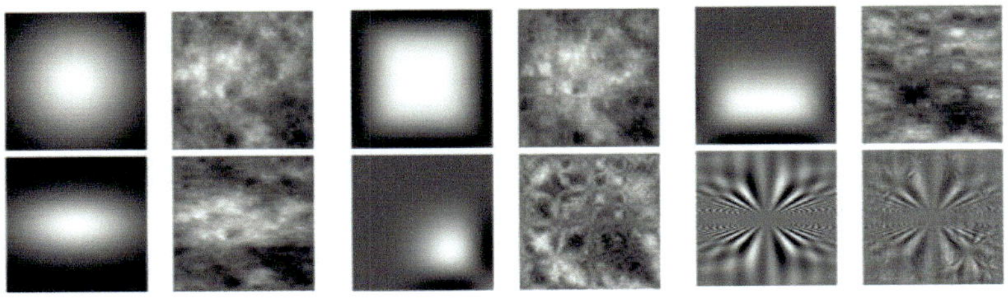

Figure 3.3: One parameter of the model in particular made it possible to play with the graphic appearance of resulting textures: what I would call 'morphlets.' I would have had to program 3 wavelets to obtain a mathematical base in 2D (the world of images); I programmed just one and called it a 'morphlet' or '*morphlette*,' as it allowed control of the shape of the elements that constituted a texture.

This bug helped me a lot as it allowed me to more easily anticipate the parameter values necessary in order to produce an image that resembled the one we were trying to obtain. Essentially, the bug made the program more intuitive and, even though it was particularly complex to implement, it inspired me, and removed a technical barrier between the user (I was its only user at the time, of course, in addition to being its creator) and the production of images.[12] I dug deeper into this vein of the model's 'expressiveness,' playing with all its parameters, such as the texture construction tree (see figure 3.4).

12: This was the first time I became aware of this fundamental aspect of software development: make it accessible and useful to the user, rather than making a tool created *by* programmers *for* programmers.

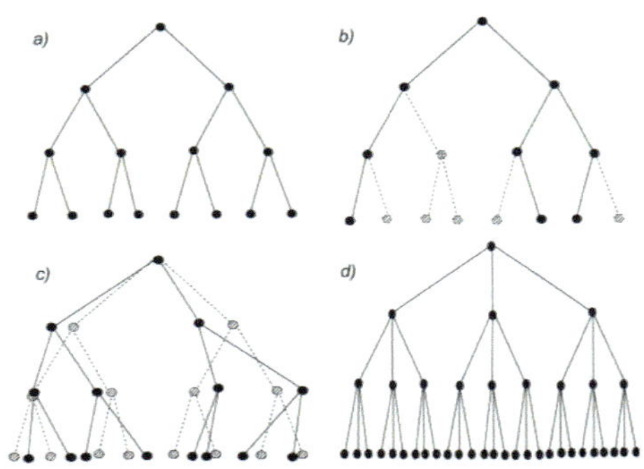

Figure 3.4: 'Dyadic' trees are a good way to code a space. These trees are often fixed in models of representation of classic signals: here I 'broke' this rule, which made it possible to create much more varied coding trees; this imposed constraints on the theoretical viability of the signals produced, but also provided a richness and expressiveness that had never been seen before. These 'free' trees were one of the fundamental aspects of the technology that would be developed by Allegorithmic, particularly in its earlier years.

3.5 TAON

This was the birth of TAON. TAON, an acronym for 'The Art Of Noise,'[13] was a program that took a number of numerical values as input, and produced an image as output. Its generation engine[14] was based on the mathematical model at the core of my thesis. Early on, its interface was very basic, and I was the only one who could make it work. A typical file for parameter definition can be seen in figure 3.5. I entered these parameters using a text editor (XEmacs, in my case) and saved them in a `.map` file, which I then 'fed' into TAON. After a few seconds (or more) of processing, TAON would then generate an output image (see figure 3.6).

13: A reference to the musical group 'Art of Noise,' as well as a description of what this program created ('noise'), and even to this form of art overall, which I felt allowed you to take something quite ordinary, and use it to create very visually interesting noises.

14: TAON is the ancestor of the Substance Engine, and its legacy can still be found inside the code of our Substance products today: some classes of the Substance Engine contain the prefix 'T3,' indicating that they date back to the third version of TAON, written by Christophe Soum (see Section 4.2).

$Dim\ T_X\ [T_Y\ [T_Z]]$

J_{max}

N_C

$$\overbrace{\underbrace{\{A_{mn}\}_{n \leq J_{max}^{A_m}}}_{m=1}}^{N_C}$$

Dim représente la dimension du bruit à générer.

T_X, T_Y et T_Z représentent la taille du bruit.

J_{max} représente le nombre de couches de l'arbre de construction de la texture (pour une image 256×256, $J_{max} \leq 8$).

N_C représente le nombre de couches d'atomes.

La notation $\overbrace{\underbrace{A_m}_{m=1}}^{N_C}$ représente une suite d'atomes A séparés par un retour chariot. Par exemple, pour $N_C = 3$, les atomes seront représentés comme suit dans le fichier :

A_1

A_2

A_3

La notation $\{A_n\}_{n \leq J_{max}^A}$ représente une suite d'atomes A écrits sur la même ligne et séparés par des espaces. Par exemple, $\{A_n\}_{n=1}^3$ sera représenté comme suit dans le fichier :

$A_1\ A_2\ A_3$

J_{max}^A représente la valeur limite de profondeur de l'atome A.

Figure 3.5: The format of TAON parameter files.

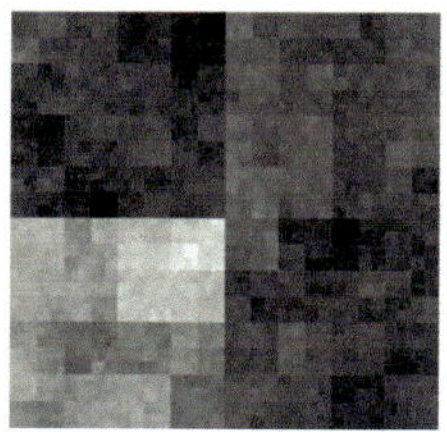

```
2 256 256
8
1
8  0.5  1.  0.   0.  G  0 0 1.   1   0 0 1 1 0 0 8 32 1 0   0
```

Figure 3.6: A first example of a parameter file for TAON (below) and the generated (above).

I'd subsequently program a graphical interface for the program, which I called X-TAON, the prefix 'X-' referring to the graphical extensions for programs running on the UNIX systems. This version with an interface, which we can see in figure 3.7, was another important step in my understanding of the software tools dedicated to artists that we would develop throughout the Allegorithmic adventure: a good graphical interface and a good user experience are essential.

Following these pretty bugs, and the power and flexibility of the TAON program, and particularly inspired by my discoveries during my teaching (see the following chapter, 4), I ultimately decided to shift the focus of

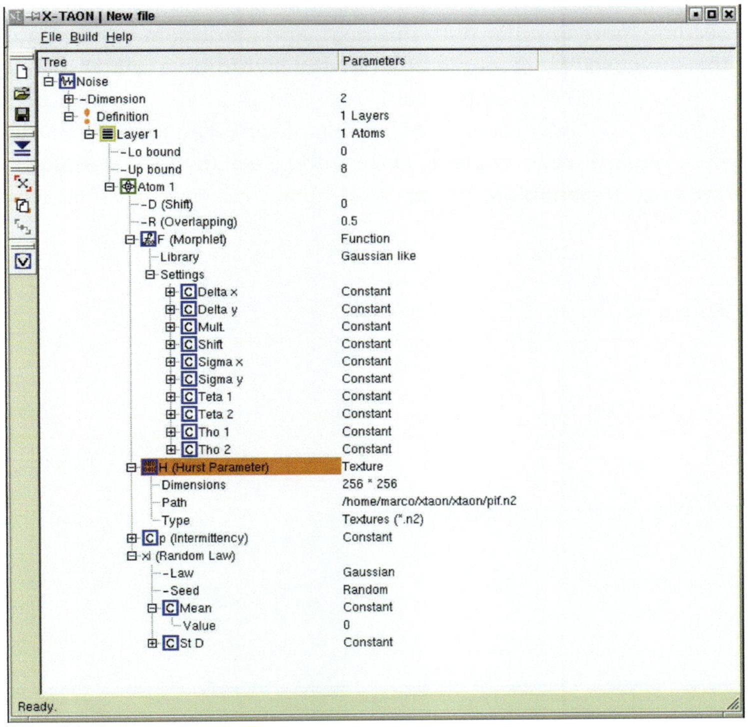


```
2 256 256
8
3
5 -1 -2 1 0 0 1 1 0 0 8 32 1 0 -3 2 256 256
8
1
8 0.5 1 0.5 0 G -1 0 1 -1 -2 1 0 0 1 1 0 0 8 32 1 0 0
0.5 0 G -1 0 1 -1 -2 1 0 0 1 1 0 0 8 32 1 0 1 5 0.5 1
0.5 0 G -1 0 1 -1 -2 1 0 0 1 1 0 0 8 32 1 0 0 6 -1 -2 1
0 0 1 1 0 0 8 32 1 0 -1 -2 1 0 0 1 1 0 0 8 32 1 0 0.5 0
G -1 0 1 -1 -2 1 0 0 1 1 0 0 8 32 1 0 1 6 -3 2 256 256 8
2 6 0.5 1 0.5 0 G -1 0 1 -1 -2 1 0 0 1 1 0 0 8 32 1 0 0
8 -3 2 256 256
8
1
8 0.5 1 0.5 0 G -1 0 1 -1 -2 1 0 0 1 1 0 0 8 32 1 0 0
1 0.5 0 G -1 0 1 -1 -2 1 0 0 1 1 0 0 8 32 1 0 0
1 0.5 0 G -1 0 1 -1 -2 1 0 0 1 1 0 0 8 32 1 0 0
8 0.5 1 0.5 0 G -1 0 1 -1 -2 1 0 0 1 1 0 0 8 32 1 0 0
```

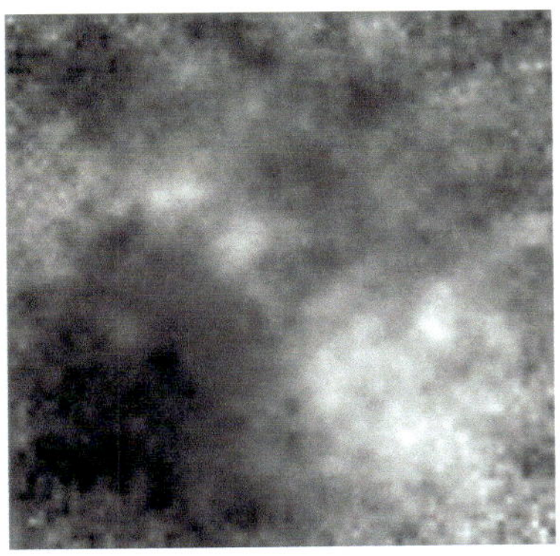

Figure 3.7: The X-TAON program (top), a graphical extension of the TAON engine. It made it easier to generate parameter files for TAON (middle), which would have been almost impossible to write manually. The texture obtained was very complex. This was the first time I really understood the importance of a good graphical interface, and a good user experience.

my work toward texture synthesis, rather than texture analysis. I started to become more familiar with this field, and made some presentations in this area, (see for example [9]), notably including a talk at the AFIG conference[10] in November 2001, an event that would prove pivotal in the Allegorthmic adventure (see Chapter 5). The idea of creating a company, which would operate at the interface of my two passions of art and science, began to take shape.

Teaching | 4

4.1 Softimage 3D

Thesis students receiving Ministry scholarships had to complete a certain number of teaching hours each year of their thesis. This was excellent training for a potential future lecturing position, as lecturers would divide their time between research and teaching at the university. I was no exception to the rule, so I found myself teaching diverse subjects like mathematics or C++ programming, to classes that were equally diverse, going from the IUT, the *Institut Universitaire de Technologie*, to the DEA. I was especially active at the IUT and the *Licence Professionnelle*, the vocational degree, in Puy-en-Velay, where my host laboratory during my thesis, the LLAIC1, was based. The links between this IUT and the laboratory were strong,[1] and I naturally found myself with a heavy teaching workload in this new branch, created only a few years earlier.

1: Denis Richard, the founder and director of LLAIC1 was also the director of the IUT in Clermont-Ferrand.

Among the subjects assigned to me was a new one: 3D, and the Softimage 3D software, from the Quebec-based company Softimage.[2] At that time, Softimage was the tool of reference in the world of special effects and was used in films like Jurassic Park. The IUT intended to teach its students the best tool available at the time.

2: Whose trajectory saw it pass through ownership by Microsoft, then Avid, then finally Autodesk

Jean-Pierre Réveillès, himself very involved in the development of the branch, knew that I was passionate about 3D and special effects, and so he entrusted me with the task of teaching the software to the Puy-en-Velay students. I admit that I liked the idea. The only small problem was that I didn't know the tool at all, and I had to start teaching it a week later...

So I began learning it as quickly as possible, immersing myself in the documentation provided with the software, which can be seen in figure 4.1. Devoting most of my time to my research work, I could dedicate a limited amount of time to Softimage, and I was about a week ahead of the students when we started,[3] which was just barely enough, and which allowed me to test out a very participatory teaching method...

3: ... and, to be honest, throughout the rest of the teaching year.

The software was divided into modules which corresponded to the different stages of creating synthetic images: *Model* (creation of the 'geometry' of objects, by connecting polygons in space), *Motion* (dedicated to the animation of these objects), *Actor* (a module focusing on rigging and the definition of skeletons for character animation), and *Matter*, which allowed the creation of textures and digital materials[4] (see figure 4.2).

4: There was also a last module, *Tools*, which was dedicated to the processing and import/export of images and geometry.

I'll return to the *Matter* module in section 4.3, as it was central to the development of my own project; first, I'll here mention a fundamental sidenote about one of my students at the IUT of Puy-en-Velay: Christophe Soum.

DOI:10.1201/9781003534624-4

Figure 4.1: The program Softimage 3D, published by Quebec-based company Softimage (in the middle, on the Silicon Graphics O2 workstation, the same as we used in Puy-en-Velay). Softimage 3D has been the reference 3D software since the beginning of the 1990s. The program's documentation, to the right, thanks to which I learned how to use the program, so that I could teach it. By Source (WP:NFCC#4), Fair use, `https://en.wikipedia.org/w/index.php?curid=43708324`

Figure 4.2: Different workshops of the Softimage 3D software: the Matter module was dedicated to textures and digital materials.

4.2 Christophe Soum

To avoid traveling too often between Clermont-Ferrand and Puy-en-Velay,[5] I tried to group my course hours on-site over one or two consecutive days. Regularly, during a busy teaching period,[6] I would travel on Tuesday morning, spend all day Tuesday in class, then spend Tuesday evening and night in Puy-en-Velay; I'd then conclude with a few more hours of classes on Wednesday morning, before returning to Clermont-Ferrand in early to mid-afternoon that day... As a teaching PhD student with a grant, I was provided with accommodation by the IUT: a very small, spartan room in a building annexed to the IUT, in the shape of a wooden cube. Barely older than some of my students, I took advantage of my Tuesday evenings there to spend a little time with them.[7] I was very close to these students, and have remained in contact with several of them.

5: A road which is, on certain sections, relatively dangerous and which I traveled at a brisk pace in my white Renault Clio.

6: Typically the first semester of the year, the following being dedicated 100% to research.

7: Notably including one evening involving a potato cannon...

Among them, one student in particular caught my attention. He was nicknamed 'God' by the rest of the class; when I asked why I was simply told, "Because he can do anything!" Intrigued, I 'spoke to God," who proved to be Christophe Soum, a particularly brilliant student,[8] who was passionate about images and who, although originally from Marseille, had decided to join the IUT of Puy-en-Velay because it was practically the only training course in its field in France. Christophe and I began a long series of discussions, each more fascinating than the last, on an incalculable number of subjects. For instance, he introduced me to anime,[9] and I talked to him about my research work. I was absolutely astonished by his IT knowledge. Christophe had a connection with computers that I'd never encountered before, a completely unique ability to program it in the noblest sense of the word—to get the most out of a machine; to make it do exactly what we expected of it. It was a knowledge and connection coupled with a love of things well made, and a willingness to demand the best of his tools.

8: I like to believe that, regardless of background, in each year group all over the world there is one student, or a few students, who prove truly outstanding.

9: Anime are Japanese animated series. I was absolutely amazed by "Serial Experiment Lain,"[11] for example, which he gave me on a series of CDs, and which I binge-watched, before the term existed, in my small cube room, on my laptop (laptops still had CD players, then).

Christophe and I started to form a close bond, and as my plans to create a company became clearer (see Chapter 6), I told Christophe about my ideas immediately. He had to be the first to join this adventure and fill the role of technical leader for Allegorithmic.

In retrospect...

I feel that I possess a talent for recognizing talent. However, what I saw in Christophe was so obvious that no great gift was needed to identify it. This meeting was crucial for the destiny of Allegorithmic, and Christophe, in addition to becoming a close friend, would become the main technical driving force of the company throughout its existence. As I write these lines, two decades later, we are still working together and I have come across few people at his level, even within the giants of the 3D and IT industry in general... Meeting him, in Puy-en-Velay, at a time when my ideas for a company were forming, was an incredible stroke of luck, and at that moment I saw a sign—the stars aligned. That he agreed to embark on this adventure with me, when nothing concrete yet existed and we still had to build everything, was one of the elements which gave me unshakeable confidence in our ability to succeed in this challenge.

4.3 Matter++

But before realizing that I wanted to create Allegorithmic, I had to finish my PhD thesis and, at the same time, handle the workload that I'd been assigned. Returning to Softimage 3D, week after week, my students and I learned all the stages of creating computer-generated images, covering the different modules mentioned above, one after the other.

When we reached *Matter*, the module dedicated to materials and textures, I realized something that lit a spark within me, that wouldn't go out: Softimage created these materials by intensively using 2D noise functions, such as Perlin noise (see figure 4.3).

However, the noises available in the tool to create new functions were very limited, and I was surprised to find that the approach I was developing for my thesis, and my prototype for generating procedural noises, TAON (see section 3.5), made it possible to go further than what I saw here—that is, further than the software of reference in the computer graphics industry!

Was it possible that the subject of my thesis could be applied to this field that I was so passionate about, that I'd put to one side in favor of my scientific studies?

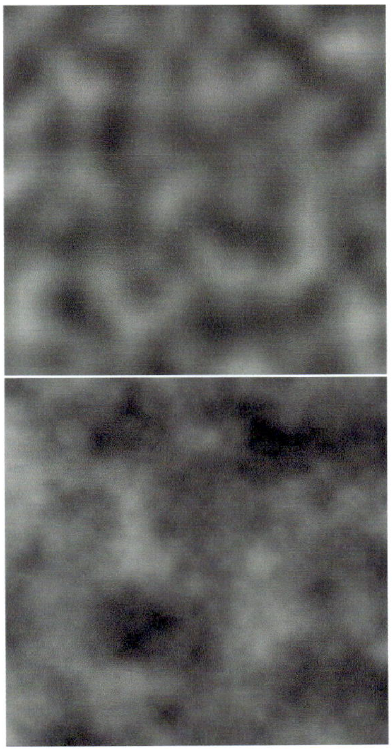

Figure 4.3: Perlin noise (above) was invented by Ken Perlin, a 3D and computer graphics legend who contributed to the visual effects in TRON at the start of the 80s, and to the world of digital graphics research overall in a particularly significant way. By adding random variations of Perlin noise several times and then applying a scale factor, we obtain a fractal 2D noise (below). Crédits: CC BY-SA 3.0, Public Domain, `https://en.wikipedia.org/w/index.php?curid=10409833`

Convergence | 5

5.1 Convergence

The realization that I potentially had something substantial—with TAON and its application in the world of synthetic images, in particular concerning its creation of digital textures and materials—gradually grew as I tested my hypotheses. It did seem like 2D noises were fundamental in the way that many textures, particularly realistic ones, were created, but they were also important for visual effects in general, beyond just textures. It also seemed that TAON permitted me to not only generate common noises, like the Perlin or 'fractal' noise, but additionally, in a very intuitive way, other never-before-seen noises which could prove extremely useful when creating new materials and textures. Perhaps here was a way to bring together two of my passions: science, with TAON and my research work, and cinema, by means of synthetic 3D images and special effects.

I wanted to go further to confirm my hypothesis and, using my students as guinea pigs, I developed this idea. Once I felt that it had been sufficiently demonstrated, and after looking into the field of synthetic image research in France, I decided to present my work to the community of researchers, whom I didn't yet know. The next key step: the annual AFIG[1] conference, which would take place in Limoges, just a few weeks before my thesis defense, from November 28 to 30, 2001. I would present my thesis results under a more computer graphics angle, rather than an applied mathematics and physics approach.[10] To do this, I translated the mathematical model at the center of my work into more natural language, as follows:

> Conditionally sum, in a non-uniform manner and with a controlled energy gain, any randomly modulated function, along scales and space.

1: The *Association Française d'Informatique Graphique*, or the 'French Computer Graphics Association.' Every year this association organizes a conference, which is an opportunity for the French microcosm of computer graphics research to meet up, and for PhD students to present their work (an excellent apprenticeship in the field). There are also some representatives from the visual effects and video game industries in the room, who come to find some good ideas and some future recruits for their internal R&D labs.

The formula was the following:

$$X(x) = \sum_{j,k \in T_{D,p}} 2^{-jH_{j,k}} F_{j,k}(2^j x - k)\xi_{j,k} \tag{5.1}$$

And the parameters were: 'conditionally' is represented by p (intermittence parameter); 'in a non-uniform manner' by the dependence in j and k, and the interval D; 'controlled flow of energy' by H, the Hurst parameter (connected to the fractal dimension); 'randomly modulated' determined by ξ (the random variables); 'any function' F, which I called 'morphlet'; 'along scales and space' T (the structure tree).

The choice of the name 'morphlet' was determined by the visual aspect of the generated noise, as we see in figure 5.1.

DOI:10.1201/9781003534624-5

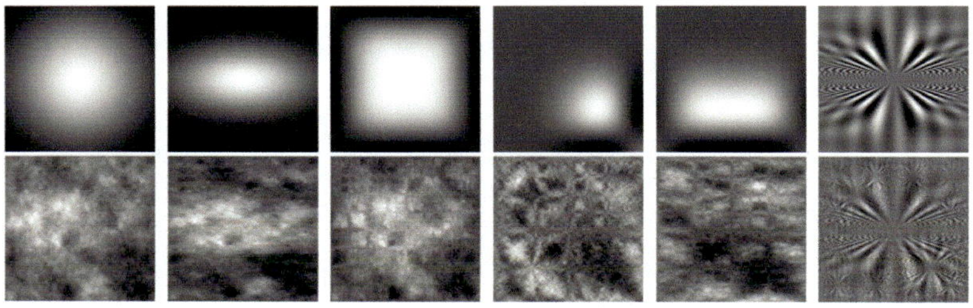

Figure 5.1: The choice of 'morphlet' *F* (images on the top line) and its visual influence on the corresponding generative process (images on the bottom line).

In this way, I demonstrated how TAON allowed me to reproduce a plaster texture by modifying parameters (see figure 5.2), then to obtain variations of the first wall by exploring 'neighbors' of the initial set of parameters (see figure 5.3).

FIG. 16 – L'image de droite est une photographie d'une texture de crépis d'intérieur. À gauche est représenté la carte de niveau, ou *map*, réalisée en utilisant le modèle tdMAP, ayant permis la construction d'un texture de crépis d'intérieur (au centre) proche de l'originale.

Figure 5.2: The noise in the left image was generated with TAON; when used as a displacement map on a 2D plane and colored blue, and once the render is placed in a lit 3D space, we can obtain the synthesized image in the middle, which resembles the photo of the wall of my office at the time of the PhD on the right (figure extracted from the text of the full presentation for the AFIG conference in 2001, including annotations in French; figure numbering in these annotations does not apply here).

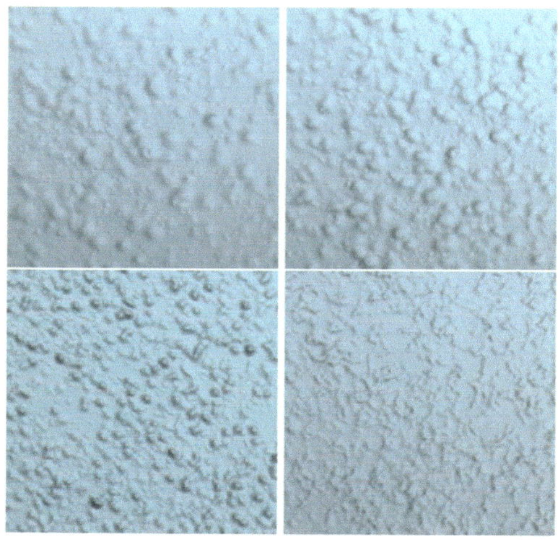

FIG. 17 – Exploration de voisinage : en changeant simplement quelques valeurs de certains paramètres du modèle (ici principalement la morphlette *F*), il est possible d'obtenir à frais nuls quantité d'autres crépis d'intérieur.

Figure 5.3: When subtly playing on the generative model's parameters (exploring the parameters' neighbors to obtain something close to the original wall in figure 5.2), we can obtain variations of the wall texture very quickly and easily (figure extracted from the text of the full presentation for the AFIG conference in 2001, including annotations in French; figure numbering in these annotations does not apply here).

In retrospect...

Rereading this article[10] 20 years later, several comments come to mind: first, the principle of construction described is still used today in the form of FX-Maps in Substance Designer and the Substance Engine. Even now, it is still useful in the world of computer graphics. Moreover, some possible avenues I evoked in my conclusion have proven to be valid and explorable and even realized. Yet, this feature of FX-Maps is now one amongst many, many others, developed over the following years. And so I realize that the path between an idea and its successful commercial application is composed of time, but also of the various elements that complete it.

5.2 BUF Compagnie

Although I'd been terrified by the idea of presenting in front of this panel of researchers,[2] my presentation went very well, and there was a sense that those in the room began to wonder where I'd come from: there was little research in the domain of computer graphics in Clermont-Ferrand, and the place was hardly a well-known hub for this field, outside of discrete geometry which was a related area. The panel asked me many questions and, following the conference a few days later, I received an email from someone named Xavier Bec. Xavier was the head of R&D for BUF Compagnie, a Parisian visual effects firm known around the world. He told me that somebody from his company that had seen my presentation in Limoges had spoken highly of my work and given him my contact details. Xavier invited me to visit him at the offices of BUF in Paris.

2: I'll always suffer from stage fright for any public presentation, no matter the size or type of audience.

Rereading the email, and on the final stretch of writing my thesis (a particularly difficult period), I was both incredibly excited (BUF Compagnie wanted to see my work!) and quite annoyed, as I was completely swamped and my mind was solely focused on the defense of my thesis. . . I decided nonetheless to answer positively and travel to Paris to meet him. I couldn't pass up the opportunity to visit such a place and to speak with such a team, whose productions had always fascinated me.

Figure 5.4: BUF Compagnie is a French special effects studio created in 1984 by Pierre Buffin. It was one of the most remarkable studios producing special effects between 1994 and 2003, notably playing an important role in the effects of films like *La Cité des Enfants Perdus* by Marc Caro and Jean-Pierre Jeunet, *Fight Club* and *Panic Room* by David Fincher, and even the two Matrix films, *The Matrix Reloaded* and *The Matrix Revolutions*, by the Wachowskis. BUF Compagnie was credited with the famous 'bullet time' effect. Image by BUF, BUF website, Public Domain, `https://commons.wikimedia.org/w/index.php?curid=7926781`.

In Paris, I met Xavier on the premises of BUF Compagnie, located in a beautiful Haussmannian building with parquet floors and moldings, filled with powerful computers and workstations with gigantic CRT screens, as well as computer graphics artists and 3D programmers who were in the process of inventing new effects for the next films by David Fincher and other prominent film-makers. Heaven. Xavier showed me some of their work and asked me questions about TAON and my approach to procedural noises. And he told me something that stayed with me and that would be fundamental in my approach to Allegorithmic: he said that 3D artists, even if they understand the potential behind procedural textures and noises, do not like using them because they cannot control them. "For example, if I create procedural wood and I don't like where a knot is placed, I don't want to click a thousand times on a button to generate another wood texture while crossing my fingers that the next one will suit me. . . I want to be able to change specific parts of the result I have in front of me!" He asked me if TAON permitted localized modifications of generated noises.

The answer was 'no.' But I had an idea. . .

Still in the process of digesting the answer and the question, he floated the idea of me joining his team. Even though I found that very flattering, I absolutely had to finish my thesis, to validate all these hard years of research, before thinking about what would come afterward. So I dove back into my work, putting aside the idea of locally modifying generated noise, and submerged myself in preparing my PhD thesis defense, scheduled for just a few days later.

5.3 PhD thesis defense

The thesis defense took place on 21 December 2001 in the large amphitheater of Cemagref, that had kindly been made available for use. Unfortunately, I don't have any photographs of the day. I imagine my parents were too nervous to think about immortalizing the moment which would put my student life behind me,[3] and that marked the official start of 'my afterlife.' I still had no idea what this next stage would comprise, but I would not remain undecided for long (see Section 5.4).

3: I would return to study later, specifically following distance learning courses, but this wasn't the same thing: here I'm describing the end of an era that had begun in my childhood. At that time of defending my thesis, I knew little else.

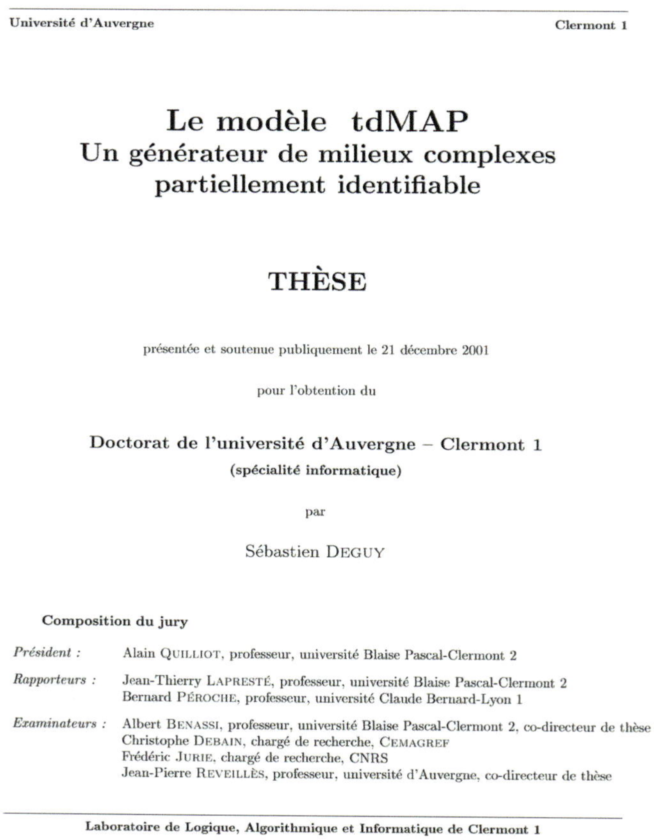

Université d'Auvergne — Clermont 1

Le modèle tdMAP
Un générateur de milieux complexes partiellement identifiable

THÈSE

présentée et soutenue publiquement le 21 décembre 2001

pour l'obtention du

Doctorat de l'université d'Auvergne – Clermont 1
(spécialité informatique)

par

Sébastien DEGUY

Composition du jury

Président : Alain QUILLIOT, professeur, université Blaise Pascal-Clermont 2

Rapporteurs : Jean-Thierry LAPRESTÉ, professeur, université Blaise Pascal-Clermont 2
Bernard PÉROCHE, professeur, université Claude Bernard-Lyon 1

Examinateurs : Albert BENASSI, professeur, université Blaise Pascal-Clermont 2, co-directeur de thèse
Christophe DEBAIN, chargé de recherche, CEMAGREF
Frédéric JURIE, chargé de recherche, CNRS
Jean-Pierre REVEILLÈS, professeur, université d'Auvergne, co-directeur de thèse

Laboratoire de Logique, Algorithmique et Informatique de Clermont 1

Figure 5.5: The first page of my doctoral thesis.

On this day I received the title of 'doctor of sciences' and, even though I was a little disappointed not to have received the congratulations of the jury, I felt a great sense of pride. The feedback that most resonated with me was that of my mother: "We didn't know you could talk like this!"[4]

4: My very dear friend Émilie Duquenne, an MBTI specialist (among other things), would most certainly tell me with a smile that this was perhaps the clearest sign that I am an 'I' type of personality (see https://fr.wikipedia.org/wiki/Myers_Briggs_Type_Indicator).

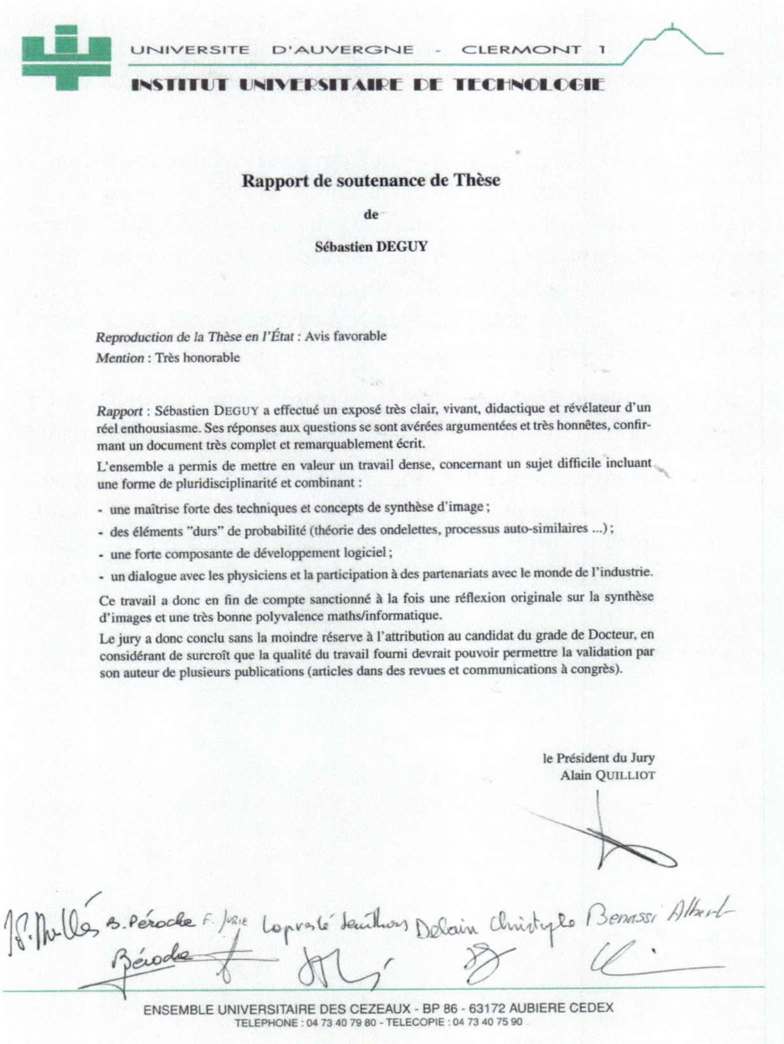

UNIVERSITE D'AUVERGNE - CLERMONT 1

INSTITUT UNIVERSITAIRE DE TECHNOLOGIE

Rapport de soutenance de Thèse

de

Sébastien DEGUY

Reproduction de la Thèse en l'État : Avis favorable

Mention : Très honorable

Rapport : Sébastien DEGUY a effectué un exposé très clair, vivant, didactique et révélateur d'un réel enthousiasme. Ses réponses aux questions se sont avérées argumentées et très honnêtes, confirmant un document très complet et remarquablement écrit.

L'ensemble a permis de mettre en valeur un travail dense, concernant un sujet difficile incluant une forme de pluridisciplinarité et combinant :

- une maîtrise forte des techniques et concepts de synthèse d'image ;
- des éléments "durs" de probabilité (théorie des ondelettes, processus auto-similaires ...) ;
- une forte composante de développement logiciel ;
- un dialogue avec les physiciens et la participation à des partenariats avec le monde de l'industrie.

Ce travail a donc en fin de compte sanctionné à la fois une réflexion originale sur la synthèse d'images et une très bonne polyvalence maths/informatique.

Le jury a donc conclu sans la moindre réserve à l'attribution au candidat du grade de Docteur, en considérant de surcroît que la qualité du travail fourni devrait pouvoir permettre la validation par son auteur de plusieurs publications (articles dans des revues et communications à congrès).

le Président du Jury
Alain QUILLIOT

ENSEMBLE UNIVERSITAIRE DES CEZEAUX - BP 86 - 63172 AUBIERE CEDEX
TELEPHONE : 04 73 40 79 80 - TELECOPIE : 04 73 40 75 90

Figure 5.6: The report of my thesis defense, signed by members of the jury, obtained December 21, 2001.

5.4 Everything becomes clear

The day after my thesis defense,[5] freshly crowned by my doctoral title, I felt a great emptiness. During the three-and-a-half years I'd spent on the thesis, I'd worked ceaselessly on an in-depth, complex, deep subject, often feeling and being very alone on the path. Now that this work had borne its fruits, and I'd received the much-coveted title of a doctor without giving much thought to what would come afterward, I found myself lacking a project, literally idle.

5: Literally, December 22, 2001.

That same evening, I went to the home of my friend Christophe Debain to celebrate my success over dinner along with his wife and their young children. The evening allowed me to relax and we drank some champagne for the occasion. Perhaps a few glasses too many.

I often make a joke when people ask me how I started Allegorithmic; the story goes like this: it was at this precise moment, while I was slightly drunk, that everything became absolutely clear in my mind: I didn't want to be a researcher; I didn't want to get hired somewhere. I realized right at this moment that I wanted to create my own company.

It would be a company dedicated to 3D software based on my research work, which would target the world of visual effects—the intersection between my passions for art and science, in particular computer graphics, a field that had always fascinated me.[6]

I'd always been enterprising and had from a very young age incessantly carried out numerous projects in parallel,[7] and so founding my own company seemed like a natural step. There was a project that suited me perfectly, and that was similar to the endeavors of my own inspirational figures, developers of software like Softimage (which seemed utterly out of reach to me, at that time), or even Kai's Power Tools (see figure 5.7), which I'd played around with a lot.

I could already see the tools developed by my company being used by 3D artists working in studios like Pixar or ILM—this was the dream!

I spoke to my father about the project in the next few days. I expressed a few doubts, but he nonetheless sensed my enthusiasm and said, "If you don't do this, you'll regret it for the rest of your life. . . " I had no obligations that could seriously hold me back; it was the right time to begin such an adventure.

So I went for it.

6: At the time of the Amiga 1000, when I was still a teenager, I even tried to convince my father to buy me a machine to make a visual effects studio in my room in Veyre-Monton, and make this my career!

7: From comic books to films, magazines, etc.

Figure 5.7: Kai's Power Tools, created in 1992 by Kai Krause, are mathematically-based filters which allow the creation of rich visual effects, patterns, and other textures. I was very inspired by these tools during my youthful explorations.

Part IV

2002–2003

Incubation | 6

6.1 The Allegorithmic Project

In the days following my decision to create a company (see Chapter 5), I was incredibly excited, even sleeping poorly—I thought about nothing but the project. The end-of-year holidays were frustrating for me because everything was closed, and I had to sit tight. I had nobody to discuss the project with, and every official institution and the Chamber of Commerce was closed. I went through all the documents on the structure of businesses in the region that I could find and learned about BUSI, an incubator for innovative companies in the Auvergne region. I promised myself to contact the organization's director, Marion Rongère, early in January 2002, so that I could ask her the thousand questions that were bouncing around inside my head (see Section 6.2).

I imagined that the Allegorithmic project would, at most, require the recruitment of two to four people, and that we'd be ready to release our first product by the end of the year at the latest... The number of chapters in this book tends to demonstrate that I was very optimistic and, above all, naive when I launched this adventure![1] Marion was one of the first people to help me be more realistic about the subject, without dousing the flame which inspired me (and which was largely fueled by my notorious naivety; the border between the two is quite subtle).

1: On the subject of naivety: around that period I read a scientific article that exposed two fundamental characteristics of an entrepreneur: naivety and a taste for gambling. I would definitely attribute these two traits to myself.

Allegorithmic, the name

One night, while I was making frantic notes in an explosion of ideas following my thesis defense and the realization that I wanted to create a company, I invented the name 'Allegorithmic'—a contraction, a catch-all word constructed by bringing together the two English adjectives 'algorithmic' (to represent the scientific side) and 'allegoric' (for the poetic side).[2] My invented adjective 'allegorithmic' would therefore describe any process that was at once both poetic and technical, at the intersection of art and science, that crossroad space that was so important to me.

Of course, I found this name much too long and complex from the start, but as I continued to look for other options, I kept returning to it. I couldn't get rid of it; I loved the depth of it. It inspired me. And so this was the name I chose when officially starting the adventure.[3] The Allegorithmic project was born.

2: During my research, I very intentionally came up with a range of ideas that would bring together two entities which were, *a priori*, antithetical, drawing inspiration in particular from 'Natural Nylon,' the name of the play and film production company created by, among others, Jude Law and Ewan McGregor, which has produced films including *eXistenZ*, by David Cronenberg; Natural Nylon is a name that has always fascinated me (as have some of its productions, of course).

3: Often mocked for its complexity and its length, and also sometimes understood and admired, it is not a name that leaves people indifferent. The funniest feedback I've received was given to me by Jensen Huang himself, founder and CEO of NVIDIA, in the early 2010s, who gently made fun of the name during one of our meetings in his office, at his company's premises in Santa Clara. He is a man who can be kind, teasing, and endearing all at the same time; in this way, he said to me something like, "Seb, I've seen some bad names, and I'd count NVIDIA among those, but this name is *awful*!"

Allegorithmic, the logo

The prospective company, which for the moment was still at the planning stage, now had a name, one that united art and science: Allegorithmic. But it already required a logo that embodied this same idea. It needed something strong.

DOI:10.1201/9781003534624-6

I turned to Julien Benassi, one of the three sons of my thesis director Albert Benassi, who happened to be a talented designer at the very beginning of his career. He worked in the Paris office of Dragon Rouge, an international creative agency working for the biggest brands. His closeness to Albert, and his knowledge of the subject of the thesis and my project overall—as well as his talent and his insightful understanding of precisely what I sought—could prove interesting.

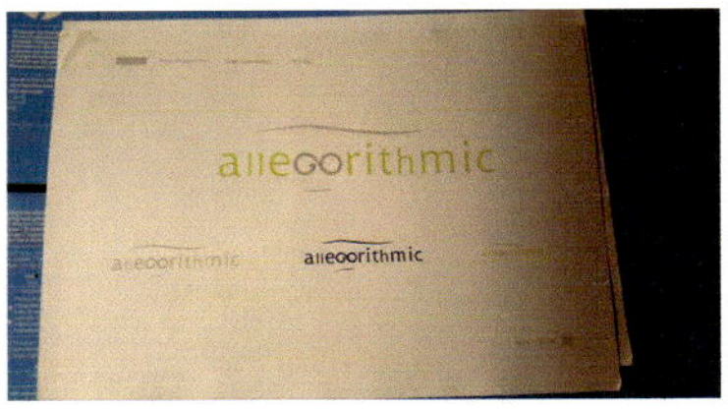

Figure 6.1: One of the logo proposals presented by Julien Benassi, which was ultimately rejected. All of his proposals were presented on these large white cardboard plates.

During this meeting in Clermont-Ferrand, while he was visiting his family for a weekend, he presented me with several options for this logo, respecting a very professional protocol, and telling me the story of each proposal, and explaining each direction he'd taken, before showing me, somewhat ceremoniously, the concepts printed on large, thick cardboard plates (such as the example seen in figure 6.1). The first two didn't really grab me, but the third caught my interest at once: before me, I had the future logo for Allegorithmic, along with its entire range of colors and some variations for letterhead paper, envelopes, business cards and a website.

Here was the logo that would accompany the project and that depicted perfectly the ambition of the name 'Allegorithmic': the fusion of art, embodied by the bird, and science, with Pi (see figure 6.2).

allegorithmic

Figure 6.2: The beginnings of the Allegorithmic logo. Designed by Julien Benassi; with a few precise lines, it transmits the core idea of the name 'Allegorithmic': the union of art and science, respectively embodied by the bird (its head top left of the image) and the mathematical symbol Pi. Moreover, this was a perfectly original creation in the world of tech, which is not typically inclined to represent birds or show subtlety in the range of colors chosen (here I only show the gray version of the Allegorithmic logo).

6.2 BUSI and Christophe Debain

At the very beginning of 2002, the time came to officially launch the project. I took the first step that I'd identified: I approached the business incubator BUSI, a recently-created organization aimed at helping young innovative companies in the region to develop. BUSI accomplished this by supporting them throughout the incubation phase, and providing assistance in various forms. The incubator had connections to a range of local industries and organizations. Being supported by BUSI opened many doors. I scheduled my appointment as soon as I could with Marion Rongère, the director of the incubator.

I was accompanied on the day of the meeting by Christophe Debain, who had agreed to give me a hand in this incubation phase of the project. During the incubation years and for some time after creation, Christophe, who would continue his career path as a researcher at Cemagref, helped me enormously in putting together the files for financial support that we'd submit to the numerous organizations that would follow the Allegorithmic adventure. Christophe's enthusiasm proved valuable, as did the credibility he brought to the project when we met with institutions. I viewed this period of putting together files and asking for financial support as a temporary step, and yet I saw it transform many business creators into experts in Microsoft Word, PowerPoint, and the files that would allow them to obtain grants and other aid, financial channels that were starting to flourish in France. And yet this focus was to the detriment of their project, causing them to lose sight of their primary objective: making products that find their users.

Marion welcomed us to the premises of the BUSI incubator, located north of Clermont-Ferrand. After the presentation of the Allegorithmic project, Marion confirmed that this type of project was very much in demand in the region, and suggested that we emphasize our local roots, rather than highlighting our Parisian connections. There were in fact few deep tech projects in Clermont-Ferrand, while the French state, which had been burned by the internet bubble of 2000 and the consequent harmful effects that were still being felt in the French economy,[4] wanted to double down on supporting more 'classic' innovation.[5] Allegorithmic was clearly a project of this type: I'd just finished a doctoral thesis and my presentations of Allegorithmic were very technical, focusing on the modeling of 'complex environments' applied to the world of computer-generated images. And while few projects could claim to have international interest from the start of their activity, this was the case for Allegorithmic, as our potential customers and partners—video game developers, special effects studios, or 3D software creators—were not based in the Clermont-Ferrand region, and most were located outside France. We therefore had a good chance of attracting the attention of all the financiers of projects of this type in the region.

4: Particularly by the banks, who didn't want to hear anything to do with 'IT,' putting anything and everything in the same bag, as long as it had something to do with a computer.

5: That is, technological innovation, rather than innovation in terms of business models, which was too often the case with so-called 'internet' projects.

BUSI was able to help guide us through the intricacies of public subsidies, which have good intentions, but can be tricky to navigate in practical terms.[6] Marion told us which organizations existed, and which were relevant to support us at which stage of our project. We had to know when and how to access these organizations, and how they relate to the flow of the project overall.

6: One of the reasons for this is that the sources of this funding are varied, ranging from national organizations like ANVAR, regional bodies like the Regional Council, departmental organizations such as those of Puy-de-Dôme or the City of Clermont-Ferrand, or even private companies, like Michelin, or semi-private companies such as export insurers or even honorary loan organizations. . .

This meeting marked the real beginning of the project. This is the first time that I'd heard someone confirm that we had, on paper, something that would be worth funding. According to Marion, the next step is to see ANVAR, as soon as possible.

6.3 ANVAR

ANVAR, the *Agence Nationale de Valorisation de la Recherche*, was a public body with the aim of supporting university or laboratory research, and converting that research into new products or services. Each year, it ran a well-known contest, the *Concours de création d'entreprise de technologie innovante*, that would highlight notable new businesses developing innovative technology, which were identified by the government as potential drivers of value creation and jobs, and support these businesses at two key stages of their development: in the incubation phase, validating the fundamental ideas and goals of the business, and just after creation, helping these businesses to get started in practical terms. When I launched the Allegorithmic project at the start of 2002 this contest had already been in place for a few years. The contest was divided into two categories: 'Incubation,' and 'Creation-Development.'

The support provided by the contest was financial, but also more than this: winning the contest was a seal of quality, as the selection process was carried out by experts who, even if their assessments didn't always prove to be accurate, would nonetheless pick out the best of the best from the list of contest entrants, an evaluation that would reassure other support organizations, banks, and so on, who would therefore be more likely to offer their own support to these selected, 'lower-risk' companies.

Projects entered in the contest were first selected region by region, by local representatives of ANVAR, then some were put forward for special prizes at the national level, with an award ceremony held in Paris. Each year, several thousand projects were initially presented, with around a hundred ultimately being recognized and awarded by ANVAR.

This contest would change everything for Allegorithmic, first for the project, then for the company. The Allegorithmic project won the contest two years in a row, once in each category: in 2002 in the Incubation category, then in 2003 in the Creation-Development category. The prizes were awarded as subsidies (which we therefore didn't need to pay back), 30K euros for the Incubation category, and around 70K euros for Creation-Development. This money made it possible for us to carry out initial business plan work (see Section 6.5) and market validation, as well as to get things moving practically and recruit our first employees, in May 2003 (see Chapter 9).

I also received one of nine special prizes, the '*Jeune Diplômé*' award, a prize for recent graduates. This was a real surprise, and a particular honor to receive. The ceremony took place in the Grand Amphitheater of La Sorbonne in Paris,[7] and the award was presented by Claudie Haigneré, an astronaut, then subsequently Minister Delegate for Research and New Technologies (see figure 6.3).

7: During the event, I met Sébastien Berthet and Pierre Bretagnolle, founders of the company N-Sided, which provides the 3D character creation software 'Quidam.' I have always found Sébastien and Pierre very engaging, and their software took the user experience very seriously. In this, they were way ahead of the rest of the market... Pierre was also involved in the development of the legendary software Amapi, by Yonowat (if you happen to speak French, 'Yonowat? Amapi,' is an excellent French-language, 3D-related pun).

Figure 6.3: July 2003. I receive the *Jeune Diplômé* award, for recent graduates, at the Grand Amphitheater of La Sorbonne in Paris, presented to me by Claudie Haigneré, a French astronaut and at that time the Minister Delegate of New Technologies, in the context of the *Concours de création d'entreprise de technologie innovante*, a contest to identify emerging businesses developing innovative technologies.

6.4 The first Allegorithmic office

Pascalis

The first official office of the Allegorithmic project was located within the Pascalis incubator and business center, located in the Pardieu technological zone in Aubière, near Clermont-Ferrand. Pascalis allowed, at a reduced cost, young workers in that region to develop and take advantage of what the building had to offer, in terms of practical facilities (such as an amphitheater, an excellent internet connection,[8] meeting rooms and training facilities, etc.) but also in terms of opportunities for contact with the network of local businesses.

This office gave the Allegorithmic project a physical presence, and even if the building was a little far from the city center, and there weren't many opportunities for synergy with other companies in the region (we were in a very specific field and for the most part, our clients and partners were not established in Clermont-Ferrand, or even in France), this concrete anchor allowed the project to truly materialize.

8: I also took advantage of this by running Napster at full capacity, putting together some compilations of music that I gave out on CD to a few friends... I abandoned this practise once I could afford to buy music, and above all to subscribe to services like Spotify. That said, I remain convinced that piracy has its place within an ecosystem, and that companies can in fact benefit from this: a very significant portion of our users come from piracy, and we do very little to prevent this.

It was in Pascalis that I met Laurent Baleydier, founder of Kartoo,[9] a company offering a very original technique for visualizing internet search results. Laurent, who became a friend and inspired me a lot with his practical intelligence and his calm enthusiasm (two characteristics which are rarely associated), also introduced me to both Réjean Lapointe, who became our intellectual property consultant (see Chapter 11), and Laurent Carrio, who soon began helping me with my financial management (see Chapter 9). Purely by facilitating these meetings alone, the Pascalis incubator had fulfilled its goal. Without that little office, I wouldn't have had the opportunity to meet these people who would play a critical role in Allegorithmic's success.

Figure 6.4: The very first office (with one workspace!) of the Allegorithmic project was housed in the heart of the incubator and business center Pascalis, at the entrance of the Pardieu tech park in Aubière.

9: Kartoo employed amongst others Nathalie Poughon, who would join Allegorithmic a few years later, as well as Tony Rochon, a childhood friend, as well as a talented designer and illustrator.

Laurent Carrio

Laurent was an independent advisor, and he offered his administrative and financial management assistance services to companies in the region (and beyond). Having previously worked in the iconic Auvergne venture capitalist firm Sofimac,[10] Laurent had a huge amount of experience and common sense, as well as possessing honesty and a connection to reality which were beneficial in the world of startups. His presence alongside an entrepreneur who had not yet proven himself also greatly reassured the future banking and institutional partners of that project, and subsequently of the company, once created.

10: With whom we would work from 2010, see Chapter 23.

After a quick presentation of Allegorithmic, its technology, and its origins, he told me he'd be happy to help us. He appreciated the ambitious, deep tech side of the project, as well as my personality.[11]

11: I mention this here because it's something that we rarely talk about, but which matters to investors and other partners: when the time comes to decide whether to invest, the project leader counts as much as the project itself. A mutual good feeling should exist, and this was certainly the case between me and Laurent.

Laurent would go on to guide us for many years, and would be instrumental in the development of the company. Like Réjean (see the following section), he would also become a good friend.

Figure 6.5: Réjean Lapointe (wearing a mask well before the COVID-19 crisis out of respect for those around him, so as not to contaminate them. . .) and Laurent Carrio, who would respectively play the roles of intellectual property and financial and administrative management advisors for Allegorithmic, for many years—in Réjean's case, perhaps its entire existence (we went on to file around twenty patents throughout the lifespan of the company).

Réjean Lapointe

Réjean, originally from Quebec, came to the Clermont-Ferrand region following an opportunity at the Michelin group. There he held the role of specialist in intellectual property, or 'IP,' drafting and filing numerous patents for the tire company. When I met him he'd been working as an independent consultant for some time, and offered his services to young technological structures in the region, which were often helpless in these areas of IP and protection of patents. A common notion at the time was that software couldn't be patented, an idea which was partly true but which was incomplete and frequently repeated in a caricatured and even dangerous way: not only could the rules vary according to geographical areas (a factor which generated risk in our case, because we were active internationally), but innovative processes including software components certainly could be protected by patent if specific technical conditions were respected (the algorithm in itself was not patentable; it had to be integrated into a broader and original solution, responding to a specific problem).

Figure 6.6: Réjean Lapointe, on the left, who would become our intellectual property advisor.

Réjean alerted me to this point in our first meeting. He then rightly explained that, given the technological depth and international scope of our project, the question of patents and the protection of our innovations was fundamental. He convinced me that we had to use this tool as much as possible, particularly because we were very small and we'd be working with behemoths. We had to arm ourselves correctly to restore a certain balance.

We went on to work alongside Réjean on several patents throughout the lifespan of Allegorithmic. Additionally, Réjean and I became close friends, and he gave me the honor of being the witness at his wedding a few years later.

In retrospect...

We never had to make use of the patents we filed, neither defensively nor offensively, but they gave us a foundation and confidence for numerous discussions. I suspect, without being able to prove it, that the existence of these patents, which we would at times mention subtly in discussions, and at times exhibit them openly and publicly with the phrase 'Patent Pending' in some of our communications, played a role in our ability to work with the industry's giants who would naturally ask the question, 'Make or buy?'—that is, would they develop software internally or buy or license a technology offered by a third party? These big companies would ultimately conclude that it might perhaps be better to work with a small company like Allegorithmic and its partially protected technology than to redevelop everything themselves (which required investment, time, and risk, because success is never guaranteed), and open the door to a legal conflict which would be unwelcome, particularly for a listed company...

6.5 The first Business Plan

The various, diverse subsidies received by the company (notably the aid coming from ANVAR, see Section 6.3) made it possible to launch the drafting of a first Business Plan ('BP'), a document which puts on paper the company's goals and its development plan, covering all the key aspects of a company: finance, marketing, products, personnel, and so on. In particular, a BP must model the future accounts of the company, over several years. One of the fundamental pieces of data required was the turnover that we thought we could achieve over the next few (three, often) years.

On the advice of Christophe Debain, who'd had excellent experiences with the company and its leadership, we began working with D&Consultants, from Grenoble, led by Dominique Carlac'h. Dominique was indeed exceptionally brilliant, and possessed a positive, infectious energy. We got to work and produced Allegorithmic's first Business Plan in just a few weeks.

Figure 6.7: Dominique Carlac'h, head of D&Consultants, with whom we developed the first Business Plan for Allegorithmic. The experience was particularly interesting. More information on Dominique: https://fr.wikipedia.org/wiki/Dominique_Carlac%27h. Image by Estelle Guillemin — Travail personnel, CC BY-SA 4.0, https://commons.wikimedia.org/w/index.php?curid=70286846

I remember feeling intimidated and overwhelmed when we talked about millions of dollars in revenue, and a team of 70 people in the company. I'd never really made these projections before (thanks to naivety...), and the simple mathematical evolution of the plan that we imagined made me dizzy. This was the first time that I became aware of what I was doing, and the means that would have to be implemented to carry out the project. Business Plans force us to reflect and to ask ourselves the right questions, and although a BP is generally incorrect from the moment it is written, the exercise that it imposes is particularly important, and can even prove life-saving.

I also remember Dominique's answer to me, when I voiced my doubts about my ability to manage a company of 70 people:[12] "You can't know this yet, Sébastien; it may very well be that you have this capacity within you..."

Dominique also used the image of a 'Top Gun' for key positions in the company: you have to hire 'a Top Gun per key position in the company.' The classic error is to believe that the leader must know how to do everything better than everybody else,[13] but this is absolutely not the case—and it is even an error which can prove fatal...

12: We would both be right on this point, as we reached this level in 10 years, rather than 3.

13: This view resonated with me, and aligned with a realization that had occurred to me while I was still preparing my thesis... Taking the image of an orchestra: the orchestra's conductor knows the music and where he wants to lead his ensemble, but he cannot play each instrument as well as most of his musicians, and certainly not as well as his soloists. There is a place for conductors, a difference place for soloists, and another place still for the ensemble. If all these skilled people can play together effectively, they can create magic. The day that I understood I was more of a conductor than a soloist, I felt greatly reassured. A place existed for me and, even if I wasn't necessarily the strongest in this or that particular position, I had a way to tell my story... That day, Dominique preferred the term 'Top Gun' to 'soloist,' and yet we were aligned on the same idea.

7 TAON 2, TAON 3

7.1 TAON 2

The first grant from ANVAR in 2002, as well as some other public assistance, allowed us to allocate a small budget to rewrite TAON, the procedural texture generation engine that I'd written the first version of, TAON 1, for my thesis. My thesis work, while certainly making it possible to demonstrate a concept, was far from a marketable product, and possessed architectural limitations which prevented us from testing new ideas. We had to rewrite the software, so that it could evolve. Knowing my own limitations as a programmer, I preferred to devote myself to all the other tasks necessary for the creation of a company. I turned to someone much more talented to code what would become TAON 2, a total rewrite and a major evolution of the engine, which would allow us to validate the concept a little more.

I asked Frédéric Jouhannel to develop it for us. Frédéric happened to be the brother of my girlfriend at the time, but more importantly he was an excellent programmer. He completed TAON 2 a few months later and, being much more complex than TAON 1, it allowed us to demonstrate the value of procedural noises a little more effectively, as well as the advantages of our particular way of producing them.

7.2 TAON 3

The life of a software product being what it is, many rewrites and 're-architectures' of the program's components take place, in order to adapt them to a constantly evolving idea of what we want the program to do. Development choices will vary depending on whether we want to emphasize performance or flexibility and at the beginning of the 2000s, programmable GPUs were not yet fully available, so we needed to 'get close to the metal' to program efficient software. Our noise generators demanded a lot of computing power, and TAON 2 clearly demonstrated the need for optimal performance and, once again, a restructure of the architecture. This time around it was Christophe Soum who would develop this new version of the procedural noise generation engine that was our particular area of expertise.

In parallel with his studies, and now that he'd agreed to join the Allegorithmic adventure as soon as possible, Christophe began working for Allegorithmic on a temporary basis, in the evenings and at weekends. He started his rewrite, with the aim of creating a component with a commercial application, rather than a simple prototype to demonstrate a concept. We needed an engine that would be able support to robust, stable products.

And so Christophe wrote TAON 3 (see figure 7.1), which proved to be incredibly efficient and effective, and which is still the basis of our

DOI:10.1201/9781003534624-7

Substance products twenty years later—a fact which demonstrates the full extent of Christophe's talent, and the durability of his work.

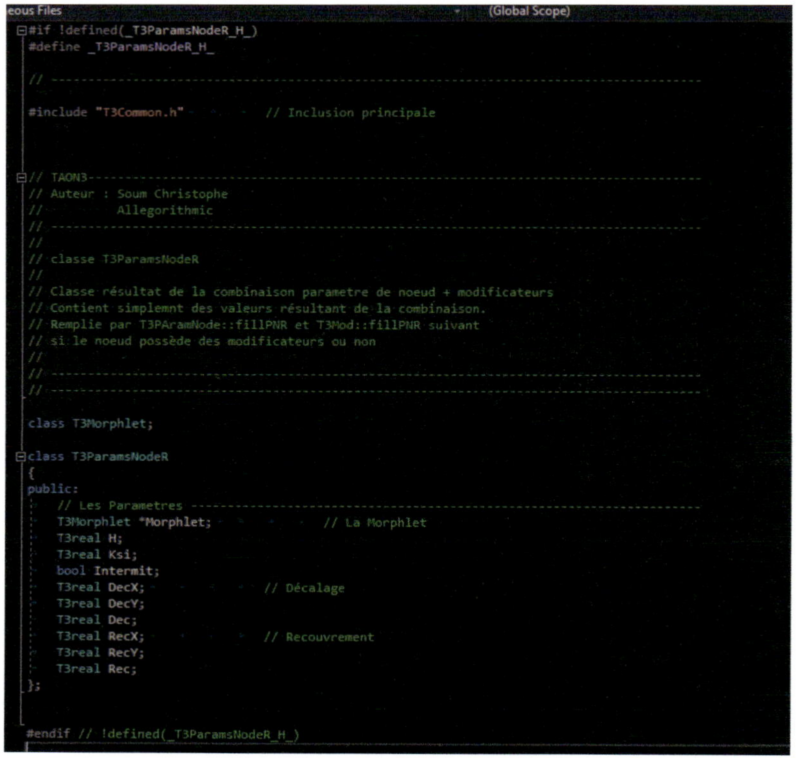

```
eous Files                                   (Global Scope)
#if !defined(_T3ParamsNodeR_H_)
#define _T3ParamsNodeR_H_

// ------------------------------------------------------------------------------------------

#include "T3Common.h"           // Inclusion principale



// TAON3------------------------------------------------------------------------------------
// Auteur : Soum Christophe
//          Allegorithmic
// -----------------------------------------------------------------------------------------
//
// classe T3ParamsNodeR
//
// Classe résultat de la combinaison parametre de noeud + modificateurs
// Contient simplemnt des valeurs résultant de la combinaison.
// Remplie par T3PAramNode::fillPNR et T3Mod::fillPNR suivant
// si le noeud possède des modificateurs ou non
//
// -----------------------------------------------------------------------------------------
// -----------------------------------------------------------------------------------------

class T3Morphlet;

class T3ParamsNodeR
{
public:
    // Les Parametres -----------------------------------------------------------------------
    T3Morphlet *Morphlet;                 // La Morphlet
    T3real H;
    T3real Ksi;
    bool Intermit;
    T3real DecX;                  // Décalage
    T3real DecY;
    T3real Dec;
    T3real RecX;                  // Recouvrement
    T3real RecY;
    T3real Rec;
};


#endif // !defined(_T3ParamsNodeR_H_)
```

Figure 7.1: A portion of the code of TAON 3, from 2002, written by Christophe Soum. Here we can see the class of the renowned 'morphlets' (see Section 3.4).

Conferences 8

8.1 Eurographics Symposium on Rendering, 2002

When we started planning commercial trip ideas and events where we could represent ourselves with the help of the financial aid we'd obtained in the incubation phase, one of the first things I thought of, with a big smile, was to participate in the biggest conferences dedicated to image synthesis that I hadn't been able to attend while writing my thesis (due to lack of means, but also because my thesis work only started moving toward image synthesis later, as seen in Chapter 3). The most iconic of these conferences was SIGGRAPH, which would take place in San Antonio, Texas, at the end of July 2002.[1] Every year, SIGGRAPH brings together scientists, artists, and studios centered around 3D and digital design in general (see Section 8.2). This makes it a prime target for meeting our potential future customers and partners.

There was also Eurographics, a purely scientific conference like SIGGRAPH devoted to the science of computer graphics. It offered a workshop dedicated to rendering, the Workshop on Rendering Techniques, that would take place in Pisa, Italy, that year. The biggest names in the field would be present, and in this case the decision was an easy one: I needed to take part in that event and present the Allegorithmic project to everyone that I could meet there!

After a long car trip from Clermont-Ferrand, I arrived in Pisa. It was June 2002, the weather was magnificent and the event program was particularly interesting,[12] with presentations from the biggest scientific names in 3D, working in leading research labs, as well as within the R&D teams of companies such as Pixar, Microsoft Research, and Digital Domain, which had become renowned for their development of the technologies used for the creation of films and special effects.

Notably, I would here meet [2] for the first time people like Sylvain Lefebvre, then a post-doc at Microsoft Research, who would at a later time become a scientific adviser for Allegorithmic (see Chapter 17), after returning to France following a brilliant research career at INRIA, or Marie-Claude Frasson, who began a thesis at INRIA Sophia-Antipolis, after working with Softimage in Montreal. With a level of English that was broken and laborious, and I imagine quite demanding for the listener,[3] I presented Allegorithmic to many people from the industry and the world of research. I also pitched to Doug Roble, from Digital Domain, who invited me to make a presentation at their legendary studio in Venice, California,[4] as well as Per Christensen, one of the developers of the Renderman render engine from Pixar, who told me to speak to a certain Guido Quaroni, in charge of tools within their studio.[5]

More surprisingly, I ran into Cyrille Damez, who I hadn't seen for a long time. Cyrille and I had exchanged Apple II C programs many years earlier, while in high school at Lycée Jeanne d'Arc in Clermont-Ferrand. Now, he

1: This conference is a point of reference in the field of 3D and digital imagery. Every year it brings together tens of thousands of attendees, including scientists, artists, journalists and industry veterans. SIGGRAPH is simultaneously a conference, an exhibition and a traveling commercial trade show that takes place between several large American cities. Inaugurated in 1974, it takes place every summer and has a large influence on Allegorithmic, playing an important role as an annual meetup, just like GDC (the Game Developers Conference) which takes place in March. I attended every SIGGRAPH between 2002 and 2019, which would make 18 in total! This was the only conference I refused to miss under any circumstance.

2: This was the beginning of my collection of business cards, which I collect and exchange avidly, as happy as any collector when I manage to obtain a card from a legend in the field or a prestigious studio. All these names that seemed so far away for me, so inaccessible, were now within reach. Allegorithmic and I were now part of this world. Nothing could have made me happier. I would go on to collect thousands of business cards throughout Allegorithmic's life. This object, in a broadly defined format, sets up meetings, and helps me classify information, to retain and return to. After a conference comes the time to sort through the cards and get back to people via email. It is an absolute pleasure to dive back into the event, reconstructed thanks to these cards, and to make contact with people who showed a spark of interest in what we do.

3: These were the first nights when I dreamt in English, which was quite exhausting at this stage of my language studies.

4: I would go to see them during my first visit to the US, passing through Los Angeles in January 2004, see Chapter 20.

5: Whom I would see during my first trip to the Bay Area, around San Francisco, also see Chapter 20.

DOI:10.1201/9781003534624-8

was doing his post-doctorate at the Max Plank Institute für Informatik, in Saarbrücke, Germany. Here in Pisa, I hadn't expected to see somebody I knew, and moreover somebody from Auvergne, with whom I'd shared a passion when we were young. Cyrille had had an impressive academic career, having written a thesis on global illumination at INRIA, under the supervision of François Xavier Sillon. I presented the Allegorithmic project to him, and said that I was in the process of building a team. Surprisingly, he told me that the project might be of interest to him once his post-doc was completed. It would be an incredible stroke of fortune to have someone of his caliber join us—it would undoubtedly boost the project, as well as provide it with an immediate international dimension. His academic career was recognized as remarkable, and he knew many prominent people in the sector of 3D research.

The appointment was made—Cyrille would ultimately join the Allegorithmic adventure 20 months later, in January 2004.

Figure 8.1: A few photos from the Eurographics Symposium on Rendering 2002 in Pisa, Italy. In addition to representing Europe during a football match organized on the outskirts of the conference, we can see in these photos some of the notable people encountered during this first event: Doug Roble (Digital Domain, orange T-shirt and arms folded), and on the group photo below, Cyrille Damez (who would join us some months later, third crouching on the right), Marie-Claude Frasson (Softimage, INRIA, first row standing starting from the bottom, fourth from the right) and to her right Sylvain Lefebvre (Microsoft Research, INRIA, who would become the scientific advisor for Allegorithmic a few years later) and my own head just next to Sylvain's.

8.2 SIGGRAPH 2002

It was the first time I'd returned to the US in over 10 years (my prior trip being a holiday with my parents), and I felt the same shock I had during that first visit: what we see in the TV shows and films I'd grown up with, I now found myself immersed in. These places had become reality—they were not merely sets or props created for a show, but simply what existed around me, so much so that I felt that I was myself within a movie. I had arrived in Texas, in San Antonio, to experience my first SIGGRAPH!

The conference delivered on all its promises, and I was stunned by the size of the event. Everything was perfectly organized, and after having first traveled between the hotel and the convention center on foot, in sweltering heat and surrounded by the nauseating odors of cooking, I was surprised to learn that shuttles were available to transport us to and from the conference, morning and evening (and with air conditioning)... Air conditioning was omnipresent in the convention center, and I still don't really understand why it was always set to 16 degrees inside conference rooms, in stark contrast to the stifling exterior. Thermal shock was a permanent state, and exhaustion was inevitable.

Figure 8.2: My first SIGGRAPH, summer 2002, in San Antonio, Texas.

Figure 8.3: SIGGRAPH 2002, in San Antonio, Texas. Pictures by Jeremy Birn www.3dRender.com http://www.3drender.com/updates/sig02/index.htm

This SIGGRAPH will always remain the one that affected me the most, and I really felt like I was in a dream throughout its whole duration. Its atmosphere was extraordinary, everything focused on a field of passion for everybody present. All of its participants, who came from the four corners of the world, were like myself dedicated to digital imagery; they were brilliant and creative, and everybody seemed delighted to be in that place, directing the future of our domain while also celebrating together. With Allegorithmic and my love for the sciences and the arts this place, with its absolute mix of these two areas, felt very fulfilling to me. It was an incredible interlude in the Allegorithmic adventure.

It was also an opportunity for me to meet as many people as possible, to present the Allegorithmic project as widely as possible, and to make contacts and try to promote our future products. My success here surpassed my expectations—the entire industry was present, and I collected dozens of business cards, each one representing an opportunity to explore once I got back to Clermont-Ferrand to follow up by mail.

I also saw some of the people I'd met a few weeks earlier in Pisa, who introduced me to new people. Once again I met Xavier Bec from BUF Compagnie, whom I hadn't seen for nearly a year, since a few days before I'd defended my thesis. Again, he told me that our techniques would have trouble finding a place at BUF, but he introduced me to several key people he knew well, who in turn introduced me to others, and so on. The network effect was working well.

At some point, the chain of contacts led me to Dave Lajoie, who worked at the well-known company Softimage[6] and who, following a brief introduction, asked me to meet him early one morning at his hotel, on the 36th floor.[7] He was impressed by what I showed him and invited me to present my project to the rest of his team in Montreal, to discuss what we could do together.

6: This firm from Quebec continued to be the ultimate reference software for 3D and was also the same software I taught during my thesis (see Chapter 4). This meeting was therefore very important to me, and I wanted to see if we could work together. The goal was to also validate what we were doing in the eyes of a true professional, whose tools were recognized by the whole industry.

7: All this seemed surreal and perpetuated the feeling that I was in a film: a building that seemed huge to me, impromptu meetings, an important figure in the field who would give me a few minutes of his time, and so on.

The trip that would ultimately take place in January 2004 (see Chapter 20) was starting to take shape, and would include include numerous stops. . .

Figure 8.4: Alexis Casas (third from the right) to my left, and Stefano Salvini (extreme right) during SIGGRAPH 2002 in San Antonio. Alexis would be very important in helping us to make contacts at the start of the adventure, in addition to becoming a friend.

Finally, it was during this SIGGRAPH that I met Alexis Casas (see figure 8.4), who was just beginning his career in 3D, working at Mac Guff Ligne, a major Parisian special effects studio. We got along extremely well and were both fascinated by this SIGGRAPH, experiencing the event to the fullest. He would have an important role to play in the next stage for Allegorithmic,[8] as he would open the doors to Mac Guff for me, which would become one of our first alpha-site studios (see Section 10.2).

8: Alexis would be play an important role in the long run, both for Allegorithmic and for me personally: it was thanks to Alexis in particular that I met my future wife a few years later when, staying with him in Paris during one of my many stopovers, I went with him to a party completely unrelated to 3D, where I met Laëtitia. She'd studied at ESSEC, and it was through her that I'd meet Alexis Khouri (see Chapter 19) in 2006; we'd work together to mine the 'ESSEC vein.'

Part V

2003–2007

Beginnings | 9

Until this point, Allegorithmic had been a project, born from a theory, desires, and dreams, then incubated to create prototypes, plans, and projections. Between mid-2003 and mid-2007, Allegorithmic truly took shape and established itself, testing its ideas on the market, and seeing whether clients were ready to validate what we thought we could bring to the world of 3D.

This era represented the 'first life' of Allegorithmic as a company, a period of building the team, management, branding, defining technological pivots, releasing our first products, presentations, and on-site visits; it represented our first successes but also, of course, numerous mistakes and sometimes crushing failures.

It was a period of intense learning, fueled by passion and great naivety, always. And despite sales results which were not always sufficient, it was during this period that some of the most important seeds for the future, and for the success of Allegorithmic, were planted. Some of these seeds would bear fruit only a decade or more later.

9.1 Incorporation

Work on the official registration of the company took place during the first half of 2003. We worked with the company Fidal, in Aubière, and in particular with Dominique Bajan, a colorful lawyer that my father knew well, who he'd worked with for many years. In looking for shareholders for the company, alongside myself, I of course approached Albert Benassi, but also my father and Christophe Debain. We defined a total capital, and distributed it in a way that seemed to me to make the most sense. I had the majority of the shares without being above 50%.[1] This money from the total capital would finance the company in its first years. To be able to contribute my part, I applied for an honorary loan, a specific type of loan mechanism dedicated to business creators, which allows them to launch their adventures with sufficient funds.[2]

Once the funds were provided, (see figure 9.1) and statues were drafted, the company Allegorithmic was officially founded, on May 22, 2003! This was the official beginning of our adventure, the official start of our financial, legal, administrative, and equipment needs. This beginning was closely paralleled by a period of searching for premises, building a team (Allegorithmic could now officially welcome its first employees), creation of a website, research and development for our products—and of course gear, specifically our first Allegorithmic T-shirt (see Section 9.4)! Once everything was ready, we could start looking for customers.

1: Which, in retrospect, is something I should have done differently: I now feel that the active founder(s) should stay well above this threshold of 50%, which makes it possible to unblock natural conflict situations between partners. In the case of Allegorithmic, this situation never reached an irresolvable point, but the risk inherent in this initial allocation now seems obvious to me. Our advisor at Fidal had already told me this, but I'd insisted that things should be different when creating Allegorithmic.

2: I would only be able to repay this loan many years later...

DOI:10.1201/9781003534624-9

BANQUE POPULAIRE

BANQUE POPULAIRE DU MASSIF CENTRAL

DEPOT N° A180/SU 22 MAI 2003

AGENCE LES CARMES

CERTIFICAT DE DEPOT DE FONDS

La BANQUE POPULAIRE DU MASSIF CENTRAL, Société Anonyme Coopérative de Banque Populaire à capital variable dont le siège social est 18 Boulevard Jean Moulin 63002 - Clermond-Ferrand
(RCS N° 775 633 878)

représentée par Mc Fortin, Directeur d'agence, certifie :

1 - qu'il a été ouvert à son agence, sous le n° 00892974957 un compte indisponible portant le libellé suivant : ALLEGORITHMIC.

2 - qu'il a été remis par chèque ou espèces, pour être créditée à ce compte, la somme de 45 000,00 euros (quarante-cinq mille euros).

représentant la totalité des versements effectués par les souscripteurs en numéraire conformément à ceux prévus dans la liste des souscripteurs :

- du capital de la sas ALLEGORITHMIC en formation (1)
- ~~de l'augmentation de capital de la sas ALLEGORITHMIC en formation (1)~~

Ces versements ont été effectués de la manière ci-après indiquée :

Sébastien DEGUY	24 750,00 euros
Christian DEGUY	6 750,00 euros
Christophe DEBAIN	6 750,00 euros
Albert BENASSI HOUBEN	6 750,00 euros

Ils resteront immobilisés dans les conditions légales et réglementaires.

Fait à CLERMONT-FERRAND, le 5 Mai 2003
en quatre originaux
(signature du directeur et cachet de l'agence)

BANQUE POPULAIRE
DU MASSIF CENTRAL
1, Avenue de la République
63000 CLERMONT-FERRAND
Tél. 04 73 98 21 98
Fax 04 73 90 05 32
775 633 878 RCS Clermont-Fd

1, avenue de la République
63000 Clermont-Ferrand
Téléphone : 08 20 34 22 30 (0,19 € la minute)
Télécopie : 04 73 90 05 32
Internet : www.massifcentral.banquepopulaire.fr

(1) Rayer la mention inutile

Figure 9.1: Certification of deposit of funds to constitute the capital of the company Allegorithmic, newly created on May 22, 2003. We can see the names of the four shareholders Christian Deguy (my father), Albert Benassi (my thesis director), Christophe Debain, and myself. We can also see the name of Marie-Christine Fortin, business affairs manager at our bank, the *Banque Populaire du Massif Central*, who would support us throughout the adventure.

9.2 The team

In addition to Christophe,[3] previously presented in Section 4.2, the team was quickly completed during the first year of Allegorithmic's existence.

3: Technically, Christophe appears fourth on the list of employees, because he was officially registered last of four initial employees, on July 1, 2003.

Catherine Debain

As soon as the company had been created, it became clear that I would need administrative assistance. Christophe Debain suggested that his wife Catherine join Allegorithmic and occupy this position of administrative and financial manager, to free me from this aspect of the work. Catherine was looking for a new project and Christophe thought, correctly, that she and I would get along well. Catherine and I went on to work together for many years, and if Allegorithmic and its team of newly graduated geeks were able to do solid work by focusing on products, it's because we owe a large part of our commercial and marketing development to Catherine.

Pierre Boy

Pierre Boy was the first person I contacted remotely to offer him a position without knowing him personally. He was a 3D rendering specialist. He answered one of our ads, then joined us; Pierre (who can be seen in one of the images in figure 9.9) stayed with us for a little over 4 years before moving to another of his passions: sculpture. Pierre was an example of something we'd observe regularly during the life of Allegorithmic: many of its members had additional talents, often artistic talents, in addition to their technical skills. This was one notable element that tended to make them a good fit for the Allegorithmic team.

Figure 9.2: Catherine Debain, who had the office opposite mine.

Cyrille Damez

Cyrille, whom I'd met again during the conference on rendering in Pisa, Italy, at the end of June 2002 (see section 8.1), officially joined us at the beginning of January 2004, once he'd completed his postdoc at the Max Planck Institute in Saarbrücke, Germany. In the same way as Christophe, Cyrille would go on to remain with Allegorithmic throughout its existence, taking on the position of Chief Technology Officer, or CTO, in the mid-2010s. Cyrille played a major role, acting as a technological caretaker for Allegorithmic through his technical and scientific contributions, as well as through his serious, constructive attitude and his exemplary professionalism.

Figure 9.3: Cyrille Damez, who joined us in January 2004, right after finishing his postdoc in Germany. Cyrille would accompany Allegorithmic throughout its existence, becoming CTO in the mid-2010s.

Alexandre Valentin

Alexandre was a young student at ISIMA who was passionate about 3D. ISIMA's 'Junior Entreprise' program carried out commissioned work for companies needing a little assistance; Alexandre was a student in this program, and the director of the school put me in contact with him. Alexandre produced the first version of a texture creation graph, which allowed us to validate certain hypotheses (and which we would push to its limits years later with Substance Designer, see Section 27.3). Alexandre (who can be seen in one of the images in figure 9.9) joined us part-time on July 1, 2003, as one of Allegorithmic's first four employees. He would remain part of the team for a little over a year before moving on to further adventures.

Benjamin Maréchal

Benjamin Maréchal, a young graphic and digital design graduate, joined us in September 2003, a few months after the first four employees. I asked him to join on the advice of Joan Da Silva,[4] who was the founder and director of Artepict, a company in the Clermont-Ferrand region, where Benjamin had done his graphic designer internship. Joan told me that Benjamin was talented, and said that having internal artists within Allegorithmic was a good idea, in order to avoid developing tools that were too far removed from the real needs of users. Having an artist like Benjamin close to the developers while they wrote the software could therefore prove valuable.

4: Joan is a pioneer in digital imaging in Clermont-Ferrand. For instance, he was the first person I ever saw using Silicon Graphics workstations and 3D software I'd never heard of. I often say that he was 10 years ahead of Clermont-Ferrand, and he always gives me excellent advice and tells me what I need to hear, albeit sometimes without any sort of filter. He was one of the first to tell me that MaP | Zone wasn't very useful, but that MaP | Time would be able to find its users. He was right about MaP | Zone, a little less so about MaP | Time (as it wasn't exactly a commercial success either. . .) but he put his finger on the deeper issues with our software in its first iterations.

Benjamin started to produce renders and textures, as seen in figure 9.4. He would remain with us throughout the Allegorithmic adventure, taking charge of the company's graphic identity for the second half of its existence, as well as managing all imagery and visual presentation of products, the company's brand identity, and more.

Figure 9.4: Left, a photo of the Getty museum, Los Angeles. Right, a synthetic render with textures produced using MaP | Zone, all created by Benjamin Maréchal.

Notable interns

Simon Brunel

Simon Brunel was an engineering student at ISIMA. He joined us for an internship around March 2004 (prior to being hired for good at the end of 2006), to help the technical teams on various subjects. Simon, who can be seen in one of the images in figure 9.9, would notably develop an idea I had at the end of my thesis, without being able to implement it, that centered on using physical phenomena to create textures, specifically the use of particles which would leave 'traces.'[5]

5: The process allowed the generation of very beautiful fractures; I nicknamed it 'Rampage,' in reference to an ATARI ST game that I played a lot as a teenager.

Figure 9.5: Textures made by Benjamin Maréchal using MaP | Zone.

The idea was to let particles evolve responding to physical laws that we could control, leaving traces and so marking their paths on matter. Albert had pointed out to us that fractures naturally create right angles (see figure 9.6), and with this in mind we obtained completely realistic 'traces.' The results were spectacular and the internship was a great success (see figure 9.7).

Figure 9.6: Albert made us realize that fractures naturally create right angles and follow the constraints of the environment (here, for example, around the stone). Once he pointed this out, we saw the phenomenon everywhere!

The idea behind this internship would become the basis of a completely original feature that would be implemented in Substance Painter almost 10 years later (see Chapter 29).

Nicolas Wirrmann

Nicolas Wirrmann (who can be seen in one the images in figure 9.9) was a 3D artist specializing in architectural renders, who was an expert with the V-Ray rendering engine created by the Bulgarian company ChaosGroup.[6] He joined us first as an intern, then began a vocational degree as an apprentice in October 2005, at the University Institute of Technology of Puy-en-Velay. He therefore divided his time between Allegorithmic and his classes.

6: With whom we would find ourselves in Sweden for a special project with IKEA about 10 years later.

Passionate about images, an extremely talented photographer, and very picky about realism in synthesized imagery, Nicolas was very doubtful about the potential of procedural generation. When he joined Allegorithmic, it was not out of love for our technology. But after several years he became one of the major contributors to the design of our product Substance Designer (see Chapter 26). He would become one of the 'Great Elders' of the tool (see Chapter 43).

Figure 9.8 shows two renders made by Nicolas while he was doing his internship in June 2005. Here we see one of the advantages of the procedural texturing that our tools made possible: the ability to change some texture parameters, and so modify the appearance of a material, in

Figure 9.7: These images were created using the 'P6' software (also known by its codename 'Rampage'), created by Simon Brunel during his internship. The idea behind this internship would become the basis of a completely original feature that would be implemented in Substance Painter almost 10 years later (see Chapter 29).

Figure 9.8: Two renders demonstrating one of the advantages of procedural texturing, the possibility of variation, here used to show the progress of time. These textures and renders were produced in June 2005 by Nicolas Wirrmann, who at the time was a skeptical about procedural texture generation. He would become one of the 'Great Elders' in that area (see Chapter 30). Also note that fracture effects on the mirror and the tiles are achieved using the software created by Simon Brunel during his internship (see figure 9.6).

this case to make it appear older and dirtier. In this way it was possible to obtain material variations very quickly, without having to remake the whole material from scratch. This could prove particularly interesting in the context of synthetic image production, when an artistic director might regularly ask for changes to the appearance of textures, avoiding the need to throw out previous work and start again.

This double image of the bathroom went on to become particularly important to Allegorithmic. It was one of the first we used to convincingly demonstrate one of the fundamental advantages of the procedural techniques that we were promoting. We used it in all our communications.[7]

7: The image greatly impressed Bernard Charlès and Pascal Daloz, respectively CEO and EVP of Strategy for Dassault Systèmes, and they mentioned it to me when they decided to invest in Allegorithmic in 2007 (see Chapter 18). A picture really is worth a thousand words. This double image caused the overall concept to 'click' in some people's minds, and had a gigantic impact overall, particularly given that it was created quite quickly.

Gilles Fleury

I was invited to give a class on 3D for a specialized training course (I forget its name, now) in Clermont-Ferrand, after its director had learned of Allegorithmic's existence in an article published some time earlier. I gave a presentation to perhaps ten students and once my presentation was finished, the Q&A phase became very much a one-on-one discussion between myself and one of the students, Gilles Fleury. As he asked me question after question, it became evident that he knew the subject well, and was passionate about the creation of video games.

I invited him to visit our office, which he did a few days later. Here, Gilles asked the whole team even more questions, and seemed to be particularly interested in our area: textures, and procedural creation. Though he wasn't an engineer or self-taught developer, he showed an enthusiasm and curiosity for the domain which, I began to think, could bring a lot to the team.

Gilles lived in an exceptionally run-down apartment in a damp, dark street in old Clermont-Ferrand. Everything at his place was dedicated to video games; he was an *Otaku*, with a passion for his interests that I've rarely seen elsewhere. His trajectory through life had been complicated, and he hadn't always passed through the healthiest environments—but our meeting struck us both in the same way: it was an opportunity for Gilles to build something unique and positive... I offered him an end-of-the-year internship, and insisted on paying him something for his work.[8]

8: Which was not the norm for internships in France at that time.

I had always shared Joan Da Silva's opinion (see section 3) that we needed to avoid a classic pitfall of software development: having tools made *by* engineers, *for* non-engineers. Our users were clearly 3D artists, so we had to have 3D artists within our team, as close as possible to these engineers, to take part in product design, provide day-to-day feedback,[9] run tests, and produce convincing demos with our products.

9: Continuously—such micro-corrections prove to be absolutely invaluable in ensuring that the product doesn't drift from its objective: market fit. Here, the market was represented by the artists who were part of the development team, and it was these artists (here, Gilles, but also Nicolas and Benjamin), who knew whether or not we were on the right track. I learned an expression in English that I felt summarized the concept quite succinctly: *Eat your own dog food*. Without offering a theoretical or formal point of view on this notion, having artists on the development team was fundamental to the success of Allegorithmic.

During his internship, Gilles (who can be seen in one of the images in figure 9.9) absolutely demonstrated the value that we'd anticipated in him. He proved vital, and we knew we had to make him stay. We tightened our belts so that the financial side worked out, and managed to make it happen. He agreed to join our team of technical artists, alongside Nicolas Wirrmann and Benjamin Maréchal and would become another of the 'Great Elders' of Substance Designer (see Chapter 30). Before that, he also played a central role in one of Allegorithmic's first major challenges: the use of our technology for the game *RoboBlitz* (see Chapter 13).

Finding such a valuable team member here, and at this time, was a surprise, and an illustration of the adage that talent can flourish in the most inhospitable and unexpected environments.

Nicolas Polo

Nicolas Polo (who can be seen in one of the images in figure 9.9) was a student at the Sup de Co—the *École supérieure de commerce*, a university-level business school—of Clermont-Ferrand, who was looking for an internship. He'd contacted me while I was still at Pascalis, and finding it interesting to have help in the commercial and marketing aspects of our work, we welcomed him on a work-study basis. Nicolas brought all of his enthusiasm to the project and contributed in a range of different areas. For a time, he was my right hand on a range of commercial subjects, partnerships, events (with the press in particular),[10] and marketing. With Nicolas, I felt for the first time the impact that a marketing director could bring, as well as the importance of certain 'horizontal' functions which filled in gaps and kept the machine running—the type of aspects represented in the role of Chief Operating Officer.

10: For instance, he organized the first press presentation of Allegorithmic at *la Maison de l'Auvergne*, a museum in Paris, which attracted a few wayward souls, drawn in more by the orange juice and champagne that we provided than in anything we had to say. However, it was here that for the first time we met some journalists from the industry, and we remained close to some of them. Once again, an event with middling success in the moment can have a major effect in the longer term.

An inner circle advisor: Patrick Dumas

I met Patrick Dumas during an Apple World event in Paris. Patrick used to be the Vice President in charge of Marketing at Avid, specifically pushing for products such as Softimage XSI (a new version of the Softimage 3D software I taught during my doctorate, see Chapter 4). He was therefore very familiar with the world of 3D and was looking for a consulting opportunity. Following a demo of our technology, that I gave with Alexandre Valentin, we discussed what he could do for us. He was very interested and had a lot of ideas—as well as many contacts.[11] Shortly after this first meeting, we found a way to work together. He would play a networking and advisory role for us during the first few years of Allegorithmic's life, and we were very lucky to be able to count on someone like Patrick. His initial contacts unblocked a lot of potential issues for us, and allowed us to get things moving: when the former Vice President of Marketing at Softimage tells you're going to meet a young French entrepreneur who will be absolutely inspiring, doors and ears open up more easily...

11: He would help me meet a number of people during my first visit to North America in January 2004, see Chapter 20.

A bank, and Marie-Christine Fortin

Allegorithmic had to open its first bank account at the moment of its creation, and we worked with the *Banque Populaire du Massif Central*, a prominent bank in the region, who welcomed us with open arms. I have to here express my gratitude to Marie-Christine Fortin, who at the time was responsible for customer relations with local companies, with whom we would work throughout Allegorithmic's adventure. Marie-Christine proved, on all occasions, to be a source of extraordinary support and enthusiasm for the Allegorithmic project. Marie-Christine was also the only one who proved willing to support my personal requirements, when all other banks refused me loans in the mid-2010s:[12] she was the only one who was willing to take the risk, being familiar with our company, seeing our evolution, and sensing our potential.

12: As an entrepreneur in debt and at the head of a company that was still losing money, I was too much of a risk for the banking establishments.

The whole team

Here we were at the end of 2003, ready to start the adventure. We had a formal company, premises (at ISIMA), legal advisors (Fidal), a bank (the *Banque Populaire du Massif Central*, and in particular Marie-Christine Fortin), an intellectual property advisor (Réjean Lapointe and his company Twenans), a financial management advisor (Laurent Carrio, and his company Digefi), a Business Plan, a range of various awards that gave the company a good name, support from dedicated institutions and organizations like ANVAR, a strong team of permanent and temporary staff (see above), and all we needed now were premises that could accommodate a growing team—as well as, of course, a product to sell, a website. . . and T-shirts with the Allegorithmic logo!

Figure 9.9: Christophe Soum (top). On the second image: Pierre Boy, Nicolas Polo, Sébastien Deguy (I am of course pretending to do important business on the phone), Alexandre Valentin, and Christophe Soum (and an English-French dictionary). On the two bottom images: Nicolas Wirrmann rolling along the corridor (bottom left); Simon Brunel, Nicolas Wirrmann and Gilles Fleury taking a break outside the office.

9.3 Premises

Once the company was created, with the latest arrivals, we needed more space, as the Pascalis office was becoming rather small. Then an extraordinary opportunity presented itself: ISIMA, the software engineering school on the Cézeaux campus, offered to house us for free, placing several classrooms at our disposal that we could transform into offices. This was an idea put forward by the director of ISIMA Alain Quilliot.[13] Alain loved the idea of technological, inspirational companies operating as close as possible to students.

13: Mathematician, and son of Roger Quilliot, the former Minister of Housing under François Mitterrand, and senator of the Puy-de-Dôme region.

Figure 9.10: The Allegorithmic headquarters in 2006, in a classroom of one of the wings of ISIMA, in Clermont-Ferrand. From left to right: Gilles Fleury, Benjamin Maréchal, Simon Brunel, Christophe Soum, Cyrille Damez, Pierre Boy.

We therefore took up residence in these premises (see figures 9.10, 9.11, 9.12, 9.13, 9.14, 9.3 and even 9.9), and remained there for the next five years.

Economie

Innovant

Du virtuel de plus en plus réel

Effets spéciaux au cinéma, jeux 3D sur consoles : le virtuel devient de plus en plus... réel. Grâce au talent d'infographistes qui savent tirer profit d'outils informatiques toujours plus innovants. A l'image de ceux que propose la toute jeune société clermontoise, Allegorithmic.

A 26 ans, Sébastien Deguy n'est pas du genre à perdre du temps. Il y a deux ans, sa thèse — sur la modélisation des milieux complexes — tout juste en poche (*), ce jeune clermontois décidait de créer sa propre entreprise. Il est vrai que peu de temps avant, il avait été contacté par BUF Compagnie, l'une des plus importantes sociétés françaises d'effets spéciaux qui a, notamment, travaillé sur diverses scènes de deux derniers films de la trilogie *Matrix*. « Ça m'a donné envie de pousser dans ce domaine-là parce qu'il y avait une attente ». Ce *domaine-là*, c'est la création d'images de synthèse. Un temps chargé de cours à l'IUT informatique et imagerie du Puy-en-Velay, c'est là que Sébastien Deguy s'est aperçu qu'il était possible « de faire plus facilement de meilleures textures qu'avec des logiciels professionnels appropriés ».

Fils de chef d'entreprise, l'entreprenariat ne l'effrayait pas : « Je connaissais les efforts que cela demande. Je connaissais aussi la satisfaction que l'on peut avoir en retour ». Et puis, d'une manière générale, confie-t-il, « j'aime créer ». Après avoir écrit, réalisé des courts métrages d'animation, pourquoi ne pas créer une entreprise ? La suite allait lui donner raison.

Le projet est accepté par BUSI, l'incubateur de la région. « Cela m'a permis de formaliser ce que j'avais en tête ». Cela lui a également permis de rencontrer les gens qui comptent dans le domaine des effets spéciaux ou de la conception des jeux 3D.

« Je suis parti aux Etats-Unis avec mon sac à dos et un CD rom de démonstration. J'ai pu nouer des contacts et l'accueil favorable m'a conforté ». Tout comme le concours national d'aide à la création d'entreprises de technologies innovantes dont il est une première fois lauréat en 2002. Un prix qui lui a permis de financer une étude de marché « qui a validé le projet sur un plan comptable ».

Productivité et créativité

Allegorithmic n'est plus un concept. Hébergée dans les locaux de l'ISIMA sur le campus des Cézeaux à Clermont-Ferrand, la jeune société compte cinq personnes qui s'attachent désormais à développer des logiciels permettant de modéliser des textures plus facilement et plus rapidement que ne le ferait un infographiste. D'en inventer de nouvelles, impossibles à réaliser jusque-là, avec, au final, une qualité inégalée en offrant un réalisme *plus vrai que nature*.

Productivité et créativité sont donc au rendez-vous de ces logiciels qui, souligne Sébastien Deguy, « évoluent sans cesse ». À côté de cela, Allegorithmic a « plein de projets en attente dans les cartons », destinés à d'autres segments intéressant des secteurs qui ont eux aussi besoin de textures : la production de plastique, le design.

Bien des perspectives s'ouvrent désormais. D'autant qu'en juillet, la toute jeune société a participé au Siggraph 2003 qui se tenait à San Diego en Californie. Le plus grand salon mondial de la synthèse d'image où Allegorithmic s'est fait remarquer tant par des éditeurs informatiques (Adobe, Visual FX) que des studios d'effets spéciaux (Pixar, PDI/Dreamworks) ont salué ce logiciel à l'instar de Scott Kirvan PDG de Splutterfish : « C'est l'une des technologies les plus intéressantes, et des plus stimulantes intellectuellement, dévoilées au Siggraph ». Et comme si cela ne suffisait pas, il y a quelques semaines de cela, Sébastien Deguy a été désigné une nouvelle fois comme lauréat du concours d'aide à la création d'entreprises de technologies innovantes.

Après un premier contrat de partenariat signé, la semaine dernière, avec MacGuffline (la pub Evian avec les bébés nageurs), Sébastien Deguy s'envolera bientôt pour le Canada afin d'y rencontrer de grands éditeurs de jeux 3D et signer ses premiers contrats commerciaux...

Jean-Pierre VACHEROT.

(*) Sa thèse a été menée au laboratoire algorithme et informatique (LAAIC) de l'université de Clermont I.

Contact : contact@allegorithmic.com ou sur le web : www.allegorithmic.com

Photos : Pierre COUBLE

Sébastien Deguy attend beaucoup des retombées du Siggraph.

Sébastien Deguy et l'équipe d'Allegorithmic : la moyenne d'âge ne dépasse pas 25 ans.

La Poste

Changement aux services financiers

Figure 9.11: One of the first articles about Allegorithmic, published in October 2003, a few months after its creation. On the photo, taken in the premises loaned to us by ISIMA on the Cézeaux campus in Clermont-Ferrand, we can see: an intern whose name escapes me, Pierre Boy, Sébastien Deguy, Nicolas Polo, Benjamin Maréchal. Missing from the photo: Catherine Debain, Christophe Soum and Alexandre Valentin.

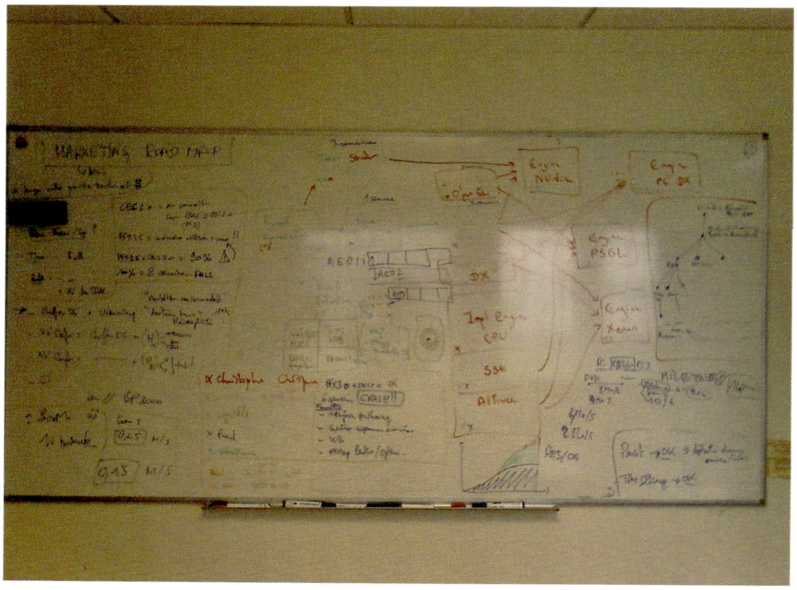

Figure 9.12: A whiteboard, a central object and general receptacle of all our ideas and whatever other information seemed relevant to display.

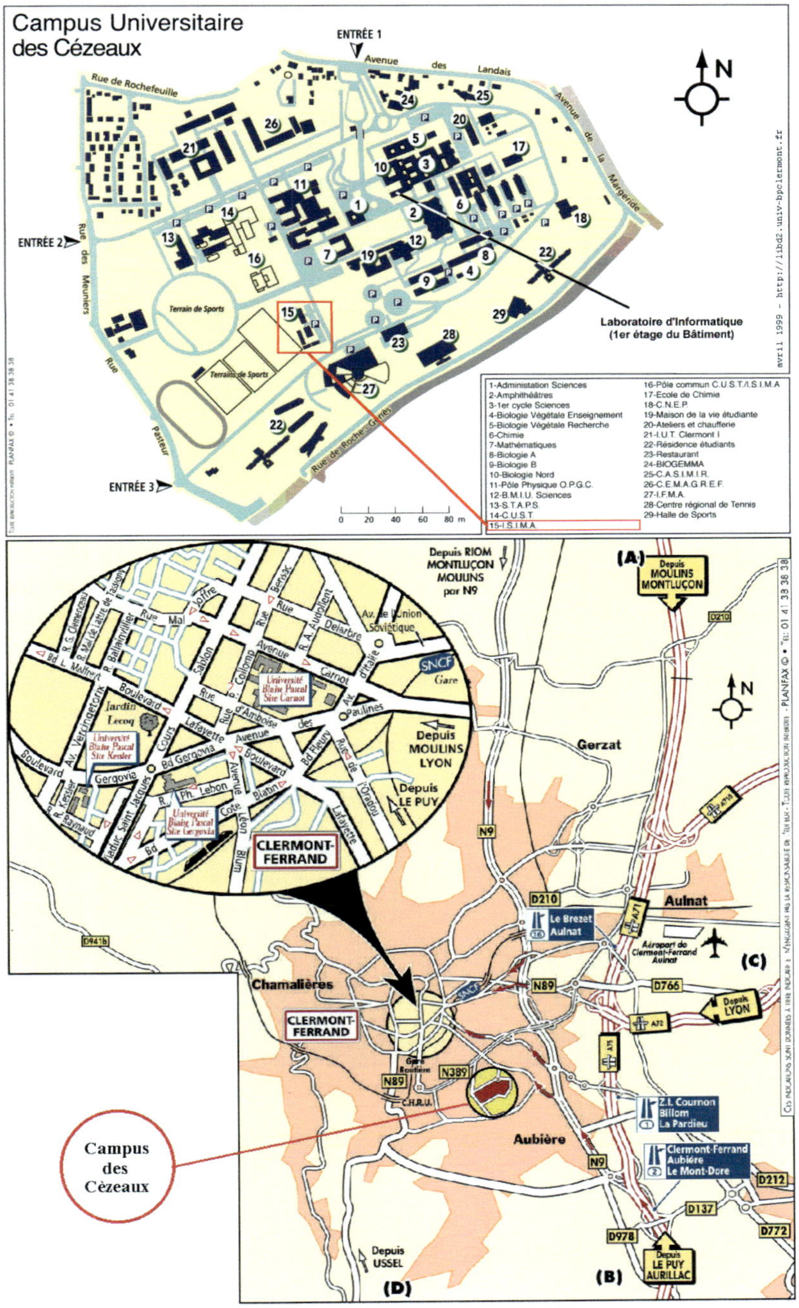

Figure 9.13: The map showing access to the Allegorithmic offices within ISIMA, as presented on the first Allegorithmic webpage.

Figure 9.14: *Espace Detente* the—very welcoming—machine providing coffee and other delicacies at ISIMA, which we used frequently (and which I managed to break, one day).

9.4 T-shirts!

I've talked light-heartedly about the importance of a company having its own T-shirt, and yet in all seriousness this is incredibly iconic. In anticipation of SIGGRAPH 2003 in San Diego, we produced a series of T-shirts and shoulder bags bearing the Allegorithmic logo, as can be seen in figure 9.15.

Placing this much emphasis on T-shirts might seem a little curious, but they served two purposes: first, they provided all the members of the Allegorithmic team with a sense of pride and belonging. This would be true for the T-shirts and all the various accessories that we would produce throughout the life of the company. Second, they signified the wearer as a representative of the company, which would sometimes bring about unexpected situations and encounters. This T-shirt, for instance, indirectly played a critical role in allowing me to meet Alexis Khouri (see Chapter 19).[14] I also had a curious feeling the first time I unexpectedly saw the T-shirt 'in the wild,' being worn in the street, on the corner of Lincoln Blvd and Washington Blvd in Los Angeles.

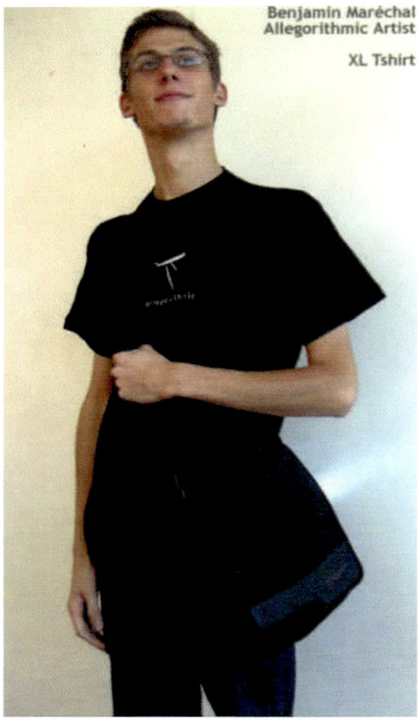

Figure 9.15: Benjamin Maréchal proudly wearing an Allegorithmic T-shirt and bag, from the 2003-2004 collection.

9.5 Website

In addition to his work on our products, Christophe developed our first commercial website. Here, you could find information about the company—and also buy our products directly! The site had little traffic for several years, but we declared it a success by late 2006—for instance, on October 4, 2006, it received 1390 unique visitors. In any case, a website is an essential tool for any company, and even more so for a tech company that aspires to sell its products at an international level.

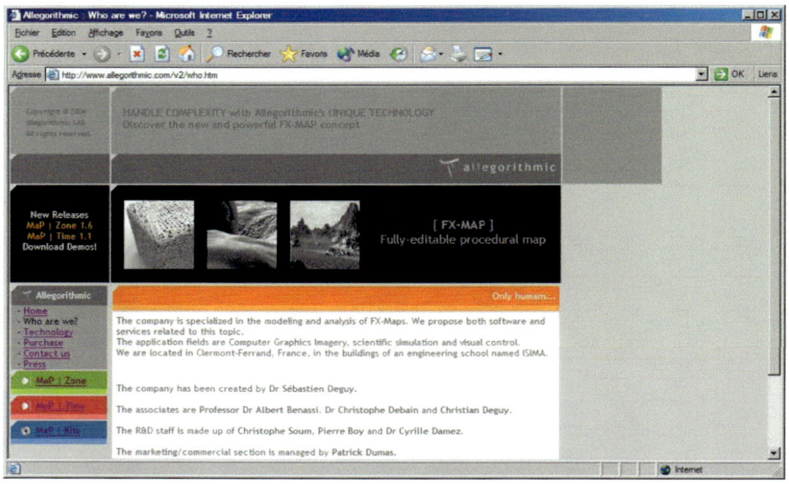

Figure 9.16: Our first website (here in 2004), created by Christophe Soum.

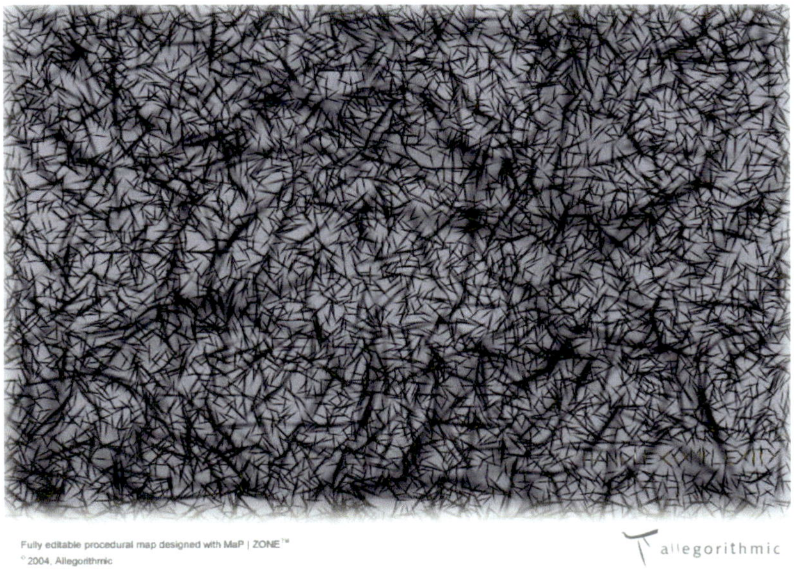

Figure 9.17: This image was iconic for our technology: due to the unprecedented level of control that we provided over the noises created with our tools, we could, for example, individually select the small spines of this noise and rearrange them to form the phrase 'Handle Complexity' (visible at the bottom right of the image), which expressed the idea of complexity control.

9.6 Products

Now we needed products to sell. And so we developed the first range of products resulting from our FX-Maps technology, specifically playing with this idea of 'maps': our outputs were images in black and white which you could use as level maps, which could then be colored and/or used to deform a surface via displacement mapping[13] or bump mapping,[14] in order to obtain a final texture that could be used for a 3D scene.

We decided that our product should incorporate the term 'MaP,' with a double meaning (that only we were aware of, I imagine, much like with 'Allegorithmic'), emphasizing the all-important 'maps,' as well as being an acronym for 'Mass Accumulation Process,'[15] which established a link with the process of constructing FX-Maps described in my thesis (see Chapter 5). And so our first product was MaP | Zone, a tool allowing the generation of procedural noises using our original approach. This was followed by MaP | Time, which added a temporal dimension and made it possible to animate the procedural noises obtained, to create new visual effects.

14: Just a few days after meeting me, my future wife spotted someone wearing an Allegorithmic T-shirt on the stairs of her apartment building in the fourteenth *arrondissement* in Paris. Surprised to see the logo of the micro-company that I managed, she spoke with this person, who proved to be my friend David Bourguignon (who had just returned from Princeton, where he'd done his post-doc in the field of 3D); he explained to her that he'd got the T-shirt from me at a conference, SIGGRAPH. Though the world is sometimes small, my wife believes to this day that I engineered this 'coincidence' to impress her...

15: I confess that I no longer remember why the 'a' is lowercase while the other two letters are uppercase...

MaP | Zone

The first version of MaP | Zone, which used the procedural noise generation engine TAON 3, recently redeveloped by Christophe Soum (see Chapter 7), took the form of a Photoshop plugin. Photoshop was by far the most popular 2D creation tool among graphic designers all over the world, but it was also used by 3D artists to create their textures. And so it seemed natural to us to position ourselves as closely to Photoshop as possible. Combining the properties of our noise generator with the options that Photoshop provided to blend and manipulate images, we hoped to vastly increase the creative capabilities of 3D artists.

Even though the product didn't find its audience immediately (that's a polite way of putting it...), MaP | Zone was nonetheless extremely useful

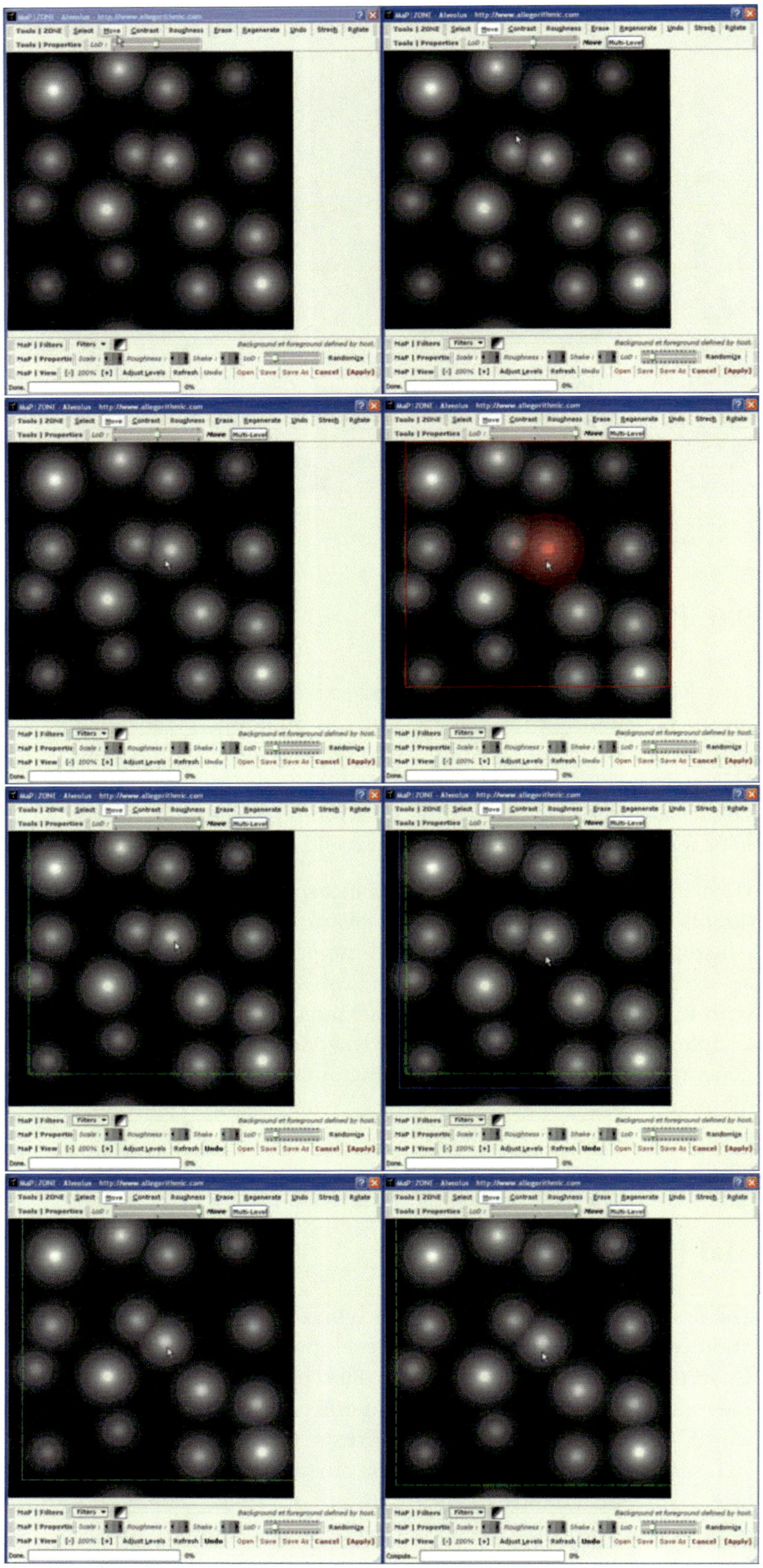

Figure 9.18: The graphical interface of one of the first versions of MaP | Zone. On this sequence of images (that reads like a comic book), we can see the specific features of the program and FX-Maps, which consisted of the unique possibility to modify some parameters locally, notably with manual, user-friendly tools. For example, here the 'Move' function lets you select one of the morphlets (optionally with its 'children' in the graph) using the mouse, and move it wherever you want. This feature, which allowed the control of procedural noise, had been requested by Xavier Bec from BUF Compagnie the first time I met him shortly before my thesis defense (see Section 5.2); Christophe Soum implemented this on top of TAON 3 (see Section 7.2), and it was a huge accomplishment—its absolutely unique character within the industry brought us a lot of attention, even if the product itself was not a huge success. It was an indication of our capabilities, and a promise of things to come.

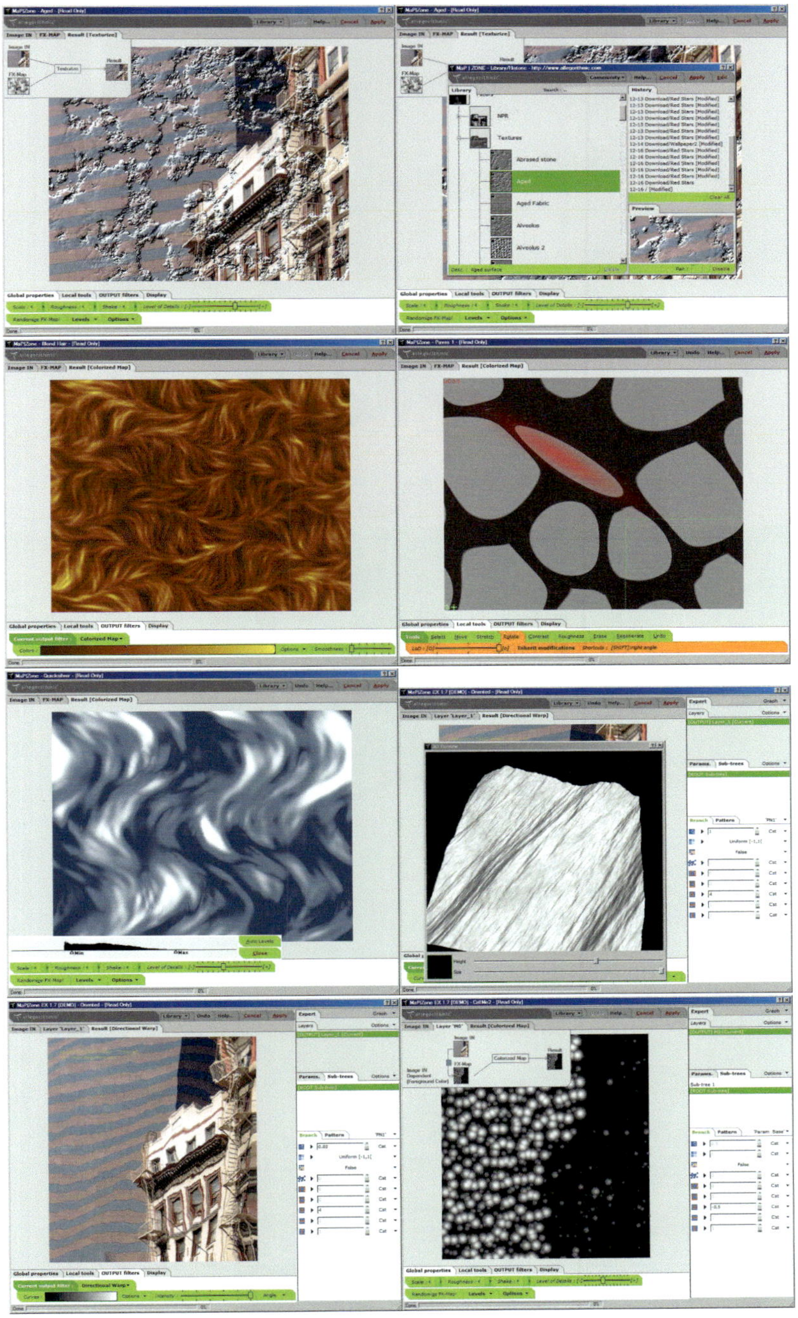

Figure 9.19: MaP | Zone, December 2005.

for us as a vehicle to meet companies and users within the 3D sector, and to confront the tool with the reality of their needs. The product remained impressive in certain technical aspects, and for specialists in particular, but most people didn't understand what MaP | Zone did.

Of course, MaP | Zone evolved over its subsequent versions, and the version we demonstrated at SIGGRAPH 2003, at our first stand (see Section 9.7) was little more than a prototype, and would only work on Linux. This product would then play a fundamental role in a key project in our development, the game *RoboBlitz* (see Chapter 13).

Figure 9.20: The (virtual) box of MaP | Zone, a plugin for Photoshop dedicated to the creation of patterns and other effects. The slogan, 'The first fully-editable heterogeneous map designer,' only meant something to a pretty small number of people. . . Also, and this a favorite joke of Christophe Soum and Cyrille Damez, my face was a 'guinea pig' for a number of graphic experiments that we can see on the cover, bottom right.

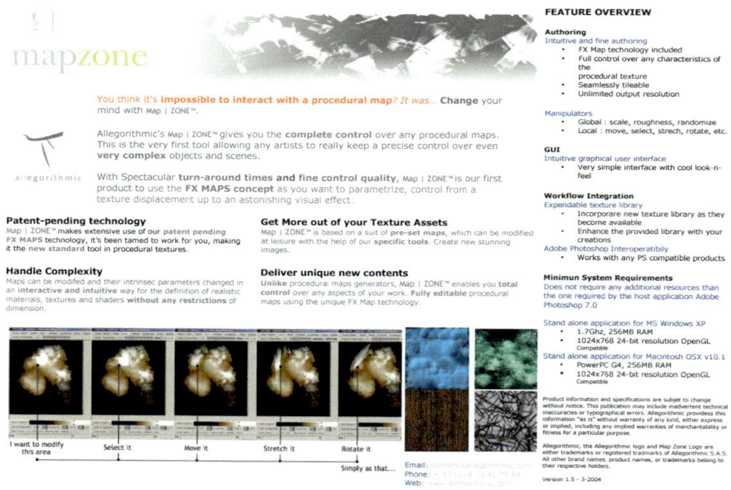

Figure 9.21: A brochure presenting MaP | Zone 1.5, which started out as a plugin for Photoshop dedicated to the creation of patterns and other effects.

MaP | Time

The second product that we developed and promoted in these first few years was MaP | Time, which used the same TAON 3 engine, but this time in the form of a plugin for After Effects, as it used an additional parameter in the generation of textures and effects: time. The noises generated were therefore animated, making each parameter of our noises a function of

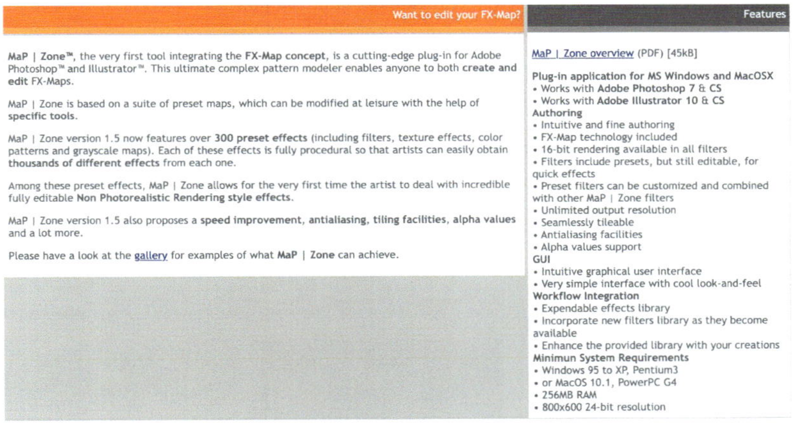
Want to edit your FX-Map?

MaP | Zone™, the very first tool integrating the **FX-Map concept**, is a cutting-edge plug-in for Adobe Photoshop™ and Illustrator™. This ultimate complex pattern modeler enables anyone to both **create and edit** FX-Maps.

MaP | Zone is based on a suite of preset maps, which can be modified at leisure with the help of **specific tools.**

MaP | Zone version 1.5 now features over **300 preset effects** (including filters, texture effects, color patterns and grayscale maps). Each of these effects is fully procedural so that artists can easily obtain **thousands of different effects** from each one.

Among these preset effects, MaP | Zone allows for the very first time the artist to deal with incredible fully editable **Non Photorealistic Rendering style effects.**

MaP | Zone version 1.5 also proposes a **speed improvement, antialiasing, tiling facilities, alpha values** and a lot more.

Please have a look at the gallery for examples of what **MaP | Zone** can achieve.

Features

MaP | Zone overview (PDF) [45kB]

Plug-in application for MS Windows and MacOSX
- Works with **Adobe Photoshop 7 & CS**
- Works with **Adobe Illustrator 10 & CS**

Authoring
- Intuitive and fine authoring
- FX-Map technology included
- 16-bit rendering available in all filters
- Filters include presets, but still editable, for quick effects
- Preset filters can be customized and combined with other MaP | Zone filters
- Unlimited output resolution
- Seamlessly tileable
- Antialiasing facilities
- Alpha values support

GUI
- Intuitive graphical user interface
- Very simple interface with cool look-and-feel

Workflow Integration
- Expendable effects library
- Incorporate new filters library as they become available
- Enhance the provided library with your creations

Minimun System Requirements
- Windows 95 to XP, Pentium3
- or MacOS 10.1, PowerPC G4
- 256MB RAM
- 800x600 24-bit resolution

Figure 9.22: Here is how we presented MaP | Zone (version 1.5) on our website in August 2004.

Figure 9.23: Examples of noise 'maps,' patterns, and effects created with MaP | Zone.

time. These functions could be simple or complex, producing effects that were potentially therefore equally complex. This time our target market was motion graphics, 2D rather than 3D, although these animated noises could be applied to 3D rendering as well. MaP | Time became pivotal in our commercial development with motion graphics studios in the Los Angeles region with Joseph Mbayen (see Section 11.1).

Documentation and EULA

Documentation

"But I've never read a software document! Who reads documentation?"[16]

But nonetheless, we needed real documentation. We couldn't release a product without it. Doing so might not even have been legal.

"Okay, then we have to find someone who will write that for us. . . " After some time searching, and thanks to a little networking, we gave the task of writing the documentation for our products (which were constantly changing, representing an additional difficulty for the writers of the documentation) to a few different external consultants. It was satisfying to see the documentation take shape for the product we were creating, but at the same time also frustrating as it took a long time to produce, and was outdated almost immediately. It also had a limited impact on

16: I wasn't being completely honest here, as I'd read one particular software user guide very thoroughly: that of Softimage 3D, which I'd taught during my doctorate (see Chapter 4). Moreover, and despite the fact that I'd been a big consumer of pirated software and games since my first Apple II C, then on my ATARI ST, and a series of Windows PCs, none of which I'd ever had the documentation for, I still at times bought books dedicated to particular software, as I'd done for example with a book on 3D Studio, the ancestor of 3ds Max[15] on MS-DOS, in the mid 1990s, one of the first 3D programs I ever used.

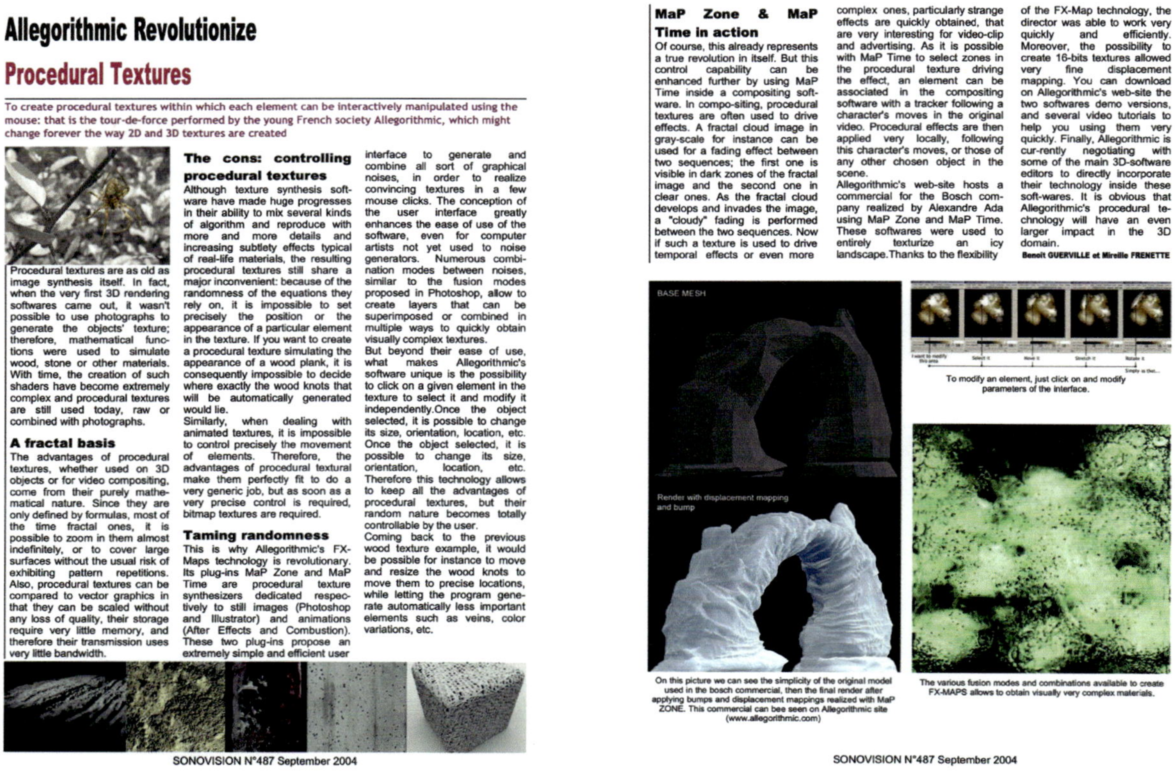

Allegorithmic Revolutionize

Procedural Textures

To create procedural textures within which each element can be interactively manipulated using the mouse: that is the tour-de-force performed by the young French society Allegorithmic, which might change forever the way 2D and 3D textures are created

Procedural textures are as old as image synthesis itself. In fact, when the very first 3D rendering softwares came out, it wasn't possible to use photographs to generate the objects' texture; therefore, mathematical functions were used to simulate wood, stone or other materials. With time, the creation of such shaders have become extremely complex and procedural textures are still used today, raw or combined with photographs.

A fractal basis

The advantages of procedural textures, whether used on 3D objects or for video compositing, come from their purely mathematical nature. Since they are only defined by formulas, most of the time fractal ones, it is possible to zoom in them almost indefinitely, or to cover large surfaces without the usual risk of exhibiting pattern repetitions. Also, procedural textures can be compared to vector graphics in that they can be scaled without any loss of quality, their storage require very little memory, and therefore their transmission uses very little bandwidth.

The cons: controlling procedural textures

Although texture synthesis software have made huge progresses in their ability to mix several kinds of algorithm and reproduce with more and more details and increasing subtlety effects typical of real-life materials, the resulting procedural textures still share a major inconvenient: because of the randomness of the equations they rely on, it is impossible to set precisely the position or the appearance of a particular element in the texture. If you want to create a procedural texture simulating the appearance of a wood plank, it is consequently impossible to decide where exactly the wood knots that will be automatically generated would lie.

Similarly, when dealing with animated textures, it is impossible to control precisely the movement of elements. Therefore, the advantages of procedural textural make them perfectly fit to do a very generic job, but as soon as a very precise control is required, bitmap textures are required.

Taming randomness

This is why Allegorithmic's FX-Maps technology is revolutionary. Its plug-ins MaP Zone and MaP Time are procedural texture synthesizers dedicated respectively to still images (Photoshop and Illustrator) and animations (After Effects and Combustion). These two plug-ins propose an extremely simple and efficient user interface to generate and combine all sort of graphical noises, in order to realize convincing textures in a few mouse clicks. The conception of the user interface greatly enhances the ease of use of the software, even for computer artists not yet used to noise generators. Numerous combination modes between noises, similar to the fusion modes proposed in Photoshop, allow to create layers that can be superimposed or combined in multiple ways to quickly obtain visually complex textures.

But beyond their ease of use, what makes Allegorithmic's software unique is the possibility to click on a given element in the texture to select it and modify it independently.Once the object selected, it is possible to change its size, orientation, location, etc. Once the object selected, it is possible to change its size, orientation, location, etc. Therefore this technology allows to keep all the advantages of procedural textures, but their random nature becomes totally controllable by the user.

Coming back to the previous wood texture example, it would be possible for instance to move and resize the wood knots to move them to precise locations, while letting the program generate automatically less important elements such as veins, color variations, etc.

SONOVISION N°487 September 2004

MaP Zone & MaP Time in action

Of course, this already represents a true revolution in itself. But this control capability can be enhanced further by using MaP Time inside a compositing software. In compo-siting, procedural textures are often used to drive effects. A fractal cloud image in gray-scale for instance can be used for a fading effect between two sequences; the first one is visible in dark zones of the fractal image and the second one in clear ones. As the fractal cloud develops and invades the image, a "cloudy" fading is performed between the two sequences. Now if such a texture is used to drive temporal effects or even more complex ones, particularly strange effects are quickly obtained, that are very interesting for video-clip and advertising. As it is possible with MaP Time to select zones in the procedural texture driving the effect, an element can be associated in the compositing software with a tracker following a character's moves in the original video. Procedural effects are then applied very locally, following this character's moves, or those of any other chosen object in the scene.

Allegorithmic's web-site hosts a commercial for the Bosch company realized by Alexandre Ada using MaP Zone and MaP Time. These softwares were used to entirely texturize an icy landscape.Thanks to the flexibility of the FX-Map technology, the director was able to work very quickly and efficiently. Moreover, the possibility to create 16-bits textures allowed very fine displacement mapping. You can download on Allegorithmic's web-site the two softwares demo versions, and several video tutorials to help you using them very quickly. Finally, Allegorithmic is cur-rently negotiating with some of the main 3D-software editors to directly incorporate their technology inside these soft-wares. It is obvious that Allegorithmic's procedural technology will have an even larger impact in the 3D domain.

Benoit GUERVILLE et Mireille FRENETTE

On this picture we can see the simplicity of the original model used in the bosch commercial, then the final render after applying bumps and displacement mappings realized with MaP ZONE. This commercial can bee seen on Allegorithmic site (www.allegorithmic.com)

To modify an element, just click on and modify parameters of the interface.

The various fusion modes and combinations available to create FX-MAPS allows to obtain visually very complex materials.

SONOVISION N°487 September 2004

Figure 9.24: One of the first reviews of MaP | Zone (page 1), in a specialized magazine, Sonovision. For the interview, we met with Benoît Guerville in a motorway rest area in Séverac-le-Château, midway between Clermont-Ferrand and Montpellier, where he was based.

the adoption of the product. Or, in any case, its impact was hard to measure.

EULA

"But I've never read a EULA[17] in my entire life! Who reads EULAs?"

17: You know, the legal text on terms of use, the End User License Agreement, that you never read when you install software, and that we're always asked to agree to. During all my years of installing pirated software, I'd never read a single one, and simply clicked on 'Next, next, next. . . ' as quickly as possible so that I could just launch the program and enjoy it quickly.

But nonetheless, we needed a EULA. This time around, the legality of the matter was clear: we couldn't release software without clearly defined conditions of use. Réjean Lapointe, as well as Cyrille Damez, were firm on this point.

"Okay, well, let's find that. . . " I soon found a solution: I found a EULA on the internet, copied and pasted it, and made a few changes as necessary. This would be our official EULA for several years.

Figure 9.25: The (virtual) box of our new product MaP | Time, an After Effects plug-in dedicated to motion graphics. Note that the English here is very approximate.

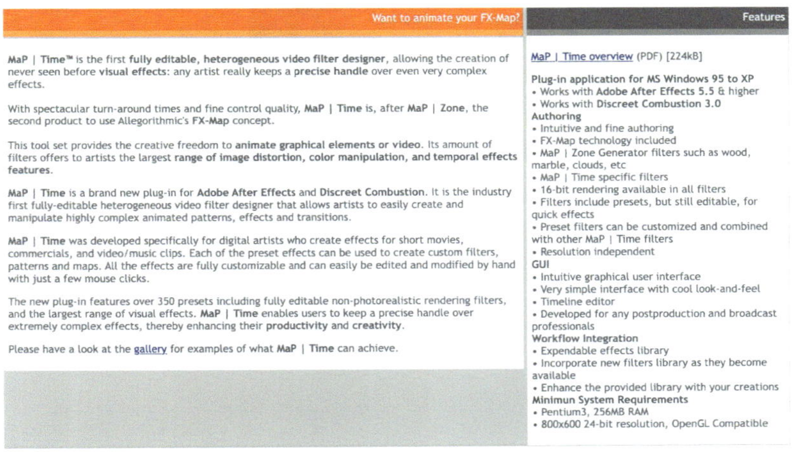

Want to animate your FX-Map?

MaP | Time™ is the first **fully editable, heterogeneous video filter designer**, allowing the creation of never seen before **visual effects**: any artist really keeps a **precise handle** over even very complex effects.

With spectacular turn-around times and fine control quality, **MaP | Time** is, after **MaP | Zone**, the second product to use Allegorithmic's **FX-Map** concept.

This tool set provides the creative freedom to **animate graphical elements or video**. Its amount of filters offers to artists the largest **range of image distortion, color manipulation, and temporal effects features**.

MaP | Time is a brand new plug-in for **Adobe After Effects** and **Discreet Combustion**. It is the industry first fully-editable heterogeneous video filter designer that allows artists to easily create and manipulate highly complex animated patterns, effects and transitions.

MaP | Time was developed specifically for digital artists who create effects for short movies, commercials, and video/music clips. Each of the preset effects can be used to create custom filters, patterns and maps. All the effects are fully customizable and can easily be edited and modified by hand with just a few mouse clicks.

The new plug-in features over 350 presets including fully editable non-photorealistic rendering filters, and the largest range of visual effects. **MaP | Time** enables users to keep a precise handle over extremely complex effects, thereby enhancing their **productivity** and **creativity**.

Please have a look at the gallery for examples of what **MaP | Time** can achieve.

Features

MaP | Time overview (PDF) [224kB]

Plug-in application for MS Windows 95 to XP
- Works with **Adobe After Effects 5.5 & higher**
- Works with **Discreet Combustion 3.0**

Authoring
- Intuitive and fine authoring
- FX-Map technology included
- MaP | Zone Generator filters such as wood, marble, clouds, etc
- MaP | Time specific filters
- 16-bit rendering available in all filters
- Filters include presets, but still editable, for quick effects
- Preset filters can be customized and combined with other MaP | Time filters
- Resolution independent

GUI
- Intuitive graphical user interface
- Very simple interface with cool look-and-feel
- Timeline editor
- Developed for any postproduction and broadcast professionals

Workflow Integration
- Expendable effects library
- Incorporate new filters library as they become available
- Enhance the provided library with your creations

Minimun System Requirements
- Pentium3, 256MB RAM
- 800x600 24-bit resolution, OpenGL Compatible

Figure 9.26: A web page presenting MaP | Time 1 on our website in August 2004.

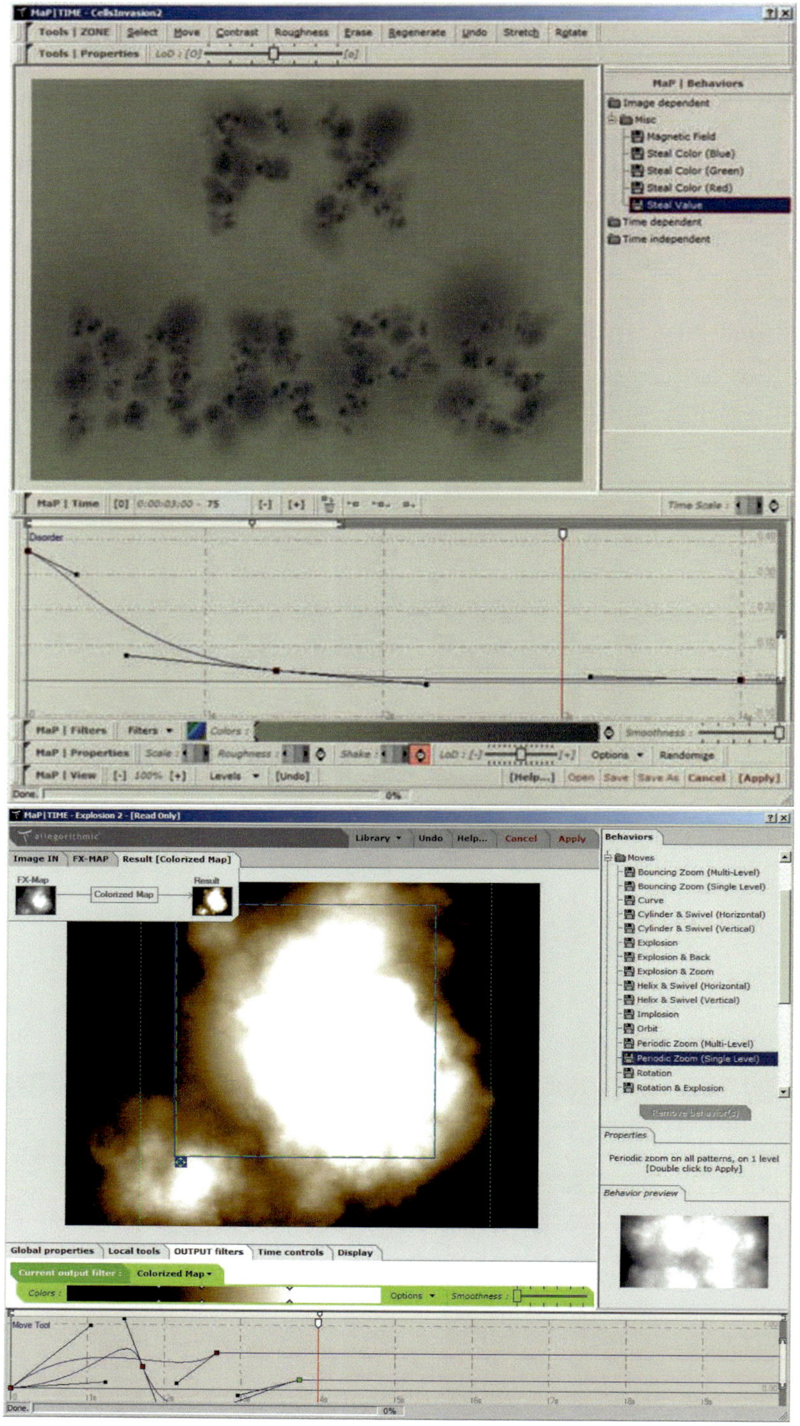

Figure 9.27: Our product MaP | Time was an After Effects plugin dedicated to motion graphics. It allowed the creation of animated patterns and effects, thanks to its timeline and animation curves that we could apply to the parameters of noises generated by TAON.

9.7 First trade shows and first tour

SIGGRAPH 2003

SIGGRAPH 2003 took place in July, in San Diego in South California. The San Diego Convention Center was huge, and the weather, like the area, was very pleasant. It was a joy to discover the surroundings, but above all this was the first SIGGRAPH in which we took part as an exhibitor! We had our own booth,[18] our T-shirts (see Section 9.4), our projector, and a folding screen which took up a large part of the space allocated to us (and behind which we'd hide our personal belongings, as well as boxes full of our T-shirts). We'd project demos of early versions of our technology onto this screen, from Christophe's laptop. The team consisted of Christophe Soum, Nicolas Polo, and myself.

18: A 20x20—20 square feet, or approximately 9 square meters, the smallest reservable space. We'd had to choose the location online, from those available on a map. We'd repeat this exercise of choosing a location many times over the following years, and it was always a pleasure to 'strategize' about the best possible location, depending on the flow of visitors, other neighboring companies (for example, the Pixar stand would consistently attract hundreds of visitors per hour), and so on.

Figure 9.28: At our stand during SIGGRAPH 2003 in San Diego. It was our first attendance as exhibitors at SIGGRAPH. I am looking at my pictures on a digital camera.

The demo ran on Linux on Christophe's laptop. The command that Christophe typed in was `demo`; on the day, the command that he'd typed in immediately prior to that was... `make`.[19]

19: `make` was the command to compile and run the program, once the coding was finished: Christophe had continued to modify the program we'd present right up until the moment the of the conference opening, and he sometimes continued making changes between meetings.

This first SIGGRAPH as exhibitors was particularly rich in encounters and would mark the beginning of a long series of participations in the conference. We stood alongside stars of the industry, companies that we'd always watched from afar,[20] and we began to create links that would be valuable in the future. We had the feeling that we'd touched on something essential—being in contact with future users, learning from other companies, and generally observing the 'plate tectonics of the industry.' The conference gave us a feeling, for the very first time, of officially belonging to the great, global 3D movement, with the name of our company and products visible to all. Our distributed T-shirts would be worn for years by members of this movement all around the world, and above all our products and technologies had been seen. I couldn't have been more proud of what the team and I were accomplishing, and this thrill of excitement that I felt for the first time as an exhibitor at a 3D conference would never leave me: I feel it every single time we return to SIGGRAPH and it fills me with immense energy.

20: For instance, we caught the attention of a special effects supervisor (the grand master of film special effects) of the next Star Wars film, which was then in production! (Star Wars!) He was interested in our flexible model of noise generation for use on terrain creation, as we can see in figure 9.29.

This SIGGRAPH was a particularly important step for the beginning of our adventure, the first in a long series, and also one of our first trips to the US, which would increasingly become a key place of development for Allegorithmic. For the next step, I had to return to the US without waiting for next year's event, and I had to stay for longer. I needed to go on tour, a bit like a rock band, but solo, and rather than singing I'd demo our products and meet potential partners and other customers.

The next step would be to return to North America the following January!

Figure 9.29: Here we can see how the unique capacity of local modification of FX-Maps allows us to manually change the position of these rocky clusters. We can literally move mountains with MaP | Zone. These images are from January 8, 2003.

North American tour, January 2004

The moment I started the car, I had a doubt. I called my father, even though it was quite late in France, and asked him, "Do you know how to make an automatic car go forward?" He told me to move the transmission to 'D,' for 'Drive' (pronounced with a strong French accent). He was right. And so I was able to drive the rental car that I'd just picked up at SFO, San Francisco's airport, at the start of January 2004. I'd just flown in from Clermont-Ferrand, with a brief stopover in Paris, for a month-long tour of the US and Canada. This would be my first visit of (very) many in this large region. I spent the month of January in, in order,[21] San Francisco, Los Angeles, Montreal, Boston, and New York.

The goal was to meet as many figures in the 3D sector as possible,[22] from a variety of different hubs. It became clear to us very early on, and particularly after the two SIGGRAPH conferences in which we'd just taken part, that the entire industry gravitated around these poles, especially on the west coast. San Francisco was home to giants like Pixar, Dreamworks, ILM,[23] and Lucas Arts, as well as large hardware manufacturers like NVIDIA, AMD, and Intel, and other software publishers like Autodesk; in Los Angeles we found all the mid-sized studios working for Hollywood and television, but also legendary studios like Blur Studios, Digital Domain, Disney, Sony Picture Imageworks and many more; in Montreal, there was Discreet Logic and even Softimage, as well as the gaming industry that was very actively present due to the aid granted by the region to companies in the area who promised to develop there and

21: This detail is important, as it was 25 degrees Celsius in LA when I boarded my flight, and -25 degrees in Montreal when I disembarked... I was not prepared for this change.

22: In particular, visual effect studios.

23: I'd be lucky enough to visit their legendary premises hidden within Kerner Optical in San Rafael.

provide jobs, and there were key individuals who Patrick Dumas (see above) had suggested I meet: people like Bill Roberts, an extraordinary character, formerly of Autodesk and Avid, with whom I discussed the industry at length over lunch. In Boston, Patrick Dumas had recommended I meet with Véronique Froment, from the PR company Bubble and Squeak—Patrick had worked with Véronique when he'd been in charge of marketing for Avid, and spoke very highly of her; Véronique and her company would go on to provide PR for Allegorithmic; finally, many effects studios for TV were based in New York, and I visited for the first time the city that I fell a little bit in love with.[24]

24: Despite the cold, I crisscrossed the city, and went on a pilgrimage to the Blue Note, and even to the letter box of Def Jux. I saw Jim Jarmush's movie atmosphere everywhere... Passionate about music, literature, art, and cinema, New York was an endless source of amazement.

This first month-long tour away from my team and closer to the industry had proven to be extremely instructive. First of all, the team could evolve without me at their side continuously, thanks to the maturity and solidity of pillars like Cyrille Damez, Catherine Debain, and Christophe Soum. I would therefore be able to repeat these tours and return regularly to North America and elsewhere, for many years. I also learned a lot from my many meetings—about the industry, how it operated, its needs, and the perceived interest in our technologies. I finally realized the gigantic gap between my level of English and the minimum level necessary for the successful development of a company that aimed to be international, and especially where most of its potential clients and partners were based on the American West Coast. And I realized one fundamental thing: I would have to come back. Often.[25]

25: And I would indeed do this, very frequently and for long periods of time. I estimate that I spent, in total, around two and a half years in the US over the next five years, during visits lasting a maximum of two or three months, though often shorter than that, and always within the limit of what my visitor VISA allowed me, and by budgeting my expenses to the dollar, which in itself would cause many nights and adventures in unsavory motels... These trips were not glamorous, far from it, but I found them enormously interesting, and I didn't mind doing these trips back to back—the travel, the stress, meetings, illnesses (nothing is more fun than getting sick while traveling to the end of the world, and having to take a plane with a temperature of 39 degrees...), the time zone differences, the distance, and the disjointed relationships with friends, family and teams—because I was on a mission. I was totally preoccupied with what we were building. At no point did I ever ask myself, "What am I doing here?"

Imagina 2004, and SIGGRAPH 2004

When I came back from my tour in January, I went directly to another conference, Imagina, in Monaco, which took place at the beginning of February. During this conference, I had the chance to meet even more people who were doing 3D in France, in Europe, and in the rest of the world. Notably, those I met included Cédric Guiard (Thalès), George Drettakis (director of research at INRIA), Henrik Wann Jensen ('Mister Photon Mapping,' a big name in 3D, particularly in rendering), Paul Debevec (an absolute legend in computer graphics, and inventor of, among other things, High Dynamic Range, or HDR...), as well as seeing Marie-Claude Frasson again (who used to be part of Softimage, in thesis at INRIA Sophia Antipolis, see Section 8.1); see figure 9.30. It was also at Imagina that I met Davide Pesare,[26] who was then an expert on shaders,[16] and particularly on *ice* shaders...

26: Davide would then join Pixar—the creators of the Ice Age series of films, amongst others—for numerous years, before finally joining Allegorithmic in 2016. The world of 3D was very small, and each conference and trip could have many repercussions many years later. If the contact was good and a certain mutual trust was established, this would only become stronger over time.

The SIGGRAPH which followed, in summer 2004,[27] was especially rich in encounters. Once again, my first travels and my first discussions led me to other contacts, people I tried to see during the conference. That year, we didn't have an official presence there, and I wandered from stand to stand with my laptop under my arm (see figure 9.31), looking for contacts and giving demos of our products to anyone who would listen. During that edition, I met Beau Perschall, from Turbosquid, a well-known online marketplace for 3D objects and components; I gave Beau a copy of our demo CD, which can be seen in figure 9.32.

27: This edition took place in Los Angeles and was much larger than the two I'd attended previously.

Figure 9.30: I gave a demo of our products and tech for Cédric Guiard (Thalès), George Drettakis (director of research at INRIA), Henrik Wann Jensen ('Mister Photon Mapping,' a big name in 3D and rendering in particular), Paul Debevec (an absolute legend in computer graphics, and inventor of, among other things, HDR) and Marie-Claude Frasson (who used to be at Softimage, in thesis at INRIA Sophia Antipolis).

Figure 9.31: Here I am (bottom right of the photo, wearing the famous Allegorithmic T-shirt (see 9.4), sitting by the Discreet Logic stand, during SIGGRAPH 2004 in Los Angeles. I was trying by any means possible (here, by 'sitting,' and preparing a demo on my laptop) to develop partnerships with major figures in the industry. Discreet Logic were the publishers of the reference 3D software 3ds Max, which would later join the Autodesk group. I wanted to meet Marc Petit, a big figure in 3D in France and throughout the world, who was in charge of the entire Media & Entertainment section at Autodesk.

Figure 9.32: An Allegorithmic demo CD, which I distributed and showed to anyone who would listen to me, during several SIGGRAPH conferences. I gave this copy to Beau Perschall, from Turbosquid, who kept it for many years; he sent me this photo of the CD fifteen years after I'd given it to him.

Special effects and projects | 10

10.1 Special projects

Inspired by the Softimage team that I'd met in Los Angeles[1] dedicated to what they called 'special projects,' I decided to set up our own special projects team, which would focus on content creation, or on training customers who showed interest in our products but couldn't afford to spend time learning and integrating new tools like ours; in these instances, the customers would try out our software with support from our team, on real use cases. For us, this was an opportunity to prove that our tools fitted our customers' needs, to develop them in response to customer requests, to learn from the industry and its needs, and at times to finance a part of this development if the customer agreed to pay for a few licenses.[2] This was exactly how Softimage's special projects team operated, allowing them to effectively integrate themselves into the production pipelines of Hollywood's special effects studios. This also gave me the opportunity to get closer to an industry that fascinated me, to see the workings and production secrets, which was an absolute joy.

1: They were based on premises next to those of Digital Domain, and the famous Rose Café, a block from Venice Beach.

2: We'd use this approach often—see the following section, or Chapters 13 or 27.

10.2 Mac Guff

Despite a great deal of help from Xavier Bec from within the company, BUF didn't seem interested in testing our tools—which were still, overall, non-existent. However, Mac Guff[3] seemed more open to the possibility, in particular thanks to the efforts of Alexis Casas, who I'd met sometime earlier, during my first SIGGRAPH in summer 2002, in San Antonio (see section 8.2). Alexis was a surprising, absolutely open-minded person with a very unconventional background. He rode a skateboard everywhere, set up his work environment in the strangest way possible, and was generally atypical in everything he did. He perpetually displayed a good mood and a passion for the world at large, and particularly for 3D. He was eternally fascinated by everything around him.

He worked, partly for fun and partly to finalize his doctoral thesis, within the R&D team at Mac Guff that worked on developing the studio's internal tools, a near-complete software suite for film production, which notably included a render engine.[4] This legendary team included many big names in 3D, pioneers in the field in France, such as Thierry 'Mammoth' Lauthelier, Frédéric Cros, and Geoff Levner. These people had all pushed the limits of what was possible in 3D, and were overall a huge source of inspiration for me.[5]

3: A visual effects studio created in Paris in 1988 by Jacques Bled and Rodolphe Chabrier, pioneers of 3D in France whom I had the please of meeting some years later; the company became one of the most renowned animation studios in the world at the beginning of 2000s. A few years later it would produce—via its extension, Illumination Mac Guff—some of the most successful and critically acclaimed animated films ever, the Despicable Me and Minions series.

4: Most of the major visual effect studios at that time worked with tools they developed internally (and some would continue to work this way for a long time; for some, it's still the case), that allowed them to create the increasingly advanced images demanded by film directors. Having their own rendering technology in particular could prove a big competitive advantage, and could cause one studio over another to be chosen to create a film's special effects. Pierre Hénon's book[17] on the history of digital animation in France provides a great deal of information on this.

5: Overall, I really liked the atmosphere of the place. It had a 'garage' feel about it—literally; the office was located in a converted garage building in the fifteenth *arrondissement* of Paris, a mythical place in the world of 3D in France. . . I felt like a wide-eyed child every time I had the opportunity to visit Mac Guff. These teams were making the most advanced digital images possible for film productions; for me, being able to mix with this world was the realization of an impossible dream.

DOI:10.1201/9781003534624-10

Mac Guff was just starting work on the visual effects for the next film by Jan Kounen,[6] an adaptation of the comic strip *Blueberry*. One scene in particular that they were working on caused them to take a closer look at our technology: the film's main character takes drugs and, in this scene, enters a sort of delirium; Jan Kounen wanted this to be expressed visually, in a wholly original psychadelic sequence. The special effects team thought about using fractal objects; shapes like this allow a sort of 'infinite dive.' I'd previously discussed my doctoral thesis with Alexis. Fractals were the basis of our technology (see Chapter 3), which could therefore be very interesting for Mac Guff.

After some initial presentations at Mac Guff's office, Alexis got the green light from the R&D team and from Jacques Bled to become an alpha-site[7] for our technologies. We signed an agreement to this effect,[8] and started experimenting with the new tools.

Despite all our efforts and the good will of the Mac Guff team, our tools were unfortunately not yet advanced enough to be effectively integrated into the Mac Guff production pipeline, and the *Blueberry* sequence was ultimately created without our tools. We learned a lot from this experience regardless and, more personally, my time on site, discussing technology and learning more about the creation of special effects, proved extraordinary.

6: Who had particular importance to me. I first met Jan Kounen when I was in high school, at lycée Jeanne d'Arc in Clermont-Ferrand, during Clermont's short film festival, the *Festival du Court Métrage de Clermont-Ferrand*, in early 1990. The Festival is a big event in the region, and a focal point for Clermont-Ferrand. Our French teacher took us to watch screenings, and invited into our classroom a young team behind a short film that would get a lot of attention that year: *Gisèle Kérosène*, directed by the very same Jan Kounen. This meeting made a big impression on me. This was the moment I realized that films were made by actual people! They weren't pulled out of a magic hat, nor created solely by expert teams far away in Hollywood. Cinema was also created by young, passionate people like Jan, with whatever was available; all it really required was a camera. My own experiments at home with my family's video camera weren't a million miles away from what Jan was doing! This experience fueled my passion for cinema, and instilled the idea that I could one day be active in this creative field as well (see more on this in Section 2.2).

7: Mac Guff would be the first *alpha-site* in the history of Allegorithmic, a studio and a partner with whom we worked hand in hand. We would provide them with our technology before it had been officially released (as a beta or even alpha version, hence the term 'alpha-site') and would try to meet their needs by implementing fixes as well as new features. This way, the studio would have access to features that corresponded to the way they used the tool, before such features were available to their competitors, with total support from us; for Allegorithmic, this was a way to ensure we were developing what the industry needed, and to test our technology under 'real conditions.' We'd work this way several times in all; see in particular Chapters 13 and 27.

8: On this occasion, my lawyers in Clermont-Ferrand drafted a document that was exhaustively and excessively detailed; Jacques discussed this with me at length, pointing out that, in seeking to cover too much with our agreement, we were within a hair's breadth of of causing Mac Guff to back out entirely. Fortunately, Jacques and his team were accommodating and intelligent enough to find common ground with us.

10.3 Akama Studio

Alexandre Ada, then a young manager of a Parisian special effects and animation company, Akama Studio, came to see us at our small stand at Imagina in February 2004 (see Chapter 25). Alexandre was a colorful character with a lot of presence, a man of great charm who always had a smile. He was also a high-level film director and visual artist, in both 2D and 3D, and a specialist in images and software such as After Effects and Maya. He was looking for products that could help him save time during production, and he found MaP | Zone and MaP | Time very interesting. We immediately struck up a very friendly rapport and had a great time together at the conference.

Some time later I met him again in Paris to discuss a project that he and his team were working on: an advertisement for a Bosch refrigerator which took place on an ice floe. He wanted a realistic representation of the ice floe and other icebergs and was struggling to produce a realistic ice texture. Here was a great special project for Allegorithmic.

I proposed to Alexandre that we'd help make this texture, without really knowing if we could fulfill his needs. Because of MaP | Zone and the talent of our internal artists (see Section 9.2), we managed to make something that was convincing, even though it took us ten times longer than it would have taken in a real production. Alexandre wanted to help us out, and was very patient with us; this gave us time to refine our work and reach a result that would get everybody talking. This was one of the very first times that textures created in MaP | Zone ended up in a production (see figure 10.1)!

A little while after this, on one occasion while we were trying to help each other and I was praising Los Angeles to Alexandre, Joseph and

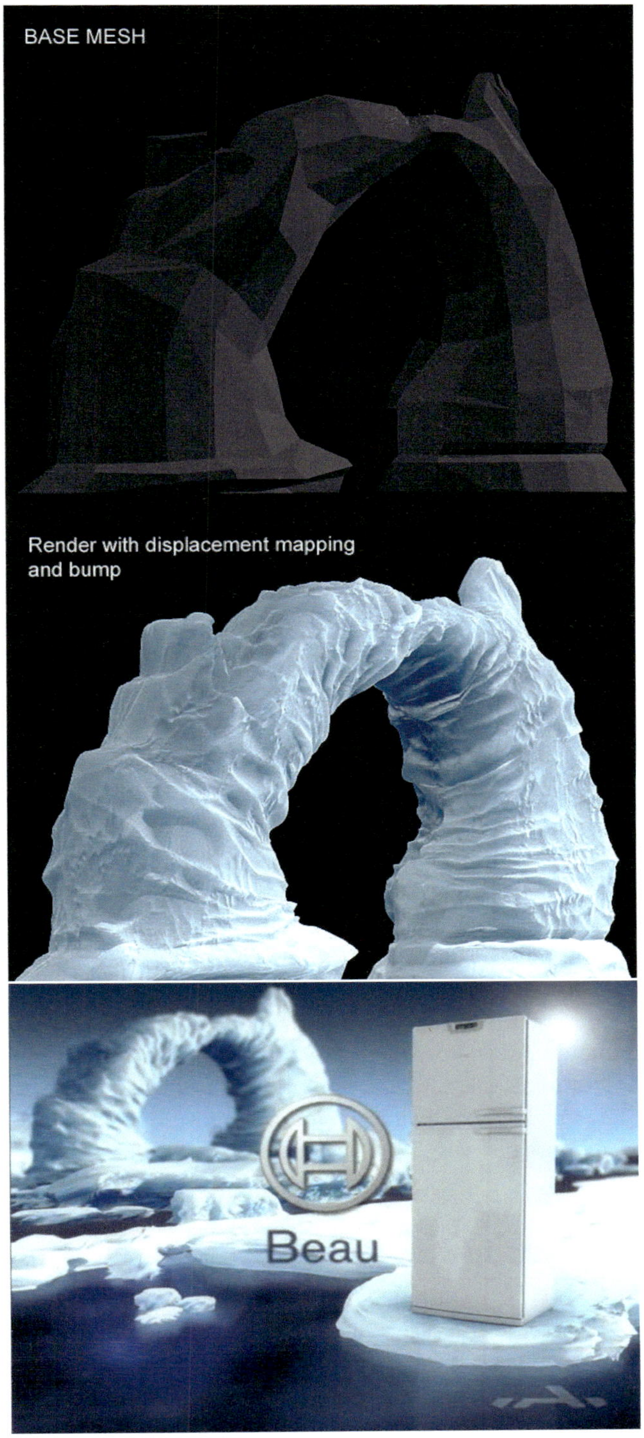

Figure 10.1: Using MaP | Zone for an advertisement, by Akama Studio. Top is a model of the ice archway without textures. Middle, the same archway with the ice texture applied. Bottom, an image from the ad with the ice archway integrated in the background. It was one of the first times that textures from MaP | Zone were used in a production.

Alexandre briefly worked together, and Joseph helped Alexandre and Akama by being a local representative for the studio, as Akama was hoping to secure contracts with producers in the region.

10.4 The Orphanage

I was spending a lot of time in San Francisco[9] in the studio The Orphanage, created by Stu Maschwitz, among others. Stu was a visual effects legend who'd previously worked at ILM, and was very open to new technologies. The studio was located in the heart of the Presidio, a magnificent former military school camp surrounded by eucalyptus trees, located at the foot of the Golden Gate Bridge. I regularly met up with Michael Spaw, an extraordinary technical artist whom I had met some time before, at SIGGRAPH, and who had a particular interest in our technology.

9: I notably spent a lot of time at the Travelodge motel on Lombard St, as they offered rooms for less than my limit of $50 per night. I'd tested out many, many hotels, and that was the best value for money that I could find. When I wasn't in the area, or visiting The Orphanage, I spent a lot of time corresponding via travel journal with the teams in France, sitting in the Grove Café on Chestnut St (now shut down). I also worked on improving my English by reading graphic novels and other books for teenagers, bought in the small bookstore across the street: Books, Inc., at the intersection of Avila St and Chestnut. If I mention these details here, it's in particular because I learned the real basics of English—something that I failed to do as a student studying the language—only once I was immersed in a completely English-speaking environment.

Michael was one of those technology lovers whose determination in seeking out new technology that would help him in his work elevated him to a category far above that of simple 'early adopters.' He was looking for a way to make original, very 'textured' renders for the next project the studio was working on: the adaptation of the graphic novel *Sin City*, by Frank Miller. Michael and I would have many fascinating discussions on the use of fractals, and of our technologies, in particular in the world of special effects. He went on to use some test assets during his work on the films *Hellboy*, *Sin City*, and *Sharkboy and Lavagirl*, though these tests didn't ultimately go much further. Even so, I learned a lot from the experience, and I found it so inspiring to have the opportunity to be so close to those projects that I consider this episode absolutely worthwhile.

I'll note too that the studio also housed the members of the small company SplutterFish, responsible for the 'Brazil R/S' render engine for 3ds Max. I felt that their presence absolutely confirmed the importance of a special projects setup, and the SplutterFish team took this concept a step further still by actually developing their tool within The Orphanage, as close as possible to production requirements. I had many engaging talks with Steve Blackmon, the co-founder of SplutterFish, which he'd created while he was still working at Blur Studios, in Los Angeles. He would ultimately sell the company to Caustic Graphics in 2008, which was in turn bought by Imagination Technologies, who wanted to port raytracing rendering technologies to mobile GPUs. Seeing the SplutterFish team embedded within The Orphanage gave me a lot of inspiration, especially for our next special projects, see Chapters 13 and 27.

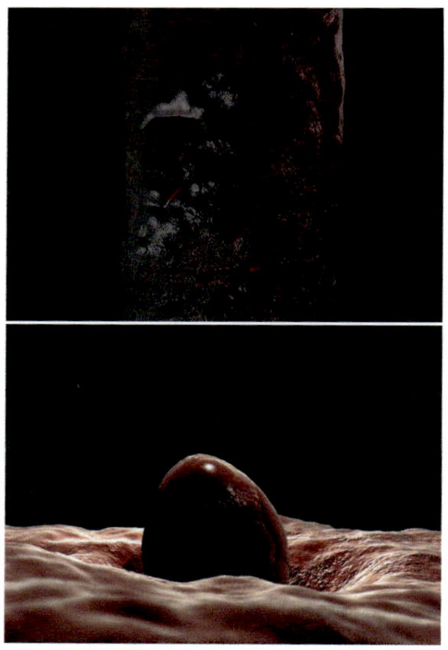

Figure 10.2: Two examples of organic textures created in 2003 by Benjamin Maréchal using MaP | Zone. The procedural textures that we could create with MaP | Zone were well suited to these organic patterns that we would later reuse for the Saskatchewan Roughriders advert, which transported us inside the human body.

10.5 Saskatchewan Roughriders

As I read the various messages from the 3D-themed mailing list that I'd subscribed to, one message in particular caught my attention: a studio was required that could produce some digital images for a TV advertisement, for a Canadian football team, the Saskatchewan Roughriders.

We were at the very start of our adventure and any source of income was welcome. The visual effects within the advertisement would have to represent the interior of the human body—which was filled, by definition, with organically textured materials, exactly the kid of thing that we knew how to create very effectively with MaP | Zone (see, for example, the two textures by Benjamin Maréchal in figure 10.2). I believed that the team could carry out the job well, and I wasn't against the idea of bringing some money into the company's coffers, which were sadly empty...

After a few email exchanges (I sent them these images as proof of our know-how in terms of organic textures), we reached an arrangement with the producers of the TV ad,[10] and we started creating the digital images. Production was stressful as deadlines were very tight and, due to a lack of experience, we had no idea how to manage content creation of this size. All hands on the team were on deck, and Christophe Soum[11] veritably leaped into producing images with Lightwave, his favorite tool.

10: I had no idea what a production like this one might cost and I tried to base myself on what they offered, without negotiating too much.

11: Who really could do absolutely anything. . .

We managed to deliver the images on time (see figure 10.3), and we could congratulate ourselves for having produced, from Clermont-Ferrand, the special effects of a TV advertisement intended for a North American audience, for a Canadian football team from the Canadian province of Saskatchewan, the Roughriders—not at all type of project we'd expected to work on, only a short time earlier. . .

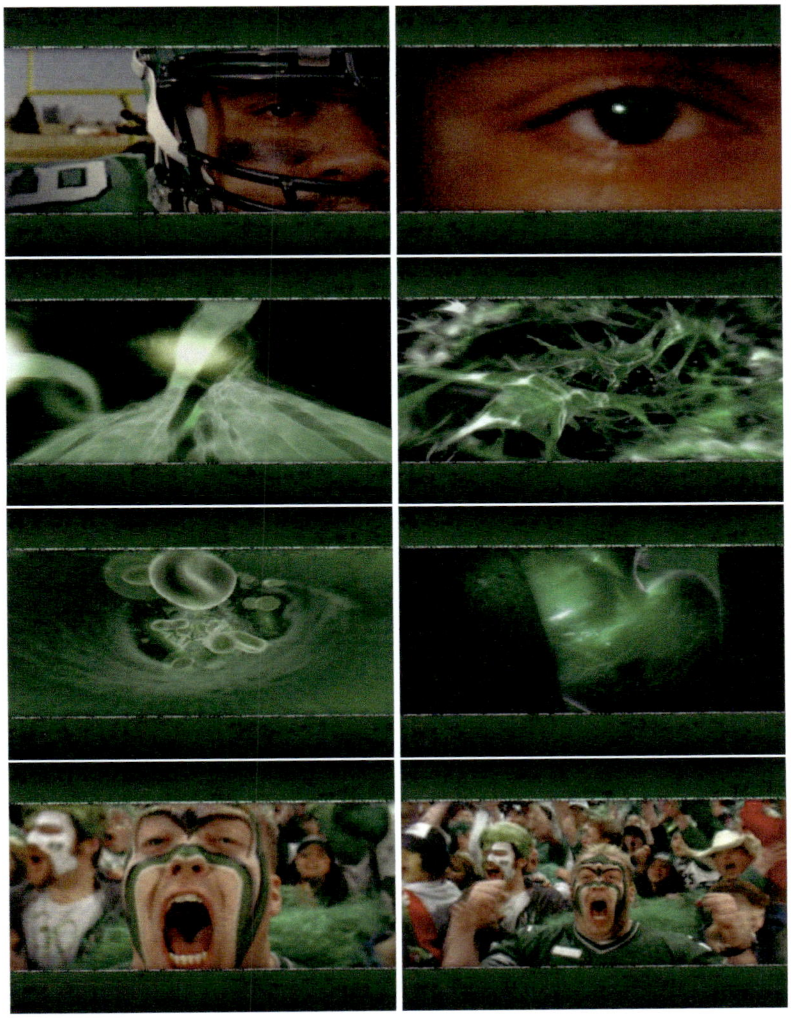

Figure 10.3: Still images from the ad for the Saskatchewan Roughriders. We created all special effects; our procedural organic textures were used to represent the inside of a human body. The whole team pitched in to deliver the shots on time.

One of the big benefits here was that our textures, created with MaP | Zone, had been used effectively in production, and we were able to use these images *ad nauseam* in future commercial communications.

10.6 Gonzo

At the end of 2005 I made one of my first trips to Japan, where I reconnected with Florian Perret, a 3D 'elder' I'd known for many years[12] who lived and worked in Tokyo, at Gonzo.[13] Gonzo was looking for opportunities to develop its 3D activities while keeping one foot in anime projects. More specifically, they wanted to develop techniques to create non-photorealistic 3D renders that evoked the familiar style of manga and other illustrations that tended to work well with the Japanese public. Seeing an opportunity, we began preparing a proposal for Gonzo.[14]

12: He was a friend of one of my cousins; they were part of the same group of skaters around Bastille, in Paris.

13: A production studio specializing in anime and original sound tracks, see [18].

14: The idea of working with a Japanese anime studio particularly appealed to Christophe Soum (Christophe was the one who first introduced me to this culture, see Section 4.2) and Gilles Fleury, who was a huge fan of the genre, and had incessantly insisted since first joining us that our procedural textures could be extremely useful for the production of this very specific style of images.

We worked on this proposal for several weeks, using our texturing technology in a very original way. I include a chart of the rendering pipeline we envisaged for Gonzo, and a few examples of the images we prepared as part of our proposal; see figures 10.4, 10.5, 10.6, 10.7, and 10.8. The commercial proposal we made to Gonzo studio, which would have almost exclusively occupied our team for several months (which is what we went on to do with *RoboBlitz*, see Chapter 13), ultimately wasn't accepted.

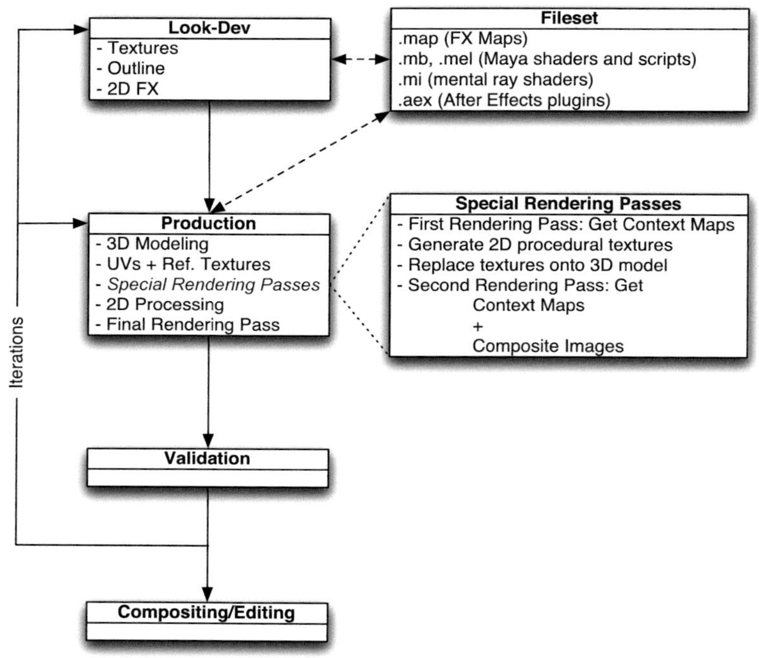

Figure 10.4: The non-photorealistic rendering production pipeline proposed to Gonzo.

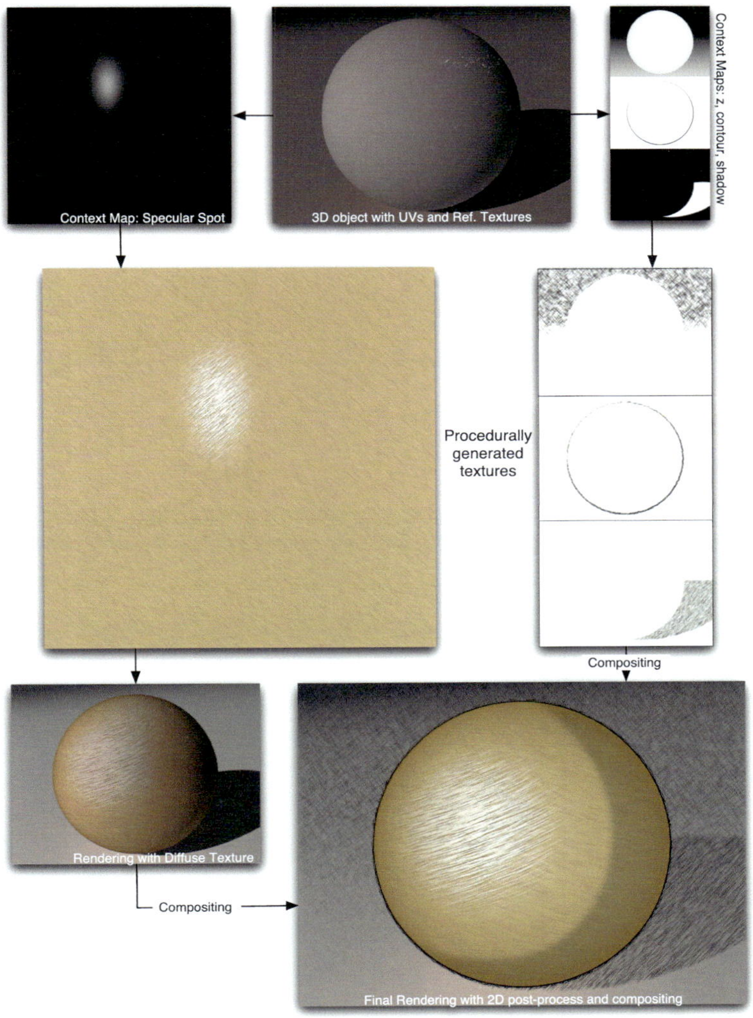

Figure 10.5: The non-photorealistic rendering production pipeline proposed to Gonzo, this time in images.

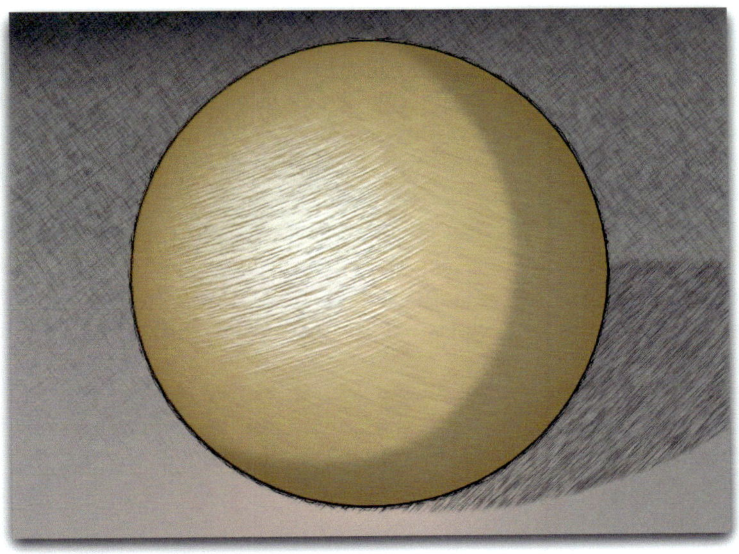

Figure 10.6: The non-photorealistic render and many textures, made for Gonzo.

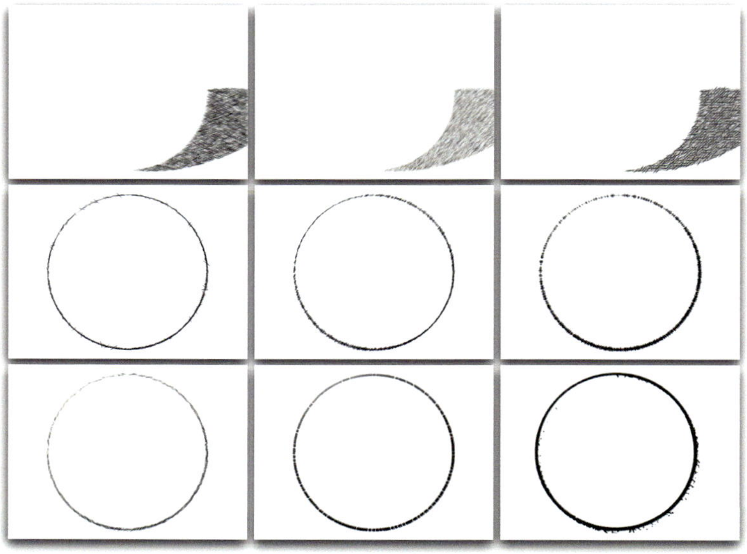

Figure 10.7: Shadows and textured outlines, created for Gonzo.

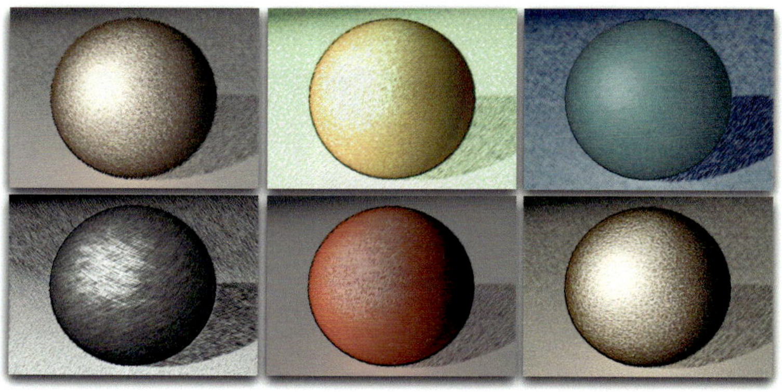

Figure 10.8: Once the pipeline was set up, we simply needed to change textures to quickly obtain a range of different renders. Created for Gonzo.

10.7 Missteps

I won't list here all the projects Allegorithmic worked on, in particular some pure service projects,[15] for which we sold development time that brought us and taught us nothing more than the amount of money we were able to invoice for, often by having incorrectly estimated the time that the work would actually require. For a young company that lived on very little, the temptation to provide service when the products are not yet present can be very strong. Such projects can bring money into the company, which allows progression and for some bills to be paid, but they also pause the development of the products which are the initial objective of the project. I've seen many young companies fall into this 'trap,'[16] and at times we too flirted with this point of balance, this area of revenue generated for service which allows the company to survive, but which doesn't provide the means to develop its products—this intermediate zone, this 'strange attractor'[17] that it's difficult to escape from organically.

15: Such as a render plugin for 3ds Max for a company in the suburbs of Paris. Or many other examples during Allegorithmic's first 10 years. . .

16: A term that should be taken with a pinch of salt, of course.

17: To reference fractals once more.

In retrospect...

Subsidies and other supports for technological innovation are double edged swords. They can keep companies moving, and give developers an opportunity to develop the first prototypes without having to chase income by any and all means, to the detriment of innovation—as was the case with Allegorithmic. A unique opportunity for French companies is the next step, which can ultimately be complicated because innovation (and in particular breakthrough innovation and 'deep' technology) always takes more time than we might imagine to find its application. After the proof of concept and the first embryos of products comes a thankless period of growth, and the search for market fit between a product and a market, and then a complex phase of marketing—in the full sense of the term, rather than any reductive use that might confine marketing to communication—and sales. Subsidies are not necessarily structured to support all of these phases, and a mistake I've seen made by heads of business is to become a champion of such subsidies, without looking for ways to go further. Such dependency locks a company into this intermediate zone, which allows it to earn just enough, through providing service, not to perish completely—but not enough to invest and innovate.

Presence in America | 11

11.1 Joseph Mbayen and our first commercial presence in Los Angeles

Meeting Joseph

Chance played a big role for us in 2004, when coincidence placed Christophe Soum and Joseph Mbayen next to each other during a train ride between Paris and Clermont-Ferrand. Christophe, as expected, spent the three and a half hours of the trip coding on his laptop, which just barely fit the description of a portable computer. At the time, Joseph was a sprinter (in the 100-meter category)[1] and, following an unsuccessful meet in Florida in which he'd tried to qualify to participate in the Olympics, he was traveling to Clermont-Ferrand to do some work with the city's athletics club.

1: When we worked together some time later, Joe took me to a few track meets at Stanford University, or elsewhere in California, while traveling to Las Vegas for a convention. On one of these occasions, I found myself standing next to Maurice Green and other world-class athletes who were warming up with him; close up like this, I was fascinated by the strength and speed of these athletic giants.

Eternally curious, Joseph asked Christophe what he was doing, programming obscure software with such intense concentration. Christophe explained his work—he was developing an app for 3D artists, for a new company, Allegorithmic, that had recently been set up in Clermont-Ferrand. When he mentioned our ambition to sell our software to 3D studios all over the world, and notably to studios in California, Joseph lit up: he'd studied marketing and finance in Los Angeles and Florida, and he was passionate about technology and startups. Moreover, he was looking to help European projects enter the US territory. He told Christophe that he'd be very interested in helping us develop in the US!

That day, I was meeting Christophe at Clermont-Ferrand's train station. When I picked him up, he told me about this surprising encounter and pointed me toward Joseph, who was walking away. Intrigued, I ran after Joseph[2] and introduced myself. After a brief discussion, I invited him to visit our office.

2: I caught up with him!

One thing led to another, and because there was a good feeling between us, it took us just a few days to find a way to work together. By working with us, Joseph was taking a big financial risk—we couldn't really afford to pay him properly. Regardless, he ended up moving[3] to Los Angeles, a hub for visual effects and motion graphics. Allegorithmic shared the cost for an apartment he rented on Sepulveda Boulevard, in Venice, which became the address of Allegorithmic's commercial representation in the US. We now had a permanent US address and phone number! And we also had a commercial representative there, Joseph Mbayen (or 'Joe,' as he preferred when he was in the US).

3: By car, from Miami, at the wheel of his Mitsubishi Spyder (see figure 11.2) !

Figure 11.1: The image we used to announce the opening of our office in Los Angeles.

Commercial prospection: the motion graphics industry

When I wasn't there, Joseph followed up on sales and organized demos and meetings to coincide with my next visits. We toured around all the

DOI:10.1201/9781003534624-11

Figure 11.2: Joseph Mbayen, the first Allegorithmic commercial representative in Los Angeles, at the wheel of his Mitsubishi Spyder. We'd travel all over LA in this car.

motion graphics studios[4] that we could find in the area,[5] such as Liquid, Brickyard VFX, and Level 3.

There were many others, and our new product MaP | Time (see Section 9.6) was a plugin for After Effects, the king of motion graphics software. Using procedural textures, and in particular, our ability to modify texture parameters using a timeline, our plugin made it possible to produce highly original and infinitely varied graphic effects.

Unfortunately the technology and the product weren't yet very mature, so our mission of selling MaP | Zone and MaP | Time was almost impossible. We worked in this way for several years, and Joseph ultimately went on to pursue new adventures,[6] just as the world of video games began to show an interest in our technologies (see Chapter 13).

4: Motion graphics are a class of visual effects that are typically found in areas such as TV credits, or advertising: a mix of rapid animations, virtual 'pyrotechnics,' and other particle-type effects, in motion, and often in short sequences. The Los Angeles area at the time was the core of American television, along with New York.

5: And beyond: for instance, I found myself giving a presentation organized by the 'Motion Graphics New York City' association, within the Apple Store in SoHo.

6: I am, as I write these lines, a happy investor in one of the companies that Joseph went on to successfully create and run in the following years.

11.2 Unit 7

Vincent Brisebois

I met Vincent Brisebois on October 19, 2004, in Hollywood during a conference organized by MGLA (Motion Graphics Los Angeles) and Ko Maruyama, whom I'd met during a previous SIGGRAPH.[7] Vincent, who was originally from Quebec and was bilingual in French and English (trilingual when he gets into 'deep' Quebec French) worked for

7: We would follow one another's work for several years, Ko being particularly enthusiastic about new technologies. He can be seen in figure 12.2.

Discreet Logic; that day he was presenting the latest 3ds Max features.[8] I approached him to discuss MaP | Zone and MaP | Time.

8: Vincent was an Application Engineer for Discreet Logic, and spent a lot of time on the road, traveling from conference to conference, studio to studio, to give presentations, provide training and give live support to users of 3ds Max software. He knew absolutely every part of the industry. He would later move to Autodesk, then Fusion IO with Steve Wozniak, and he currently works at NVIDIA

Figure 11.3: Slides from the presentation I gave on October 4, 2004 at MGLA, in Hollywood. I first met Vincent Brisebois during this evening.

At the end of the event I saw that, as often happened, my presentation had impressed one person out of every hundred and left the other ninety-nine confused by the complexity of what I'd discussed. Procedural textures and effects were not widely used, nor widely understood, at that time; we could provide the technology to make procedural textures accessible, but this nonetheless required a certain level of investment to grasp them. For that one person in every hundred, however (often the most technical artist in the room), we could clearly provide something unique, and this person would often bombard me with follow-up questions, before jumping into the trial version of the software.[9]

That evening, that one person in a hundred was Vincent. He told me how much he'd appreciated the presentation and the demo, and that he felt we had the potential to impact the 3D industry as enormously as the introduction of normal maps once had.[10]

Vincent and I immediately got along particularly well.[11] We continued our evening, and I told him about everything we'd been working on, and in particular about my increasingly frequent trips to this part of the world. Vincent was based in Marina del Rey in Los Angeles, and offered to host me at his place the next time I passed through. I readily accepted his invitation, especially as he also offered to introduce me to several people and companies who he thought would be interested in

9: We'd take advantage of this phenomenon some years later by explicitly separating Substance Designer and Substance Painter, addressing two different audiences; I presented this idea in an internal white paper, introducing 'Left-Brain Artists' and 'Right-Brain Artists,' many years later.

10: Vincent was clearly way ahead of the curve. His support was enormously encouraging, and inspired me to persist in my efforts.

11: This was totally down to Vincent; he gets along well with everybody, and everybody likes him immediately. He is kind, open-minded, and helpful, and people can't help but appreciate this.

what Allegorithmic could provide. This was the best possible point of entry for us: a recommendation from someone the studios trusted.

When I was back in LA a few weeks later, I stayed at Vincent's, and his apartment, which was part of one of those marina condo buildings in Marina del Rey, was a geek's paradise, with an endless number of books, figurines, DVDs, and other technological rarities that represented a treasure trove for someone like me. He introduced me to many new areas of interest—in addition to introducing me to numerous people and companies in the 3D industry.[12] Our friendship grew each time I visited the area, so much so that we eventually became roommates.

12: From many studios, of course—notably Ben Girard from Digital Dimension, John Chalfant from Red Engine, Adam Watkins, Chris Vienneau, Alex Alvarez, Claude Robillard, Gary Davis, Jean-François Yelle, Keith Chamberlain, Ken Pimentel, Mark Noland, Michel Besner, Michel Kripalani, Paul Norman, Sébastien Lavier, Shane Griffith, Yannick Leblanc, and many others still... The list is too long to fully include here, but Vincent, in addition to being a dear friend, was an incredible help in making connections, both for Allegorithmic and for myself.

Unit 7

From the start of 2004, I spent a lot of time in the Los Angeles area and, in order to avoid the too frequent, exhausting trips between California and France, I decided to stay for several months at a time each time I visited, within the limits of what my visa allowed me (that is, a cumulative maximum of 6 months a year, in individual visits of no greater than 3 months each). Vincent and I had the idea that we should become roommates; he was thinking about moving to a bigger apartment anyway, and we got along very well.

Figure 11.4: 'Unit 7' was located in this building (top), at 117 Catamaran St, in Marina del Rey, Los Angeles. Below, my desk—at the back), facingVincent's.

Following a quick, successful search, the two of us soon moved into 117 Catamaran St, in Marina del Rey, into Unit 7 of the complex, along with a third roommate, Lee Roderick, an independent film director and visual effects creator who divided his time between his family home and Hollywood, and who (like me) needed a place to stay while he was around. He was very rarely present, and Vincent and I often had the apartment to ourselves.

Figure 11.5: Lee Roderick and Vincent Brisebois, with whom I shared an apartment in Venice, California, which we renamed 'Unit 7.' We organized technical presentations, and would invite some key figures from the world of 3D.

Unit 7 became a magical place for us, and we organized it around our work on digital imaging. The apartment was filled with equipment, magazines, DVDs, and books, all of it dedicated to the realm of the imagination. We also organized a few mini-events there, inviting 3D personalities to give presentations, such as Dominique Pouliquen, founder and director of the company Realviz, which he would sell to Autodesk a few years later. Unit 7 played a pivotal role in my life, allowing me to have a strong presence in Los Angeles (in addition to the permanent commercial representation provided by Joseph), so that I could also spend some time with Dave Taylor (see Chapter 13), with whom I would soon be working, as well as giving me the opportunity to meet as many notable figures as possible within the 3D industry.

A very special project

The people that Vincent worked with a lot (alongside John Chalfant) included the well-known director David Lynch. Vincent was Lynch's technical advisor, and he and John produced several 3D images and animations at the director's request.

Lynch's projects at that time included an animated film written by his wife, Mary Sweeney. Vincent discussed this project with me as he felt that our technology and knowledge could prove of value, also knowing that David Lynch liked to surround himself with people he trusted, and didn't immediately want to bring a major production studio into the project. Lynch had full confidence in Vincent on everything related to technical and visual effects.

I read the script,[13] and discussed it with Mary; to allow David Lynch, as director, to have full control of the production (this is what he wanted, particularly in the context of an animated film), I had the idea of a production created with game engines and real-time techniques.[14] This way, David would get feedback on the animation immediately, and set up a positive feedback loop, giving him the control he needed. I called the project 'Game of Director' (GoD).

13: I read it on the plane from LA to Paris—so Hollywood!

14: Which wasn't entirely new at the time—notably, a number of creators were working on 'Machinima,' [19] using game engines to tell animated stories—but which was nonetheless far ahead of production trends at that time; this approach would only be used in major productions in the early 2020s.

After several months of intermittent work, the project fell through. In a sense, this was a good thing, as our tools at that time weren't yet able to really execute the idea. We could have potentially gotten lost in this project that was just a little too far outside the norm. . .

Luxology and Imagesynth 12

12.1 Luxology, Imagesynth

Luxology

On August 2, 2005, I was lucky enough to attend a special event connected to SIGGRAPH in Los Angeles: a presentation organized by the newly formed company Luxology at a prestigious venue, The Orpheum Theater. They were going to present what they called "Nexus," their 3D modeling core (among other things), which would become Modo.[1] The audience was very enthusiastic, and the head of Luxology,[2] Brad Peebler, was particularly charismatic. His appeal as a former American football player, who was still very athletic, and his art of communication and natural, genuine enthusiasm, worked to great effect as he presented his project. The future would be Modo!

Figure 12.1: Luxology's special event on August 2, 2005, took place at the legendary Orpheum Theater in Los Angeles.

This was one of the first times that I met, following the event, Brad and his team, notably including Greg Duquenes, whom I would visit a few weeks later in Bordeaux.[3] We'd been put in contact a few days earlier, during this same SIGGRAPH, by Wanda Meloni,[4] an analyst of the 3D universe; Wanda in turn had been introduced to me by Bill Roberts (if I recall correctly), and I'd recently presented Allegorithmic to her. During our discussion, Wanda, who was always very well intentioned and who had a lot of good-quality contacts based on respect and trust, gave me some valuable advice and pointed me toward Brad, feeling that he and I would get along well together...

1: A major 3D software tool in general, known particularly for its modeling capabilities.

2: Luxology was founded by former members of the team behind LightWave, iconic 3D software of the late 90s, published by NewTek. It is interesting to note that Christophe Soum had been an advanced user of Lightwave for many years. Christophe and I had a great deal of admiration for this legendary team—legendary in our eyes, in any case!

3: Greg worked for Luxology from home, in Bordeaux. He was a particularly endearing character and one of the principal programmers of Modo, particularly of its materials and textures module. This was one of the first times I'd seen a successful example of remote work.

Figure 12.2: On this photo from 2006: Brad Peebler, Bob Benett (both at Luxology), Sébastien Deguy, Ko Maruyama (who oversaw the future of MGLA, Motion Graphics Los Angeles), and someone named Dave who I do not recognize.

4: To this day, I still have a great relationship with Wanda, one of my favorite people from the 3D world, and somebody who I respect enormously. I also developed a friendship with Brad and Greg, which remains strong today.

Imagesynth

Brad told me that, although he liked procedural texturing, he had another idea in mind for us: he'd like to see us develop a tool for his company Luxology, who would publish the product. That product would be

DOI:10.1201/9781003534624-12

analytical texture synthesis software—that is, software that could take a photo of a texture as input, and then copy and extend that texture. In particular, the goal here was to obtain a higher resolution version of the input image, which could be repeated without any "seams" being visible. This process would use relatively recent techniques that had been developed in the world of research in the second half of the 90s, and which had caught Brad's eye—Brad felt that purely procedural textures couldn't match the richness of a photographed texture.[5]

5: Back then we couldn't really say otherwise, even though Allegorithmic would later demonstrate the opposite.

After my return to France, and following some further exchanges by email, we reached an agreement. Part of the team, with Cyrille Damez as head, would develop and implement the central algorithms, and would launch the production of a Photoshop plugin for the legendary Luxology—and all of this was coming out of Clermont-Ferrand! I had a hard time believing it.[6]

6: And I take my hat off to Brad for placing his trust in us from the very beginning. . .

The "Imagesynth" software was released in September 2006.[20] We'd set up a royalty agreement with Luxology that meant that, if the product sold well, we'd all make money; if it didn't sell, we'd all fail together.

Figure 12.3: The ImageSynth software, which we developed for Luxology, was released in September 2006. It was a plugin for Photoshop which took an input image and generated an extended texture that repeated without any visible edges. The product wasn't a commercial success but, thanks to its technical capabilities and appreciation within the 3D community, it opened some doors for us. It was also an opportunity for us to develop cutting-edge graphical software, in Clermont-Ferrand, for a company that we greatly admired, who would publish our software.

Even though the product was highly regarded, bringing us some respect within the industry,[7] it didn't make us rich. . . In any case, I don't regret having had the opportunity to work with Brad and his team, and trying out a project that, for me and my team, was very prestigious—even though it briefly took us away from our long-term path, our focus on procedural textures. We'd go on to make other "errors" in the future when it came to our services (see Chapter 30, for example), but this was one that we still regard with great affection.

7: The tool was well known, and the technical capabilities it represented opened some doors for us.

Dave Taylor, *RoboBlitz*, and ProFX | 13

13.1 Dave Taylor

I met Dave[21] in March 2006 during the Game Developers Conference (GDC),[1] one of the last to be held in San Jose, the capital of Silicon Valley, an hour South of San Francisco. This was my first GDC and one of my first forays into the world of video games. Dave was a legend in the video game universe. He was one of the developers of *Doom*[2] and *Quake*, when he worked at id Software,[3] in Austin, Texas. He then worked entirely alone to develop a new game, *Abuse*, in the mid-90s—when it was still possible to do so. The game was an enormous success, which allowed him, as he told me himself, 'to make his first million.' After this, he moved to Hollywood to develop a film project with American McGee. Due to a disagreement with McGee, this project was halted, and when I met Dave he was navigating between several projects as a business developer or adviser.[4]

Dave notably advised me to approach a young gaming company, Naked Sky Entertainment; we'd end up working with them very soon afterwards. Dave was an exceptional person. He was brilliant and whimsical; when I met him he had long, curly, platinum blond hair that he liked to play with, and that gave him an air of being slightly crazy. He was flamboyant, and always looking for the little (or big) thing that would somehow make a big difference. With his flowery language, he made me think of a more technical Jim Carrey character. Spending time with him was a delight.

13.2 Middleware

During this first encounter at GDC, I pitched Allegorithmic and our products to Dave. I told him that we'd so far been trying to sell our products to visual effects and motion graphics studios, but we had a feeling that video game developers might be interested in what we had to offer... without really knowing what precisely they'd find interesting, nor having any contacts in the industry.

Thanks to his technical background, Dave understood our technology very quickly, and in great depth, which I found remarkable. Then he pointed out one element I'd discussed that could be interesting for game developers: he thought that the procedural aspect[5] of our textures could be very useful if we could extract the procedural texture generation engine from MaP | Zone, and implement it as a library within the game engine, in order to allow developers to generate the final texture images (bitmaps) at any point they wanted. The idea would be to make TAON 3, the procedural texture engine at the heart of MaP | Zone, a technological product in its own right, a library that could be integrated into game engines like Unreal Engine, and to port it to various platforms such as the XBox 360. Unlike MaP | Zone, which was a product aimed at 3D artists,

1: At the same event, I also met Marc Rein and Jay Wilbur, of Epic Games, for the first time. Jay and Dave had worked together at id Software.

2: And things came full circle for me once again: see Section 1.3.

3: The book *Masters of Doom* by David Kushner, which tells the saga of id Software, mentions how Dave would regularly collapse to the ground in the offices of id due to dizziness brought on by extremely long, intense sessions of Doom. The id team went so far as to mark out the shape of his body on the floor with tape.

4: When I later worked with Dave (see the following passages), I was fascinated by his method of doing business: fluid, without complications, and at times very blunt—and it worked! I'd always had an image of the business world as something complex, formal, 'legal,' and serious. Dave showed me an approach that was very uninhibited and direct—and perhaps very American? It was an approach I'd go on to see again, particularly among certain investment bankers. In the US, it seemed perfectly fine to conduct business all by yourself, in the corner of your small office—it was possible to make big, or even huge, business deals over the phone, based on just a few poorly formatted emails. All of which made it possible to take full advantage of life in the Los Angeles sun... I saw this as a very positive thing, and this way of working that I discovered with Dave proved very reassuring, and helped alleviate some of the anxiety I felt in my own approach to work.

5: Which was therefore compact—that is, the procedural texture description file was very light, weighing just a few KB, whereas textures themselves, the bitmap files, could weigh several MB, or even much more. Our generated textures would therefore require around one thousandth of the space that might otherwise be required, or even less!

DOI:10.1201/9781003534624-13

the 'TAON 3 product' (we'd name it a little later; see below) would target programmers, who were a very different audience.

The idea was particularly impactful, and it was the first time I heard someone mention 'middleware,' the layer of software between the app and the hardware. Middleware was a booming field in the gaming world, and enough of an umbrella term that a number of different techniques and libraries, ranging from sound libraries to video compression and decompression, as well as physics solvers, could claim to be a part of it. Above all, it was sufficiently new, and had been sufficiently hyped, that the tech world overall was drawn to it. Dave, as a business developer, was always looking for a good opportunity, and sensed potential within our technology. Already, he was beginning to visualize a link between Allegorithmic and one of the companies he worked with, Microsoft—who, just then, were preparing something new for the XBox 360: the XBox Live Arcade.

13.3 XBox Live Arcade

Dave told me about a Microsoft project called XBox Live Arcade, an online game distribution platform dedicated to the brand-new XBox 360. It was one of the first services whose goal was to distribute console games via the internet. Microsoft wanted to strengthen the game development ecosystem, and offered here an opportunity and a platform for a class of smaller games, by more independent creators.

Microsoft therefore imposed a maximum size constraint of 50MB per game, so that they could be downloaded quickly;[6] this would offer the best possible experience to players without having to wait: 'I want to play a new game, I click, I play (almost) immediately.'

6: Internet connections at that time were not very good, particularly in the US where we were just entering the ADSL era.

It was also a way for Microsoft to test out new business models, especially 'free2play,' which was quite new at the time (but fundamental in South Korea, see Chapter 20). This model allowed players to play a game for free, with a monetization system based on purchases within the game (a special power, a magic weapon, a different appearance etc.). With this setup, a significant link existed between the time required to access the game and its success—and so, it was crucial to reduce as much as possible the time required to download the game, to prevent players from moving on to something else before even starting to play. Microsoft therefore encouraged us to optimize as much as possible the size of games on the platform.

50 MB was a comfortable size for a 2D game, but very, very limiting for a 3D game. "Yet what element takes up most space in a 3D game?" Dave asked me. "In general, the textures!" Planets began to align in the heavens above us, and I finally saw what Dave was driving at. Our procedural textures occupied next to no space on hard drives and so, if the game was textured mostly with MaP | Zone, it would require very little space and fit within the 50 MB limit imposed on games available on the XBox Live Arcade. These textures would then be generated on the player's XBox 360 once the game had been downloaded, thanks to our middleware based on TAON 3.

And so there was, potentially, a real need for technologies like ours. Dave had put his finger on this potential application, seeing the connection between one of the strengths of procedural textures and the constraints imposed by Microsoft. In theory, we were even in an ideal situation: we saw a clearly defined need in the market, which could be answered with our new technology... If we were only able to create a real, functioning product, success would be guaranteed!

When Dave suggested he'd be interested in helping us grow in the gaming world and push our middleware product once it was ready, I jumped at the opportunity. Dave had the technical background to understand our technology, and he'd spotted the opportunity available to us if we were to transform it into a product that we hadn't even thought of until that moment. Moreover, he knew the gaming market intimately, and he even had an idea of who our first customer—or our first alpha-site—could be...

We quickly found a way to work together, and Dave became our business developer specializing in the video game sector.

Figure 13.1: In this photo from 2008, Dave (second from left) no longer has his extravagant haircut. Dave worked with me for many years as a business developer and advisor. On this photo: Sébastien Deguy, Dave Taylor, a friend of Dave's, and Justin Lassen, a musician who spent a lot of time between Phoenix, Arizona, and Los Angeles, who I became friends with. He composed the music for *RoboBlitz*. He later worked extensively with Intel as an artist in residence. He left us very suddenly at the beginning of 2021...

13.4 Naked Sky, alpha-site

The companies and projects in which Dave was active included Naked Sky Entertainment, a young game development company based in a skyscraper in downtown Los Angeles. Dave knew several members of the team well (notably genius developer Josh Glazer, Jake Carvey,[7] and Tariq Soliman, all talented artists who would become my friends), and worked well with the company's CEO, Tian Mu, as an advisor. Naked Sky had secured funding from investors, in part with Dave's aid, and was now in the process of developing a game for XBox Live Arcade: *RoboBlitz*.

7: Jake lived in an industrial complex in Los Angeles used as an artists' squat. It was a unique place, full of various and eccentric creations, like a permanent mini-Burning Man. Jake was also an extraordinary cook, and we benefited from his talents on many occasions.

RoboBlitz was a 'physics-based puzzle' game, offering three main innovations and differentiators: first, it was one of the first games to use the brand new game engine Unreal Engine 3, developed by Epic Games. Epic had used this on their own game, *Gears of War*, but also licensed it to any developer who was interested and willing to pay their fee. Second, *RoboBlitz* incorporated a massive use of 'physics'—that is, the movements of objects and characters (robots) in the game were *calculated* in real-time, responding to the laws of physics (in terms of impacts, gravity, ballistics, etc.) and not simply *played* according to a previously recorded sequence. This allowed the game to unfold with infinite possibilities available, making the experience overall extremely realistic. Finally, it was an entirely 3D game; it was able to provide numerous levels while remaining under the 50MB size limit imposed by Microsoft for the XBox Live Arcade (see Section 13.3). And so, the game was one of the only 3D games on the platform and did, in fact, stand out from the crowd.

Figure 13.2: The cover of the game *RoboBlitz*,[22] developed by Naked Sky Entertainment, which was released on XBox 360, and distributed on the XBox Live Arcade. It was the first game that used MaP|Zone and ProFX. Image Fair use, `https://en.wikipedia.org/w/index.php?curid=21270219`

To optimize the size of the game, Dave proposed that Naked Sky use Allegorithmic's technology and become an alpha-site for our middleware, which didn't yet exist (see Section 13.2). The idea was to generate a significant part of the game's textures in a purely procedural way. If the byte weight of a classic 3D game was largely due to textures, we could theoretically reduce this size very significantly. This would allow Naked Sky to include more game content—or even more freedom to 'force' the game down to a specific size, such as the 50 MB limit in this case. Once downloaded, the game's textures would be generated during installation and saved on the hard drive of the XBox 360. It didn't matter if the final size of the game exceeded 50 MB once installed; only its size during the initial download was important.

We therefore had to succeed both in producing procedural textures that were good enough to be approved by Naked Sky's artistic director, for use in the game, while also ensuring that the generation of textures on the XBox 360, by the 'extracted' engine of our middleware, was fast enough—otherwise, any time saved during the download time would be replaced by calculation time, which would make the use of our technology pointless... The risk was big for both parties, because if the middleware didn't work, or if the procedural textures that MaP | Zone produced were not of a sufficiently high quality, then it would be impossible to release the game (which would be catastrophic for Naked Sky)—and such a failure would put us in a very bad position (which would be catastrophic for Allegorithmic). This was a critical moment for our technology and, despite the very high risk,[8] the opportunity to finally demonstrate the power of our software, in a real application, was too good to pass up. We had to try.

Thanks to Dave, we all found a way to work together. And so, Allegorithmic's development team in Clermont-Ferrand (led by Christophe Soum) focused on the development of our middleware, and on porting this to the XBox 360,[9] while another part of the team, our technical artists, created the procedural textures for the game. Naked Sky paid us (a little) for this production of specialized textures. This was therefore a content production service, but 'in the service of the development' of our middleware.

8: But in a sense, this risk is inherent to all innovation; seeing such risk in this case was just another sign validating the fact that we were indeed at the cutting edge, in an area of absolute innovation. If we'd been in more familiar territory, there would have been less risk—but this would have implied a very weak level of innovation...

9: It was indeed necessary to port the code of the texture generation engine, TAON 3, which ran on Intel processors and under Windows, to the hardware and software environment defined by Microsoft for the XBox 360. The teams therefore had to use development tools that were different to those they typically used. Above all, we had to get an XBox 360 'development kit' from Microsoft—a strange, dedicated machine; we couldn't even plug it into a French outlet until one of my father's friends created a homemade transformer for us, finally allowing us to switch it on... During this period, we established a good relationship with Microsoft, and in particular with Tracy Frankcom, who managed developer relations at Microsoft; we ended up making several trips to the offices of this historic company, in the Seattle area.

13.5 The birth of ProFX

With the game due for release in a few months, the teams got to work. Gilles Fleury set up the production pipeline with the rest of the team in Clermont-Ferrand, then flew to Los Angeles to work within the teams at Naked Sky, close to the various artistic directors who successively worked on the project. All of these artistic directors were very demanding concerning the quality of the textures produced, and some of them had little faith in what we are doing... Gilles stayed in a particularly shabby hotel in LA's city center.[10] Gilles didn't drive and so—because it's impossible to travel around Los Angeles on foot—he was stuck in this environment for several months. This was a difficult period for him, but he heroically pushed through to the end. This was also a tense period for Allegorithmic, because the project was so complex and we didn't know for sure if we'd be able to deliver what Tian and his team were expecting from us. Tian was very vocal and direct with his concerns, and was at times putting pressure on us. He and I had some heated discussions.

10: In one instance, he literally broke through the wall of his room by leaning on it a little too much...

Nevertheless, after several months of intense work between Los Angeles and Clermont-Ferrand, we managed to deliver something of a sufficient standard artistically (our textures) and technically (the texture generation engine on XBox 360). Naked Sky's artistic director approved the textures,

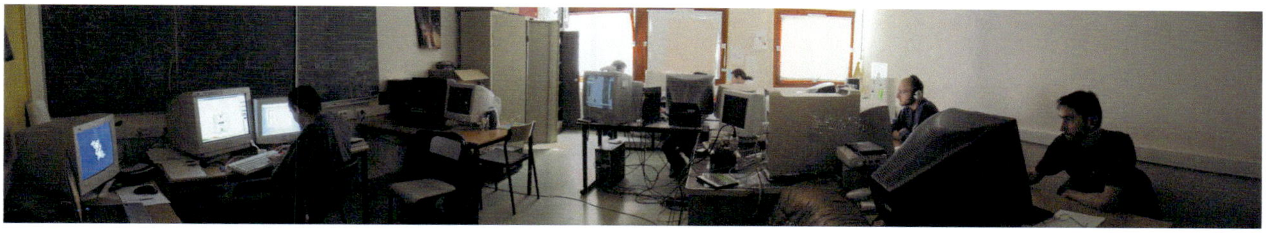

Figure 13.3: May 2, 2006: the Clermont-Ferrand team working hard on our middleware for *RoboBlitz*. In the center, we can see an XBox 360 development kit, connected to a TV displaying results of a calculated texture. We can see, from left to right, Gilles Fleury, Christophe Soum, Cyrille Damez and Pierre Boy.

and the engine ran smoothly while generating images at a sufficient speed!

Our middleware product was born, and we named it ProFX.

By the end of the project, the usage statistics for MaP | Zone and ProFX on the *RoboBlitz* game were very good:

- The game had 18 levels in 3D;
- It weighed 50 MB instead of 400 MB, due to ProFX;
- 80% of its textures were created procedurally using MaP | Zone 2;
- The ratio of weight between MaP | Zone's procedural textures and traditional bitmap textures was 1 to 300;
- Textures were generated with ProFX on XBox 360 at a speed of 20 MB/s.

Figures 13.4, 13.5, 13.6, and 13.7 illustrate the work carried out, and the pipelines set up for *RoboBlitz*. Figure 13.8 shows the general way that ProFX was used, and how it related to MaP | Zone.

Figure 13.4: Some procedural textures from the game *RoboBlitz*. They were made using MaP | Zone (in version 2 here, and from now on) and helped reduce the game's size with the goal of making the game as fast to download as possible. These textures were generated during installation by our middleware ProFX, which we ported to XBox 360 for this project.

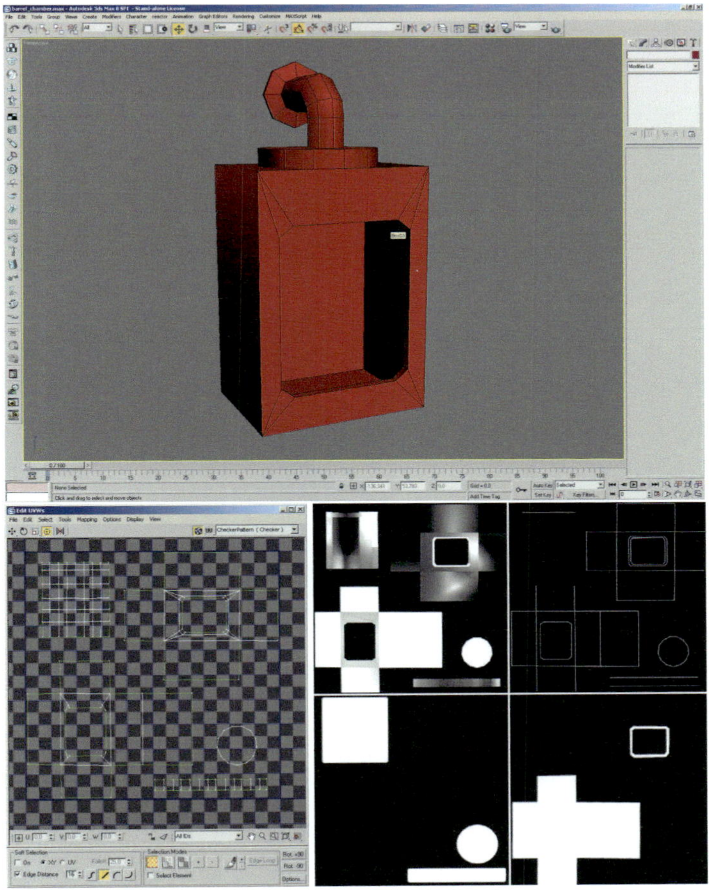

Figure 13.5: Stages of texturing an asset for *RoboBlitz*: a blank model without textures; an 'unwrapped' model in 3ds Max; some 'baked maps,' such as curvature, ambient occlusion, and various masks.

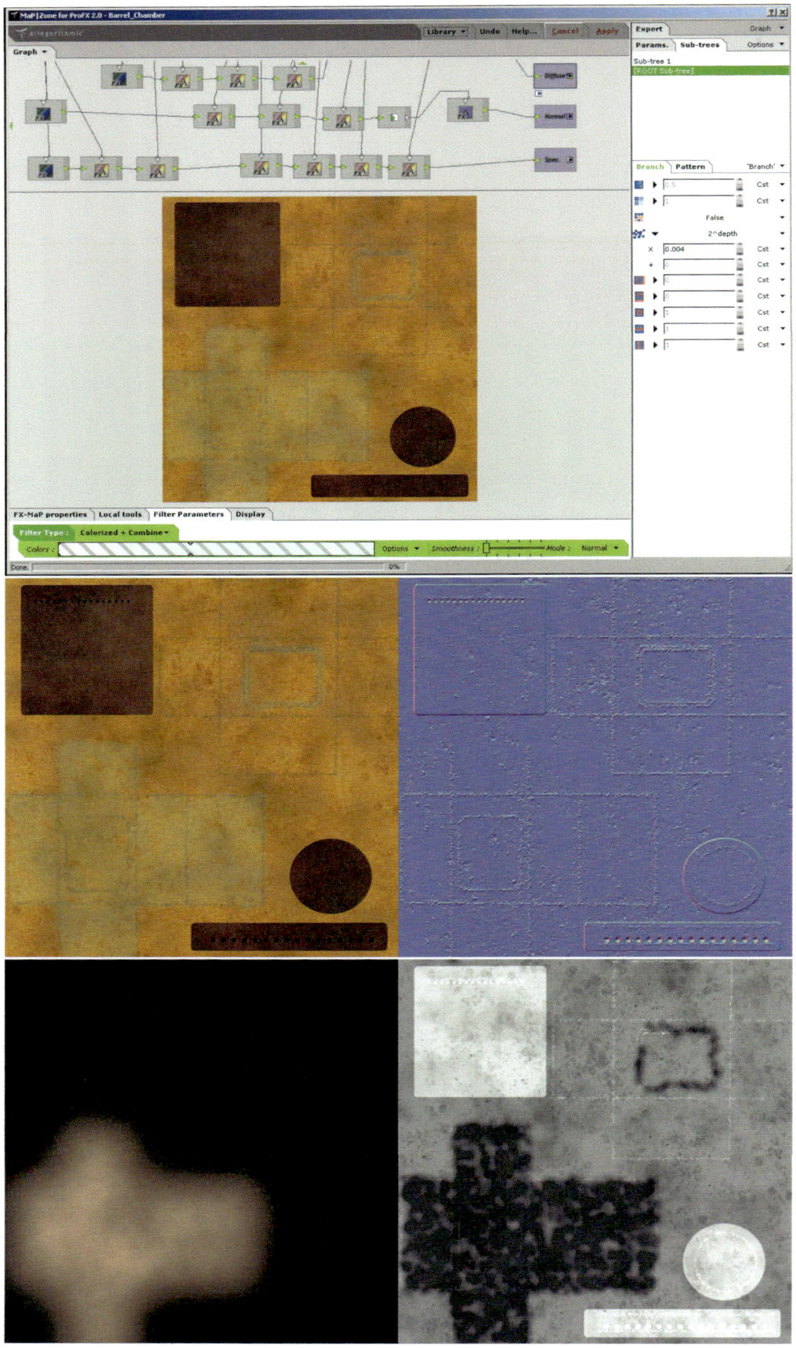

Figure 13.6: Stages of texturing an asset for the game *RoboBlitz* (continued): texture creation in MaP | Zone; the diffuse map obtained; the normal map obtained; the emissive map obtained; the specular map obtained.

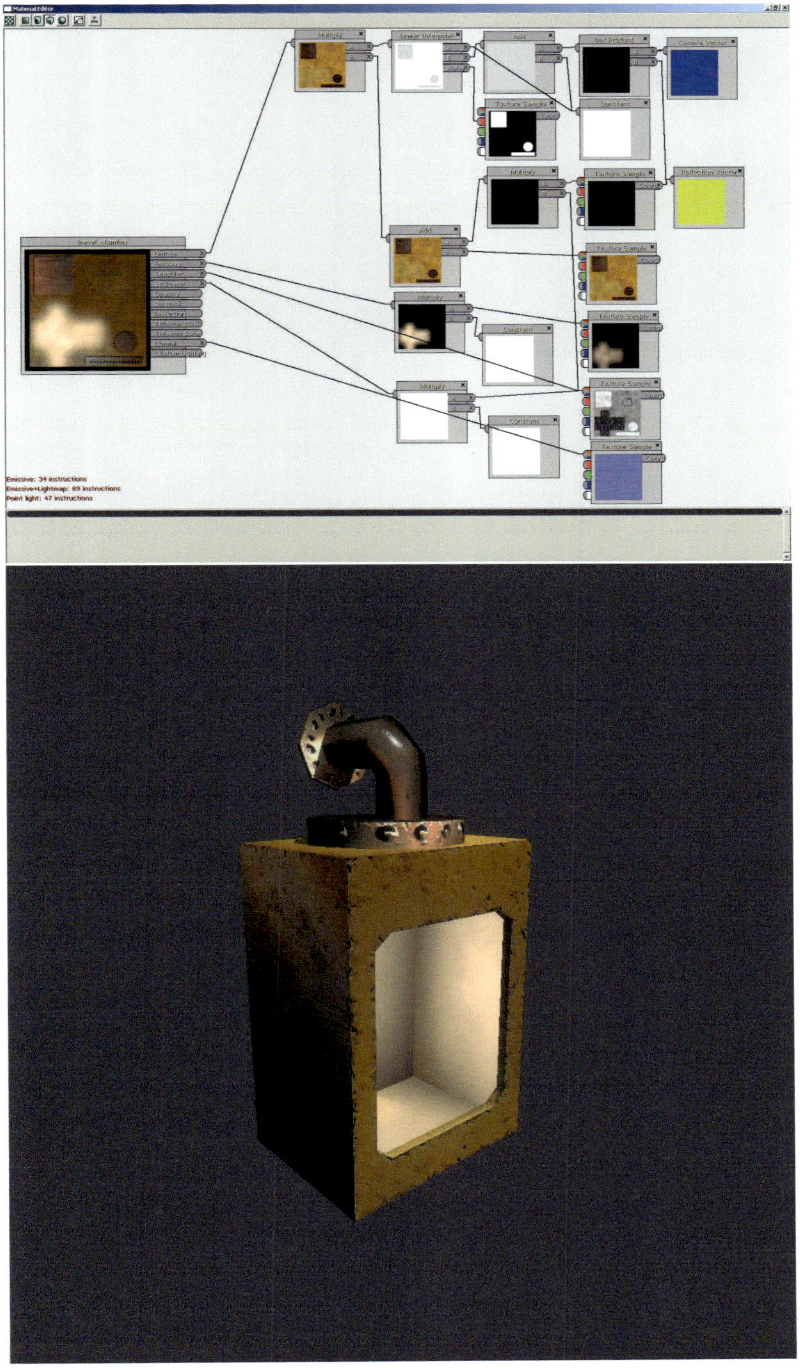

Figure 13.7: Stages of texturing an asset for *RoboBlitz* (continued and concluded): the shader in Unreal Engine; the final in-game result.

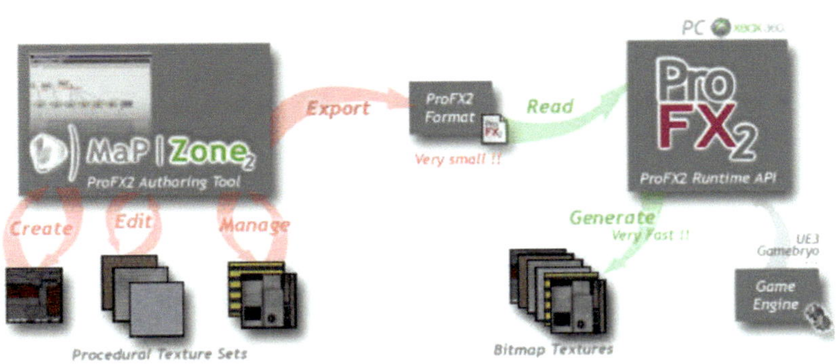

Figure 13.8: Texture production pipeline with MaP | Zone and ProFX, as presented in 2007.

Figure 13.9: A promo flyer for ProFX that we distributed at conferences. Dave Taylor proposed the slogan'2k Textures in 2kb,' which highlighted one of the advantages of ProFX: its ability to create high-resolution textures from very small files (2KB, or 2 kilobytes).

13.6 *RoboBlitz*, precursor

When *RoboBlitz* came out on November 7, 2006, it was the first Unreal Engine 3 game to be released publicly, a few days before the release of *Gears of War*. It was also one of the very first 3D games to be released on XBox Live Arcade. Despite these advantages, the game did not completely achieve the commercial success expected by Naked Sky.

For us, however, it was a great technical success: the project pushed us to our limits and allowed us to release ProFX, our middleware product, which was functional, as had been demonstrated in a quantifiable way. Moreover, it could create procedural textures of a reasonably good graphic quality; this highlighted the value of MaP | Zone, which we released in version 2 at the end of the project, integrating all the improvements requested during the work on *RoboBlitz*.

We believed we'd found the key to our success and, in our minds, we now had to reach out to the rest of the industry with our new offer, our new know-how, and a proof of concept that anybody could test: they'd just have to download the game *RoboBlitz* on their XBox 360 console to see MaP | Zone 2 and ProFX at work!

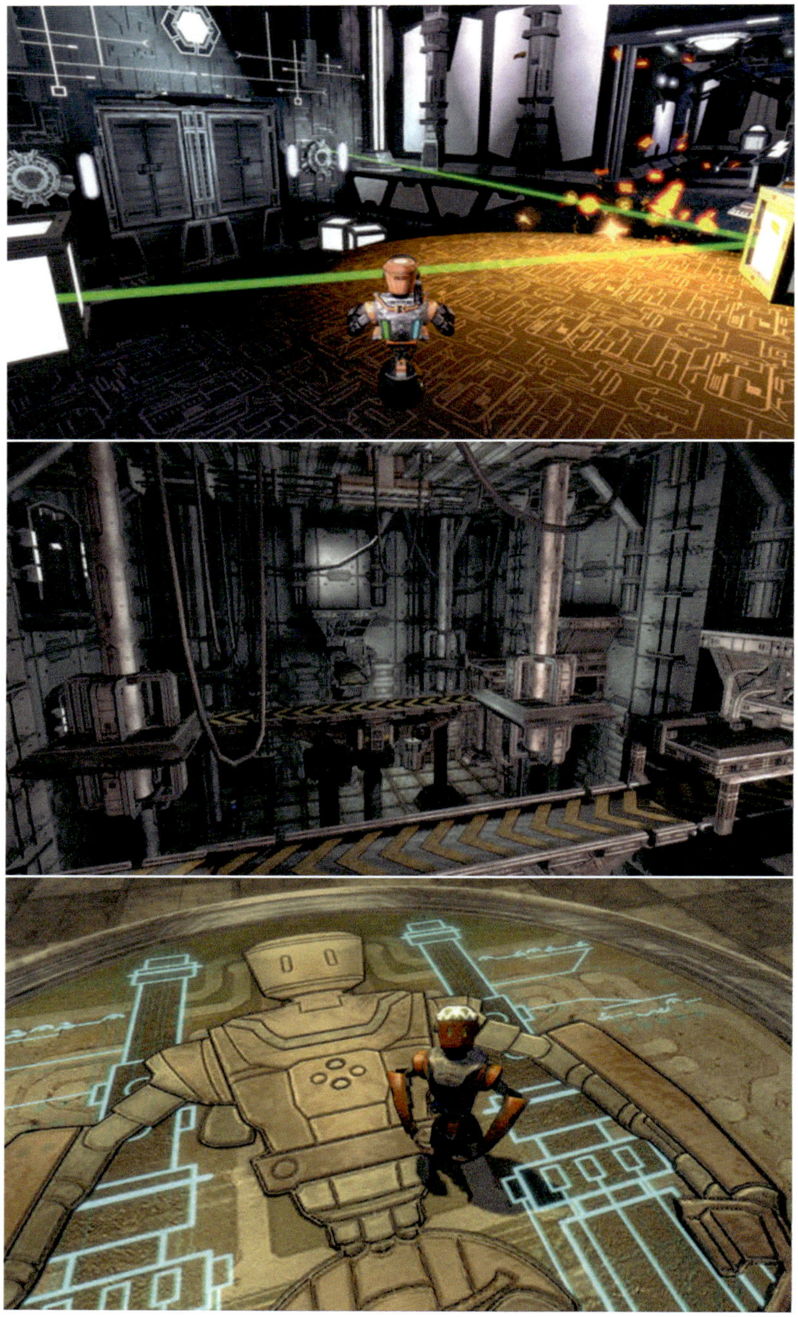

Figure 13.10: A few images from *RoboBlitz.* The majority of textures are procedural, and were created using MaP | Zone 2. They were generated at installation by our middleware ProFX. Images by Naked Sky Entertainment, Inc. CC BY-SA 3.0

13.7 Pivot

This move toward the world of game development constituted one of the first major pivots for Allegorithmic: from software for 3D artists, visual effects, and motion graphics, with MaP | Zone in version 1, to middleware for video games, with MaP | Zone 2 and ProFX. This pivot not only added a new technical dimension (as well as a great difficulty, as we will see) to the project, but it provided us with a very clear objective, and an identified market need, that we could provide a solution to. Allegorithmic's next few years would focus on this new challenge.

During the *RoboBlitz* project and for years to come, I spent a lot of time with Dave, including at his West Hollywood apartment, which effectively became the new site of Allegorithmic's presence in California, from where we'd promote our new product. Dave introduced me—notably while we were driving around in his Acura NSX Coupé—to a side of Los Angeles that I hadn't known, as well as making introductions to some particularly interesting members of the 3D industry, notably including Jordan Mechner, the brilliant developer of *Karateka* and *Prince of Persia*, Trey Harrison, an international *Tetris* champion who also developed 'Salvation,' an extraordinary real-time motion graphics tool that was used during huge shows and concerts. Dave helped me understand how Hollywood worked—the model of setting up a company around a film project, or a particular IP, which would then be dissolved, and replaced by other projects.

Dave also taught me English. Real English—colorful English, full of imagination and slang and wonderful expressions; the effective and polished English which makes people laugh, or think.

Figure 13.11: Dave Taylor, in 2007. Dave guided me for several years as a business developer and advisor.

These years were also difficult for the team, not only from a technical point of view, because the middleware was very demanding, but also from a commercial point of view, as the 3D gaming market on XBox Live Arcade was not sufficiently developed, and few studios would take the risk of this new approach for a return on investment that had not yet been demonstrated. Also, Microsoft ultimately loosened the 50 MB limit, which killed the interest of our offer for this particular market. The 3D game market on XBox Live Arcade would not sustain us, and we'd have to look further afield.

In retrospect...

Dave Taylor played a major role in the development of Allegorithmic, and in my own personal development as well. He was behind our first major pivot into the world of middleware and the video game market, which would become our focal point for many years to come. We would try to meet the needs of this universe with our future tools.

RoboBlitz (see Chapter 13) was our alpha-site, the first beneficiary of this pivot, and the demonstrator of our technology and new middleware product, ProFX. And even if ProFX didn't experience sufficient commercial success, the technical success of the product itself, our unique technological approach to procedural textures, and the first successful demonstration of our approach with *RoboBlitz* opened doors for us, and brought us new customers, and even investors, which proved extremely important for the development of Allegorithmic: first with NVIDIA, for the 'Pachinko' project (see Chapter 16), and then with Dassault Systèmes and Microsoft (see Chapter 18).

From a personal point of view, the years I spent with Dave were extraordinary, and I have fond memories of our work sessions, and the times we spent laughing together—which often overlapped. He helped me to grow, particularly in terms of business, and inspired me to always look for the biggest *bang for the buck*![11]

11: One of the many expressions that Dave taught me, obviously.

Technical Demos | 14

Starting in 2006 we produced a graphic and technical demo every year, showcasing our technology. Allegorithmic's team of internal artists loved making these mini-games or real-time films, which were developed under significant constraints, as they had to above all demonstrate a technical point; the demos also had to be produced with (our) tools which were still a work in progress, which at times was complicated to manage as they simply might not work, or would change constantly during production.

14.1 The Bathroom and Aging Boat demos

These two demos (see figures 14.2 and 14.1), which we released at the beginning of 2007, demonstrated three aspects: firstly, that procedural textures obtained with MaP | Zone were of high quality; secondly, that textures could be animated with ProFX, changing from one state to another in real-time during the execution of a game or demo, this change being carried out by recalculating the textures as needed, or via interpolation in a shader of a few key textures calculated by our middleware; finally, that our procedural textures were compact—that is, that the texture files were very small compared to the images they generated.

The Bathroom demo (part 1[23] and part 2[24]), specifically, was the first demo where we made an effort to stage the scene. Not only did we work on the technical aspect of texturing, but we also developed the script, lighting, plans, editing, etc. so the tech demo would be visually interesting.

DOI:10.1201/9781003534624-14

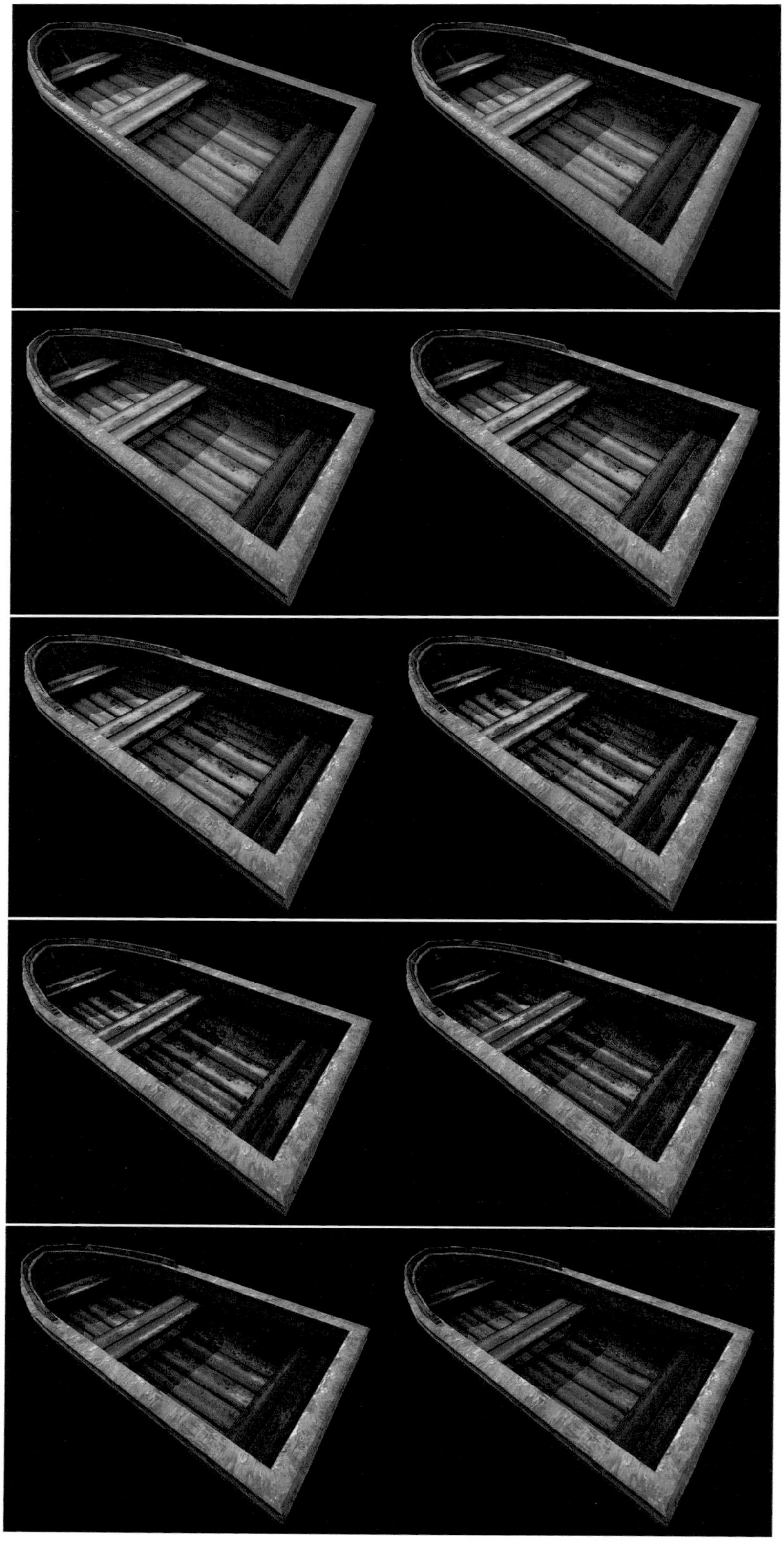

Figure 14.1: The Aging Boat, that we prepared for GDC 07 and another conference we took part in that year, demonstrates the evolution of textures thanks to ProFX. The boat becomes more and more weathered as time passes. Our middleware allowed us to rapidly generate this type of effect, which could be played out in real-time in a game engine. A small anecdote about this GDC: as I was about to begin my presentation with the audience already in place, I found that the demo didn't work... I then spotted Jérémie running into the room, making his way through all the chairs with his arm outstretched, waving around a USB which contained a working version of the demo, which I immediately installed on the PC used for the presentation. This image of Jérémie running toward me with a USB stick will remain with me forever.

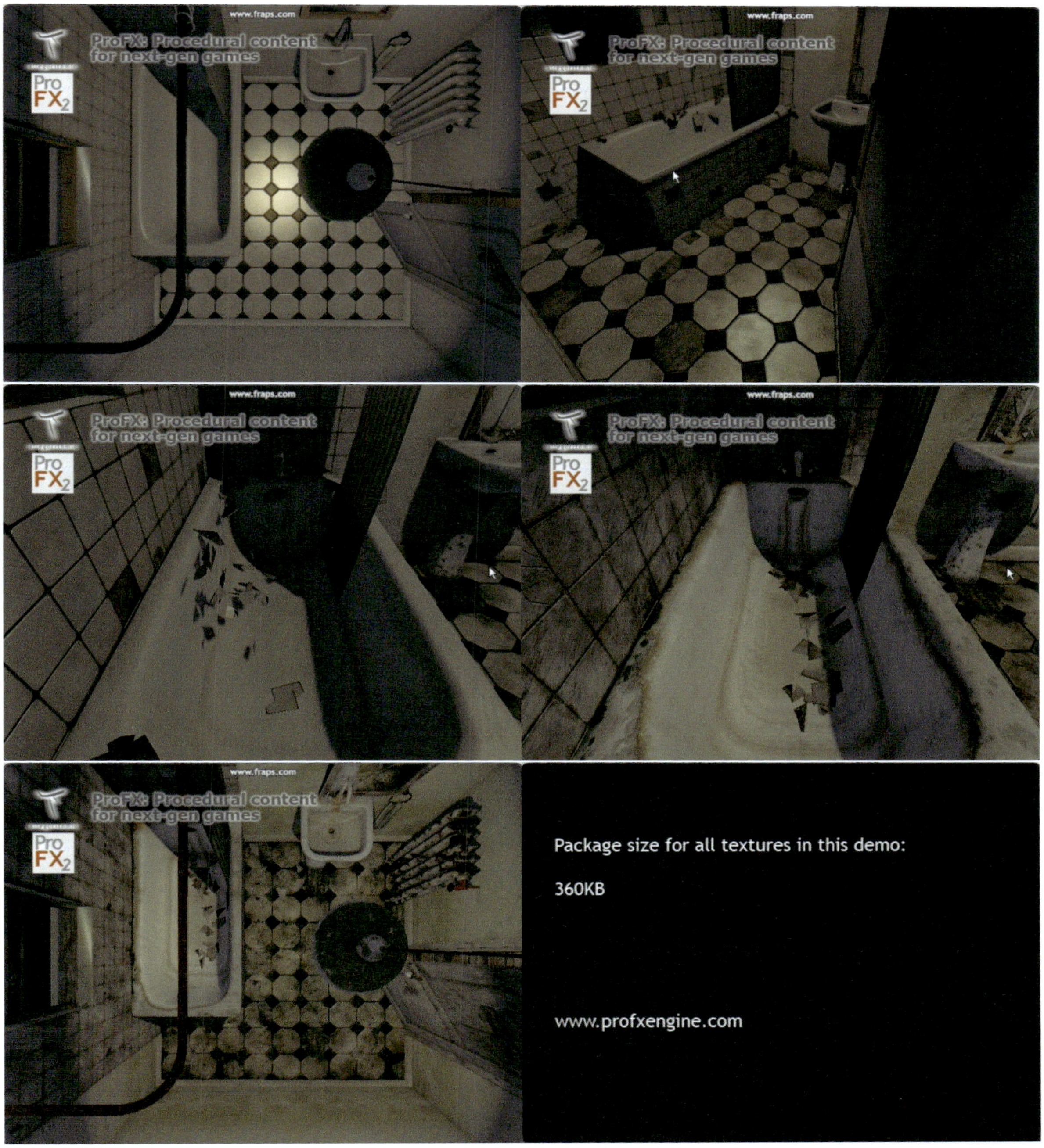

Figure 14.2: The Bathroom was an entirely real-time demo with a multiple-camera setup. It highlighted textures shifting from clean to dirty and broken. Our middleware allowed users to create this type of effect, that could be played out in real time in a game engine.

14.2 The Bryo demo

We applied the same concept to the 'DemoBryo' demo, which we made in September 2006, this time using the GameBryo game engine, which was looking to differentiate itself from the rest of the industry. An integration of our texture generation engine was carried out within GameBryo, and we produced this demo with the sort of obligatory element that appears in any good 3D demo: wooden barrels and crates. Textures in this demo evolved over time to create an original effect.

Figure 14.3: The 'DemoBryo,' a technical demo for ProFX using the GameBryo game engine, which sought to stand out from the rest of the industry.

14.3 The Bayou demo

We pushed the concept a little further with the 'Bayou'[25] demo, which we developed over the course of 2007 and which aimed to demonstrate the use of ProFX as middleware capable of transporting a large number of high-quality textures with minimal size. All of the textures in the animated version weighed just 318 KB, as opposed to the hundreds of MBs thart would have been required if we'd used classic texture bitmaps.

The demo was made completely internally, by Benjamin Maréchal, Gilles Fleury, Mélinda Esponda Diaz, Nicolas Wirrmann, and Jérémie Noguer, who were totally dedicated to the project for months. It was made using Unreal Engine 3, the same game engine that was used for *RoboBlitz*.

A year after *RoboBlitz*, we made this demo with the goal, as always, of pushing our ProFX middleware as a mature commercial product. As we'd done with our Bathroom demo (but in a much more ambitious way), we also developed the staging, as well as music and sound effects.

Figure 14.4: The Bayou demo, produced internally in 2007 using Unreal Engine 3. All textures weighed just 318 kilobytes thanks to our middleware ProFX, versus the hundreds of megabytes needed had we used traditional bitmap textures.

15 Autodesk: first contacts

15.1 Commercial bundle

In 2006, building on our success with the game *RoboBlitz* (see Chapter 13), and thanks to the contacts obtained from Autodesk (in particular, Marc Petit), we proposed to the company that we create a bundle bringing together the tools MaP | Zone 2, 3ds Max, and Maya.[1]

1: With such a commercial bundle, everyone who had a Max or Maya license would get a MaP | Zone license for free.

The advantage for users of Autodesk tools would be to get these other tools for free, and to be able to create procedural textures with MaP | Zone, useful as it was for any type of 3D applications. The interest for Allegorithmic was to take advantage of Autodesk distribution, and its extensive presence in the world of 3D, and specifically game development, which would allow us to reach a greater number of potential users. These game creators, if they had the possibility to easily discover for free the power and flexibility of our tool, might see the value in extending their use and moving to ProFX. This wouldn't be part of the bundle, so these game developers would have to turn to us to get a ProFX license for their game projects. It was a kind of 'foot in the door' effect.

Figure 15.1: First page of the proposal to make a bundle with MaP | Zone 2, 3ds Max and Maya by Autodesk, April 2006.

This idea of a commercial bundle in which we would distribute our tool for free and hope to ultimately make money by selling our middleware was a strong step forward and a direction we thought to be correct. Autodesk, however didn't want to commit to this direction, partly due to the complexities of technical implementation, but also most likely due to the newness of our technology, having proved its success in just one production.

15.2 Textures for architecture

Discussions with Autodesk continued for several years, following multiple trips to Montreal, notably with a certain Pierre-Félix Breton, who proved to be very interested in what we were developing. He was open, very friendly and wanted to help us demonstrate our point and showcase our tech to the world of architecture, a domain we were not at all familiar with and that needed the most realistic textures possible, and that met criteria that we hadn't until then understood in our work with *RoboBlitz*, or in the world of video games and animation more generally. But if we were to achieve the level of realism required, procedural textures could theoretically answer other issues encountered by architects: personalization and non-repetitive application on large surfaces.

Pierre-Félix sent us examples of textures we would try to reproduce, and which would potentially interest users of 3ds Max (a large portion of those users were in the domain of architecture). We can see the (very successful!) results of some of these reproduced creations in figures 15.2 and 15.3.

DOI:10.1201/9781003534624-15

Although they didn't lead to business opportunities, these first connections and common projects with Autodesk were the starting point of several collaborations and discussions to come (see Chapter 22), which would multiply in the coming years.

Figure 15.2: Pierre-Félix Breton from Autodesk gave us examples of textures used in architectural rendering, so we could try to reproduce them with MaP | Zone, which we did in figure 15.3.

Figure 15.3: Reproduction of textures, using MaP | Zone 2, common to architecture, as provided by Pierre-Félix Breton from Autodesk (see figure 15.2).

NVIDIA and Pachinko | 16

While having lunch on the edges of a conference in San José, Neil Trevett, who was Vice President in charge of mobile development at NVIDIA, and the president of the Khronos Group, the organization for the definition of standards for mobile phones,[1] suggested that we might use what Allegorithmic had been developing for an NVIDIA project. NVIDIA was interested in procedural textures, and what we had with ProFX was by far the most powerful tool, and the most usable in production, that he'd seen. Of course, the work done on *RoboBlitz* (see Chapter 13) was compelling, and served as convincing proof that our technology worked well. ProFX, he told me, might be the ideal solution to a problem that he'd wanted to solve, and all we needed to do was port the generation engine to mobile hardware.

1: They were in charge of standards like OpenGL, OpenGL ES, WebGL, Collada, Vulkan, and so on.

He then told me about a special project that NVIDIA was carrying out, based around Pachinko gaming machines from Japan (see figure 16.1). Then, in the mid-2000s, machine constructors wanted to provide these machines with better 3D visual effects, which would make them stand out, and attract more players. As the Pachinko was essentially a gambling game, significant constraints were imposed on its construction—any computer in the machine would be closely scrutinized by regulatory bodies, to avoid any risk of piracy or other interference. NVIDIA had positioned itself in this market with its mobile GPUs[2] which made it possible to display real-time, high-quality graphic animations, while respecting applicable constraints, notably including requirements around embedded data memory.

2: NVIDIA is less well known for embedded technologies, but since this time has been producing many SoCs, or 'Systems on Chip,' mini-motherboards which contain all the components necessary to allow embedded technologies within devices to function correctly—such as in mobile phones, for instance, or car navigation systems.

Neil and his team understood that our procedural texture technology could generate high-quality textures from files that weighed only a few kilobytes. They therefore believed it was possible, by using the computing power of embedded NVIDIA GPUs, to generate an almost infinite amount of data from very little information.

Based on what Neil could share with me, I understood that the situation was similar to what we'd experienced with *RoboBlitz* (see Chapter 13). This seemed like a textbook case for our ProFX technology and a potential new market for us. Neil explained to us the potential in the world of mobile gaming, which was developing at a great pace, and would explode in the next few years.[3]

3: This would indeed be the case, in particular with the arrival of the iPhone by Apple, and all Android devices. These machines were mostly used for 2D rather than 3D games, however, due to a lack of graphics calculation capabilities, which evolved more slowly than we or NVIDIA would have liked.

We managed to find a commercial agreement, and when we signed this agreement in January 2007, it was by far the biggest deal in the history of Allegorithmic. In a single contract, we managed to not only 'make our entire year', but that amount also represented more than all revenues from all our previous years, cumulatively! It was a one-off deal; we'd receive a single payment, although I tried to make it a deal based on royalties.[4] Two hundred thousand dollars! Allegorithmic had never signed a deal of this magnitude before. And, moreover, with a company like NVIDIA!

4: My dream was that every time a machine generated images, we'd receive a fraction of a cent... Of course NVIDIA, who couldn't afford such an arrangement even for themselves, couldn't provide this for us. So we calculated an amount based on the estimated number of machines that would use our technology, multiplied this number by a very small amount, and ulimately agreed on two hundred thousand dollars.

This opportunity marked a turning point for Allegorithmic, because even though the product would ultimately be abandoned by NVIDIA, we'd

DOI:10.1201/9781003534624-16

managed to convince a large, cutting-edge technology group to trust us, and take a risk on our still somewhat nascent technology.[5] Furthermore, this contract and its associated turnover placed the company in a very different position, particularly from the point of view of financiers and other institutions who, in France, had for some years been following our progress, or preparing to potentially support us more closely—including, for instance, Dassault Systèmes (see Chapter 18).

5: I applaud Neil Trevett and his team for seeing the potential in what we showed him, which was nonetheless still far from being a usable product. . .

Figure 16.1: The Pachinko is a game of money and chance, which is played in specialized rooms in Japan. Small metal marbles fall and collide with small metal rods which change their trajectory, until the marbles finally land in receptacles positioned at the bottom of the screen. Winnings are calculated according to the distribution of the marbles. Pachinko rooms are filled with the constant, alarming noise of millions of metallic collisions; the game is a real institution in Japan. Images by Tischbeinahe, own work, CC BY-SA 3.0, `https://commons.wikimedia.org/w/index.php?curid=12746666` and by MichaelMaggs, own work, CC BY-SA 3.0, `https://commons.wikimedia.org/w/index.php?curid=6812565`

17 Summary of progress up to mid-2007, and conclusion of this period

17.1 Summary of this stage

This first stage of Allegorithmic's existence as a company came to an end around mid-2007, with mixed results.

The team

The team continued to grow until there were a dozen of us by mid-2007. New members included Jérémie Noguer,[1] Mélinda Esponda Diaz, Thierry Frey,[2] Frédéric Scherma, and Jérôme Hummel, who had a lot of experience in 3D, having worked for a 3D modeling company based in California.

Completing the internal teams, we were lucky enough to work with Sylvain Lefebvre, an incredibly talented researcher based at INRIA who would take on the role of scientific advisor for us, bringing a wealth of knowledge in the field of 3D, as well as his kindness and infectious enthusiasm.

1: Who would play an absolutely key role in the rest of the Allegorithmic adventure, see for example Chapter 27

2: Previously of Dassault Systèmes, who became our first COO (Chief Operating Officer), and who would play an important role in the upcoming investment, see Chapter 18. Thierry's arrival, and his role of COO, generated anxiety among the teams, who had the preconceived notion of a COO as a whip-cracking slavemaster; Thierry and I therefore had to work to break this stereotype.

Figure 17.1: The full Allegorithmic team during a 'Global Gathering' (where we bring together all employees for a few days; we would uphold this tradition throughout the life of our company. . .). In March 2007 the team included: Gilles Fleury, Catherine Debain, Nicolas Wirrmann, Mélinda Esponda Diaz, Simon Brunel (who is attempting to escape from the photo), Benjamin Maréchal (on the first photo), and Jérémie Noguer, Thierry Frey, Cyrille Damez, and Christophe Soum. Bottom left: a *Guitar Hero* session played in one of ISIMA's amphitheaters that we'd 'borrowed,' with Christophe Soum and Laurent Carrio, our financial adviser. Bottom right: Benjamin Maréchal, during one of our first brainstorming sessions for Substance Designer. It was perhaps our first use of Post-its. Thousands have been used since.

Finally, we began a partnership that was both very friendly and professional with a public relations (PR) company called'Liaison.' Its manager, the very endearing Heidi Lowell, who was based in Portland, had been recommended to us by Brad Peebler, of Luxology (see Chapter 12). We would work with Heidi and her teams throughout the Allegorithmic adventure! It sometimes proved difficult for the Liaison teams to promote our progress to the press, as this little group of French people, who spoke English with strong accents and who always wanted to discuss procedural textures and obscure algorithms was sometimes slightly confusing. . .

DOI:10.1201/9781003534624-17

Figure 17.2: On these photos from mid-2007, we see: Gilles Fleury and Benjamin Maréchal (in the top photo), Nicolas Wirrmann, Thierry Frey, and Christophe Soum (bottom left) and Gilles Fleury, Benjamin Maréchal (standing), and Nicolas Wirrmann (bottom right).

The products

During this period, we introduced and developed many products and technologies, from MaP | Zone, which now offered a construction graph to produce more complex textures, as can be seen in figure 17.3, similar to what would later appear in Substance Designer (see Chapter 26), to ProFX, via MaP | Time and Imagesynth (see Chapter 12). We also laid the foundations for future products like Substance Painter, including the internship of Simon Brunel (see Chapter 9) and the concept that we called 'Lifeform' (see figures 17.4 and 17.5).

I'll note that, while we pivoted to ProFX and gaming middleware during this time in order to focus on the uniqueness of our procedural textures and their useful characteristics in the world of video games, the beginnings of a good general tool dedicated to 3D artists, in MaP | Zone and in Lifeform, were already present. We would return a few years later to pure texture creation, with Substance Designer, and we would move from the creation of procedural textures to the procedural creation of textures... for which the market would be ready about 10 years later (see Chapter 26).

Sales and financial results

If our technical challenges were met with success, our sales had been practically zero[3] since the beginning of the adventure despite the immense efforts of everyone involved, whether we sold our tools via distribution

3: If we don't take into account the meager work we got from orders and service work that we managed to invoice for, or even a pivotal deal with NVIDIA, which finally brought us into the big leagues.

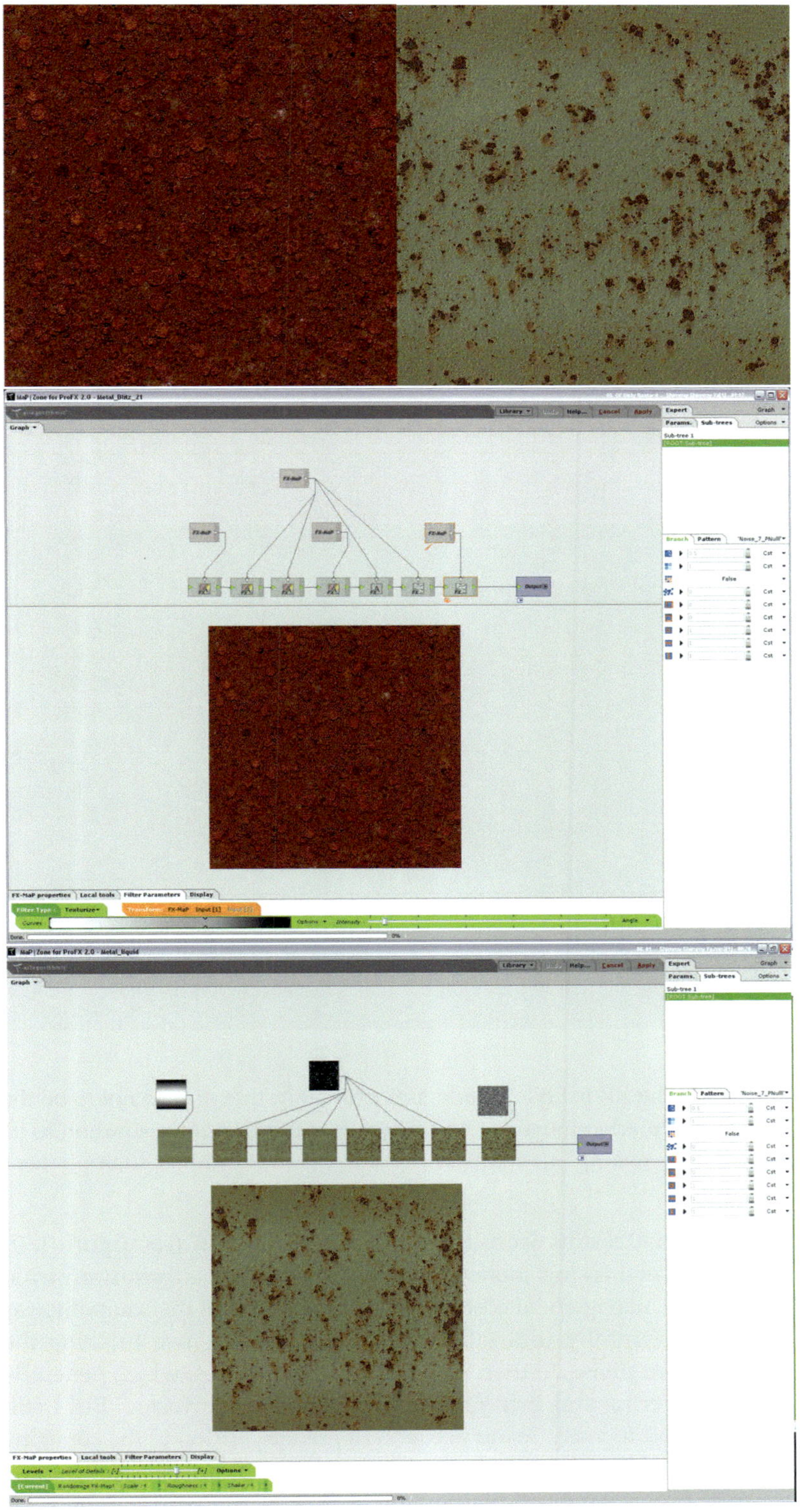

Figure 17.3: Two material textures made using MaP | Zone 2, by Benjamin Maréchal. In this version of MaP | Zone a texture construction graph can be seen.

through our own channels (see for example the version of our website in May 2007, in figure 17.6), via our local representatives in California, or even via resellers and partners such as Luxology (see Chapter 12). We were perfectly in line with an expression that Dave Taylor taught me: *We built a hammer, and we're looking for a nail.*[4] We thought we'd identified a

4: That is, we started by developing a technology, and then looked for an application for this technology, a problem expressed by the industry that we could solve.

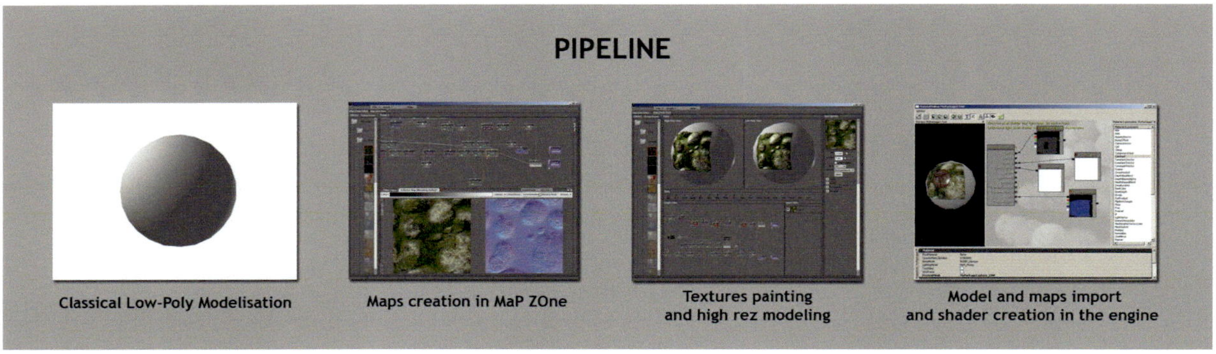

Figure 17.4: Future pipeline model of MaP | Zone, establishing the basis of Substance Painter.

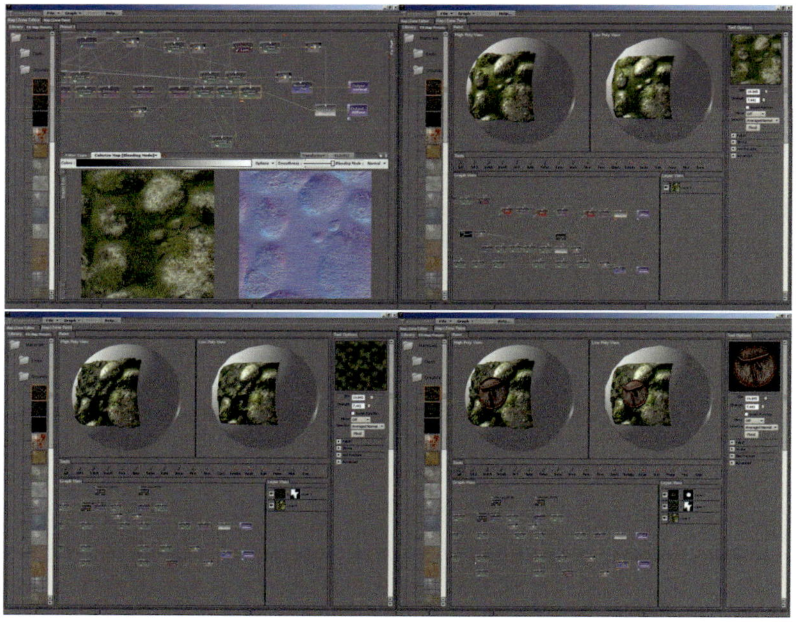

Figure 17.5: Project 'Lifeform,' January 2007, the future we were imagining for MaP | Zone, which was the precursor for Substance Designer and Substance Painter... as well as a vague hope for a sculpting and concepting tool 'Michelangelo,' which we would start developing many years later.

need with the XBox Live Arcade; unfortunately, this proved not to be the case as this market transformed before we could provide a solution to its constraints, making our solution obsolete, and too complex to implement anyway.

Our financial results were therefore not very good (see figure 17.7) and we'd been losing money since the start of the adventure,[5] even though our management costs were extremely low, as the company was very lean. Typically, innovation companies have to invest during the development phase, to then reap the rewards of sales, which generally end up covering and then far exceeding the sums invested. But I still regularly had to reassure our accountant Frédéric Virion of the company MB&A in Aubière, as well as our auditor, Didier Roiron, telling them that we were progressing and on the right track, and that we, therefore, had to continue our development, and not sound the alarm prematurely.[6] Still, one thing was becoming clear: up until now we'd been financed entirely by our original shareholders and our meager income, but we now needed investment in our structure to be able to continue, and even accelerate our adventure.

5: My father would save the day for us twice, with loans of 15K and 20K euros in associates' current accounts. Without these small injections of cash at a few key moments in the company's development, we wouldn't have been able to pay salaries. I didn't even pay myself a salary throughout this entire period...

6: It would be more and more difficult to maintain this discourse and this trajectory, which pushed me a little more to look for investors to support us in the next phases of Allegorithmic's development. This search would be successful very quickly, see Chapter 18.

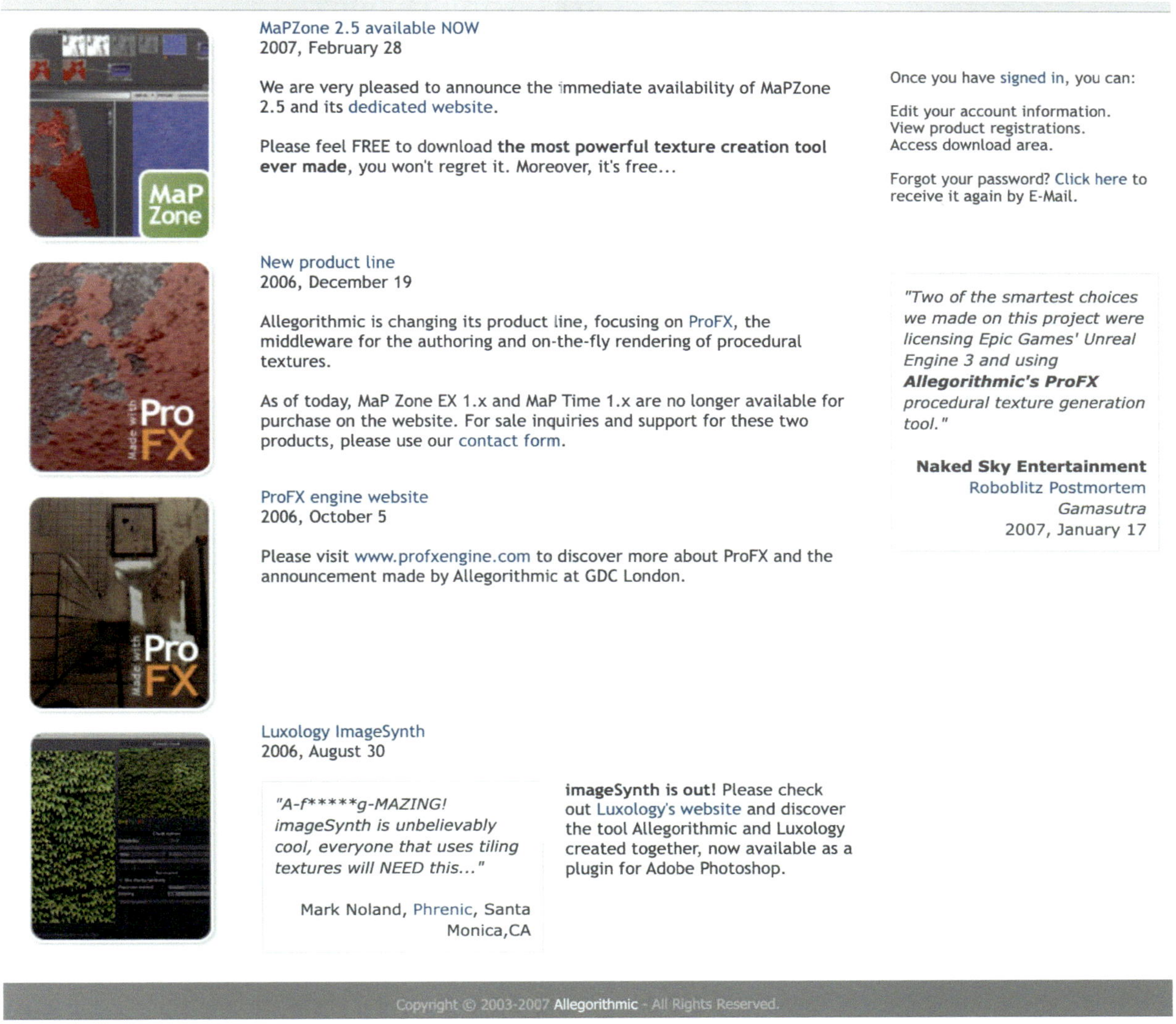

Figure 17.6: Homepage of the Allegorithmic website in May 2007. All our products at that time are represented here.

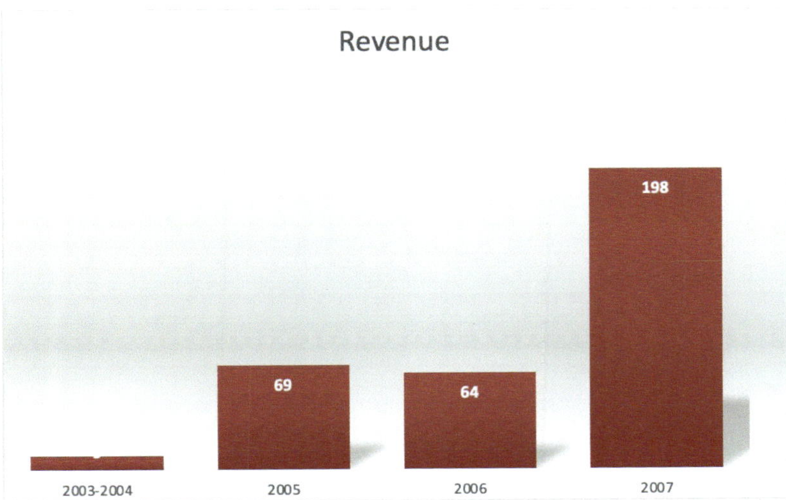

Figure 17.7: Allegorithmic's revenue between 2003 and 2007. The first few years between 2003 and 2004 were combined for a total of 9K euros of revenue. We'd reached a total of 198K euros by the end of 2007.

17.2 Conclusion, 2003–2007

This early period of Allegorithmic's life, from mid-2003 to mid-2007, was a time of construction, of trial and error, of success and failure, and of excitement and hope, always. Despite the hard times, I don't remember ever questioning whether it was the right path for me,[7] or for all of us working in those small offices at ISIMA, or on the other side of the planet, to develop technology that few really understood the benefit of. On the contrary, I remember how personally driven I was, and proud of what we were doing, of our technological advances, and of the team that was on a mission to make Allegorithmic a successful, recognized publisher in the field of 3D software, the world that we were all passionate about.

7: However, it was a physically challenging time for me, with a direct impact on my health, due to the stress, my total dedication, a lack of sleep, energy spent non-stop, constant long-distance travel and jet lag, and so on. When I started the adventure, I'd felt invincible, ready to move mountains—but by the end of this period all the company's problems provoked a range of health issues for me, all the way up to panic attacks, a result of my little hypochondriac side. Some of the health issues that came out of that time still trouble me today... I'll also note a phenomenon that in my experience is quite unique to me: time differences have a very strong effect on my memory, and operate as a sort of 'reset button,' rebooting my thoughts for a few hours or even a few days.

If I had to take away one particular lesson from this period, it would perhaps be this: what we sold to Naked Sky, to Autodesk, to NVIDIA and soon to Dassault Systèmes (see Chapter 18), was not technology, and certainly not products, but *trust*. Our technologies were nascent, our products immature, and what brilliant people like Dave Taylor, Neil Trevett and soon even Pascal Daloz bought were technological promises coupled with trust in the Allegorithmic team not to let them down. And to deliver.

This first part of Allegorithmic's life was all about creating trust.

Part VI

2007–2011

Investment from Dassault Systèmes

18

18.1 Dassault Systèmes

Here, I'll allow my narrative to take a brief chronological step backward, of one year, to July 2006. At SIGGRAPH that year, which took place in Anaheim, California, Thierry Frey organized a meeting with a delegation from Dassault Systèmes,[1] where he'd worked before joining Allegorithmic. Thierry was very familiar with how things tended to work at the conference,[2] and reserved a large room in the Anaheim convention center. When I arrived, I was a little surprised—I hadn't expected to see so many people present. I began my presentation and demo, in French, to this company I could have met up with in Paris—although I could see that the general atmosphere at SIGGRAPH, on the other side of the planet, helped create conditions where people would listen carefully.

1: Dassault Systèmes, which is a relatively unknown company, is a French software giant, particularly in the field of CAD, Computer-Assisted Design. Their flagship application, CATIA, is used by companies such as Toyota and Boeing (the Boeing 777 was the first plane to be entirely designed on a computer, notably thanks to tools developed by Dassault Systèmes).

2: Thierry had been very involved with SIGGRAPH for many years. He was part of the organizational team, being a huge 3D and digital imaging enthusiast.

Among the people present at this meeting were Arnaud Ribadeau-Dumas, Philippe Loeb and Jean-Luc Cuinier, who would play an important role later, pushing for an investment in or purchase of Allegorithmic. I ended the meeting without really knowing what to think about it, as I couldn't really imagine Dassault Systèmes being interested in what we did. But we arranged to follow up on this first meeting in Paris, in Suresne.

18.2 Pascal Daloz, Virtual Earth

When I gave this presentation again at our next meeting, in the autumn 2006, I met someone else who'd have a big impact on Allegorithmic, and on me personally: Pascal Daloz.[3] Pascal was in charge of strategy within the Dassault Systèmes group, and he told me about several of their projects currently in development. Some required more realistic 3D imaging to improve the visualization of products developed within CATIA, which was partly achievable by using more attractive textures; another project in collaboration with Microsoft would provide 3D technology allowing the creation of a 'Virtual Earth,'[4] the equivalent of Google Earth. Microsoft wanted to allow users of their platform to create their own models in order to fill the virtual map with 3D duplicates of the entire world.[5] The platform was available online and, to guarantee a good experience for users, it was fundamental that the download data required to display the 3D elements representing any particular place had to remain minimal. And the heaviest elements of these 3D representations were always the textures.

3: Pascal made an extraordinary impression on me. He was absolutely brilliant, open-minded, attentive, and possessed a level of empathy and self-control that I've rarely encountered. I saw a potential mentor in him, and I felt honored that he fulfilled this role over the next five years.

4: Known today as Bing Maps Platform.

5: A great example of crowdsourcing before its time.

Figure 18.1: Virtual Earth, from Microsoft, who wanted to allow users of the platform to create their own models in order to fill the virtual map with 3D duplicates of the entire world. Dassault Systèmes, partnering with Microsoft for this project, wanted to use our procedural texture technology.

With its lightweight procedural texture engine, Allegorithmic could provide the solution to the problem. All we had to do was send procedural texture description files (weighing just a few kilobytes) and generate the corresponding bitmaps directly on users' machines. . .[6] This was an extraordinary opportunity. Allegorithmic, a small company from Clermont-Ferrand with barely a dozen employees, might license one of

6: This was of course exactly what we'd done for *RoboBlitz* (see Chapter 13) and what we would later try to sell to online game developers in South Korea and China, see Chapter 20.

DOI:10.1201/9781003534624-18

its technological components via Dassault Systèmes to Microsoft, for their highly ambitious Virtual Earth project!

Pascal suggested to me that, in addition to this licensing opportunity, Dassault Systèmes might be interested in investing in Allegorithmic. He also said, "I imagine that you want to continue, and that you don't want to sell at the moment, do you?" I confirmed this was correct... We therefore agreed on a minority investment, rather than a total buyout.

He then proposed if I was available to have lunch with someone named Bernard Charlès, that same day. Unfortunately, I had a meeting planned with Thierry. When I called Thierry and mentioned this, he shouted at me. "You're crazy—Bernard Charlès is the CEO of Dassault Systèmes! Don't worry about me—go eat with him!"[7]

7: I confess that I hadn't done my homework, and didn't know who Bernard Charlès was...

18.3 Investment

A few minutes later I found myself on the top floor of the Dassault Systèmes offices, in Suresnes, in a small, reconfigurable meeting room where a dining table for four was set. A moveable partition blocked one side of the room, its limited soundproofing making it clear that a meeting was in progress on its other side. After a few minutes, Bernard came in and greeted me.[8] As we ate, Bernard asked me a few questions about my background. He was a mathematician with a passion for that area and for new technologies and, as he seemed to understand and appreciate our 3D technology, I explained at some length what we were developing, its advantages, and our ambitions. He told me that Dassault Systèmes wished to take part in the ecosystem of French startups, potentially investing in some companies—in particular companies whose domains converged with the areas of interest of Dassault Systèmes, as was the case here. I left the lunch feeling somewhat dazed.

8: I think I will remember the strength of his handshake, and his piercing regard, full of fierce intelligence, for the rest of my life.

Sometime later, Pascal confirmed to me that Dassault Systèmes intended to invest in Allegorithmic, in order to help us develop and to begin to establish a strong commercial partnership between the two companies.[9] We then began the process of implementing this investment. In this way, I discovered a universe that until then had been completely unknown to me, made up of lively discussions between lawyers and terms like 'right of first refusal,' which my lawyer called an 'atomic bomb,'[10] which we would, however, end up accepting, in large part because we didn't really have a choice, but also because this agreement seemed fair to me at this stage of Allegorithmic's development, and because Dassault Systèmes was the first major company to display belief in us, and was getting us out of a difficult situation.

9: There are several reasons for a large company to invest in a smaller society like this; in our case, this was to ensure the survival of a technology supplier (we were going to sell technology to Dassault Systèmes, who would in turn sell technology to Microsoft), and to get involved in our development and help us grow, with the additional benefit of obtaining special rights, such as the famous 'right of first refusal' (see next note).

10: The 'right of first refusal' is a particular right that certain investors, in particular 'industrial' investors (like Dassault Systèmes in this case, which is actually not an institutional investor), want to obtain when taking a stake in a company. It allows this investor to take the place of a potential buyer of the company in which he has invested, forcefully and without possible recourse, paying the same price and accepting the same conditions of sale. This is a very strong right that can repel any potential buyer, because if another company wanted to acquire Allegorithmic, going so far as to make a firm offer, this would have allowed Dassault Systèmes to snatch us out from under that prospective buyer's nose. We can clearly see the dissuasive power of that law, here...

The negotiations were very complex overall, and would take several months. I spent my first sleepless nights trying to measure the impact of this or that clause in the successive drafts of contracts. This was one of the first times that I understood that negotiation, in this type of situation, is not a zero-sum game, as well as that you have to know how to 'tell the lawyers to stop,' and to fight on the subjects that really matter. For example, it was important for Dassault Systèmes not to take too large a stake for accounting reasons, while it is important for me to retain my absolute decision-making power, and that we could begin to open capital to employees.[11]

11: Dassault Systèmes was very aligned with us on this point.

Many months later, we found an agreement which allowed Dassault Systèmes to take a stake of just under 20%, backed by a loan which would provide an additional influx of cash, for a valuation that was accurate for our level of development. We also created a pool of BSPCE (*Bons de Souscription de Parts de Créateurs d'Entreprises*, a specific type of stock option), which we distributed to employees, in order to generate interest in the overall success of our structure. The agreement would be implemented in 2007. In one step, we went from 4 shareholders to a dozen, in addition to Dassault Systèmes. This was the first time that I found my influence on the company diluted, which was a concept to consider in itself, but one that had to be accepted in order to move forward. Risk is always necessary, in any case, and the investment by Dassault Systèmes came at the right time when we needed to accelerate, to 'get out of the garage' (and we would use these newly-acquired means immediately, to hire people, see Chapter 19).

And so here we were with a new investor to support our development, who would also play the role of commercial partner in this joint adventure with Microsoft, a first partnership which promised to be exciting.

18.4 Microsoft, and a partnership

The partnership would prove to be a disappointment for me, however. My first proposal to license our engine was negotiated downward by Dassault Systèmes, and the final price was approximately 15 times lower than my initial proposal.[12] Our deal with Dassault Systèmes, who I naively thought would place a much higher value on the technology, therefore wasn't enough for us to hit our targets for the year. We had at least managed to find a licensing agreement with them, including a joint opportunity to work with Microsoft and its Virtual Earth.

12: This was one of the first times that I realized that we'd have to change our business model, ideally sooner rather than later—that is, it wouldn't be possible to sell at a very high price to a small number of buyers, especially when these buyers had too much control over the price they wanted to pay, and that we'd have to reach out to more potential buyers of our technology, with a more affordable price.

Working first indirectly then directly with Microsoft also proved to be a reality check: as our product had to run on Windows, we had to go through Microsoft's testing and QA (Quality Assurance) processes, which were absolutely Dantesque. We had to ensure the robustness of our technologies on a staggering set of machine and system configurations, which had been targeted by Microsoft for many years, and would continue to be for years to come. Unlike the Apple ecosystem, where the combination of machine and software remains contained, the Windows world is a merciless jungle. When our engine was tested, it lit up too many red lights in Microsoft's headquarters in Redmond, near Seattle. This was a problem we needed to resolve, requiring a great deal of work from the team.

In addition to QA issues, we also had a performance problem. Here, we were saved by one of our latest recruits, Charles Bauchet, who had just arrived and who managed to implement an extraordinary image processing algorithm that unblocked the whole process at the last mmoment. We finally managed to get the green light from Microsoft!

In retrospect...

Pascal and Dassault Systèmes, much like Neil Trevett and NVIDIA around the same time, were among the rare few in large companies who understood in sufficient depth what we were doing and saw an interest in it, before anyone else. I have immense respect (and great gratitude) for Pascal, not only for seeing this potential but also for placing his trust in my team and in me. Few people are able to see beyond the small, emerging structure. Those like Pascal understand a potential, buy a promise, and count on trust. And sometimes with a premium: in the case of Dassault Systèmes, an investment in Allegorithmic.

Pascal would also be a mentor to me for many years. Dazzlingly intelligent and with rare finesse, he told me, during each of our meetings, what I needed to hear, just before I needed to hear it: not only was he a great advisor, but a man with a unique power of anticipation which let him know, before me, and in many cases before everyone else, what obstacles would arise before us, and what I'd need to implement in order to overcome them...

The team grows, new offices 19

Following the investment by Dassault Systèmes (see Chapter 18), we now had the means to accelerate our development.[1] The first step was crucial: hire! We also needed to look for new offices that would support our expansion, as our time at ISIMA was coming to an end.

19.1 The team grows

New arrivals in 2007

In the months following the investment, in 2007 alone, we were joined by Guillaume Cerdan, Gaëtan Lassagne, Alexis Khouri (see below for more information), Maxime Delavergne, David Dublanchet, Sylvain Nouveau, Raouf Béjaoui, Matthew Boerjan, Vincent Ganachaud and Benoît Barbier (some of these can be seen in figure 19.1).

This rapid influx of new arrivals, after a period of very slow evolution of the structure, gave the project new life. All of them had a big impact on the development of the society, whether over the short term or throughout the whole duration of the Allegorithmic adventure. This would be the case for Benoît, Gaëtan, and Alexis, for example. These three would become pillars of the company. For others, Allegorithmic was sometimes a sort of springboard to other jobs in the 3D industry, and this was a source of pride for us. For example, Guillaume and Raouf went on to join the game studios Ubisoft and Splash Damage, and Sylvain even ultimately pursued a brilliant career in the world of visual effects.[2]

Notably, Alexis, who was one of the first to join in this wave, would play a special role in the development of our structure, right from the moment of his arrival.

Alexis Khouri

One day in 2007 my future wife Laëtitia told me, "A very good friend of mine would like to speak with you. He studied at ESSEC with me, he composed a musical comedy pretty much on his own, and was about two years ahead of his studies—he's a real little genius... It turns out he's also interested in video games, and would like to know more about Allegorithmic. His name is Alexis. Alexis Khouri."

During our first discussion on the phone, I found Alexis a little too 'bullish,' but he was undeniably passionate about video games, a world that I hadn't personally followed as much as the world of special effects over the last 10 years,[3] and which was a market that was starting to take a close interest in our products, as mentioned in previous chapters. Allegorithmic could be in great need of someone like Alexis, somebody internal who could take over from Dave Taylor. I clearly needed a right

1: As we often say, 'to get out of the garage.'

2: 'Springboard,' in Sylvain's case, is a big word; Sylvain is incredibly gifted, and knows how to naturally get noticed through his work and his talent, as evidenced by the way I discovered and hired him: I spotted his student work, the remarkable short film *Hugh* on the front page of a French magazine specializing in 3D, 'Computer Arts,' in 2007. In an interview with 3DVF,[26] Sylvain had mentioned using MaP | Zone! When I read that, I contacted him and offered him a contract on the spot.

3: Ironically, I almost stopped playing video games when most of them moved to 3D, in the mid-90s. I remember being disappointed by the quality of these first 3D games, and, beyond the technical level that they represented at the time, the difference between these games and the 2D games I'd grown up with, which had reached a high level of artistic finesse, was too much for me. I lost interest in games for a few years and focused on special effects for cinema.

DOI:10.1201/9781003534624-19

Figure 19.1: Among the new arrivals of 2007: Raouf Béjaoui and Sylvain Nouveau, Gaëtan Lassagne, Guillaume Cerdan and Benoît Barbier, here in January 2009.

Figure 19.2: A beautiful image created by Sylvain Nouveau using our texturing tools in 2008.

hand to help me grow Allegorithmic in the area of sales. So I suggested that we discuss this further.

I met him a few days later in a restaurant in the twentieth *arrondissement* in Paris, next to his job at the time: he was Managing Director of PlaySoft, a company that ported games to mobile phones. Our discussion was particularly exciting. Alexis was clearly brilliant, passionate, and a good listener. He very quickly understood Allegorithmic's present stage of development, and clearly saw how he could help us.[4] I saw in him someone who could support me and develop the commercial aspect of the company, on a large scale. At that time, I focused on 'big deals,' major opportunities, which I followed up personally, one after the other—an approach which doesn't scale naturally, and which requires a lot of interactions, travel, and overall work. The time that passed between a first meeting and the signing of a contract could be counted in years... We needed someone who was able to develop our commercial branch so that we could sell software at a large scale without needing to communicate and negotiate directly with each buyer or, if it proved necessary at any point, to find the right price and reduce the time for contract signatures. We needed incoming opportunities, a processing pipeline for sales and follow-up that was as automated as possible.

4: Alexis notably has a dizzying (and therefore sometimes very disturbing for many) ability to explore at high speed a tree of possibilities, analyzing both the breadth of branches available as well as looking at each one in depth. He can therefore completely change his mind between two sentences if logic is respected—without any regret for his previous idea, or any misplaced ego that might make him cling to it, even if that idea had been proven to be most likely wrong. This intellectual honesty coupled with this extraordinary ability to not get hung up on his own ego were incredibly important: they allow him not to lie to himself!

I also needed somebody I could depend on who would support me in my overall strategic thinking. I was indeed starting to feel the strain from the effort I'd invested in the project. I was reaching my physical limits and the stress was beginning to affect me. Alexis impressed me a lot and gave me the impression that he could be the standout person I needed.

As the discussion progressed, it became obvious to me that we should work together. I asked him to join us, without really knowing yet how we would manage to pay him, particularly in a way that seemed interesting in relation to his current work. Discussions with Dassault Systèmes were progressing well (see Chapter 18) and this would perhaps give me the means to employ him if he was willing to wait a little while. And yet I also had to convince him to join the project. He had a good position in a company that worked well, in Paris, in a sector that he liked. The equation to solve was therefore complex.

It was during our second meeting, in the restaurant *Le Train Bleu*, in Gare de Lyon in Paris (which I passed through very regularly when traveling between Clermont-Ferrand and Paris), that I managed to convince him. This restaurant had a strange atmosphere, and it offered 'discreet' rooms, which apparently lend themselves particularly well to meetings—and meetings that don't necessarily fall under typical work responsibilities... Alexis loved secret agent stories, so the context was perfect. The investment from Dassault Systèmes was now finalized, and so at last we could decide on his role with Allegorithmic.

Alexis and I went on to work together for many years, and he would have an extraordinary impact on Allegorithmic's destiny, as I'll discuss later in this text.

In retrospect...

This encounter was one of the more fundamental meetings in the history of Allegorithmic. Alexis would play an extraordinary role in our adventure. He was the first person to 'tire me out' in a long time: his energy is superhuman, and his involvement and professionalism are limitless. He would be continuously on the road, finding himself in the most improbable situations, but would never express any doubt or desire for something different. He was the embodiment of going 'above and beyond,' his impact at Allegorithmic ranging from strategy to business development, as well as product design and interpersonal relationships.

Alexis was one of the people involved in our adventure who would also take the most tangible risks, through substantial financial investment when I opened up capital, or at times when it was necessary to be particularly clairvoyant (or naive, or a little crazy, or both) to predict a bright future for our company... He and his family would settle in the US a few years later, to establish closer relationships with our customers, and with Naughty Dog in particular (see Chapter 27). This required courage and a good amount of faith in Allegorithmic to move his entire family to a new continent. A deep and lasting friendship between Alexis and myself is one of the great things to come out of the Allegorithmic adventure; as I write these lines we are still working together, and I am a proud godfather to his second daughter, Mila.

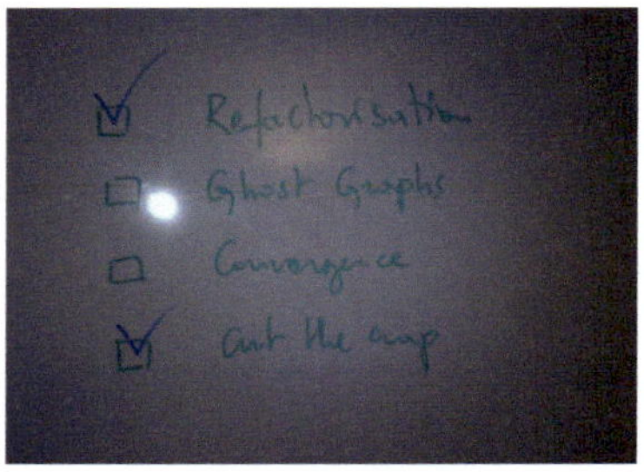

Figure 19.3: 'Cut the crap,' a phrase that Alexis and I often used. Alexis tried to convince me that this originated in a presentation we made to potential clients when I'd cut him off, saying, "This is just some marketing crap; don't listen to it too much." I personally feel that this cannot be entirely true...

Figure 19.4: Alexis and I during one of our trips to Japan in 2017. It is at times difficult for me to express this connection—the chemistry—between Alexis and me. This photo is worth a thousand words...

2008 and 2009 arrivals...

Recruitment continued at a good pace in 2008 and 2009, with the arrival of Emmanuel Laurent, Caroline Noyer, Amandine Lorrai, Lucie Poureau, Antoine Gonzalez, Fred Moreau, Igor Pilleux Kravtchenko, Nathalie Delfour, and Sylvain Paris.

Emmanuel, who had a rich background as director of an animation studio, joined us as head of the content production team that we were developing internally (we went so far as to call it ADS, 'Allegorithmic Design Studio') in order to address the needs of some customers, as we will see for example in Chapter 20.

Amandine Lorrai and Sylvain Paris would remain throughout the Allegorithmic adventure. Sylvain became the technical lead of our future product Substance Designer (see, for instance, Chapter 26), and Nathalie, who joined us after having worked at Kartoo (see Chapter 6), would stay for another ten years, taking over from Catherine Debain, who left to work on another project led by one of Christophe Debain's PhD students.

Nathalie, working with our financial advisor Laurent Carrio (see Chapter 6), gradually built up an accounting team around her, and became the administrative and financial backbone of Allegorithmic, essential for the smooth operation of the company.

. . . and afterward

Arrivals continued naturally thereafter, according to needs as well as Allegorithmic's ability to not only attract talent to join a company still under construction, and which had not yet demonstrated its full potential, but also, more pragmatically, it ability to pay its team. The task was further complicated by the fact that we were based in Clermont-Ferrand,[5] a city that was not known to be particularly attractive.

Among the roles we needed to fill was a new director of operations. I asked Alexis if he by any chance had anybody in mind who had the right profile for the position.[6] He told me that he did, but clarified: "He still works at Playsoft, running the company's Polish studio. Asking him to join us is a bit touchy, as I've already put Playsoft in trouble myself by coming to Allegorithmic. . . Let me talk to him and see if he might be interested."

After a few months of discussions, and against the advice of one of his fellow managers who strongly advised him against joining Allegorithmic, this 'company with no future,' Nicolas Liatti joined us in May 2010. He would take part in our adventure for the rest of its duration, assuming the thankless and largely misunderstood role of COO, Chief Operating Officer, this connector and facilitator working in the shadows, responsible for the tempo of the production teams and the correct execution of strategy.

Many more recruitments followed, such as Alexandre Chambriat, Benoît Mayaux, Alexandre Chassany, Grégory Allègre, Stéphane Guy,[7] Vincent Graveleau, Benoît Bigeard, Gaëlle Thomarat, Eric Batut, and Clément Jacob, the majority of whom would go on to become pillars of Allegorithmic's technical team throughout its life.

5: Which would prove to be a real difficulty throughout the existence of the structure. The region was far from overflowing with 3D developers, and we therefore had to try to attract people from all over France, or even from abroad. Encouraging talent to move to Clermont-Ferrand, a small provincial town poorly served by train and 'far from everything' often proved impossible. Conversely, once employees had decided to come to the city they tended to have a good feeling about the place, get invested in the community, and remain long-term.

6: Alexis had previously recommended Maxime Delavergne, somebody he met at ESSEC some time earlier. The source of talent that Alexis provided proved very important.

7: See Chapter 22 to learn more about the arrival of Stéphane Guy, Alexandre Chassany, and Benoît Mayaux.

Iñigo: the team grows. . . or not.

The previous sections don't fully convey the difficulty in recruiting new talent, for a young, unproven technology company which happened to be based in Clermont-Ferrand. Our field was particularly technical and there were few specialists in graphics programming in the *Clermontois* region. . . I therefore regularly had to contact people that I'd spotted online.

This was how I came across the work of Iñigo Quilez, a demo-maker who had been getting a lot of attention thanks to his real-time demos involving astonishingly beautiful fractals. With a little research, I learned he was based in San Sebastian, in Spain, and I managed to find a contact email. I decided to try my luck, and wrote to him, asking him to work with us, to take part in the crazy adventure of Allegorithmic, and join my team in developing a 'new wave' of procedural tools.

He answered me quite quickly, which was already a good sign that we could work together,[8] but after thanking me for the proposition, he told

8: At the time, I thought that being responsive to emails was a rare and valuable characteristic. . .

me that he was already busy—"An opportunity I can't let pass," was the phrase he used. Sometime later I found out that he'd joined Pixar...[9]

9: I understand completely why he chose Pixar rather than Allegorithmic; at Pixar, he would leave a unique mark and would be responsible for a large part of the sets and environments (forests, mountains, etc.) for the film *Brave*, much of which takes place in the wilderness. All of these environments are created procedurally, with mathematical formulas! Iñigo is a one-of-a-kind genius in his domain, capable of drawing with mathematics as nobody else can. He continued through the industry, very much making his presence felt. He is the creator, for instance, of the website Shadertoy.com, an absolute reference in programming shaders. After Pixar, he joined the world of VR, within Oculus Story Studio, and ended up developing Quill, a unique tool for graphics creation in VR.

In retrospect...

The arrival of new members brought its share of difficulties and the discovery, sometimes painfully, of the complexities and challenges associated with 'human resources' (even though I've always had issues with this particular term, which I find reductive). We made, and in particular I made, mistakes in recruiting, in employee follow-up, and in management. We sometimes had to part with team members when performance was not as expected, when the new recruit wasn't a good fit with the rest of the team, or simply when our priorities changed, and we had to halt certain initiatives. Throughout the lifespan of Allegorithmic, however, we never had any major HR issues, and I like to think that this is because we first focused on recruiting the 'right people,' with strengths and values aligned with those of the company. I also like to think that we've always considered each employee an integral part of the adventure, someone with whom we would build something, rather than a simple resource. Perhaps the opinion of those who left the company, or those who we forced to leave, might be less glowing. Still, I am sincerely proud of what we accomplished and the trust we established throughout the life of Allegorithmic with all the women and men who were a part of it.

19.2 The Jaude offices

The team was growing. Not wanting to push our luck with ISIMA,[10] and now that we could pay rent thanks to the investment from Dassault Systèmes, we needed to find new offices. Thierry Frey tackled the task of finding us a new development center, capable of supporting potential growth over several years and being, ideally, located in the city center of Clermont-Ferrand, where the majority of our employees were based, and 'close to daily life,' which wasn't the case in the business incubators in La Pardieu, or even at ISIMA.

10: Thanks again to ISIMA for welcoming us for several years; this help was extremely valuable in the beginning phase of our activity.

After several months of visits, we finally found the perfect place, at 31 rue Gonod, in Clermont-Ferrand. The premises were within the 'Centre Jaude' building, the most visited and lively place in the heart of the city, next to the shopping center, cinemas, cafes, bars, sandwich shops, and restaurants, all of which we'd take advantage of for many years. The windows of the office also provided a stunning view of Place de Jaude, a major square in the center of the city. We would go on to experience some fantastic times in this office, which we can see in figure 19.5, photos taken during our first visits, before we'd moved into the office, as well as in the series of black and white photos taken by Nicolas Wirrmann, in figure 19.6, once the team had moved in.

Figure 19.5: Jaude office in February 2007, before moving in. Thierry Frey (whose reflection we see in the last image) can take the credit for finding them. We would have some great times here.

Figure 19.6: Jaude offices in 2011 with some of the team. This office would always have special significance for us, as it was one of the major steps in Allegorithmic's development.

Figure 19.7: The team in the Clermont-Ferrand office a few years later in January 2014. In the foreground, with backs turned: Sylvain Paris, Benoît Barbier and Clément Jacob (working on Substance Painter). Further back, facing forward: Alexandre Chassany, and behind him, Nicolas Wirrmann, Fabrice Piquet and Christophe Soum. On the wall, a whiteboard showing development sprints. On the ceiling, some decorative CDs.

Prospection in Asia, and Redux | 20

As soon as he arrived, Alexis Khouri (see Chapter 19), immersed himself in our products in order to fully understand them. The level of involvement he exhibited in trying to understand MaP | Zone and ProFX was extraordinary, and after long exchanges with the technical teams and artists, and having attended numerous demos and commercial presentations (often with me), he began to be able to lead meetings on his own, and give demos himself.

Drawing an analogy between the MIDI format in the world of music (a compact and synthetic representation of music) and the format of our procedural textures from MaP | Zone, he wanted to emphasize our unusually small file sizes that we'd successfully implemented in *RoboBlitz* (see Chapter 13) and even for Microsoft's Virtual Earth (see Chapter 18). The XBox Live Arcade market hadn't taken off for us, as Microsoft had decided to relax their game size limits, so developers had less need for ProFX. However, there was a certain type of game, in a particular territory,[1] which might need smaller-sized games which were quicker to download. 3D games with a lot of textures...

1: We can see here one of the subtleties that Alexis brought in his analysis of the problem and the market, with a particular dimension we hadn't considered before: geographical segmentation!

20.1 Korea and free2play

Korea

At that time, Korea possessed a notable characteristic compared to the rest of the world: they had the fastest internet on the planet, by far. Fiber optic connections were standard, and transmission speeds in Korea were up to 1000 times faster than elsewhere. This particularity, combined with other elements such as a ban on American and Japanese game consoles throughout this territory, contributed to the creation of unique types of games, players, and business models. These would ultimately spread like wildfire throughout the rest of the world.

PC and online games

Korea's ban on imported games consoles from Japan encouraged PC gaming on Windows. Combining this constraint with the specificity of the Korean internet network, many local game developers naturally specialized in online gaming for PC. Distributing a PC game over the internet, even if it was heavy,[2], was very quick and simple in Korea. This unique trait was liberating for Korean developers who offered grand, complex sagas[3] without having to worry about loading times and knowing that their target market was captive and receptive. They also evolved their games constantly, with regular updates, again taking advantage of their nature and intangible distribution: fixes, developments, and new game maps were released regularly, and games would potentially

2: As is often the case with 3D games...

3: Such as the Lineage saga by NCSoft.

DOI:10.1201/9781003534624-20

have a long life, as opposed to to a more traditional approach of being printed on CD once, and then being sold in specialist shops.

Korea would then specialize in the development of complex online games, sometimes in 3D, which were often graphically rich and evolved regularly, only on PC. Aside from games like *World of Warcraft*,[4] Korea was leading the way for online games of this type at that time.

4: Published by the Californian company Blizzard.

PC Bang

Most households did not have a computer at home at that time, so another trend arose on a large scale: 'PC Bang,' 'internet and gaming' cafes where, for a very low price, players could connect for long hours to their favorite games and social media. These cafes were everywhere in the poorer areas of Seoul and other major cities of the country, and players sometimes spent entire days and nights there.

Figure 20.1: Top, Alexis visiting a PC Bang, in Seoul, in May 2008. Bottom, a classic PC Bang. By Hachimaki: https://www.flickr.com/photos/robfahey/146145429/, CCBY-SA2.0, https://commons.wikimedia.org/w/index.php?curid=2689737

Developers offered players the possibility of connecting via an account, which wasn't linked to any particular computer. This decentralized, client-server approach is very widespread today but was quite new at that time. The owners of PC Bangs would pre-install the most popular games on their fleet of PCs, and players would connect using their own credentials.

A regular phenomenon took place, usually during the night: games would be updated simultaneously on PCs all over Korea, and in particular on those in PC Bang, who wished to be able to continuously offer the latest version of the game, to satisfy and keep their clients. Here, developers applied limited optimization intended to ensure rapid transfer, as internet connections were excellent.

Nevertheless, the side effect was felt in the business models proposed by the game developers.

free2play

A new business model emerged: free2play. With this model, developers didn't require players in PC Bangs to pay for a game license and an account immediately. The idea was that the game was offered to players for free, for as long as they wanted, and that monetization would take place via micro-transactions linked to the sales of virtual goods which would allow for faster progression in-game (for example, a very powerful sword, some highly protective armor, or more devastating spells than those that could be acquired in the free version of the game, or that would otherwise simply require more game time before they become accessible). This was the free2play model with its micro-transactions, which today is a reference business model for developers.

Korean game developers were very successful with their games and this business model, particularly due to 'whales,' a small number of players that spent an enormous amount of money and compensated for a large majority who spent hardly anything.[5] Once the Korean market was largely conquered, the developers naturally wished to multiply their success and export their games to the rest of the world, and in particular

5: A wonderful example of 'long tail,' described by Chris Anderson in his book with the same title,[27] which had just come out in 2008

to China, where a new generation of players were emerging along with an attractive market size.

Export

Unfortunately, Korean developers found themselves facing an unanticipated problem: in comparison with what existed in their country, the internet connections were horribly slow outside of Korea. And the size of the games, as well as their need for regular updates—essentially, everything that characterized the essence of Korean games—became a huge obstacle abroad, bringing Korean developers' plans to a halt, and invalidating their business model. . .

The developers naturally first focused on countries that had decent internet speed, and smaller games. They also searched for technical means allowing them to distribute games more effectively. . .

. . . and this was where Alexis spotted an opportunity for us: the majority of a 3D game's weight was taken up by textures (as we'd seen with *RoboBlitz*, see Chapter 13), and so with ProFX we had a potential solution to the problems of Korean game developers, these giants of online PC games and their free2play model.

Compression

This was the beginning for Alexis and for Allegorithmic of a major commercial development campaign in that region, in Korea but also in China. We visited a lot of developers at this time to introduce them to ProFX, and had the chance to carry out tests on games like *Kart'n Crazy* and *Pangya*. In this way, we managed to secure a first deal for the game *Ragnarok*, thanks to the presence of Gravity Europe, to whom we were able to show, in-depth and from France, the interest in this technology.

Sales and adoption were complicated, however, largely due to a combination of two factors: first, the textures for the games the developers wanted to export already existed in the form of bitmaps and were at times far from what we could call a texture (they were closer to graphical elements, and didn't respect the 'good practices' of 3D texturing) and had already passed through the stages of artistic validation before being integrated into the game. To use ProFX in an optimal manner, these textures would have to be entirely redone in procedural form, using MaP | Zone.

Our first tests confirmed that only a few textures from the games we were working on could indeed be remade using MaP | Zone, and the space saved like this would be fairly limited.[6]

6: At the time, 3D game textures were made in a very artisanal way, without any real technical rigor, whereas MaP | Zone textures were well suited to a precise formalism, which was nonetheless still far from the reality of production methods. The market would change its approach and eventually get closer to this formalism and to our tools a few years later, when PBR arrived (see Chapter 26).

Second, producing textures using MaP | Zone's graph-based approach was very different to the traditional way of producing those same textures using tools like Photoshop. Not only were the 3D artists in these game studios untrained (though they were perfectly capable with Photoshop), but one simple training course would not necessarily be sufficient, as the profile of an artist capable of manipulating tools like MaP | Zone was very different to that of a conventional 3D artist. The effort required to remake a large portion of textures with our tools was therefore significant.

To find a solution to this problem, this time on a bigger scale than we'd done with *RoboBlitz*, we went so far as to build an internal content production team, the same way Gilles Fleury, Mélinda Esponda Diaz, Benjamin Maréchal, and Nicolas Wirrmann had produced the textures for *RoboBlitz*, as they were the only people who knew MaP | Zone well enough. We 'made our technical artists available' to developers integrating ProFX, but who didn't want to train their own artists just yet. A ProFX license could therefore include a number of hours of texture production. . .

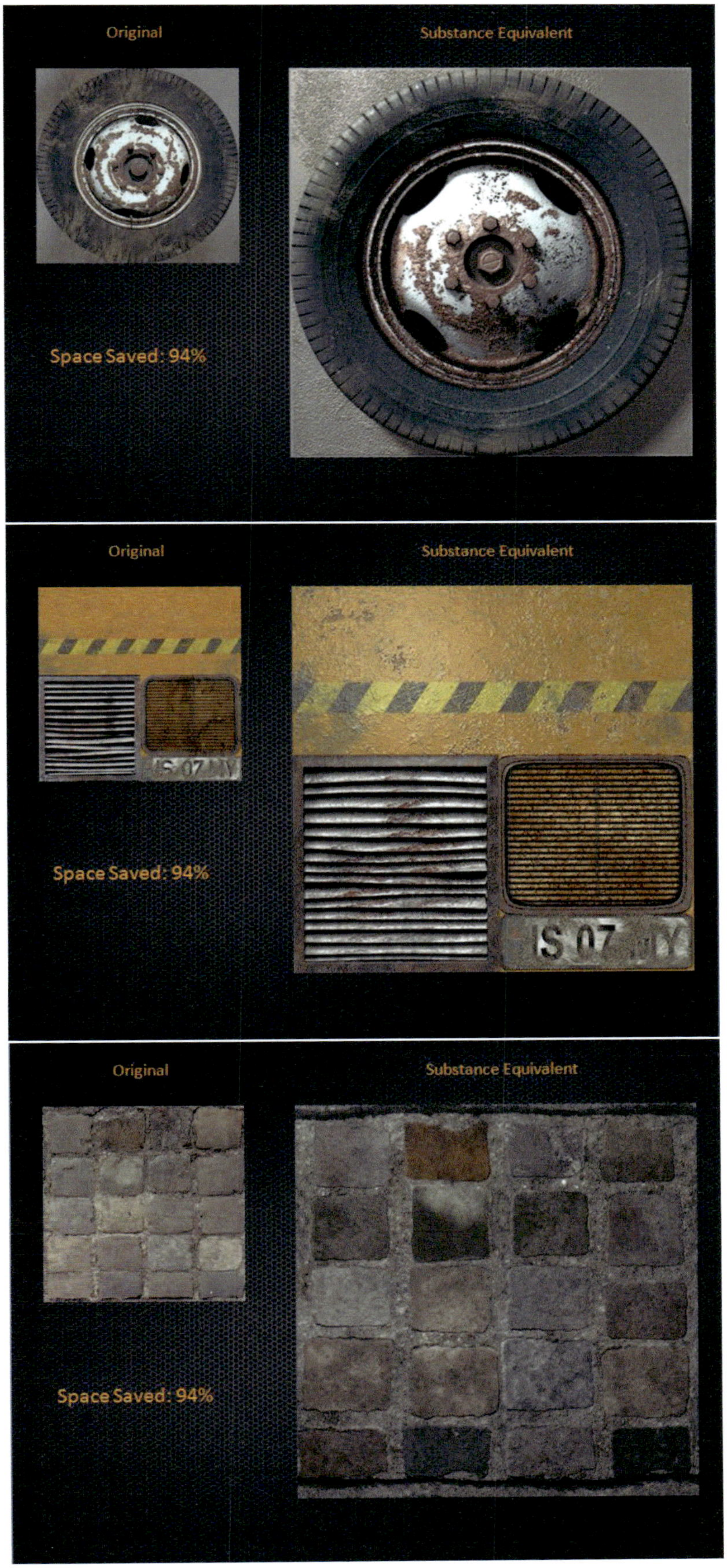

Figure 20.2: Several examples of procedural texture reproduction, using MaP | Zone, and size savings obtained versus their equivalent with bitmaps.

Figure 20.3: Alexis and I during G-Star 2010 in Seoul. Bottom, our stand.

We carried out more and more tests, on games like *Parabellum* by Acony,[7] and in companies like GameHi, Nexon, Tencent, P PM (for the game *Panshel*), Shanghai NorthStar and The 9 (one of our rare clients who stayed with the process right to the end). The work was particularly tedious and, despite some successes, commercial development for the ProFX solution associated with texture production was too complex, even though we had some particularly valuable help with local representation, particularly from Christian Kim, whom I met during the G-Star conference in 2007 in Seoul. Christian would become Allegorithmic's representative in Korea for many years to come, ceaselessly demonstrating extreme professionalism, implication, selflessness, and loyalty.

Figure 20.4: A monsoon descending on Seoul in August 2007. I came to Seoul with one goal: signing a ProFX license with Sebastian Ryu. But when I arrived at the GameHi offices, I learned that Sebastian Ryu was no longer part of the company, and no one else was aware of the negotiation. I left the next morning on a plane that I wasn't sure would take off, as a typhoon was approaching. I didn't sleep well that night. . .

7: A free2play MMO on PC,[28] on which Benjamin Maréchal (who traveled twice to the premises to help with development, sometimes in difficult conditions), Jérémie Noguer, Gilles Fleury, Guillaume Cerdan, Gaëtan Lassagne, Sylvain Nouveau, Raouf Bejaoui, and Lucie Vodeau worked.

Figure 20.5: Christian Kim (here with me in 2018), who would become head of Allegorithmic Korea from 2008, and for the entire adventure onwards. Christian possesses incredible professionalism, selflessness, and loyalty.

20.2 Redux

Alexis was the first to put his finger on the potential solution to the problem.[8] For these Korean game companies, the best-case scenario would be to have tools able to automatically compress textures without needing to recreate them which made the process more complicated. His idea was that, contrary to using the generic texture compression tools (like ZIP and other similar lossy methods[9]), we should focus only on textures, and exploit certain particularities, such as the presence of specular and normal maps that were often connected together, and put in place some technical bricks that only belonged to us, to obtain an ad-hoc method of texture compression.

This was the birth of Redux,[10] a product that the team, and in particular Antoine Gonzalez and Charles Bauchet, would develop in addition to our procedural texturing offer. Redux was the perfect answer to the problem

8: And it is extremely rare for someone on his first commercial development mission to develop product ideas answering problems expressed by the market! Alexis's exceptional contribution to Allegorithmic's progress can clearly be seen here.

9: Which resulted in loss of image quality.

10: An article covering the press release at the launch of Redux, published on March 4, 2010, in GameIndustry.biz, can be found here: [29].

identified for this particular market.[11] The tool allowed the compression of texture packages for Unreal Engine 3 by a factor of 2 or even 3, which was very significant.[12] The mechanism can be seen in detail in figure 20.6.

11: One of our first examples of market pull versus techno push: we made a tool in response to the demand of the market, whereas ProFX and our other products until then had been products and technologies straight out of the lab, looking for a problem to 'fix.'

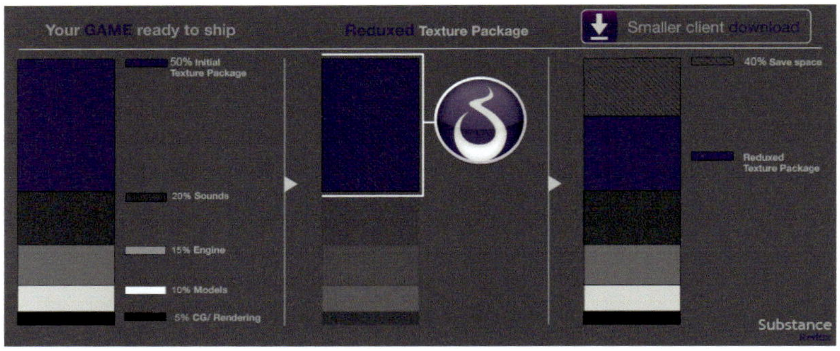

Figure 20.6: The principle of Redux's operation.

12: The tool worked particularly well when developers used the game engine Unreal Engine 3, which compressed textures in a very basic way. Redux compressed JPEG textures, decompressed in DDS and recompressed in DXT with a DXT real-time compressor that we were the only ones to possess, thanks to the work of Charles Bauchet. The trick of passing through JPEG, combined with this unique key of the DXT real-time compressor, made all the difference.

20.3 China

We had our first commercial successes with Redux in China, and even though the product was suitable, nothing was ever simple, and meetings with developers were not easy to schedule for a small company from Auvergne, nor always typical in the way they took place. As was for example the case in a meeting where Alexis, having just arrived for a meeting after a long trip was told, "Take off your clothes! And put on these overalls!"

Alexis, surprised to say the least, nonetheless complied with the demand. He had just arrived at Snail Game, a Suzhou game developer. The building was impressive: on the outside, it was in the shape of a giant snail, on the inside was a tower which evoked the pyramid of Babel, with the boss's offices at the very top.

Alexis, dressed in orange overalls,[13] was accompanied to a meeting room where he would present our technology. He had to pass through a safe zone full of servers and other equipment that was highly sensitive to dust and insects[14] that Alexis could potentially have brought in on his clothing. Of course, once he'd passed through the zone, no one told him he could put his normal clothes back on, and so he ended up being the only one in the meeting wearing bright overalls...

13: Which were reminiscent of the clothing worn by Tintin (and Snowy!) in *Destination Moon*.

14: The origin of 'computer bugs.'

There was another incident at the end of 2010 in Fuzhou, when visiting Netdragon, a Chinese online gaming heavyweight. Alexis managed to get a meeting with the CTO after long months of discussions with one of the team's product managers, who had done a study exchange in La Rochelle, France, and took advantage of discussions with Alexis to practice his French. Netdragon had three game projects in development, all using Unreal Engine 3, for which Redux could be of particular interest.

Alexis had arrived after a long trip all the way from Paris, and having freshened up at his hotel, showed up at the premises at 1:20 in the afternoon. He was met by his contact, who looked at him strangely when Alexis said, "I'm a little early for our meeting at two o'clock—but that will give us a bit of time to set everything up." His contact replied: "You mean the meeting at two o'clock... in the morning?"

Once Alexis recovered from his shock, he learned that the CTO, who regularly worked with the US, had readjusted his schedule and worked during the night. After a long tour of the city with his contact, it was time for Alexis to do the demo, in spite of his intense fatigue. The CTO didn't utter a word throughout the meeting. He was the only one dressed in a baggy band T-shirt, surrounded by members of his team who were all wearing suits, asking questions and translating for him what Alexis was presenting. At last, at the end of the meeting, he said, "Thank you very much mister Khouri, very impressive," with a fluency in English that left his level in no doubt. . .

Alexis continued his journey with a flight to Tokyo the next morning. When he landed, he'd received an email from the CTO in his inbox: it contained the signed copy of the term sheet, for two Redux licenses for a total of 50K dollars. This was our first major deal for Redux.

In retrospect. . .

Redux would prove to be a very useful tool for a very specific need in the world of online gaming, and it would sell in a very satisfactory manner, but it was also proof that the middleware market was particularly complex and unrewarding. The technologies we had to put in place were extremely complex, and the sales process was long and difficult. The market remained a very limited size. In the end, this tool was unfortunately not the booster Allegorithmic had been looking for.

21 Demos, products, and conferences

21.1 Our products

Even though products tend to evolve at a rapid pace, having few clients gave us a lot of freedom to try out new ideas, and iterate rapidly on new concepts. Here I list all the products we worked on throughout the entire period 2007-2011.

After endless discussions and brainstorming sessions, filling up every whiteboard we could find, we soon converged on the concept of an ecosystem of products dedicated to texturing comprising three tools, as seen in figure 21.1. We can see among these concepts three distinct tools with different functions, notably including a tool for creating graph-based procedural textures (replacing MaP | Zone, which would become Substance Designer) and a more 'artistic' tool allowing users to paint masks and apply materials, which would several years later become Substance Painter.

Substance Designer

For some time we'd wanted to help our tools evolve, and imbue them with new energy. An ecosystem composed of a procedural texture generation engine (TAON 3), a tool for authoring these textures (MaP | Zone) and a middleware that would integrate into game engines (ProFX) seemed like the right direction to take. The authoring tool, however, needed to be updated.

We also wanted to find a new name for our products, to mark the arrival of a new generation of tools. We needed an umbrella name that would encompass all our tools more elegantly than our current nomenclature. After a generalized brainstorm, we chose the name 'Substance,' which notably had three points in its favor: it evoked the quality of our 3D surfaces (textures), it described a certain depth of concept, and it was easily pronounceable by a team of French people who expressed themselves poorly in English, as well as by our potential customers almost everywhere in the world.

We therefore had to find a new name for all our products, which would identify them under the Substance umbrella. We chose Substance Designer for the authoring tool (to replace MaP | Zone), Substance Air for the middleware (to replace ProFX), and finally Substance Engine (to replace, or rather to finally give a name to, an almost standalone product, TAON 3).

This was the beginning of the adventure for what would become the suite of products that would establish itself as the absolute reference in the world of texturing—the Substance adventure. Here, however, we were still a long way from that moment; this was only the beginning of the suite's development. . .

DOI:10.1201/9781003534624-21

We presented an alpha version of Substance Designer, much too early in its development cycle, at GDC in March 2008, as seen in figure 21.3.

The first version of Substance Designer, version 1.0, was finally released two years later, in June 2010. Christophe Soum put a finishing touch on the new format for procedural texture creation just a day before the launch! The SBSAR format, still in use today as I write these words twelve years later, was born. It's worth noting that the product development team was quite heavily opposed to releasing the product, feeling that it wasn't yet mature enough for commercial use. Nicolas Liatti, who had arrived just a few weeks earlier and was taking on his new role as COO, was not yet able to judge the quality of the product, so he asked the views of the technical artists we had on the team. They confirmed that the product lacked many features *but that it was functional*. This was enough for Nicolas, always a fan of large-scale public tests and agility in product development, to approve the launch of Substance Designer 1.0 right away.

Although there were only a few dozen downloads of the product in the following months, an important cycle had begun for Allegorithmic: a pivot toward tools for texture creation, slowly moving away from middleware, and also the first step toward agility in development, a notion that Stéphane Guy (see Chapter 19) would push even further as we developed Substance Painter (see Chapter 29).

The next major iteration of Substance Designer was released a year later, after a lot of hard work to make it more well-rounded, and also taking into consideration feedback that we often received: the tool was complex, procedural textures were complex in and of themselves, and the graphs within the tool were hard to understand...

In June 2011, we launched Substance Designer 2.0 and a new tool, Substance Designer Lite, on both Windows and, this time around, Mac. The latter tool didn't display creation graphs for textures, but rather a layer stack like those of Photoshop, which we hoped would be simpler to understand. The goal here was to appeal to a wider base of users, also in part thanks to lower pricing.

We didn't reach this goal; we only sold a few dozen licenses for Substance Designer 2.0, mostly to beta version users of the Unity plugin (see Chapter 24), and fewer than 10 licenses of Substance Designer Lite! Two months after its release, we dropped Substance Designer Lite, and gave Substance Designer 2.0 licenses to its unfortunate early customers. We also heard the message loud and clear that users didn't want a 'Lite,' limited version of our tools. They wanted the same version as the pros, without any compromises.

Substance Air and Substance Redux

These were our middleware tools, that we renamed to make them an integral part of our 'Substance' offer (see the following page for the brochure presenting the two products, dating from March 2010). The focus for Redux was very clearly on saving space, and we developed it to be very simple in what it had to offer (see Chapter 20).

For Substance Air, the offer was more complex and involved saving space resulting from the procedural quality of textures and their compact representation, but also by the possibility of 'customizing' those textures at runtime, for example when configuring a character at the beginning of a game as we choose their clothing and other equipment.

The middleware for bitmap compression

- The first solution to automatically reduce the size of your bitmap textures by about 50% (compared to zipped dds dxt).
- No noticeable loss of quality ingame.
- No impact on ingame performances.

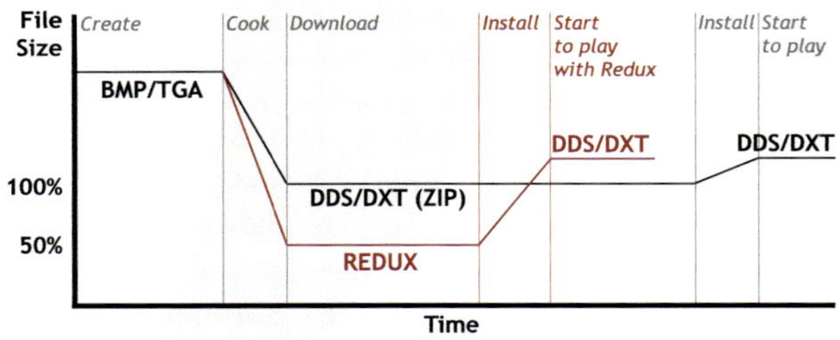

Substance Redux Editor | Optimized compression with real-time feedback

A complete toolset

- The Redux *Editor* can load any kind of bitmaps (TGA, BMP, PNG, etc).
- You can fine-tune your compression parameters with realtime visual feedback.
- Plugins are available for Unreal Engine 3 and Gamebryo.
- The Redux *Engine* offers detailed texture map analysis and optimal compression scheme.
- Ultra fast in-house DXT compression at runtime.

Create with Allegorithmic's Substance Air

The first middleware solution 100% dedicated to texturing

Create with Substance Editor

- Mix bitmaps, vector graphics and procedural elements through a unique hybrid and non-linear creation process.
- Create high quality materials with complete sets of texture maps (diffuse, normal, specular, etc).
- Create tiling textures or textures for complex objects based on their UVs.
- Create dynamic textures that can offer hundreds of variations from just one asset.

Substance Editor | First authoring tool entirely dedicated to texturing

Bathroom Demo | Runtime texture aspect change

Generate with Substance Engine

- Substance textures are saved in a lightweight format that can be up to 99% smaller than their bitmap equivalent, allowing to save gigabytes of textures in just a small package.
- Final outputs are generated on the fly at install, loading or run-time, whenever you need them.
- Substance textures can be imported and tweaked at run-time from any game engine once integrated.
- Substance is already integrated in Epic's Unreal Engine 3, Emergent's Gamebryo and Lightspeed, and Unity 3D.

Bitmap2Material, or B2M

On the return train after our meeting with the game development studio Asobo[1] in Bordeaux during spring 2010, Alexis and I unpacked how our meeting had gone. The feedback we'd received from the Bordeaux team had mostly been negative and fairly depressing. In particular, Sébastien Wloch, then Technical Director and an incredibly talented programmer, was developing a fully procedural game (which would become *Fuel*); on paper, our procedural tools were well suited to their project, but Sébastien re-developed everything himself and didn't really need our tools. In addition, the studio worked with textures based on environment photos, which they then combined in a way that was suitable for their procedurally generated topology. Even though we tried to push for our procedural approach to textures, their concern for absolute realism forced them to use photos. We weren't yet able to meet this need.

1: Asobo was in the process of developing *Fuel*, a game that would be released a little while later. Asobo would ultimately become hugely successful with the remake of *Flight Simulator*, which would come out in 2020.

Vincent Dedeine, the Creative Director of Asobo, had specified, "What we really need right now is a tool that allows us to make high-quality normal maps from these photos." We didn't have anything like that, and other tools on the market, like Crazy Bump, were already specialized in this area that we'd always looked down on: our view was that this pragmatic approach was not 'pure' enough in comparison with our procedural approach.[2] And so we'd clumsily allowed a competitor to occupy an important position in the game development pipeline, right under our noses, without reacting at all.

2: Obtaining a normal map from a single image back then was a task that no algorithm could carry out perfectly, and all approaches were quite approximate and heuristic.

And so, on the train back, Alexis had to express his thoughts. "Good God, it's unbelievable—is it really possible that *fake* normal maps are not *good enough*? Because if, using Substance, we can do *good enough*, we have a hell of a tool on our hands; we could do Crazy Bump but with way more flexibility—we can generate normal maps at runtime,[3] and so on." He was right, of course, and it stung both my curiosity and my ego, which were both already sore from the frustrating meeting we'd just had. I pulled out my laptop...

3: At the moment when a game is executed. It was the principle we'd used for *RoboBlitz* a few years earlier, see Chapter 13.

I opened Substance Designer, and within literally 5 minutes made a graph that could generate a normal map using a photo as input.[4] 'Well, it doesn't look so bad...' I showed Alexis my results, and his face lit up. We'd just created the prototype for our normal map generator using photos as input. I immediately proposed a name for it, inspired by the trend in the Unix world to use as few characters as possible—a '2' in place of 'to,' in this case—to represent a transition from one state to another. Here, the tool would transition a bitmap to a material state (with multiple bitmaps representing a material). My proposition was b2m, as in, 'bitmap to material.'

4: My approach was 'dirty' and very simplistic for this first test, but it was good enough to conclude that if we weren't too attached to the form and purity of our methods, the results we could get, even though imperfect, were totally suitable in many cases, and particularly for gamers who weren't even thinking about normal maps...

Once we returned from the meeting, we shared the prototype and the story behind it, as well as the idea for a new product, with the wizards of our team. Subsequent versions of the b2m algorithm (which we ultimately called B2M) would come from Jérémie Noguer and Gilles Fleury.[5] The tool became particularly powerful and soon overtook Crazy Bump in terms of the quality of its results.

5: Here I'll mention something very important to me: the B2M algorithm was created directly in Substance Designer, in the form of an operational graph, and is a perfect example of 'visual programming,'[30] the art of programming without using code, using graphs for a range of diverse operations. It was a way for someone like Gilles, who didn't have a programming background but could 'see' algorithms, to develop ideas very rapidly, free of any entry barriers of programming, and of the dry, technical shell that can make this area inaccessible for non-specialists. This phenomenon of freeing artists who are not programmers but who nonetheless have a technical affinity, whom the industry calls technical artists, and whom I would later call 'left-brain artists,' jumped out at me while watching Gilles work, producing algorithmic magic without having a traditionally scientific education...

The fact that B2M was a Substance graph allowed distribution on a large scale and using simple methods, just as Alexis had predicted, via integration plugins using the Substance Engine within tools like

Autodesk (Flame, Max, Maya, and so on: see Chapter 22), as well as Unity (see Chapter 24). It allowed the rapid generation of complete materials from a single input image. It also made it possible, in a roundabout way, to reduce the size of texture packages using a simple operation: from a single input image, B2M generated three or four. The gain was immediately visible, and it was very simple to set up the tool to create textures when installing a game (which is exactly what we'd done with *RoboBlitz* (see Chapter 13).

We decided to sell it separately, only available in its 'compiled' form, distributed using the SBSAR format, like a recipe whose secret ingredients we didn't want to reveal. Our latest product to date, B2M, was born and its version 1.0 was launched on April 8, 2011.

In retrospect...

It isn't my intention to provide lessons in this book, but it was clear that this event was a learning experience for me and my team. We'd previously looked down on a tech that we judged too simplistic. Having been in a hyper-specialized techno push for years, we sometimes found it difficult to be pragmatic, and to set aside our pride for a little while, just to see how we could adapt our cutting-edge technology to what the market needed *at that moment*. Sometimes this would take on a different form, perhaps a simpler form, than what we'd originally imagined.

Alexis was a master at this! He was the most pragmatic person in our company. He was the one listening to the market and having us develop Redux (see section 20.2), and the one who refused to accept our elitist approach to normal maps, instead pushing me to try a 'dirty hack' that would become B2M. It was also Alexis who, alongside Jérémie, pushed to adapt our tools to a newly emerging rendering paradigm, PBR (see Chapter 26)...

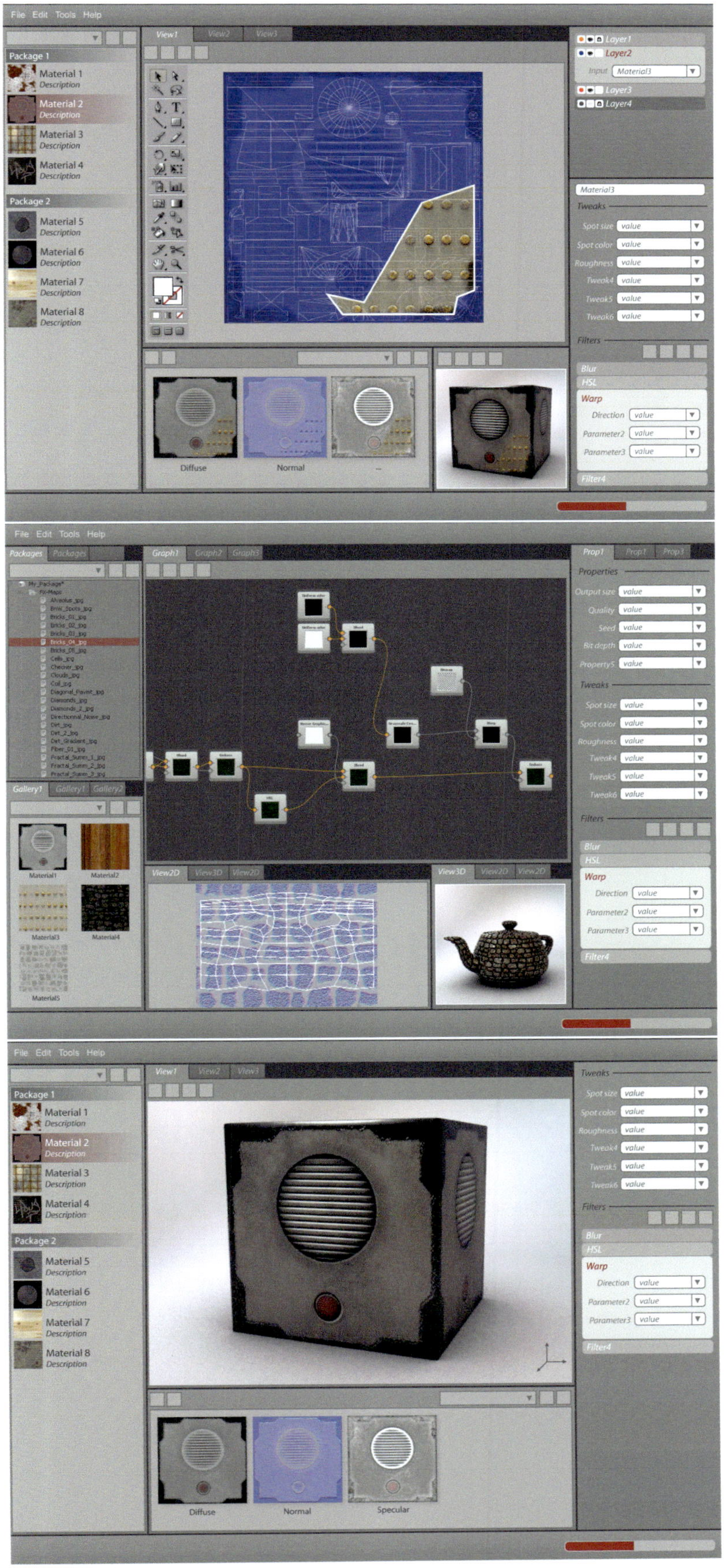

Figure 21.1: The 'wireframes' for future Substance tools. We can see among these concepts three distinct tools with different functions, notably including a tool for creating graph-based procedural textures (replacing MaP | Zone, which would become Substance Designer) and a more 'artistic' tool allowing users to paint masks and apply materials, which would several years later become Substance Painter.

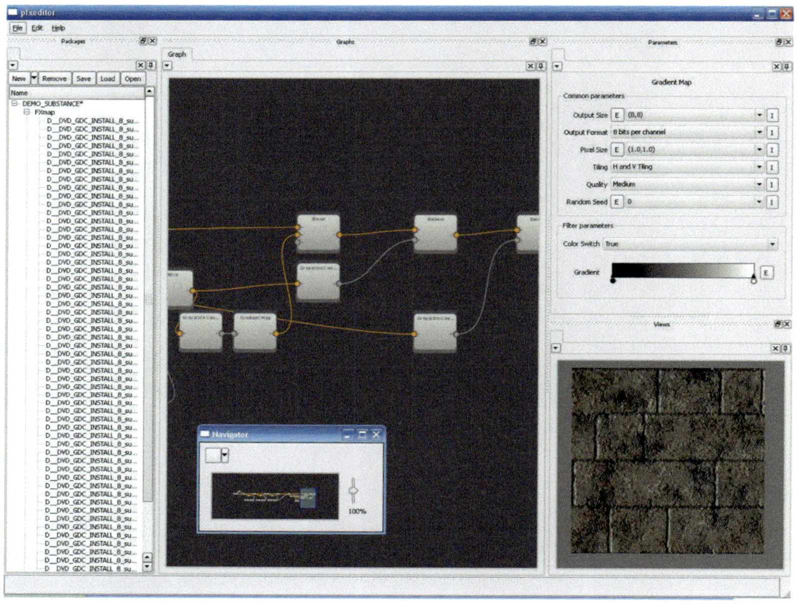

Figure 21.2: The first iteration of what would become Substance Designer. The program here is still called 'pfxeditor,' as in ProFX Editor.

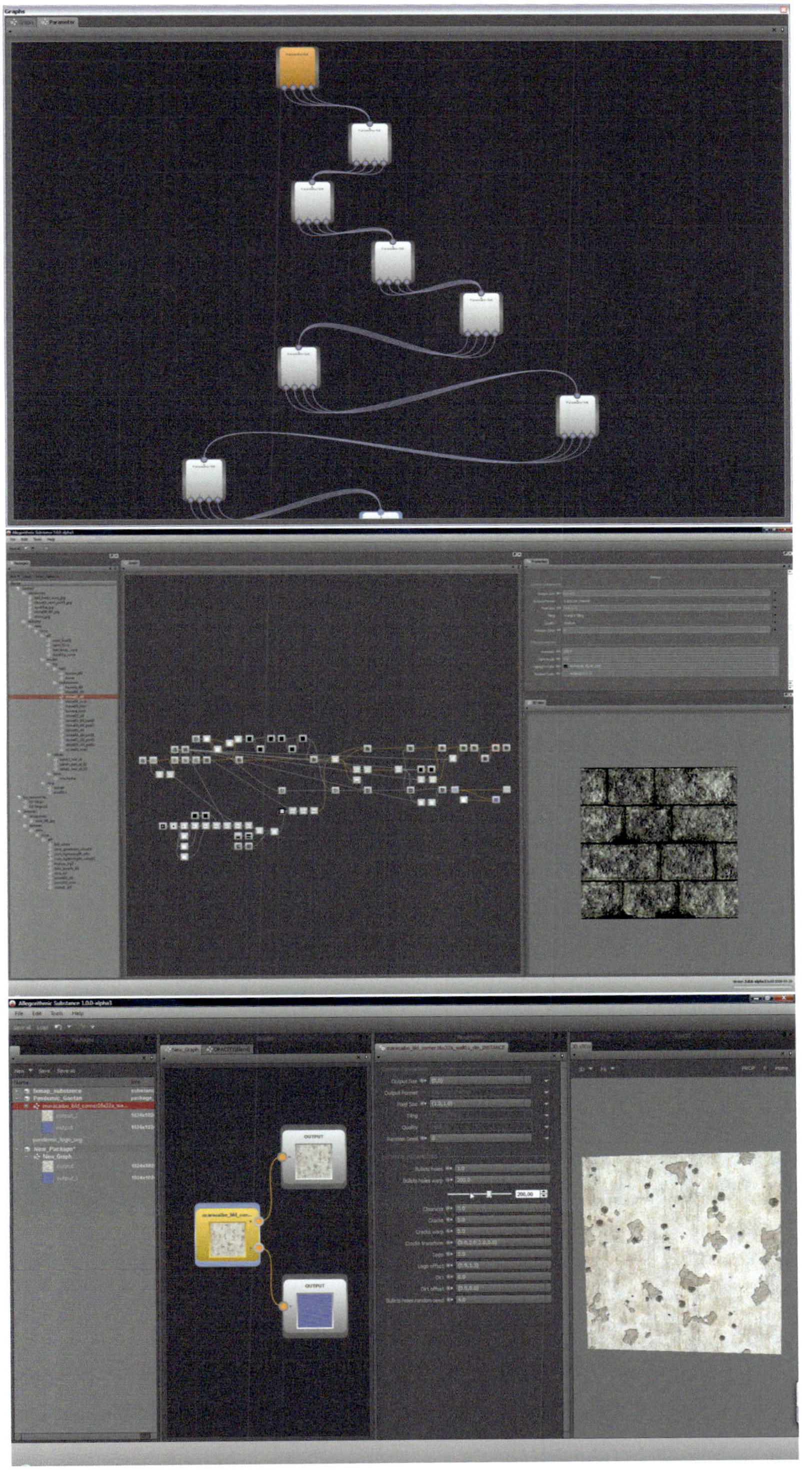

Figure 21.3: The graphic interface of Substance Designer's alpha version in 2008.

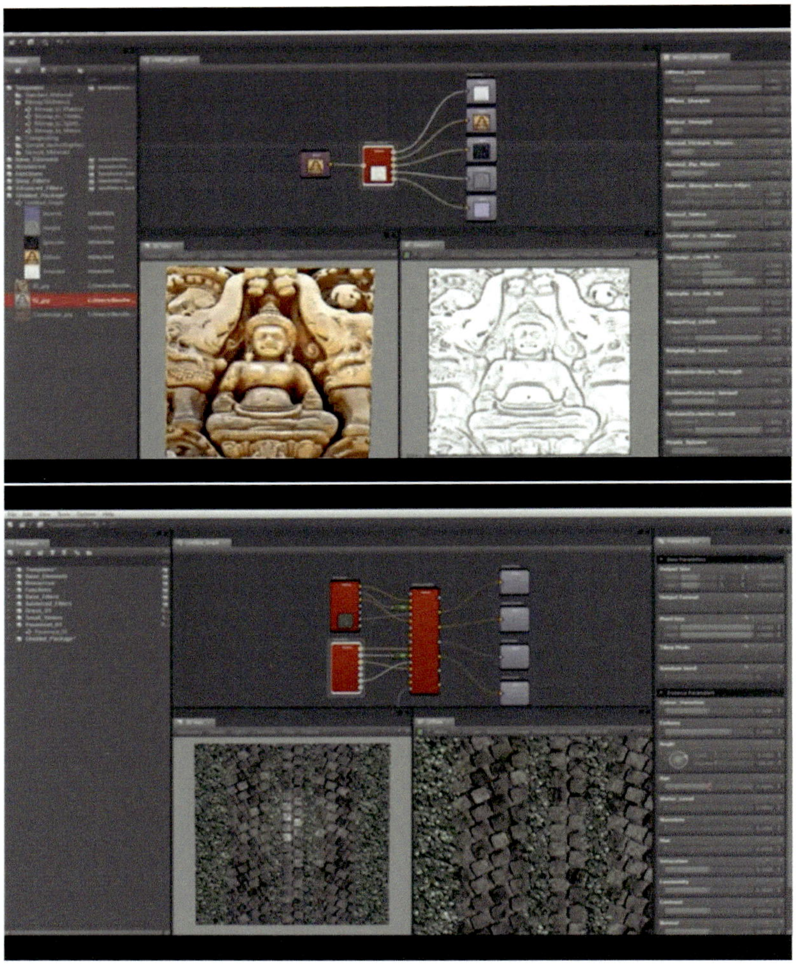

Figure 21.4: Substance Designer 1.0, June 2010.

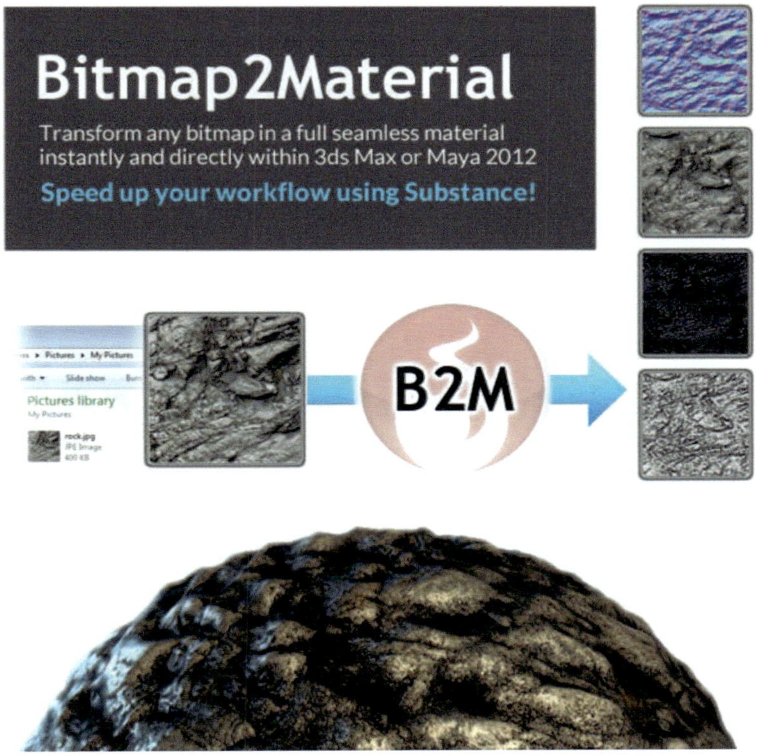

Figure 21.5: B2M or Bitmap2Material, released April 8, 2011. We sold 3 licenses on the day of release, and celebrated copiously! Version 1.5 came out only a little while later.

21.2 Technical demos

Namacius

A year after Bayou (see Chapter 14), the team, composed of Gilles Fleury, Jérémie Noguer, Sylvain Nouveau, Gaëtan Lassagne, Guillaume Cerdan, Raouf Béjaoui, and Benjamin Maréchal, tackled a large-scale demo, which took place in Clermont-Ferrand's cathedral. It was called 'Namacius,' a map for the game *Unreal Tournament*, by Epic Games.

Figure 21.6: The Namacius demo, made completely internally, was a map for the game *Unreal Tournament*. With the use of ProFX, the 233 textures on this map fit in a package weighing 270 KB instead of 257 MB for the same bitmap textures, compressed in DXT5.

The video can be viewed here: [31]. We also created a making-of: [32]

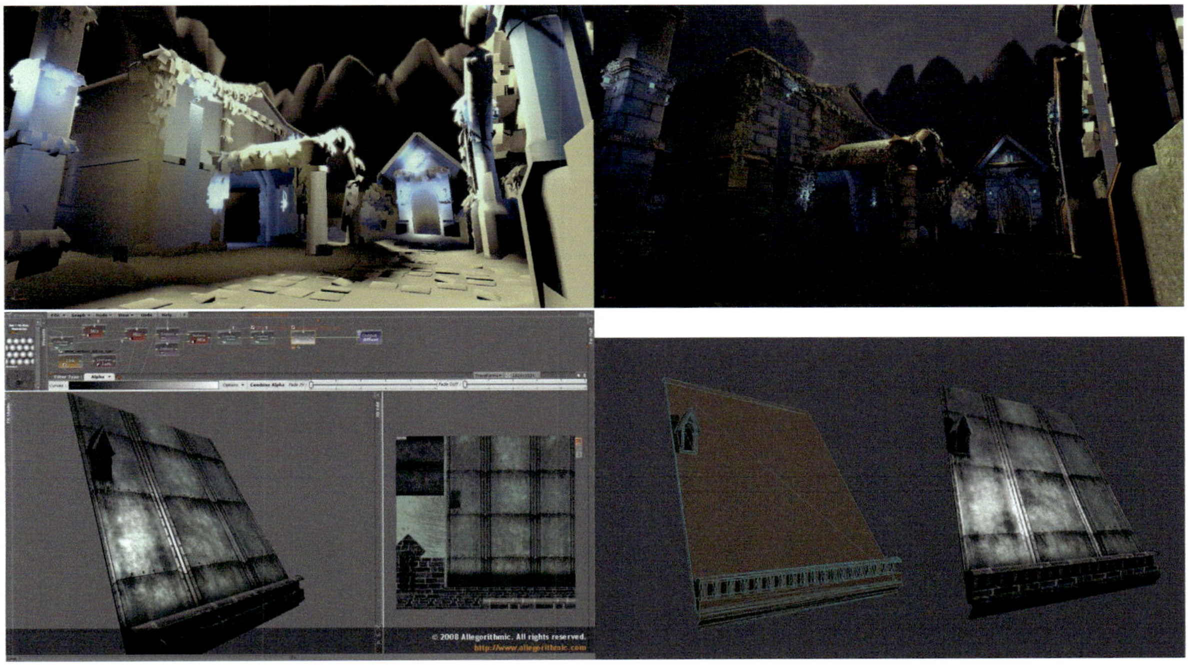

Figure 21.7: The Namacius demo: top right, texture input; top left, textures applied to bare 3D models; bottom, one of the demo's textures made using MaP | Zone.

Once again the goal of the demo, which was made in the second half of 2007 for GDC 2008 taking place in March in San Francisco, was to show the technical benefits of our middleware software ProFX, which allowed the 233 textures of the map to be contained in a package of 270 KB instead of 257 MB for the same bitmap textures, compressed in DXT5.

Airstream

Three years after the Namacius demo, and this time using the new Substance product range, the team created a new technical demo that in particular demonstrated what the integration of the Substance Engine within Unity could provide. Again, the idea was to illustrate an evolution of procedural textures and, after numerous creative brainstorming sessions, the team settled on the concept of an Airstream-type caravan, alone in a desert, whose textures could evolve (degrading, getting dirty) in real time, as in the case of the Bathroom demo that we'd created several years before (see Chapter 14). This was also a way to demonstrate the benefits of B2M (see the dedicated section, earlier in this chapter) in Unity.

The demo was presented quite successfully in 2011. It was very useful for our demos and presentations when talking to potential customers.

Figure 21.9: The notorious Rock Pillow by Jérémie Noguer, which he improvised during the Substance Engine demo in Unity, at GDC 2011 in San Francisco.

21.3 Conferences, trade fairs, and tours

This entire period was full of numerous trade fairs and conferences that we took part in, and the commercial tours which echoed them. In particular, the big events for us were the Game Developers Conference (GDC) and SIGGRAPH. Each event was an opportunity to present our new products, and to meet our community, our partners, and our competitors. The following images provide some photos of these events.

Ultimate texturing solutions designed to optimize the distribution process and 3D production workflow of tomorrow.

Tweakable environments in Unreal Engine 3

"As digital distribution is becoming more important than ever, the move towards procedural textures was a natural step for Funcom. After thorough evaluations we found Allegorithmic to be a professional partner with solid technical solutions. Collaborating with Allegorithmic has been a pleasure for Funcom."

Rui Casais
CTO

"One of the biggest challenges of this game was keeping the game size as small as possible. **By using Substance, we could increase the amount of high-quality content and optimize the download size by factor 10.** This technology is paving the way for F2P developers and gamers."

Frank Trygub
Founding Partner

Substance Editor from Substance Air

Dramatically reduce client size

Create hybrid, dynamic and lightweight textures

Boost your productivity

Integrated in

Unreal Engine Partner · Gamebryo · unity

Substance **Redux**

REDUCE THE SIZE OF YOUR EXISTING BITMAP TEXTURES BY 50%

A no-brainer solution for online games

At any stage of your game development, Substance Redux allows you to automatically reduce the size of your bitmap textures (DDS DXT) by about 50% without noticeable loss of quality ingame and without any impact on ingame performances.

A complete toolset

The Substance Redux *Editor* is a compehensive compression tool that can accept any bitmap format (TGA, BMP, PNG...) and compress any kind of maps (diffuse, normal, specular..) with a realtime visual feedback.
The Substance Redux *Engine* allows detailed texture map analysis and optimal compression schemes, and features an ultra-fast in-house DXT compression at runtime.
Plugins for Unreal Engine 3 and Gamebryo are available for a complete pipeline integration.

Some Substance licensees:

Funcom · Acony · Virtuos · the9 第九城市 · NCsoft · T3 Entertainment · Autodesk

Substance **Air**

CREATE SMART TEXTURES AND GENERATE THEM AT RUN-TIME

The unique solution 100% dedicted to texturing

Substance Air is the first hybrid texturing middleware solution that allows game developpers to create high-quality textures that can fit in only a few kilobytes and that can be generated them on the fly.

Create with Substance Editor

Substance Air includes Substance Editor, the first authoring tool entirely dedicated to texturing. Using a node-based interface with real-time 2D and 3D views, users can mix bitmaps, vector graphics and procedural elements. Its completely non-linear process allows to create lightweight textures with all the output maps needed for modern shaders (diffuse, normal, specular, etc) in just a few clicks.
Advanced users can create parametric textures that can be tweaked from any game engine and offer hundreds of variations from just one asset. The combination of Substance Editor with traditionnal texturing tools offers unlimited creative and workflow possibilities.

Generate on the fly with Substance Engine

All the textures created with Substance Editor are saved in a lightweight format that can go down to only a few kilobytes, allowing to create texture packages that can be up to 99% smaller than their bitmap equivalent. All outputs are then generated on the fly by the Substance Engine at install, loading or even run-time.

Contact us
Alexis Khouri
VP Strategy & Sales
alexis.khouri@allegorithmic.com
+33 (0)6 79 78 38 28

Allegorithmic
31 rue Gonod
63000, Clermont-Ferrand,
France
+33 (0)4 73 34 70 80
www.allegorithmic.com

allegorithmic

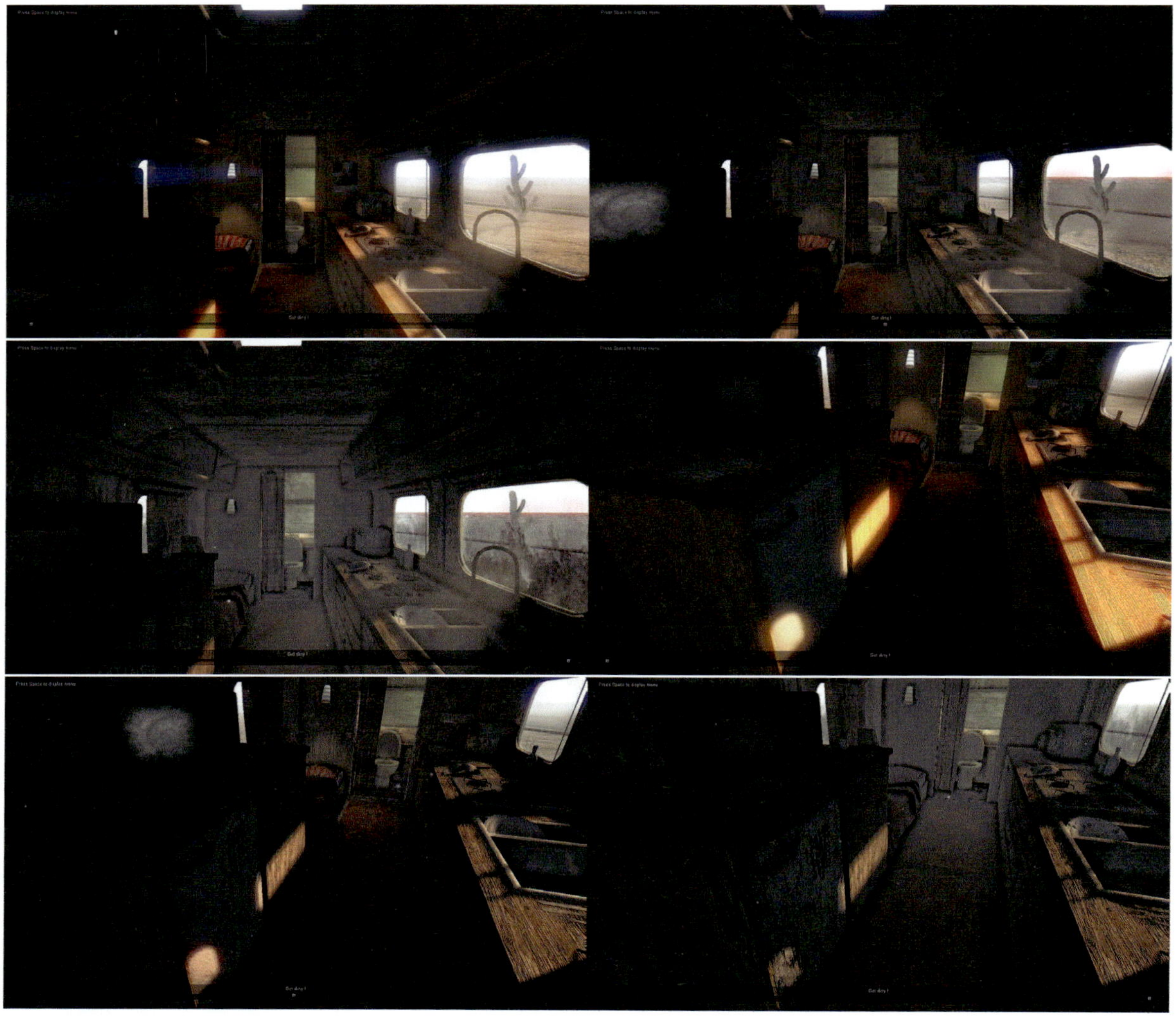

Figure 21.8: The Airstream demo was made in 2011, demonstrating the Substance Engine and B2M integration in Unity.

These conferences and trade shows were sprinkled throughout the development of our company, and allowed us to find our way into the economic fiber of 3D and video game development. Among these events, one in particular had a singular impact (see Chapter 24)...

Figure 21.10: GDC 2007. The team (Jérémie Noguer, Nicolas Wirrmann, Benjamin Maréchal, and Gilles Fleury) in the streets of San Francisco. The little meeting room we were renting with a banner dedicated to ProFX.

Figure 21.11: SIGGRAPH 2007. The team (Jérémie Noguer, Gilles Fleury, Thierry Frey, Sébastien Deguy, Cyrille Damez, and Benjamin Maréchal, crouching) in our hotel room, in August in San Diego. Bottom: well deserved rest for Benjamin Maréchal, Cyrille Damez, and Gilles Fleury.

Figure 21.12: GDC 2008, San Francisco. In these images we can see: the shipping label for our stand's materials (built in Montréal); before construction; the stand with an integrated meeting room and a monolith—one of the first times we significantly invested money, consequently establishing a notable presence; our legendary tag-line *'fullfill your stream'* didn't quite hit the mark; Gilles Fleury preparing the stand's computers; our meeting room and the inside of our stand; Jérémie Noguer and Benjamin Maréchal at the stand.

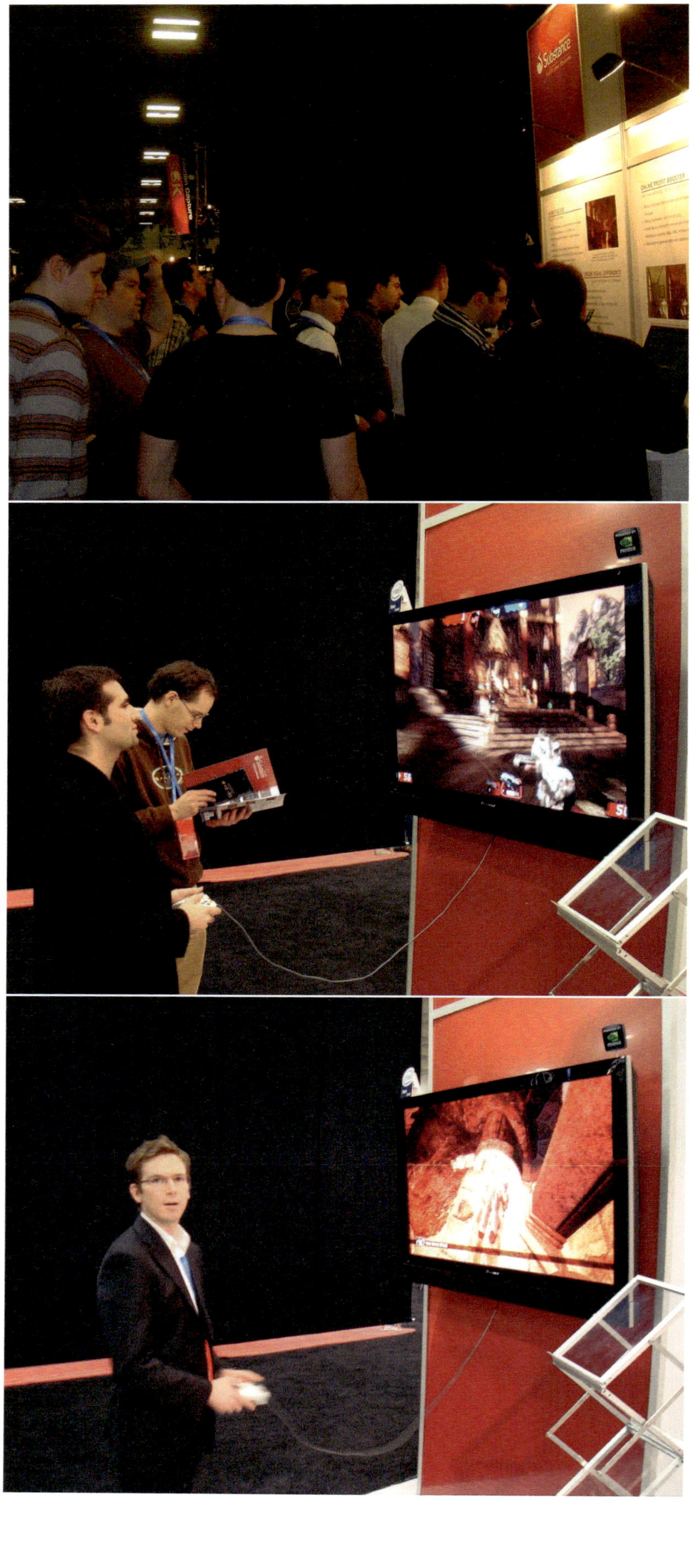

Figure 21.13: GDC 2008, San Francisco. From top to bottom: demos going strong; a surprise visit from Tim Sweeney, CEO of Epic Games (whom Alexis was ignoring superbly); for reasons I'm unaware of, I decided to wear a suit to a conference for video game developers...

Figure 21.14: GDC 2008, San Francisco. Charles Bauchet and Gilles Fleury lost in thought. Alexis, Thomas Bidaux, and me.

Figure 21.15: A talk during FMX 2008, in Stuttgart (organized by my friend and lifelong inspiration Jean-Michel Blottière, to whom we owe, amongst other things, the magazine TILT, the first magazine in France that was dedicated to video games, which was tremendously important to me as a child; I am very lucky now to count Jean-Michel as a friend!). I was scheduled to present just after Ken Perlin, one of my idols in the world of 3D, the creator of the noise bearing his name (Perlin noise). He'd participated in the creation of films like the original *TRON* and made a huge contribution to the field of 3D. It was such an honor to be able to speak right after one of the legendary names in 3D. My presentation was titled, 'Animated Textures—New Creative Opportunities Through Living Content.' On this occasion, we received the Deutsche Telekom Award for best innovation for ProFX. It was presented to me by Neil Trevett (see Chapter 16), Vice President of Mobile at NVIDIA.

Figure 21.16: Walking the Golden Gate with Alexis and Fred, after GDC 2009. Watching a 3D film with Fred and Cyrille.

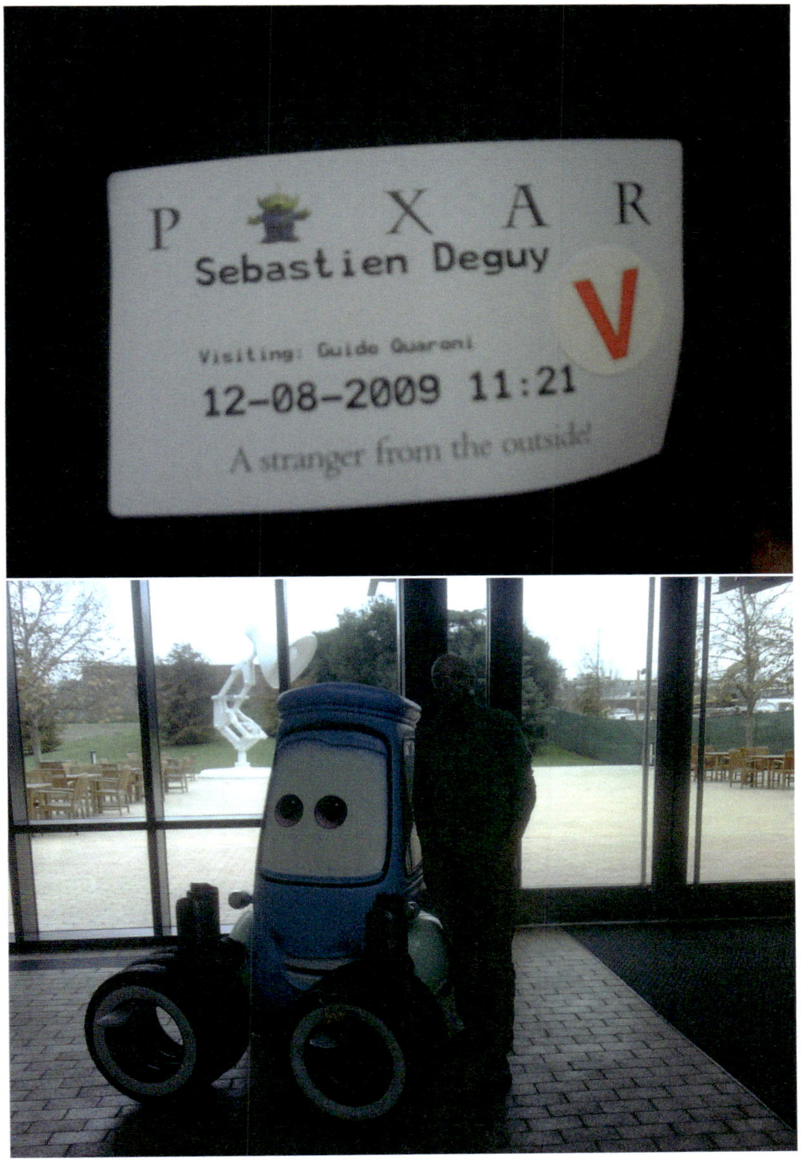

Figure 21.17: 'A stranger from the outside!' This was written on our Pixar visitor badges. I was lucky enough to be welcomed by Guido Quaroni on December 8, 2009, to present the latest developments from Allegorithmic. Guido was the technical leader for Pixar's internal tools. He also voiced... Guido, in the film *Cars*!

Autodesk again 22

22.1 Softimage XSI, 3ds Max, and Maya

The company Softimage wasn't yet part of Autodesk in June 2008, when we offered to integrate the Substance engine within their software Softimage XSI. Discussions went well with Dave Lajoie and Marc Stevens, Softimage's CTO, and the goal was to allow Softimage users to take full advantage of the power of parametric textures, thanks to native integration inside their 3D reference app, of what we'd announced as the successor to MaP | Zone: Substance Designer.

This was a fundamental pivot from our first attempt to bundle MaP | Zone with Autodesk tools, when we'd tried to sell our middleware (see Chapter 15): here, by contrast, we hoped to integrate the generation engine Substance Engine by default (the successor of TAON 3, which was at the heart of ProFX) within Autodesk's tools to encourage 3D artists to license our creative software Substance Designer (the successor of MaP | Zone)!

A few months later, and while we were still negotiating, Softimage was acquired by Autodesk, in October 2008. This changed things, removing an independent actor from the market. If we wanted to license our technology for integration in any of the 3D tools of reference, 3ds Max, Maya, or even Softimage, we had to go through one single company: Autodesk. And its head of Media & Entertainment division: Marc Petit.

Discussions were going well with all the divisions and product teams at Autodesk, both in Montreal at 10 Duke, on the banks of Saint Laurent, and in San Francisco, at One Market, on the bay. All the apps (see for example the series of images beginning with figure 22.2) went through this process, with the same idea: establishing a strong technical partnership with this formidable actor of our industry. I had a feeling we could find a way to collaborate.

DOI:10.1201/9781003534624-22

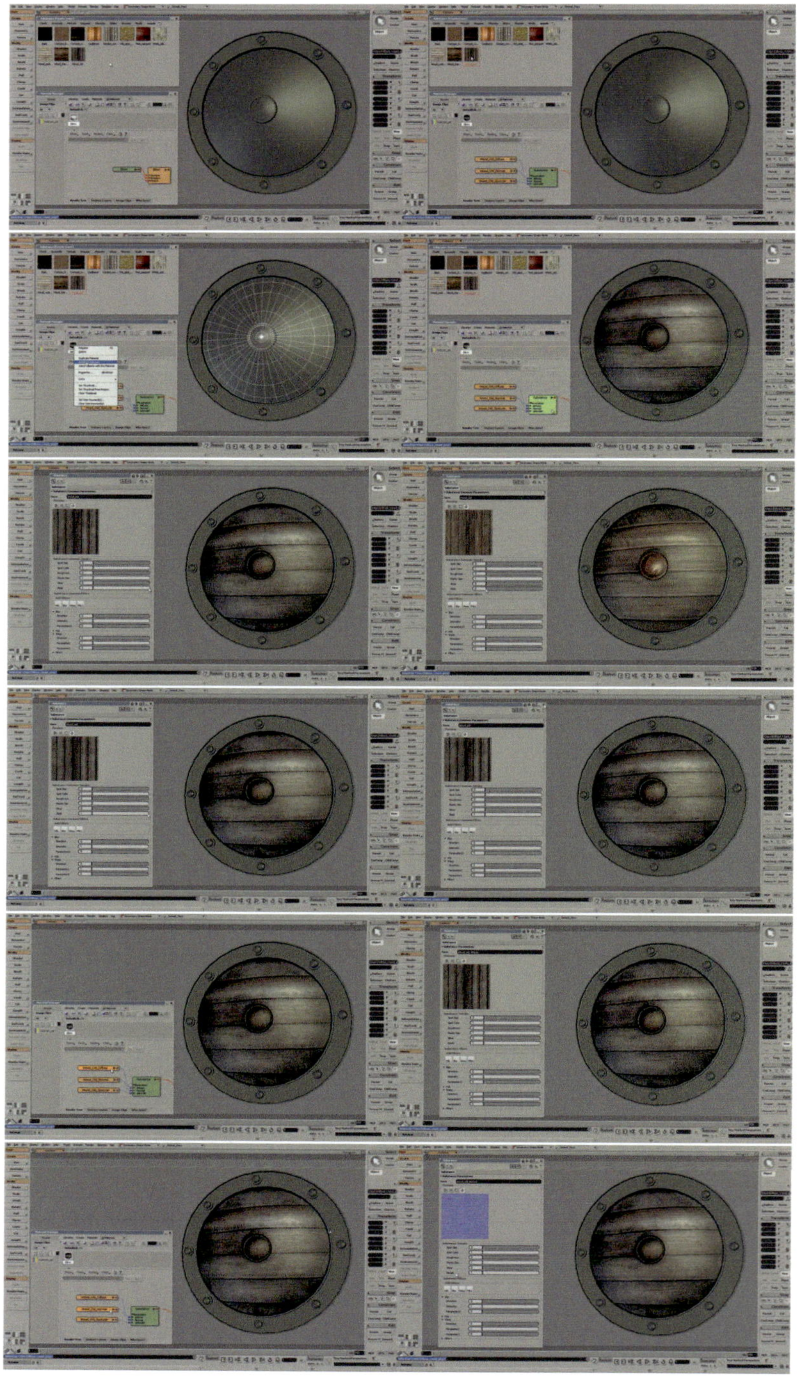

Figure 22.1: These images are proposition mockups for Softimage in the context of Substance Engine's integration inside Softimage XSI in June 2008, a few months before their acquisition by Autodesk. We see a library of Substance file presets, three textures (diffuse, normal, specular) automatically connected to a material graph in Mental Ray, and from the fifth image, a change made directly in Softimage XSI with exposed parameters of that texture. The retained material convention was 'diffuse, normal, specular': we were not yet in the PBR era (see Chapter 26).

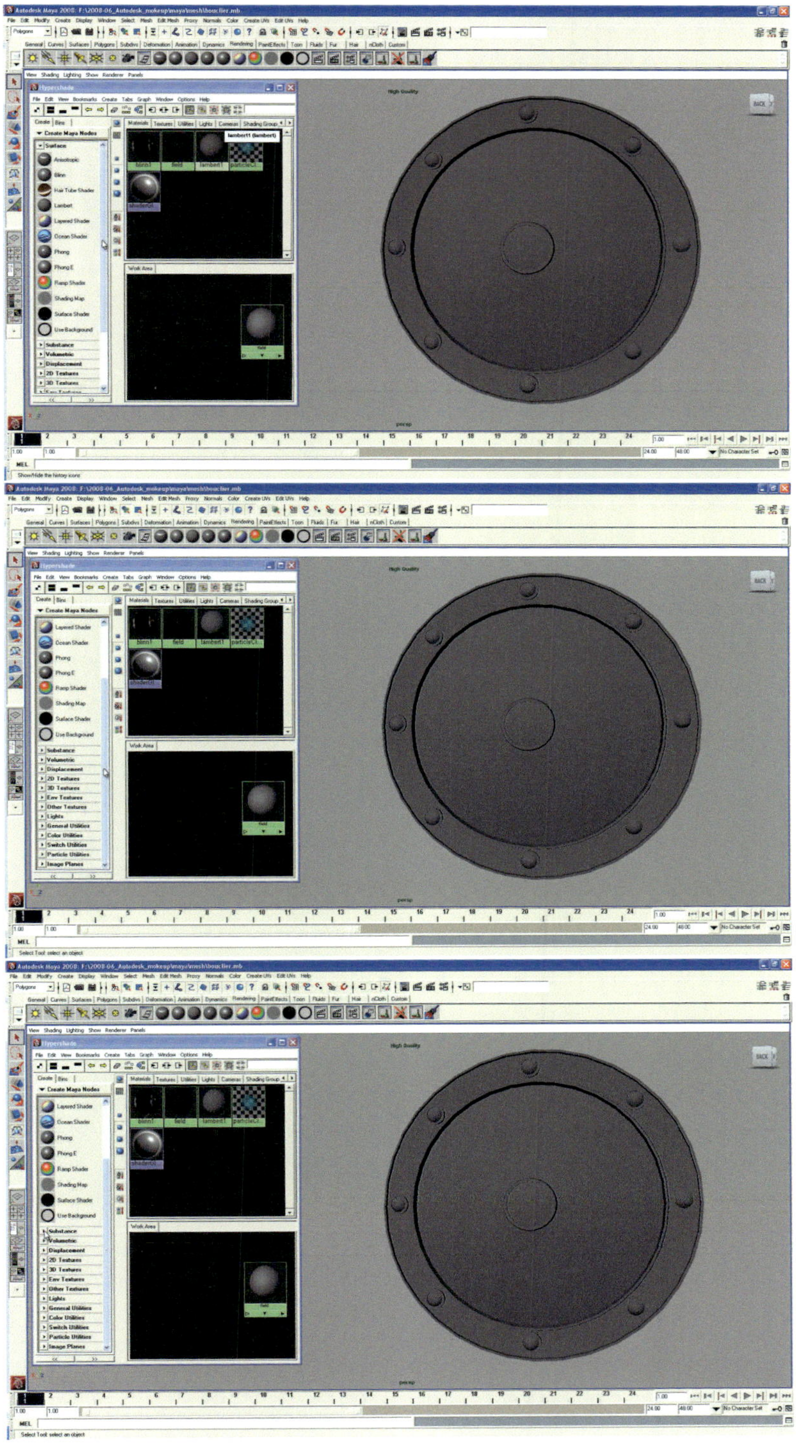

Figure 22.2: (1/4) These images are proposition mockups made for Autodesk to integrate Substance Engine inside Maya, in June 2008. We see a library of Substance file presets, three textures (diffuse, normal, specular) automatically connected to a material graph in Hypershade, and a change made directly in Maya with exposed parameters of that texture.

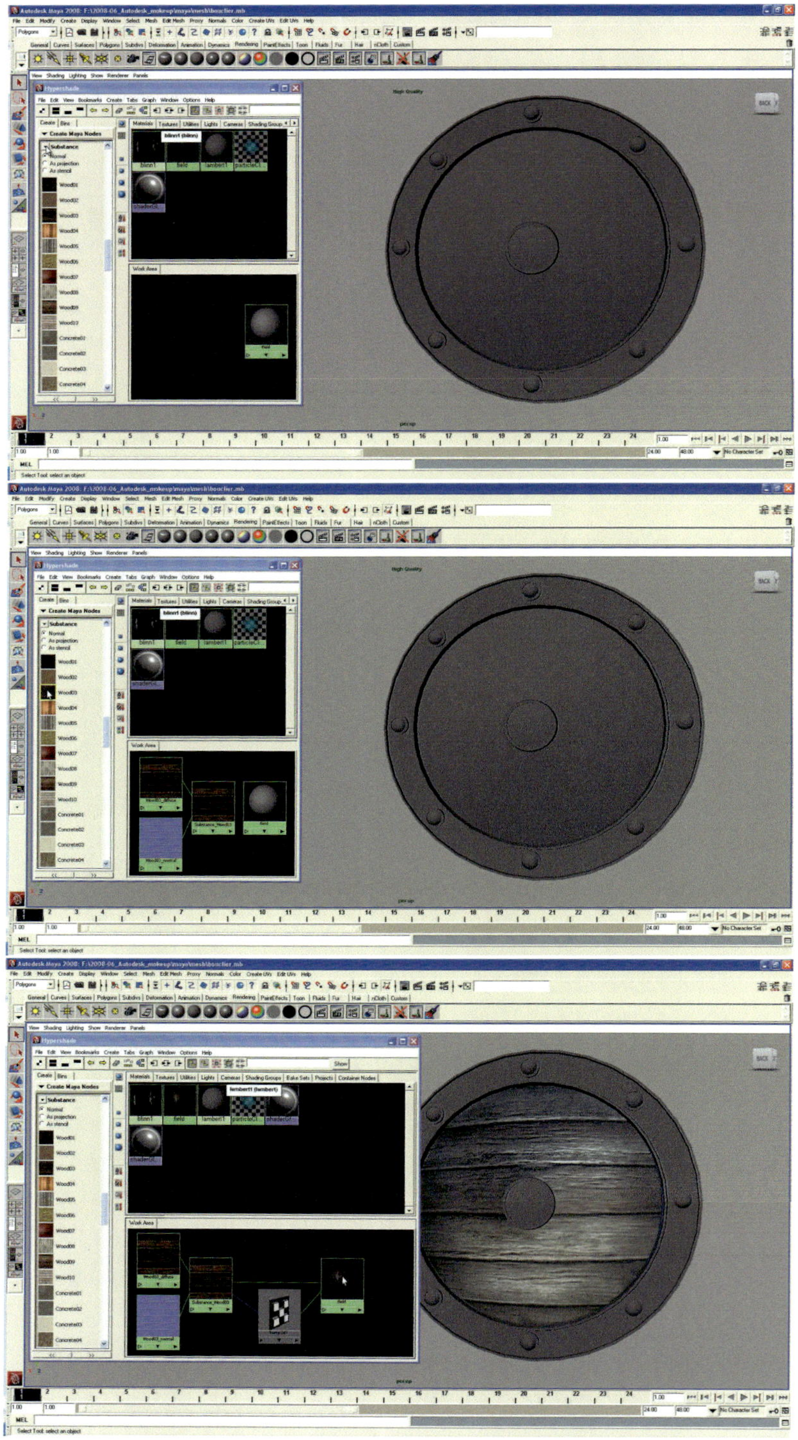

Figure 22.3: (2/4) These images are proposition mockups made for Autodesk to integrate Substance Engine inside Maya, in June 2008. We see a library of Substance file presets, three textures (diffuse, normal, specular) automatically connected to a material graph in Hypershade, and a change made directly in Maya with exposed parameters of that texture.

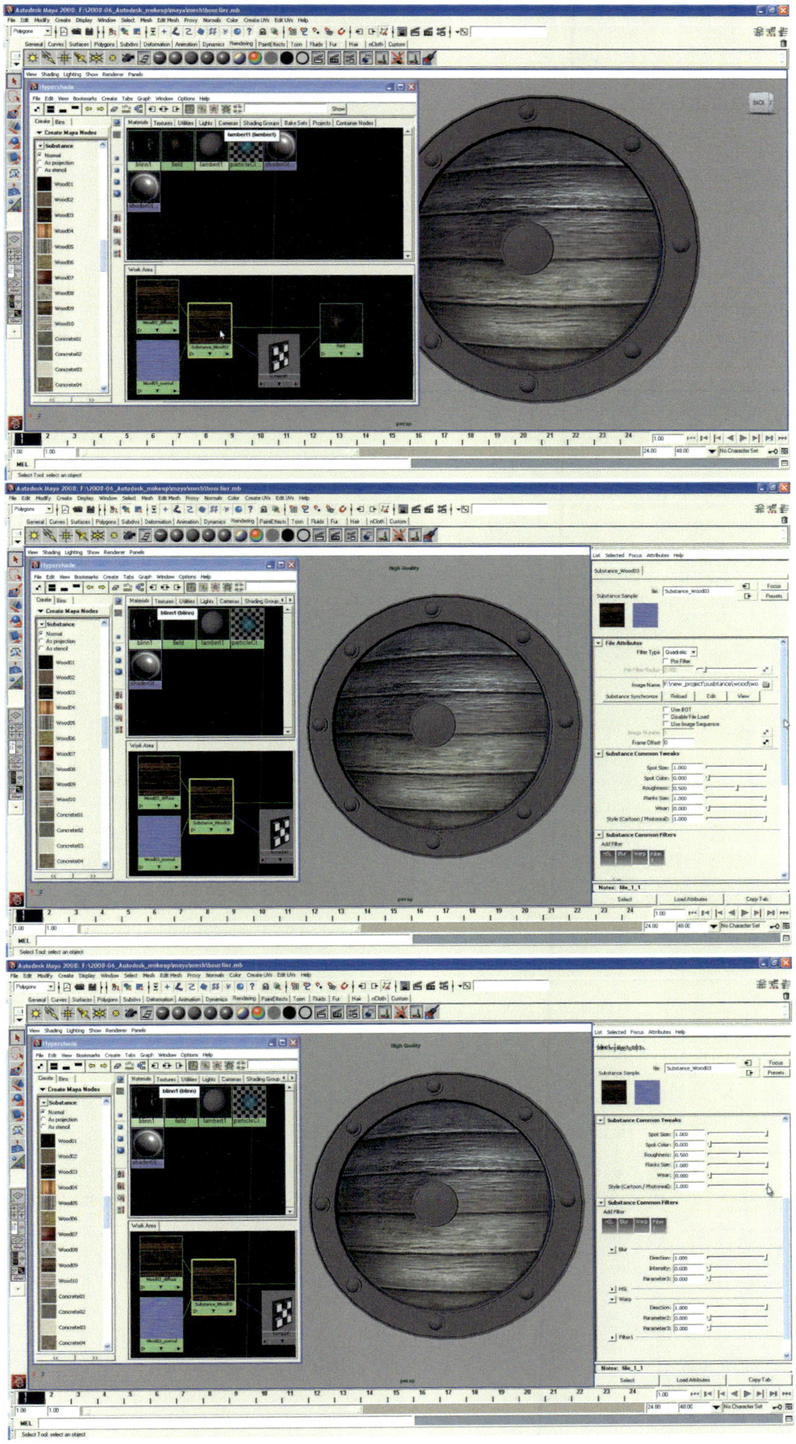

Figure 22.4: (3/4) These images are proposition mockups made for Autodesk to integrate Substance Engine inside Maya, in June 2008. We see a library of Substance file presets, three textures (diffuse, normal, specular) automatically connected to a material graph in Hypershade, and a change made directly in Maya with exposed parameters of that texture.

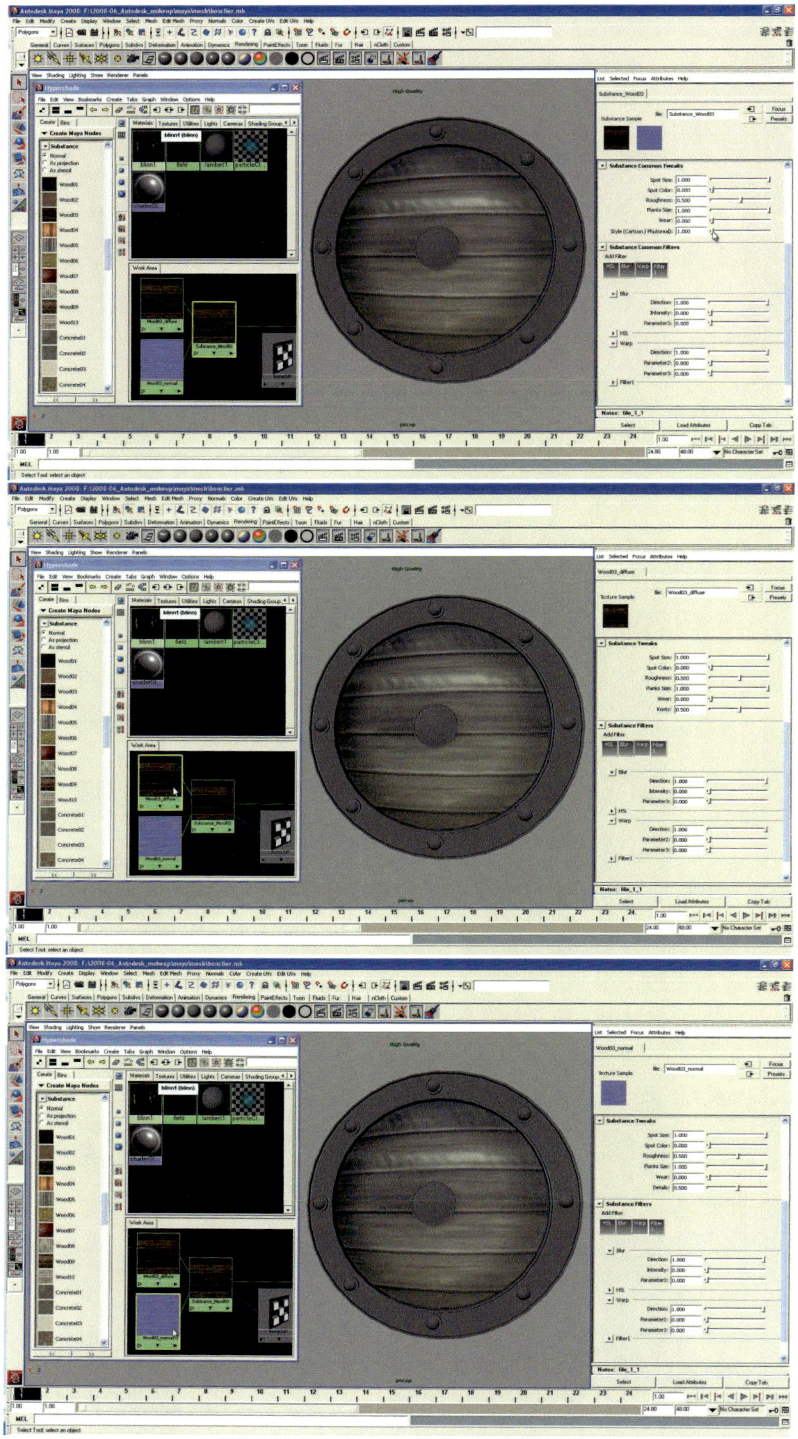

Figure 22.5: (4/4) These images are proposition mockups made for Autodesk to integrate Substance Engine inside Maya, in June 2008. We see a library of Substance file presets, three textures (diffuse, normal, specular) automatically connected to a material graph in Hypershade, and a change made directly in Maya with exposed parameters of that texture.

22.2 Flame...

It was finally inside the Flame software that we tested out our first integration and licensing plan at the very beginning of 2009. This major step for Allegorithmic's development happened in large part thanks to Philippe Soeiro,[1] who was the Lead Product Designer in charge of Autodesk's compositing products, specifically Flame,[2] and Diana Colella, who was the Director of Product Development in charge of Flame, would cut short the endless, internal stagnant discussions pushing for a global license. Diana ended up imposing a license for Flame only, as a starting point: "There's no time for this bullshit, we need to move forward!" Philippe, for his part, was a visionary with a unique strength of character.[3] He wanted differentiation for his tool which was attacked on all sides by solutions that were simpler to access, and that required less investment than Flame, both financially and in terms of a learning curve.

Flame had just integrated a new 3D compositing engine, and Philippe wanted to use 3D textures and effects inside this tool, feeling that this addition could add a great deal of graphical richness. In a sense, this integration within an app like Flame represented the successful continuity of what we'd started a few years earlier with MaP | Time, an After Effects plugin for motion graphics, for compositing and visual effects (see Chapter 11). Our work had come full circle.

1: Indeed, it often takes THE person, the visionary early adopter with enough influence to get things moving, especially in big companies which have a hard time working with new startups that move quickly and need to be responsive. This notion of tiered adaptation in the context of innovation is perfectly described in a book by Geoffrey Moore, *Crossing the Chasm*[33] (I acquired and immediately devoured this edition as soon as it came out in 2009).

2: Flame was a high-level tool dedicated to compositing and visual effects. It was used by all major special effects studios and required very high-end hardware configurations. The 'Flame artists' were some of the highest-paid artists in the VFX industry, because they made the final touches to films, often working directly with the film director, crammed into a small, windowless room. Their time was therefore very valuable and their mastery of the tool had to be perfect to meet the needs of directors live.

3: The association of Philippe Soeiro + Diana Colella was explosive (in a good way) and allowed us to arrive at something concrete.

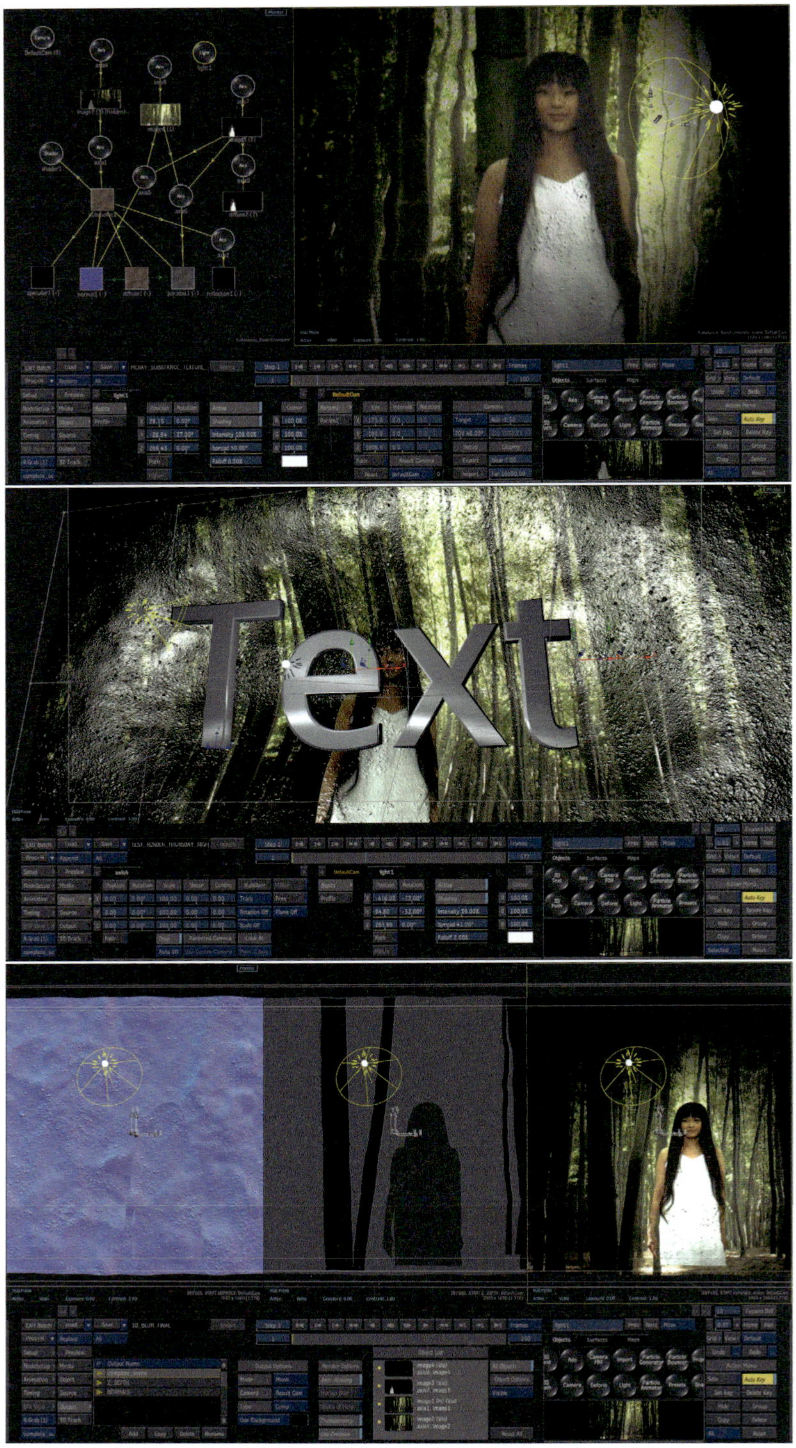

Figure 22.6: Substance Engine integration in Flame in action, allowing for 3D visual effects that were rich in. . . textures.

Figure 22.7: A series of visual effects made with Substance inside Flame.

22.3 ... and all the others

One successful integration led to another, and the trust between Autodesk and Allegorithmic grew. As one contract ended we'd sign another, until we ultimately signed a global agreement allowing Autodesk to integrate our technical bricks in their present and future tools.

All these contractual discussions were the source of my first gray hairs. Due to a lack of legal expertise in these areas in the immediate Allegorithmic circle, I had to be the one to manage all discussions and negotiations directly.[4] This was a totally new universe for me, and I had to learn quickly. Which were the elements of acceptable language, and what were the limits of terminology that couldn't be exceeded? Concepts like governing laws, representations and warranties, liabilities, indemnifications, change of control, right of first refusal,[5] source code escrow, grants of licenses, IP rights, upgrades versus updates, termination, consequences of termination, infringement, limitation of liabilities, assignment, severability, and even force majeure... All of this had very specific meanings, and all of this had to be negotiated. Some aspects had deeper implications than others, notably those for which we'd accept some level of responsibility and risk.

4: Here, some advice from lawyers at Dassault Systèmes, as well as from Réjean Lapointe, proved invaluable. Réjean also introduced me to an American lawyer, specializing in intellectual property, with whom I spent numerous hours on the phone trying to decipher legal texts I had received.

5: And it had no place in a commercial contract: it was an investor's right, not a partner's right. Nonetheless, I had to put in considerable effort to get rid of first drafts of some of these contracts...

During this period of discussions, I spent some troubled nights trying to understand these concepts, and anticipating and evaluating the possible consequences going forward. An unintentional, seemingly trivial error might result in a total loss of value (if we gave away the whole appeal of the company without necessarily even realizing it), or crashing in flames in the case of litigation (if, for example, we were to distribute and sell code we didn't own (IP infringement)): in both cases, this would have been the end of the company.

But we did manage and, although imperfect, these contracts would survive throughout Allegorithmic's existence. The experience I'd acquired was useful for years to come, while I played an active part in contract acquisition.[6]

6: I admit I never imagined that this would be my role, and I was happy some years later when we put in place a dedicated and highly skilled team to do the job (see Chapter 35)!

During these years of discussions, integrations, negations, and first successes, the question of Autodesk acquiring Allegorithmic naturally came up.[7] However, I had the impression that the focus was more on our technology than our products, and we had not yet proven our worth. We still had many things to build... Even though their interest was much appreciated and I considered the idea, it was not the right moment,[8] nor necessarily the right choice of partner.

7: Especially encouraged by John Hutchinson, who was our big supporter inside Autodesk. We got along particularly well, and he did everything in his power to help us out and push us in the right direction. He liked the idea of us joining the Autodesk group, and I had some discussions on the matter with M&A Autodesk teams in San Francisco (in addition to my overall discussions with Marc Petit in Montreal).

8: The world was hit by a full-blown financial subprimes crisis, and this had an important impact on our results and on my reflections. We had to once again pull in new funds (see Chapter 23), which was what made us consider the offer of this industry heavyweight. The fact that Dassault Systèmes and Autodesk were rivals complicated the situation...

22.4 Custom development for Flame

The relationship of trust we'd developed with the Flame team overall, and with Philippe Soeiro in particular, led us to a new opportunity at the end of 2008, on which I positioned Allegorithmic through our presence and discussions in Montreal: Flame's development team wanted to evaluate a product proposing new features and visual effects, like atmospheric effects, particles, bump/displacement mapping, edge detection, and other graphic elements necessary for the mastery of 3D tools. The Autodesk team was limited by the number of hires they could make, but they could use the budget for consulting/work for hire. People who were able to master these subjects weren't easy to find, and I proposed that Allegorithmic should be the company to develop these new features. We had internal specialists who were capable of creating what they needed. Philippe accepted my offer, and we began the project.

Here was a new 'special project' for Allegorithmic, and even though it borrowed some of our more seasoned developers for a little while,[9] it was for a very high-level task which would allow Allegorithmic to stay afloat. Additionally, I used the pretext of this project, and its associated benefits, to carry out a series of recruitments. The gamble was that once this service project for the Flame team was done, we would have the means to keep the talent and enrich our permanent team. This bet could be won either through a significant increase in revenue during this period, or by raising funds, which seemed increasingly inevitable.

The project took place between the end of 2009 and the beginning of 2011, and allowed us to hire additional developers like Benoît Mayaux, Alexandre Chassany, and Stéphane Guy, all three coming from gaming studios based in Lyon,[10] and who went on to spend a lot of time on site in Montreal,[11] to carry out work directly within the offices of Autodesk.

9: Removing them from the development of our own tools: this was a classic danger I discussed in Section 10.7... But we were ready to take the risk at this stage of Allegorithmic's development, as we were in dire need of the revenue.

10: I would use the 'Lyon network' on several occasions to find talented developers like Benoît, Alexandre, and Stéphane, and even Sylvain Paris, who joined us in July 2009 and who would become the lead developer on Substance Designer. I was helped by Pierre Deltour, ex-Technical director and co-founder of Widescreen Games, a Lyon game development studio which unfortunately ceased its activity at the end of the 2000s. I had a lot of faith in Pierre's judgment when it came to the technical quality of the developers, and he would always refer me to people of great personal qualities, equally happy to see them join a new adventure after the closure of Widescreen Games and many other studios in the region.

11: We went so far as to rent an apartment in Montreal for Allegorithmic, so that we could house the personnel who had to spend a while there.

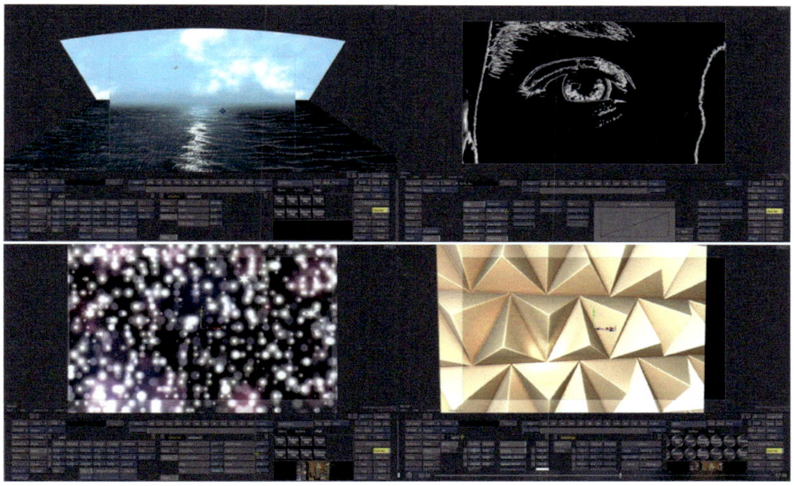

Figure 22.8: Some examples of 3D visual effects we developed for Flame, as work for hire.

A second round of investment 23

Despite a few commercial successes, the impact of Alexis, and the increasingly rapid development of our products, this period was complicated to manage. We were investing a lot, without yet seeing a sufficient return that would allow us to move up a gear, or even to ensure the survival of the company...

2008 saw the whole world hit by a historic financial crisis, which for us translated into a very poor turnover for 2009 (see the graph in Chapter 25). The future was uncertain, and Dassault Systèmes didn't want to place more money into Allegorithmic by themselves; this encouraged us to look for other investors, with the aim of a second round of financing.

23.1 Sofimac and new BSPCE

And so we began our search, ramping up our efforts to make contacts and present the company, mostly in the Paris region, with funds that expressed lukewarm interest in meeting us. Few of these organizations knew anything about 3D, and even less about our very specialized domain ('Procedural textures ... ?'). The meetings all ended with the same feedback—a refusal—justified by our lack of presence on the market (we hadn't yet concluded our deal with Unity at that time, see Chapter 24), a technology that was difficult to understand, a product line that wasn't yet very mature, the fact that we operated within distant, uncontrollable markets, and generally working within conditions that weren't favorable.

Only one investor expressed interest: Sofimac, an investor in capital risk based in Clermont-Ferrand and in Italy. Laurent Carrio, who had worked in this structure for a while, put us in contact with Philippe Vuagnat, who managed several funds supported by a European body that wanted to help regional projects. Sofimac had obtained a matching contribution from this organization with the goal of acquiring a significant number of stakes in companies from Auvergne.

Sofimac's investment committee considered the Allegorithmic project risky. Regardless, the constraint imposed on their investment meant that our Clermont-based company[1] represented a good opportunity for them. We had numerous discussions with them and ultimately convinced them to invest in us. We had at last found our first investor in this new round.

1: One of the few in the region at that time, and one which was developing real technological innovation.

This round of investment would keep Allegorithmic afloat and relaunch our activity for our next major period (which would include a significant pivot point, see Chapter 26); it would take place in three stages, in 2009, 2010, and 2011.

The first step consisted of creating a pool of BSPCE[2] for employees, at a fair value; all participants around the table—namely Sofimac, Dassault Systèmes, and longstanding Allegorithmic shareholders—wanted to see this happen. The BSPCE makes it possible to provide employees

2: *Bon de Souscription de Parts de Créateur d'Entreprise*, essentially a form of stock options.

DOI:10.1201/9781003534624-23

with stock options that they could opt into at any point, and if the company appeared to be growing in value it would be possible to sell those options.[3] They were the most practical tool to set up this employee participation, and were starting to become increasingly popular in France. And so in 2009 we created this pool of BSPCE and distributed them to employees who had been part of the company for a certain length of time.[4]

3: This opportunity occurred for the first time nearly 10 years later, in 2017; see Chapter 39.

4: I'll note here that Alexis, in order to demonstrate his faith in the company to our investors, immediately bought up 100,000 euros ofBSPCE, half of this paid for with (all of) his savings from his previous career, and half paid for by a loan acquired at an extremely high rate of interest. That is commitment, and then there's *Alexis-level* commitment...

In 2010 and 2011, we negotiated the precise terms of Sofimac's investment. This involved many complex negotiations with numerous lawyers around this or that critical point within the contracts,[5] and I spent a lot of time considering the impact of specific details—throughout the night, sometimes. But finally, Sofimac entered Allegorithmic's capital.

5: See for example the information on the right of first refusal, in Chapter 18, which again resurfaced here. Sofimac wanted to be added to this particular right, and I had little other option than to accept once again... Overall, certain clauses slipped past me, and their consequences would only surface a few years later, see Chapter 39.

This round of investment would be completed by a very special business angel: Cédric Littardi, who was introduced to us by Thomas Bidaux.

23.2 Thomas Bidaux

Alexis and I met Thomas Bidaux for the first time during Game Connection, in Lyon, in 2008. He worked at NCSoft, a big Korean online video games development company that had opened a European division in 2004, based in Brighton, in the United Kingdom (see Chapter 20). Thomas was in charge of developing a branch and assembling a team dedicated to finding opportunities for NCSoft games in Europe, but also of analyzing the European game development market to find possible gems that NCSoft could then import to Korea, or even publish in all their target territories.

With this objective in mind, Thomas[6] was also looking into technologies that could have a positive impact on online games. After what we'd accomplished with a game like *RoboBlitz*, and now with our packaged offer around ProFX, we were on his radar.

6: Thomas was very analytical, with a deep enthusiasm for data.

We met during the event, and Alexis and I presented our technology and its potential benefits to Thomas and Diane Lagrange, who was also part of NCSoft in Brighton. The technology was young but Thomas and Diane liked it, enough that they bought licenses for ProFX.

We also got along very well with them, and developed a friendly relationship which allowed us to discuss a wider range of subjects, about which they gave us excellent advice. Thomas also provided game-related advice to a man called Cédric Littardi, who would very shortly also offer us his support.

23.3 Cédric Littardi

Cédric Littardi was at times described in the French press as the 'Patron Saint of Geeks' [34]. In the 1990s Cédric Littardi had possessed the visionary awareness to anticipate the massive impact that anime[7] would have on the world; he therefore founded Kazé, the first and most significant import and distribution company for this genre of Japanese

7: Japanese cartoons.

films, TV series, and mangas. When we met Cédric, he'd recently sold this company.

Cédric wanted to invest a part of his profits from selling the company to support projects in the sector that he was absolutely passionate about: the universe of imagination, and everything that could be described as 'geek culture' overall—he was very familiar with board games, role-playing games, anime, and manga, but he was by his own admission, lacking in knowledge of video games. Nonetheless, this was an area in which he wanted to invest and involve himself.

And so Thomas was Cédric's specialist in the area of video games. And, knowing that Allegorithmic was looking for investors, Thomas spoke to Cedric about us. We needed to finish this new round of investments and were looking at all possible sources.[8]

8: At this time, I made a lot of presentations to investment funds and business angels.

The meeting took place in the Kazé premises in Paris. Cédric welcomed us into his office which was overflowing with DVDs, CDs, books, manga, and figurines; this very much had the effect of transporting us into a rich, fantastical universe—Cédric's universe. And it was a very welcoming universe, a great change to the sterile meeting rooms of the many investment companies we'd visited. Cédric was a very impressive person—he was physically imposing, first of all, and also somebody with very strong opinions. He was a true fan of the domain he worked in, and possessed a degree of generosity that I've rarely seen. He was, overall, an inspiration for me in many ways.

The meeting was pretty short; we quickly moved on to the presentation of our products, and of our company itself. Cédric tends to judge the person in front of him, and he judges quickly. We spoke for a few minutes, and he asked us a few questions—and then he told us that he wanted to invest. He had faith in Thomas's opinion and, visibly, he'd decided that Alexis and I were trustworthy. This was a great opportunity for us, and we'd potentially found Allegorithmic's next investor!

Cédric would go on to play a very special role throughout the life of Allegorithmic, through his advice and the opportunities he presented us with, and through his unconditional support.

In retrospect...

Sometimes, the existence of a company can very easily go one way or the other. In 2009, having reached the end of the funds invested in 2007 by Dassault Systèmes, we were in great financial difficulties. After numerous unsuccessful searches for investors wishing to participate in this new round of investment, we were finally fortunate enough to be able to count on Sofimac, and the fund that they were obliged to invest in the Auvergne region—one of the supports set up to stimulate regional and national businesses, which here worked exactly as intended. Without this constraint on the investment fund, Sofimac would certainly have refused to help us, and we would have had to redefine our project.

Meeting Cédric, our business angel, was an unexpected stroke of luck, and the result of the relationship of trust that we'd built up over several years with Thomas Bidaux. Cédric in turn trusted Thomas's opinion, and very much saved the day for us—even before the co-investment he made with Sofimac in 2010 was finalized. In mid-2009, while we were experiencing some short-term cash flow difficulties, Alexis met Cédric in a bar in Paris, and mentioned our problems to him. Without hesitation, Cédric took out his checkbook, and wrote a check for 100K euros—without Alexis even asking him. Alexis ran to the bank to deposit it, and we were able to pay our teams that month. . .

Unity 24

24.1 Unite

I first heard about Unity from Thomas Bidaux (see Chapter 23). During a phone call in 2008, he told me, "You should take a look at Unity; they're getting a lot of attention at the moment. If I had to bet on a game engine, it would be Unity." They were notably present on Mac and the engine seemed perfect for iOS game creation. The App Store for the new Apple iPhone had become El Dorado, and Unity was selling a tool that allowed 'gold mining' game developers to try their luck.[1]

Holding my Blackberry in one hand and grabbing a pen, I made a note on some scrap paper, in very large letters: "Unity: take a look!"

With a little research, I soon found that the game engine seemed interesting and exciting. It appeared to be uniquely positioned to attract the booming iOS mobile game development market. Providing a 3D engine (for games or other experiences) to as many people as possible was a dream of Dassault Systèmes, who had previously acquired Virtools, a French game engine, sometime before. But Unity seemed to be the engine of choice for developers, mainly because of its presence on Mac,[2] which was the obligatory entry point, imposed by Apple, to compile games on iOS, and the whole increasingly popular ecosystem on iPhone and iPad. For its part, Virtools had been in difficulty lately: a large part of the team had left following the acquisition, notably after they'd been required to move from their Paris office to the general headquarters of Dassault Systèmes, out in the suburbs of Paris, which many in the team had perceived as cold and too 'corporate.' The tool was struggling to progress and Dassault Systèmes was torn between an open or closed system—and consequently missed this wave of gaming popularity.[3] Unity filled that gap,[4] with immense success.

I first met the Unity team in 2009, during an event the company organized in San Francisco, the aptly named 'Unite.' I signed up for the conference, as did more than 350 others; over several days, I attended the conferences, training sessions, and other events expertly organized by the Unity team. I was very impressed by the connection between the team and their users and by the exceptional atmosphere throughout the event. Everyone was part of an adventure that was unique and particularly promising; game developers had a tool that met their needs, and the Unity team was ready to listen to their requirements, train them, and provide them with everything they needed to succeed. It was clear, seeing them, that the Unity team found it difficult to believe that this dazzling, worldwide success was really happening to them. Originally from Copenhagen in Denmark, the members of the team were trying to remain in line with their values and culture, and to invest all their energy and good humor into their project.

During this event, they announced that Unity would be free for students. This had a big impact on the room and inspired me to do the same

1: The big winners of the gold rush were of course the tool makers; this analogy always plays well with investors. The iPhone, released in 2007, created an ecosystem of applications, in which games were among the biggest winners. A new market was developing, and many people dreamed of conquering that market with a game that would be a huge success. These mobile games didn't necessarily require large development teams—sometimes, even one developer could be enough, if they had the right idea, and the right tools. Unity was very clearly in the right place at the right time to support this movement in mobile gaming.

2: I always saw the developers of the game engine, in Copenhagen or San Francisco, working on Macs, which was extremely rare in the world of 3D. The CTO and co-founder of Unity, Joachim Ante, was also one of the first legendary developers in the gaming world to start out on this platform.

3: I'd say, in retrospect, that this was the point that Dassault Systèmes started to lose interest in the world of video games, and by extension in Allegorithmic.

4: Without even really noticing their competition from Virtools; they simply advanced toward their goal.

Figure 24.1: Unite 2009, the conference organized by Unity, took place in San Francisco, at Fort Mason, on the edge of the Bay. I took this photo on my way to the conference, admiring the city's incredible natural scenery.

DOI:10.1201/9781003534624-24

thing several years later (see Chapter 38). At the conference, I met the company's three co-founders, CTO Joachim Ante, CCO (Chief Creative Officer) Nicholas Francis, and CEO David Helgason. They were people with very different backgrounds and personalities, but all three were incredibly passionate about their work and somewhat stunned by their current success.

I had the opportunity to present to them for the first time the technology that Allegorithmic was developing; they liked what they saw, and understood the potential benefits of our technology for mobile and web games, where the size of data was critical. We briefly discussed the idea of a licence, or potentially even more—though I explained that we'd recently raised money from Dassault Systèmes, and I wasn't interested in anything more for the moment. And so our discussion turned toward a possible partnership. Our technology could allow mobile game developers to compress the size of their textures, or even customize their game textures using their procedural aspect at runtime. Joachim in particular asked a lot of technical questions and expressed doubts about our ability to obtain a sufficiently fast and portable generation engine, as Unity was not only aiming for iPhones but wanted to target all platforms on the market. We then spent some time thinking about how we might integrate our technological bricks inside their engine, and how to integrate Substance Engine in particular, both in the editor and in the Unity Engine, which was distributed with every game, allowing the game to run.

24.2 License

After several months of demos, visits and technological developments,[5] we managed to establish an agreement for a Substance Engine license.

5: The technical side of things turned out to be very complex, both for the integration to be good enough in the editor, as well as making sure that the integration within the Unity Engine, the component which is included within games, was robust and efficient enough to effectively run on all hardware platforms supported by the Unity Engine, particularly on the internet browsers.

Unity bought the right to integrate Substance Engine in Unity Editor and Unity Engine by default (that is, their users wouldn't have to pay for this component). For our part, this deal provided us with not only a financially attractive license, but also access to an exponentially growing community of 3D artists; we'd focus on selling licences for Substance Designer, the newest version of our procedural texture creation tool, to this group. This was a unique opportunity to reach a market that had a particular interest in using our tools, thanks to the native support of our textures in the game engine they used. We did ultimately find many new users this way, though this didn't necessarily change our situation from a financial point of view. Nonetheless, this was an important step in Allegorithmic's development and the use of our tools within the gaming world.

Many interactions followed between the two development teams, some simple, some more complex. We ensured continuous follow-up between Clermont-Ferrand and Copenhagen, handled in particular by Christophe Soum, Eric Batut, and Alexandre Chambriat, who didn't always have an easy time trying to reach a level of integration, performance, and portability that satisfied Unity.

In retrospect...

Figure 24.2: Alexis and I having dinner with Nicholas Francis and Joachim Ante, two of the Unity co-founders, in December 2012, in Copenhagen, Denmark.

Like the license that we implemented with Autodesk (see Chapter 22), the structure of the Substance Engine license we set up with Unity constituted a pivot for Allegorithmic—a change in our business model. With this opportunity, we used the integration of Substance Engine within Unity as a gateway to game developers using this game engine, hoping to sell them our procedural texture creation tool Substance Designer. A Substance Designer license only costs a few hundred dollars, but the large, and growing, number of Unity users meant that our sales volume could potentially be much higher than we could make by selling the technology directly.

And this is exactly what happened: this deal with Unity marked our first big commercial success with our texture creation tool Substance Designer, and with B2M (see Chapter 21). The symbiosis was so effective that we even discussed the possibility of acquisition in 2011, just as we'd previously done with Autodesk a little earlier (see Chapter 22). For the same reasons, I shut down these discussions.

This pivot toward a new business model for Allegorithmic would become even more pronounced a few years later, when the world of game development needed our tools even more (see Chapter 26)...

Summary of progress up to mid-2011, and conclusion of this period

25

The period from mid-2007 to mid-2011 was difficult and can be called the 'weak point' in Allegorithmic's history. After a strong start thanks to the investment from Dassault Systèmes (see Chapter 18), which allowed us to get out of the garage and settle into a place that we loved right in the city center of Clermont-Ferrand, and to grow a team with talent from all over France, exploring specialized and structured subjects (see Chapter 19), the objective difficulties that we encountered in selling our products and our technologies were emerging rapidly, and would increase throughout this entire period.

In every area we were striving to get the business off the ground and position the structure well with a view to the profitability that we wanted to achieve quickly (after all, the investment and the loan received with the capital of Dassault Systèmes had its limits, which we would see emerge very quickly.[1]) Inspired by the licensing of our technologies to NVIDIA in particular (see Chapter 16), we tried to reproduce this approach with other major companies in the world of 3D, successfully so with Autodesk and Unity (see Chapters 22 and 24 respectively). These major deals were particularly important steps for Allegorithmic, because they of course brought revenue and 'fuel' into the machine, but also because they validated our work and our technologies, firmly positioning them among the more effective middleware tools in the industry.

1: Our strained cash flow very nearly found itself deeply in the red when, during a routine VAT check, a particularly zealous tax inspector (the type you see in storybooks. . .) pointed out one of the invoices from one of our content providers based in Shanghai: at the very bottom of the invoice, in very small letters, appeared the three letters 'BVI.' He asked if we knew what that meant, and we admitted we didn't. And so he told us that it signified the British Virgin Islands, a small state which appeared in the list of tax havens identified by France and several other countries. This was potentially serious because a tax could be applied to what we'd paid to get the content we ordered in Shanghai, which had been billed to us via this buffer state. . . and this tax could ruin us! Fortunately, after a few exchanges, and because the content produced was not only resold in France but internationally, everything was finally validated and we didn't have to pay any penalty (this would also be a source of pride for the management of Allegorithmic throughout its existence: almost perfect financial management, officially recognized as such).

These licenses also allowed us to pivot over several years toward a business model which would make the sale of texturing tools, rather than the sale of middleware, the heart of our activity and our future success. Our integration within Unity would be the first to bring revenue from sales of Substance Designer to game developers using this engine.

We would also, as is often the case for a young technology company, sell development time on order, or custom content production produced by our internal artists. In the case of licensing to Autodesk, for example, we developed a range of high-level graphics components for the Flame system (see Chapter 22).

Finally, we did everything we could to try to sell our products and set up from scratch a team dedicated to commercial action, led by Alexis Khouri, who demonstrated his importance more and more. The result of our countless discussions and strategic reflections fueled by hundreds of meetings with video game developers and other figures in the world of 3D, all over the planet (particularly in Asia, see Chapter 20), was that we decided to develop one particular product rather than another, then finally decided to pivot toward the sale of authoring tools, which seemed more accessible to us, and potentially more profitable than middleware.

So, after the complicated years 2007-2009, during which revenues didn't seem to progress amidst the backdrop of the 2008 crisis which affected the whole world, our customers included, the figures looked better in 2010 and 2011. That last year, we achieved 'our first million,' which was a very significant step in our development. Our products, in particular B2M and Redux, without being particularly elegant, sold well, bringing

DOI:10.1201/9781003534624-25

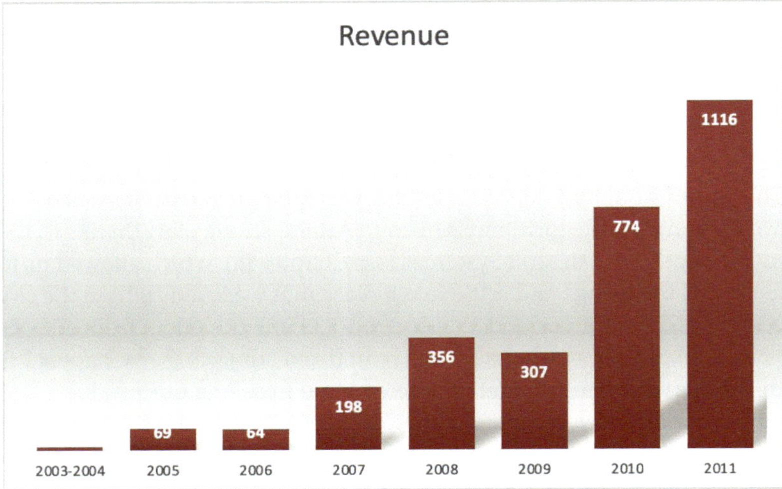

Figure 25.1: Allegorithmic's revenue between 2003 and 2011. The progression was exceptional! We made our first million euros in 2011, which beautifully marked the end of this middleware period, a complicated time. It's notable that the subprimes crisis of 2008 can be seen on the curve, with 2009 results appearing 'flat,' but the curve goes back to its exceptional growth trajectory in 2010, as if the 2009 bump had never existed. I think our revenue, which came mostly from abroad, started climbing again at the same time as that of countries which were quick to recover from the crisis. This was a big advantage from having international reach when it came to our sales.

us around 700K euros; we could also add around 100K from the sale of various services, as well as our major licensing agreements with Autodesk and Unity, bringing a total of approximately 300K.

This symbolic step of one million euros, however, still didn't cover our expenses, and we weren't yet profitable. This accounting reality, mixed with our unceasing ambition, seemingly confirmed by signs from the market that our pivot was the correct approach, pushed us to consider the need for a new round of financing and investment. The time wasn't quite right for that, as seen in Chapter 23. The sub-prime crisis of 2008, which was felt for many years in France, had made investors cautious. This was a very complex period, and this was the first time that we had heated discussions with our investor Dassault Systèmes.[2] However, we managed, through a lot of effort and stress during these years, to find investors who were sufficiently confident in the project to follow us. This meant we were ready for the next stage of accelerated growth.

2: The new representative of Dassault Systèmes on the board of Allegorithmic was Didier Gaillot, and he was very picky about our financial management which, I must admit, wasn't my strong point at that time. He pressed me a lot on the solidity of the structure, and when results were strained, discussions also become strained. . .

3: Which I relate here because it would have an indirect role in the evolution of the structure, as it determined that Alexis, rather than I, would relocate to California, which played a big role in the exponential commercial development that we would experience during the next period of the company's life.

A Personal Pivot. . .

At the same time as this pivot for Allegorithmic, another more personal pivot occurred,[3] when my wife Laëtitia announced to me in June 2010: "I'm pregnant!" Wow.

The previous few days had been a roller coaster already. I'd been planning to relocate to California; for several months, my wife, my team, and I had been preparing for the move. And then, three days earlier, in his office at Dassault Systèmes, Pascal Daloz had told me: "I don't think it's the right time for you to move to San Francisco. The company isn't ready." Wow, shock. I wondered how I was going to tell Laëtitia about this change. . .

I tried to convince Pascal, telling him about my objective to base myself in San Francisco, so that I could spend a large part of my time with my customers. I explained to him that the team in Clermont-Ferrand was very independent, and that I already traveled constantly—I made a transatlantic trip every month and a half on average; I spent about half my time in the US, so this ultimately wouldn't change much for our teams... I tried everything, but nothing worked; he only answered: "It's too early, the team isn't ready."

I'd known for a few months that I had to change my way of working—I was exhausted from my incessant trips between Clermont-Ferrand, Paris, and the rest of the world (Europe; Asia—Tokyo, Seoul, and Shanghai in particular; and lots of time in the US and Canada, most frequently the West Coast and California). I could no longer stomach the smell of the Teoz rail service from Paris to Clermont-Ferrand, whose jolts I could anticipate with my eyes closed.[4]

4: There was no WIFI in Teoz trains. One of my 'catch-up' moments was reconnecting to WIFI in my apartment and sending out batches of emails in response to the floods of messages I'd received while disconnected.

Since 2006, I'd been out of sync with two of the three pillars of my 'ordinary' life (here I'm excluding friends and family): when I was in Clermont-Ferrand, I was with my teams but not in contact with my customers nor with my wife. When in Paris, I was with her, but far from my teams and my customers (even if there were already more customers in Paris than in Clermont-Ferrand, at that time there were still very, very few). When I was in California, I was with my customers and partners, but far from my teams and my wife... It would have been good, for both my physical and mental health, to be able to combine two of these three ingredients wherever I was.

Laëtitia worked in Paris, and couldn't easily find something to do in Clermont-Ferrand. The team was well established in Clermont-Ferrand, and was developing well there. And of course, I couldn't move my customers... The only remaining solution was for Laëtitia and me to relocate as close as possible to my customers, to California.[5] I discussed this with my teams, who understood and supported this choice. Cyrille even told me, "It seems inevitable to me."

5: Laëtitia loves the US, has worked there in the past (in New York), and liked the idea of expatriation while we were still young. There is so much to learn from an experience abroad. We were torn between Los Angeles and San Francisco, and it was ultimately on the latter that we'd set our sights.

And yet, "It's too early." The words of Pascal were still bouncing around inside my head. He'd explained why, and I understood the rationale—but I couldn't turn back now! Laëtitia had left her job and we were in the process of speaking to lawyers in California to set up visas. We'd announced the move to our families. How could I turn back now? I think it's fair to say that when I told Laëtitia that our investor didn't support the move, and had strongly advised me against it, the news was very difficult to accept.

And, as was often the case when Pascal told me something that I didn't agree with... he was right. The very day after he'd told me his views, a small conflict emerged within the teams, nothing particularly serious but a small indicator that echoed what Pascal had said. Indeed, this may not have been the right time.

And then, as is often the case with life and its sense of irony, three days later Laëtitia told me she was pregnant. Wow—we'd make a little French person, then!

And ultimately it was Alexis who finally settled in California, as we will see in Chapter 28... And here, a new period began for Allegorithmic, for Alexis, and for me, now essentially a Parisian.

Part VII

2011–2015

PBR and Substance Designer 26

26.1 Physically based rendering (PBR)

In 2010, during that year's SIGGRAPH conference, Naty Hoffman, who was then at Activision, made a presentation in the form of a masterclass that would have an explosive effect on the entire video game industry: "Crafting Physically Motivated Shading Models for Game Development" (see [35]). He developed a BRDF ('bidirectional reflectance distribution function,' a function that describes the surface of a material) which possessed properties that were very close to reality (the term 'physically based' was used in this context); this BRDF was called 'Blinn Microfacet,' and it permitted very realistic simulation of the interaction of any type of light on a large number of surfaces, the surfaces characterized by different variables of this BRDF. Moreover, it accomplished all of this at a very low performance cost on modern machines, so this BRDF was suitable for real-time use in game engines.

This approach promised to allow developers to make game shaders much simpler and, if textures respected the 'PBR'[1] industry standard, it would avoid any major concerns about where to place lights to highlight this or that material; with this new approach, all surfaces and all materials defined using dedicated textures would naturally interact correctly with light sources positioned within the virtual environment (a digital sun, for example). Following Naty's presentation, all the technical directors from all the game studios wanted to know more about this technique.

1: PBR standing for 'physically based rendering.'

One of the first studios to adopt this approach, at the insistence of Sébastien Lagarde, was the Parisian studio DONTNOD, who in 2013 released the game *Remember Me*, using a modified version of the Unreal Engine 3 game engine, and adopting the PBR approach. The game was very impressive for, amongst other things, its graphic quality, and was the first game to use this new rendering format. The rest of the industry would ultimately follow this example—but other studios first had to adapt to this new texture format, and Allegorithmic took advantage of this giant pivot in the industry to position ourselves accordingly.

Figure 26.1: PBR, also a beer brand. This was a popular joke amongst game developers at the time.

26.2 The video game industry pivots toward PBR

Naty Hoffman's article on PBR and the example set by *Remember Me* didn't go unnoticed, and the heads of R&D at the most advanced game studios around the world quickly understood the advantages that PBR techniques would provide: a higher-quality render,[2] that also required less work from artists, who no longer had to circumvent the limitations of the non-PBR techniques that had been used until that point. The question of whether to adopt PBR techniques was not difficult. The only disadvantage was that this required studios to alter their existing

2: But really—*significantly* higher. . .

DOI:10.1201/9781003534624-26

production workflows, and begin creating textures respecting the PBR standard,[3] and nobody really knew how to do this.

3: It was thanks to textures that this new method was adopted; more specifically, it was necessary to move away from textures defined by characteristics such as 'diffuse,' 'normal,' and 'specular' to textures defined by 'albedo,' 'normal' (this remained the same), 'metallic,' and 'roughness.' Few artists understood how these new maps worked...

This meant turning away from techniques that artists had used and mastered for over a decade, and which predated the GPU-accelerated cards manufactured by NVIDIA and AMD, amongst others, to a new approach that nobody was yet trained in. Studios therefore turned toward the industry for tools that allowed them to create these next-generation textures.

And so here we were at the back of the room, waving our arms and shouting, "Yes, over here! Over here! We know how to do PBR! Take a look at Substance Designer!"

Jérémie, Alexis, and Alexis's team had been visiting customers, particularly in California; again and again, they provided feedback that all their customers were talking very insistently about integrating PBR. With this in mind, we needed just a few hours to adapt Substance Designer to this new paradigm. New exports were implemented (set up by Gilles Fleury, Gaëtan Lassagne, and Nicolas Wirrmann), and Cyrille added a new visualization shader...[4] and *voilà*.

4: Cyrille designed the shader to use the same format as Unreal Engine, so we could ensure perfect continuity between textures produced in Substance Designer and Unreal Engine.

The studios we met with were astonished that we'd been able to perfectly, and almost immediately, adapt Substance Designer to their new pipeline, and they were also impressed by the maturity of the tool. By this point, we'd already been developing it for a few years, and it showed: particularly considering that it was the first PBR tool on the market, it was very robust and complete.[5] We didn't know it yet, but this shift in the industry, this new appetite for PBR, would potentially mark the biggest pivot in Allegorithmic's history. Though, of course, this would take more time than anticipated... Our frustration grew month after month, as the studios didn't reach out to us. But, fortunately, one studio in particular did get in touch: Naughty Dog. But before our story alongside this legendary studio began to unfold (see Chapter 27), we had a little surprise...

5: We had the advantage of all the years we'd spent developing FX-Maps, then MaP | Zone, then finally Substance Designer, with the freedom to explore and to search for a clear application of our technologies; even though users had been hard to find, the product had continued to evolve without interruption throughout this time, and little by little we'd created an advanced, mature tool, in our little hidden laboratory in Clermont-Ferrand, biding our time. With the needs of PBR, Substance Designer's moment had arrived, and the tool was ready.

26.3 *Assassin's Creed Unity*

I looked at the parquet floors with longing... The new game by Ubisoft, *Assassin's Creed Unity*, which came out in November 2014, was absolutely magnificent. It was one of the first games to adopt PBR—and to do it well. The game's graphics were breathtaking, the materials in the game particularly so. Notably, I found myself staring at the parquet floors of French palaces and mansions, and thinking: "These are exactly the kinds of textures that Substance Designer is perfect for! Why isn't Ubisoft using our tool? It's ideal for PBR... "

And then the team in charge of the game posted a huge art-dump[6] on the website Polycount.[36] And here, we received a shock: the artists revealed that these parquet floors, as well as many other textures in the game, actually had been made using Substance Designer! We hadn't known that a little team from Ubisoft, based in Annecy,[7] had implemented Substance Designer into their pipeline of asset creation.

6: An 'art-dump' is a massive publication by several artists, in a short time, of 2D and 3D artwork created for a particular game.

7: Amongst them an artist named Vincent Dérozier, who would go on to become an absolute master of Substance Designer.

This was a wonderful surprise. This art-dump marked the beginning of a growing wave of questions around Substance Designer, this new tool that the artists from Ubisoft were showcasing, on the specialized website Polycount. The rumors were spreading: "Substance Designer is the future of PBR texturing, Ubisoft used it on AC Unity, Naughty Dog is currently using it for *Uncharted 4*," and so on.

The AAA video game industry had its eyes on us.

In retrospect...

Assassin's Creed Unity was the first game to make significant and successful use of Substance Designer with the goal of producing textures in line with the industry's pivot toward PBR. This art-dump by the Ubisoft artists who'd used the tool had taken us by surprise, and caught the attention of the industry overall, which now turned its attention our way .

The PBR revolution in the video game world was, in retrospect, the external event that placed us at the center of the map. It was potentially the most important industry pivot in the history of Allegorithmic. The tide had therefore started to turn for us at the end of 2014, and we were well positioned to take full advantage of this pivot for some time afterward, particularly thanks to all the work carried out with Naughty Dog (see Chapter 27).

Naughty Dog, alpha-site for Substance Designer

27

27.1 First contact

The game studio Naughty Dog is responsible for creating masterpieces like *Crash Bandicoot*, *Jak and Daxter*, and *Uncharted* (and more recently, the series The Last of Us). Part of Sony since 2001, Naughty Dog is a legendary studio, the 'Pixar of video games,' generally considered to be the best and the most unique studio in the world. Everything they do is scrutinized, observed, and then copied. Whatever tools they use will likely be adopted by the rest of the industry. So when we were contacted in 2011 by Tate Mosesian, a visionary 3D artist from Naughty Dog, who was curious about our work, we were more than a little excited.

Tate was particularly interested in B2M, our texture generation tool using photos as input. Naughty Dog bought five licenses for B2M following these discussions—a modest beginning. And yet for us this was exceptional, as we didn't usually sell multiple licenses for a product in one go. And even more so because this was, after all, Naughty Dog.

The relationship developed, and at the beginning of 2013 we gave them an in-depth presentation of Substance Designer, along with special training for Brad Smith, an exceptional technical artist who ultimately went on to become a grand master of Substance Designer, and who would have a significant impact on me.[1] Jérémie Noguer subsequently dedicated a big chunk of his time, in Los Angeles, to helping Brad and the rest of the Naughty Dog team integrate Substance Designer into their pipeline, and to get the most out of it. He also collected requests for features to pass on to the Substance Designer development team, headed by Sylvain Paris, in Clermont-Ferrand.

1: When we visited the Santa Monica premises of Naughty Dog, I had two big shocks when I arrived at Brad's cubicle: first, I saw Substance Designer open on one of his two screens—and back then it wasn't a widespread tool, and seeing it there, used by such a prestigious client, was startling. Second, a few minutes later Brad showed me what he'd been working on, and what he'd managed to create with the tool—notably including absolutely perfect procedural rock textures, something I'd tried to produce during my thesis work over ten years ago, without success. That failure, at the time, had pushed me to integrate other processes in the middle of a texture creation pipeline, particularly the influence of physical forces, to reproduce some natural effects. This work led to Simon Brunel's internship in 2004 (see Chapter 9), which in turn led to working on Substance Painter a few years later (see Chapter 29). Brad clearly hadn't needed these effects, and what he was able to produce using only what was present in Substance Designer was breathtaking. His rock materials were absolutely perfect. In retrospect, I'm glad I didn't possess Brad's talent; if I had, then Substance Painter, which then came to fill what I thought of as a gaping hole in Substance Designer, wouldn't have been necessary.

Figure 27.1: Brad Smith, at his desk in the offices of Naughty Dog, using Substance Designer, in January 2013. Brad was a maestro of the tool and pushed it to its limits.

DOI:10.1201/9781003534624-27

27.2 Alpha-site

In August 2013, we took an important step and established a very significant middleware contract,[2] with the original goal of reducing the size of the game so that it could launch faster once installed on the Sony PS4.[3]

2: Christophe Balestra, the co-CEO of Naughty Dog, and a former demo-maker of a very high standard, called Alexis before finalizing the contract to make sure that we would provide them with the maximum level of support. He was afraid we might simply disappear, as small companies like us sometimes did, at that time…

3: An objective 'à la *RoboBlitz*' once again, see Chapter 13.

And so, from mid-2013 to mid-2014, Naughty Dog and Allegorithmic worked together, in a strong partnership. It was a period of almost 'co-development' of the next version of Substance Designer, version 4. We considered the studio to be our 'alpha-site'; they had access to everything we developed in real time, and tested our tools in production, while giving us feedback on what they needed from us. This was the best way of learning, and of developing the tool, so long as what they asked of us remained generally applicable enough that we could then propose it on a larger scale, once the new features had been integrated into the tools, and therefore tested on a full-scale production of the size of a game like *Uncharted 4*.

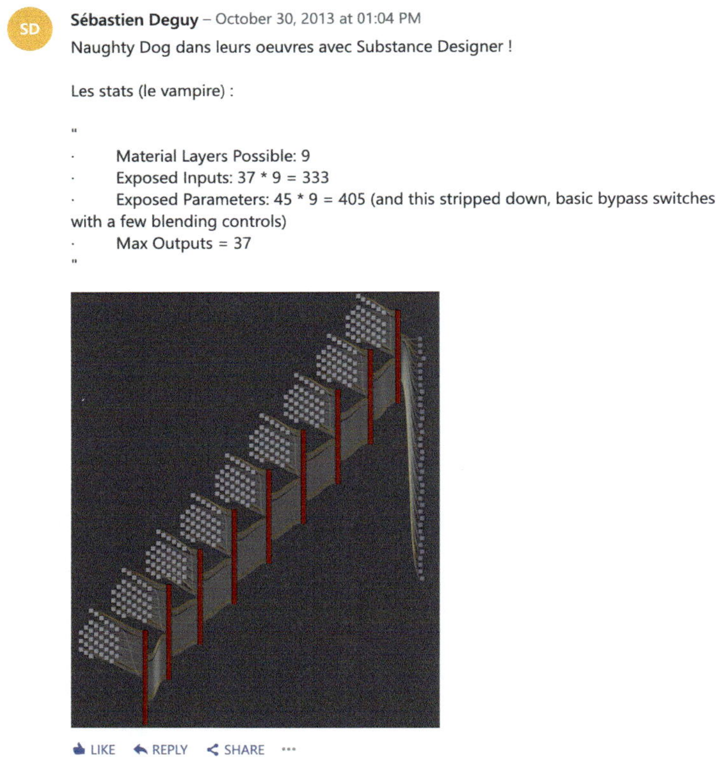

Figure 27.2: In this image we can see a huge Substance Designer graph, an extreme test case for the tool sent to us by Naughty Dog. This was the type of advanced use case that we wouldn't have been able to imagine without seeing the tool in the context of real production, which allowed us to sufficiently develop the tool so that the larger industry would be eager to adopt it.

Jérémie and Alexis spent about two days a week at Naughty Dog, to provide them with a sufficient level of support.[4] Alexis in particular tried to ensure a good connection between Naughty Dog and the outsourcers[5] they worked with, notably Virtuos in Shanghai. These outsourcers had to integrate Substance Designer into their production process, so that they could provide the right textures in the right format (in this case, the Substance format) to Naughty Dog in California, who would integrate these assets into their game. Alexis traveled to China many times to help with this process, coordinating with Gilles Fleury who was based in

4: This was following the creation of our Los Angeles branch: Alexis was already based there, and Jérémie soon moved there permanently as well. So did Nicolas Liatti a little later.

5: The outsourcing companies in the video game world are there to produce content, like on an assembly line—they'll create 3D objects, textures, animation, and so on for the studios who hire them. Depending on the needs of the developers and the phase of production for the games, these outsourcers can temporarily join the development teams. A lot of these outsourcers tend to be based in China, South Korea, and Vietnam.

Shanghai, and performing much the same role as Jérémie within these outsourcing studios (see also Chapter 28).

After considerable effort, the pipeline was set up, stretching across Naughty Dog's office in California, the outsourcers' studios in China, and Clermont-Ferrand with the ongoing development of our tool. Across the three continents, the teams did everything they could so that Substance Designer[6] could support and provide value to the teams at Naughty Dog for *Uncharted 4*, which promised to become an iconic video games.

6: From mid-2015, Naughty Dog also started using our next product, Substance Painter (see Chapter 29). This early adoption was in particular championed by Christophe Desse. Christophe is an extraordinary character, who over the years became a good friend of Jérémie, Alexis, and myself, and a great friend and supporter of Substance and Allegorithmic in general.

27.3 Substance Designer 4, then 5

Substance Designer 4 launched in March 2014, at the same time as the Game Developers Conference in San Francisco. It incorporated many of the features we'd developed during our partnership with Naughty Dog. Word of our software was growing in the game development world, and we started to sell more meaningful numbers of our tools. Almost all the publishers of 'AAA' games came to see us and learn more, to see a demo and to find out how we'd been working with Naughty Dog. Without going into too much detail.[7], we could confidently say that a tool like Substance Designer could bring significant benefits to a production: we'd seen and experienced this ourselves. This was the beginning of Substance Designer's undeniable, ongoing success.

7: We've always been very respectful of our customers' and partners' confidential information and NDAs (non-disclosure agreements) I believe that the trust we inspire in our community is one of the key elements in our commercial success—especially at the beginning of our adventure, when we were essentially selling a promise, without any sort of reassuring corporate solidity.

Figure 27.3: Substance Designer 4 was released in March 2014. It benefitted from the work that we'd carried out for Naughty Dog, our alpha-site.

Substance Designer 5 came out a year later, to coincide with GDC 2015. And, even though *Uncharted 4* hadn't been released yet, we were able to cite these sorts of quotations, which were pure gold for us:

> *It didn't take long for Substance Designer to carve out an important role within our artists' toolset at Naughty Dog.*
> **Brad Smith**, Senior Texture Artist, Naughty Dog

Figure 27.4: Substance Designer 5 was released in March 2015. This image was created by Christophe Desse from Naughty Dog.

27.4 *Uncharted 4*

Figure 27.5: *Uncharted 4* marked a major milestone in video games. At the time of its release, it was considered the most beautiful game ever made, thanks to the breathtaking quality of its artistic direction and the graphic coherence of all its environments. It was also an excellent game, well received by the gaming community, as well as by the press and specialized sites.

Everything possible has already been said about *Uncharted 4*. It was clearly the most beautiful game ever made at the time of its release in May 2016, thanks to the intrinsic quality of the assets that constituted it, its artistic direction (it wasn't a hyper-realistic game), and the consistency and graphic coherence of all its environments, right down to every detail despite its vast setting. Naughty Dog had accomplished something truly outstanding.

And Substance Designer had been used for 95% of the game's environment textures!

In retrospect...

The adventure with Naughty Dog and *Uncharted 4* represented a turning point in Allegorithmic's history.

The risk taken by a few visionary artists from the game studio allowed us to establish an alpha-site, and a partnership of almost co-development; in this way we could develop our tool Substance Designer, corresponding exactly to the needs of 'AAA' game developers.

When *Uncharted 4* was released, we could communicate about the use of Substance Designer on a large scale, in the context of the most beautiful game in the history of video games. We'd be lucky enough to feature several artists from Naughty Dog at the Game Developers Conference in San Francisco, in March 2016 (see Chapter 32). Artists such as Christophe Desse, Brad Smith, and Rogelio Olguin presented their workflow, and discussed how they'd used Substance Designer, and how the tool had helped them to create their universe.

This 'street cred' positioned us as the only PBR tool of the new generation. Our success exploded in 2015 and kept on growing thereafter.

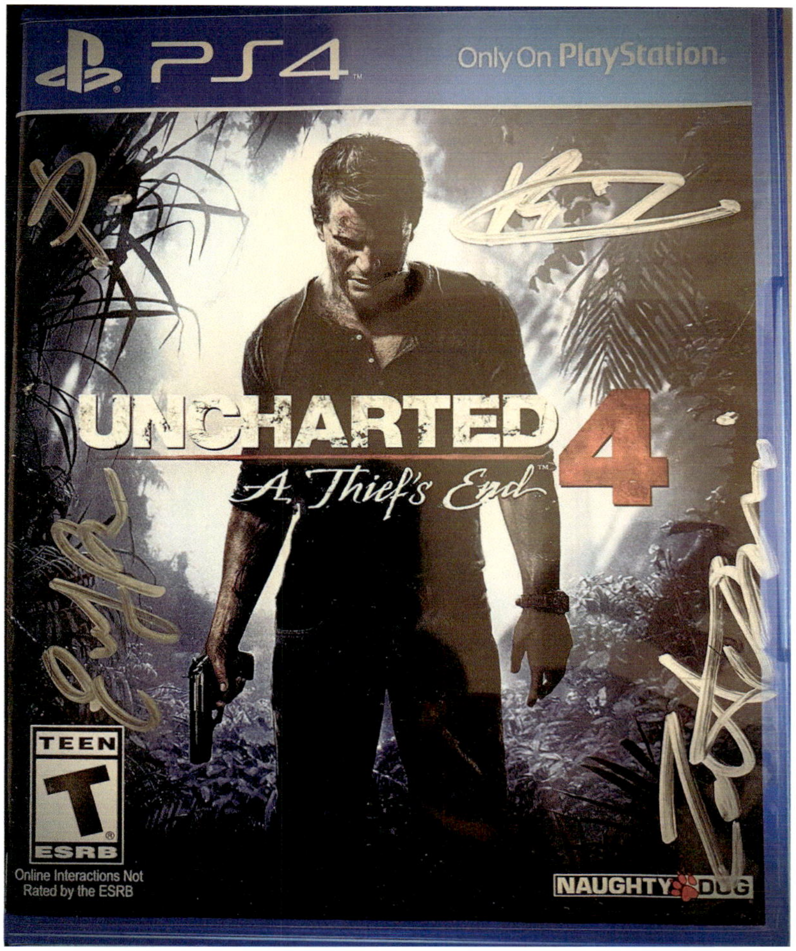

Figure 27.6: The box of the game *Uncharted 4*, signed by the leads of the Naughty Dog development team.

SUBSTANCE DESIGNER
NEXT GEN TEXTURING
Substance Designer is a comprehensive tool made for 3D artists who want to create more assets in less time and with fewer software packages.
NEXT-GEN TEXTURING
• Fully Non-destructive process
• Multi-output projects
• Real-time preview
• Parametric templates
UNIQUE FEATURES
• Material layering workflow
• PBR library and preview
• Mesh baking and batching process
• Seamless integration with 3D packages
"It didn't take long for Substance Designer to carve out an important role within our artists' toolset at Naughty Dog."
Brad Smith,
Senior Texture Artist, Naughty Dog
SUBSTANCE DESIGNER 4.0
Linux
590 USD per seat
SUBSTANCE PAINTER
NEXT GEN PAINTING
We have been thinking for a bit about what next gen painting should be.
NEXT-GEN PAINTING
• Non-destructive 3D/2D Painter
• Multi-Channel Brushes
• PBR Preview
• Dedicated to game assets
UNIQUE FEATURES
• Particle-Based Painting
• Automatic UV Reprojection
• Parametric Brushes
• Live link with Substance Designer
A particular buzz
"This is seriously awesome. I've wanted something like this since I started art."
"This is juste mind blowing. Now that I see particles used to paint stuff, I wonder why no one else thought of it before. It's such a logical idea when you thinbk about it."
SUBSTANCE PAINTER 1.0
Linux
Coming on STEAM soon
SUBSTANCE ENGINE
Substance Engine allows your game to benefit from the power of Substance at runtime.
"With Substance Engine we can simply provide AAA content to the masses, instantly"
REDUCE DOWNLOAD SIZE
• Parametric Substance files are typically 100X smaller than traditional bitmaps.
• A smart Hybrid approach allows to pack 10x more content in a single file.
AAA PIPELINE INTEGRATION
• Unique versatile runtime component allowing in-depth studio pipeline implementation.
• Expose texture parameters tweak them in real time and rapidely iterate over materials.
SUBSTANCE ENGINE is available for:
PS4 XBOX ONE Windows Mac os X Linux android iOS
SUBSTANCE ENGINE is natively integrated with:
Autodesk 3ds Max Autodesk Maya Autodesk Flame unity UNREAL ENGINE MODO MARMOSET TOOLBAG FUSE
allegorithmic
innovation matters
Contact us:
ALEXIS KHOURI
VP Strategy & Sales
alexis.khouri@allegorithmic.com
+1 (310) 754-0171
allegorithmic
USA / FRANCE / CHINA
Twitter: @Allegorithmic
facebook.com/AllegorithmicSubstance
www.allegorithmic.com
SUBST4NCE
SMART TEXTURING
allegorithmic
innovation matters

Figure 27.7: The Naughty Dog team taking on the task of integrating Substance for *Uncharted 4*: Brad Smith, Glauco Longhi, Erick Pangilinan, Tate Mosesian, Christophe Desse, and Rogelio Olguin. On the right, Alexis Khouri and Jérémie Noguer from Allegorithmic, who spent a lot of time at Naughty Dog to provide the maximum level of support during the development of the game. This photo was taken on April 28, 2016, shortly before the game's release.

Premises 28

28.1 Clermont-Ferrand

With a little success, our team began to grow, and were starting to take up more and more space in 31 rue Gonod, with its fantastic view of Place de Jaude. We expanded our presence by taking over the offices next to ours, which we transformed into a break room and meeting room. A little later we'd sub-rent a portion of that space to the 3D artist and filmmaker Damien Climent there, from the production company Autour de Minuit, famous for the production of short (and generally very high quality) films, founded and headed by Nicolas Schmerkin,[1] who was in the process of setting up a branch in Clermont-Ferrand, called Autour du Volcan—Around the Volcano.

1: We took part in the development of Nicolas's project, both by hosting Damien, but also by developing an augmented reality app for him called "Babioles"—"Bugs," in English—based on an animated TV series project.

Figure 28.1: Scenes of everyday life, in April and October 2014, then June and July 2015, in Clermont-Ferrand...

DOI:10.1201/9781003534624-28

Figure 28.2: A team photo in July 2013, taken in Clermont-Ferrand at Place de Jaude. On the photo from top to bottom, left to right: Nicolas Wirrmann, Gaël Granier, Gaëtan Lassagne, Alexandre Chassany, Eric Batut, Alexis Khouri, Sébastien Deguy, Clément Jacob, Stéphane Guy (bottom), and Christophe Soum, and on the photo below: Cyrille Damez, Benoît Barbier, Sylvain Paris, Amandine Lorrai, Jérémy Matichard, Benjamin Maréchal, Nathalie Poughon, Antoine Grimond, and Céline Dameron.

28.2 Allegorithmic Paris

Starbucks, Regus

Allegorithmic's first premises in Paris, as I was settling in with my wife and first child in 2012, was a spot in Starbucks on the crossroads of rue de Rivoli and rue des Mauvais Garçons, not far from our apartment in the fourth *arrondissement*. Upstairs at Starbucks, I took advantage of the free Wifi and a place to work, all for the price of a coffee for the day. When I[2] wasn't in meetings, I'd write emails and chat with my teams in IM.

2: I'd regularly see a few other independents there who, like me, took advantage of the fairly quiet, and almost free, environment to work. As Jerry Seinfeld said in one of his sketches: "I bought a coffee, I live here now."

As I spent more time in Paris, I met more and more people and, as Allegorithmic was growing, several people joined my team, and we ended up creating a real branch in Paris. In particular, it was from here we launched commercial development operations in 'non-entertainment' universes, or 'new markets,' as we called them internally, with François Cottin driving the team which was soon joined by Jérôme Derel, Anthony Salvi, and Frédéric Kohler (see Chapter 33).

Figure 28.3: Our premises, a small, simple office in Paris, at the Regus on rue d'Amsterdam, at the start of 2015. Here we see Jérôme Derel andAnthony Salvi.

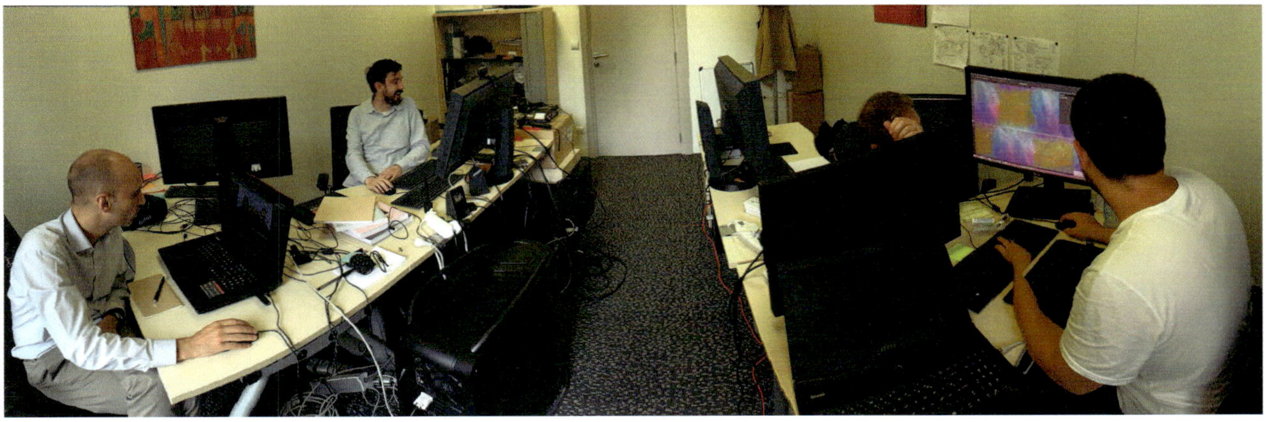

Figure 28.4: Our (very temporary) office in Paris, at the Regus on rue de Londres, in June 2015. Here we see François Cottin, Anthony Salvi, Jérôme Derel, and Damien Bousseau.

28.3 The beginning of our presence in Lyon

As is often the case, it was one person who made the difference, and led us to open a mini-office in Lyon. Damien Letournel, who had joined us during this period, wanted to stay in Lyon. The city was interesting for us as it contained a pool of present and past game developers, and so we took the opportunity to set up a branch within the premises of Pôle Pixel, a business center focusing on creative industries in Villeurbanne. We were hosted by a talented team within the game studio UpperByte, notably including Camille Masson, who would join Allegorithmic a few years later (see Chapter 35).

Figure 28.5: Our first branch in Lyon, with Damien Letournel (in the reflection, on the right) in 2013, at the heart of Pôle Pixel in Villeurbanne. We were hosted by a talented team at the game studio UpperByte, notably including Camille Masson, who would join Allegorithmic a few years later.

28.4 Allegorithmic Los Angeles

In order to reinforce our commercial activities in North America and to support Naughty Dog in particular in its integration of Substance within its pipeline (see Chapter 27), at the end of 2012 we created an American subsidiary (see figure 28.6). A little while later, Jérémie Noguer joined Alexis Khouri there, at the very beginning of 2013.

By the end of 2013, the team had grown even more with the arrival of Wes McDermott, an absolute 3D enthusiast known as '3D Ninja' on social media. I met him during a SIGGRAPH, where he was presenting the tool Modo by Luxology. His way of giving demos, of listening to users, and his generosity and evident empathy were incredibly engaging. He was disconcertingly comfortable connecting with people, and everybody immediately trusted him. He was working at UPS at the time, and was extremely excited about what we were developing; he ultimately agreed to join Allegorithmic Los Angeles, while working remotely from his home in Louisville, Kentucky. He then played an important role as an 'evangelist' for us, during conferences but also online, producing video tutorials that greatly helped our development.

And so the team comprised Jérémie, Wes, and Alexis, right in the heart of this market, and we were taking steps to conquer the US!

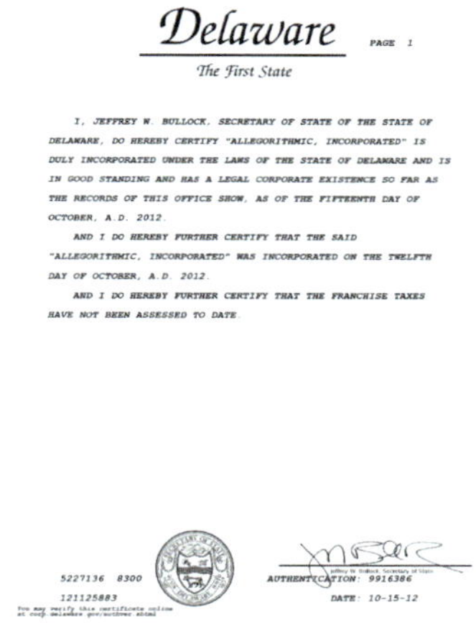

Delaware PAGE 1

The First State

I, JEFFREY W. BULLOCK, SECRETARY OF STATE OF THE STATE OF DELAWARE, DO HEREBY CERTIFY "ALLEGORITHMIC, INCORPORATED" IS DULY INCORPORATED UNDER THE LAWS OF THE STATE OF DELAWARE AND IS IN GOOD STANDING AND HAS A LEGAL CORPORATE EXISTENCE SO FAR AS THE RECORDS OF THIS OFFICE SHOW, AS OF THE FIFTEENTH DAY OF OCTOBER, A.D. 2012.

AND I DO HEREBY FURTHER CERTIFY THAT THE SAID "ALLEGORITHMIC, INCORPORATED" WAS INCORPORATED ON THE TWELFTH DAY OF OCTOBER, A.D. 2012.

AND I DO HEREBY FURTHER CERTIFY THAT THE FRANCHISE TAXES HAVE NOT BEEN ASSESSED TO DATE.

5227136 8300

121125883

AUTHENTICATION: 9916386

DATE: 10-15-12

Figure 28.6: Proof of incorporation of the American subsidiary of Allegorithmic, 'Allegorithmic, Inc.,' in October 2012.

Figure 28.7: Wes McDermott giving a demo to the legendary Ed Catmull (one of the founders of Pixar and one of the most important scientific contributors in the history of 3D) at SIGGRAPH in 2017, a few years after having joined us in December 2013.

Figure 28.8: February 21, 2013, Jérémie Noguer's big day of departure to the US—the start of a great adventure, and ultimately even a family in California.

Figure 28.9: I joined the Allegorithmic Los Angeles team at the start of 2013. I am surrounded by Alexis Khouri (left) and Jérémie Noguer (right).

Figure 28.10: Alexandre Bagard, in March 2015, in the small Allegorithmic office in Los Angeles, in Venice.

28.5 Josh Coyne and the Akron/Cleveland team

Josh Coyne

In 2014 we placed an ad, for the first time, in a specialized section of the website Stack Overflow, a site dedicated to developers from all over the world, a high-level platform for exchanging good practices, pieces of code, and discussions between 'coders.' The platform had launched a new job posting service, just as we were looking for a new member of the team to manage Substance Engine integrations in third-party applications, particularly game engines. For this, we needed someone with game development experience if possible, based in the US, and who spoke perfect English, capable of providing a high-quality support service to our customers. Our idea was to push for the use of the engine in runtime, and several studios had already expressed interest. We now had a good idea of the work involved, and we absolutely needed someone solid who was dedicated to this task.

I saw the profile of someone named Josh Coyne, who answered the ad and wanted to know more, and Eric Batut confirmed that Josh's background was very impressive. Josh was working at Crytek at the time, publisher of games such as *Far Cry*, as well as of the AAA game engine CryEngine. Crytek had bought the game development studio Vigil Games,[3] where Josh worked. He was based in Austin, Texas, and on paper he presented us with an extraordinary opportunity.[4] After some technical interviews, we made him an offer and he agreed to join Allegorithmic, Inc. Josh was our first American employee!

3: Responsible for the Darksiders series of games.

4: Josh was one of our first 'outside the box' hires, thanks to Allegorithmic's good business development: this recruitment was out of the ordinary in the sense that it was rare for a small company passionate about video games (particularly one based in Clermont-Ferrand) to hire someone of Josh's level, who had participated in the creation of games that we'd all enjoyed as players!

The Akron team, in Ohio

After some time, and having gained the respect of the team, Josh asked us if we had any problem with him moving closer to his family based in Ohio, next to Akron, a little town best known for being the birthplace of LeBron James, the famous basketball player. Josh had proven to us, from Austin, that he could work remotely just fine, while the rest of the team was based in Los Angeles; whether Josh was in Austin or Akron didn't make a big difference for us. So he moved there and, one thing leading to another, and to meet the needs of a growing 'Integrations' team, we gradually expanded the team around him, in Akron. At first we used the basement of Josh's house as an office for a little while, then ultimately set up in an actual office in the center of Akron (see figures 28.12 and 28.11).

Figure 28.11: The Akron offices: the official presence of Allegorithmic Inc. (our US subsidiary) in a city center building in Akron, Ohio.

Figure 28.12: The Akron team, which was formed around Josh Coyne. Top: Wes McDermott (left) visiting us at Josh's house (which was Josh's and the team's office for some time, early on). Below, the Akron team in October 2017: Laurent Lussier, Dan Stover, Josh Green, and me. Also Keston Gregory with open arms.

28.6 Allegorithmic Shanghai

Naughty Dog, with whom we'd been working closely in the context of their use of Substance, was working with some outsourcers from the region of Shanghai, notably with a company called Virtuos (see Chapter 27). Just as Jérémie Noguer was doing in Los Angeles, it seemed crucial to us to have a presence there as close as possible to Virtuos, to ensure the success of our partnership with Naughty Dog. This led to Gilles Fleury spending a lot of time in Shanghai, and ultimately falling in love with China. He settled there; so did Nicolas Liatti, who moved there with his family in 2012. We assembled a team locally to support Virtuos, among others, and to address this booming Chinese market, which greatly impressed us. We saw huge potential for our products in this region, where the digital sector in general, and video game development in particular, was rapidly growing.

Figure 28.13: Our Shanghai office, in May 2013. Here we see Gilles Fleury (standing), Nicolas Liatti (from the back), Wang Cong, and Meizi Yan.

As we'd done in Paris, we setted in a Regus office building (after some unsuccessful explorations of our own), within a lively neighborhood in Shanghai. Wang Cong and Meizi Yan joined the team, two technical artists that Gilles had worked with during training sessions in local studios. Meizi Yan would play a big role in the development of Allegorithmic in the region, being a real driving force throughout the life of the company in China.

Figure 28.14: A visit to Virtuos (we can see Philippe Angely on the right) by the Shanghai team: Gilles Fleury (standing) and Nicolas Liatti (sitting).

28.7 Allegorithmic Korea

We didn't really have an office in Seoul, South Korea, but we had a commercial presence led by Christian Kim, whom Alexis and I met in 2007 during the G-Star conference in Seoul (see Chapter 20). The remarkable and uncompromising work of Christian allowed us to develop a continuous presence there, supported by regular visits, which made it a unique site for us.

Figure 28.15: A historic visit to Seoul with Nicolas Liatti.

Figure 28.16: Commercial prospection, a dinner with Webzen in 2012, and Alexis at the KGC (Korea Game Conference) in 2013.

Figure 28.17: Commercial prospection with Unity in 2013. Christian Kim presented.

Figure 28.18: Commercial prospection at NCSoft in 2014. Gilles Fleury gave the demo.

Figure 28.19: Signing a partnership with DevTree (a training company for careers in 3D), in Korea, in May 2014.

Substance Painter 29

29.1 Emergence

Non-destructive 3D painting, multi-maps, everything on GPU

We wanted to bring an evolution to Substance Designer centered around the possibility of painting in 3D directly on textured objects. The purely procedural approach offered by Substance Designer was very powerful, and provided significant advantages, but many users had asked for the ability to retouch their work, or even to texture everything manually using painting tools 'à la Photoshop.' Our first idea was to add this feature to our flagship app; we prototyped this change—and then, without initially really knowing why, we questioned whether we should implement this functionality in Substance Designer. Designer was a 'pure' tool, specifically for creating procedural textures; this capability was linked to Substance Engine, which was 'detachable,' and could be integrated into various host applications. Adding manual 'strokes' wouldn't really be compatible with this approach, and would partly break this pure element of the tool, which worked well for our users. Additionally, the software architecture for Substance Designer at that time made us wonder whether it would be the best receptacle for such a feature, which imposed strong constraints, particularly on hardware: we absolutely wanted to use the latest GPUs, just as we'd done for Substance Engine. We dreamed of a new type of never-before-seen 3D painting, where everything was in the GPU, that was non-destructive and allowed users to paint, with one stroke, all maps at once, by defining a PBR material (see Chapter 26).

With this vision in mind, Clément Jacob began writing a prototype for painting 3D PBR materials, that was non-destructive and entirely GPU-based. He produced something very quickly and, testing it out, the sensations it evoked were extraordinary: the crucial sense of fluidity was present, and we could paint several maps in 8K simultaneously! Moreover, each action we carried out was saved as part of a long sequence of actions in the 3D space, and could be modified in the stack without having to redo everything—which was a unique approach in the industry, and very aligned with Allegorithmic's approach to procedural texturing.[1]

1: This particularity would appear in the final version of Substance Painter in the form of UV independence on textured objects: that is, once all painting actions were saved, it was entirely possible to change *a posteriori* the object's UVs without destroying all work previously carried out. The various saved actions were then 're-played' and reprojected onto this new UV parametrization. This, therefore, was a 'non-destructive' approach.

Particles

Previously, in 2004, we'd had an intern called Simon Brunel who was doing work focused on the use of particles and random movements (but following strict rules, see Chapter 9). This work had allowed us to confirm an idea that I'd formed during my PhD thesis several years earlier. It consisted of using iterative processes to simulate physical phenomena such as fractures and leaks. These phenomena, which often evolve over time, can be observed everywhere in nature, and so it seemed that, if we wanted our software to create textures that were absolutely as

DOI:10.1201/9781003534624-29

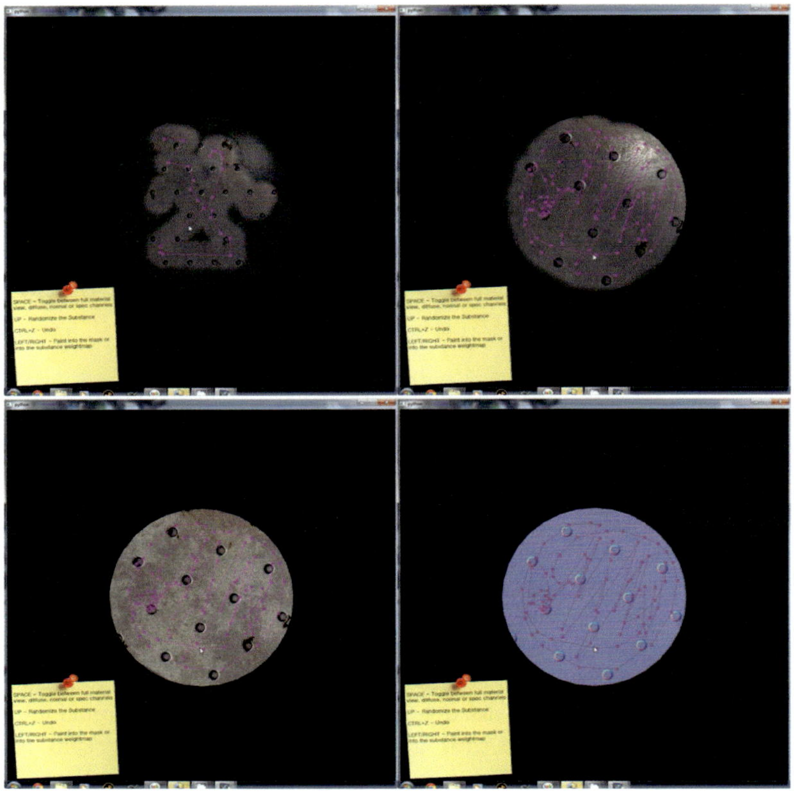

Figure 29.1: A first prototype of GPU painting developed by Clément Jacob. The process only used the GPU, making it possible to paint all of the material's channels in a single stroke (see the bottom two images, showing the result of painting in the diffuse channel, which determines basic colors, and on the normal channel, which defines the relief of a surface). It was also 'non-destructive,' as we can see on the top images, where each movement in space in saved as a curve that can be edited afterward; the sequence of operations can also be re-executed following any changes. This was a veritable tour de force, and this prototype was extremely promising for the future.

true-to-life as possible, we had to be able to recreate these phenomena as well. Integrating this capability into Substance Designer was complex; regardless, we'd seen that particularly advanced users like Brad Smith from Naughty Dog (see Chapter 27) had already achieved this to some extent, and so we resolved to focus our attention on this problem, to make this feature more accessible and powerful for our users.

The particle systems that we saw emerging in the industry at that time were mostly real-time, and allowed artists to create spectacular effects. They all benefited from advances in hardware, whether CPUs or GPUs. 3D games were making increasingly significant and sophisticated use of effects created with particles. A few months before GDC 2012, I came across a new particle system called Hell Heaven FX,[2] which was soon renamed Popcorn FX (I'll use this name from this point on), created by a small Parisian company, Persistant Studio. Their system produced particularly impressive results, and I made a point of going to see them during GDC.[3]

2: For French speakers, it's a pun on the world 'Eleven,' as neither 'H' sound is typically pronounced; the joke doesn't really work for native English speakers, who would pronounce the 'H' sounds. . . I mentioned this to its developers when I met them, and they ultimately changed their name to Popcorn FX. I imagine I wasn't the only person who'd provided this feedback.

3: One of my great pleasures during conferences is to tour the stands and discover the new technologies and latest products from developers in the industry. It was, for example, during one of these tours that I met the Japanese company Silicon Studio, which develops extraordinary graphic libraries, including Yebis, which we went on to license, and integrate into our tools.

Popcorn FX

During GDC 2012, in March in San Francisco, I introduced myself at Persistant Studio's little stand. They were demonstrating their real-time programmable particle software Popcorn FX. I introduced myself, and met Maxime Dumas, Camille Mirey, and Julien Bilalte, the people behind the product. They gave me a demo, showing how they could program the physical behavior of the particles very deeply, and flexibly. Then, making the link with Simon Brunel's intership work eight years earlier, I asked,

"With your system, is it possible to make it so that a particle emitted with a certain type of behavior, changes to a different type of behavior once it comes into contact with a 3D object?" I explained my thinking, giving the example of a particle of paint coming out of a spray pistol; it follows a classic ballistic curve depending on its initial emission speed, its weight, wind, turbulence of the surrounding environment, and so on—and then, when it arrives at an object it stops dead (by crashing on impact). It then begins to flow along the object, now following a second type of behavior, defined this time by the viscosity of the particle's material, the type of surface of the object, the roughness of that surface, its position in space, and, of course, gravity. . .

Julien's answer would remain with me: "Today, no. But I think we'll be able to do that!"

He specified, "We could certainly program two different behaviors, but we don't yet know how to constrain the particle to the surface of an object." I was especially excited by this discussion, and I in turn told them my idea: I wanted to use a system of particles like the one they'd developed directly on a 3D object in real time,[4] so that we could create trickles, fractures, impacts, and other marks that would look credible, as they followed simulations of physical processes. This was the idea of particle painting.

4: By contrast, during his internship Simon worked on a system that was far from real-time, and that operated on 2D images.

I suggested that I visit them in Paris once we'd all returned from GDC, allowing me to explain my idea to them in detail, so that they might implement it. There was a potential opportunity for us to license Popcorn FX for integration into a future product in the Substance suite, which would be very interesting for them, as well as the key to a unique feature for our potential next tool.

Prototypes and working together

Back in Paris, at the end of March 2012, I began visiting the Persistant Studio office in Paris about once a week, so that we could directly develop this idea. I worked in particular with Jordan Galby, a developer of the particle solution attached to the project; week after week, Jordan implemented the missing functionalities that would allow them to achieve the effects that I'd presented to them (see for example figure 29.2).

After the first few sessions, we saw some extraordinary results. The feeling of painting with physics, of seeing these complex effects created so easily and in a fun way, was simply unique. And this was perfectly aligned with the spirit of Allegorithmic—a mathematically complex tool that was controllable by an artist. In this way, we extended the purely artistic act by using the power of the machine to open further possibilities.

If we could implement this feature in our future 3D painting tool, we would clearly have an important differentiator, one of these 'black magic features' which made a tool stand out from the rest. These results, along with the multi-map GPU-based painting prototype, were extremely promising, and we decided to officially launch development in the form of a separate application from Substance Designer. This was the beginning of Substance Painter!

Figure 29.2: Inspirational photos for particle painting, taken during Eurostar and plane trips.

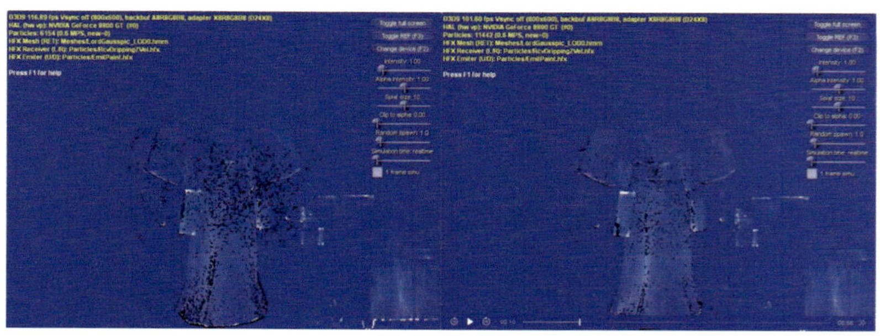

Figure 29.3: The first prototype of 'particle painting,' developed by Jordan Galby from Popcorn FX. Particles (small black dots) were launched in the direction of a 3D mesh (a magician character, transparent here for the demo) in real time, using a virtual spray pistol. Once they touched the surface of the mesh, these particles would slide downwards following the surface, adapting to the geometry and leaving a trace behind! This was a first; the feeling of painting with particles, just like you'd spray an object with paint, was utterly unique.

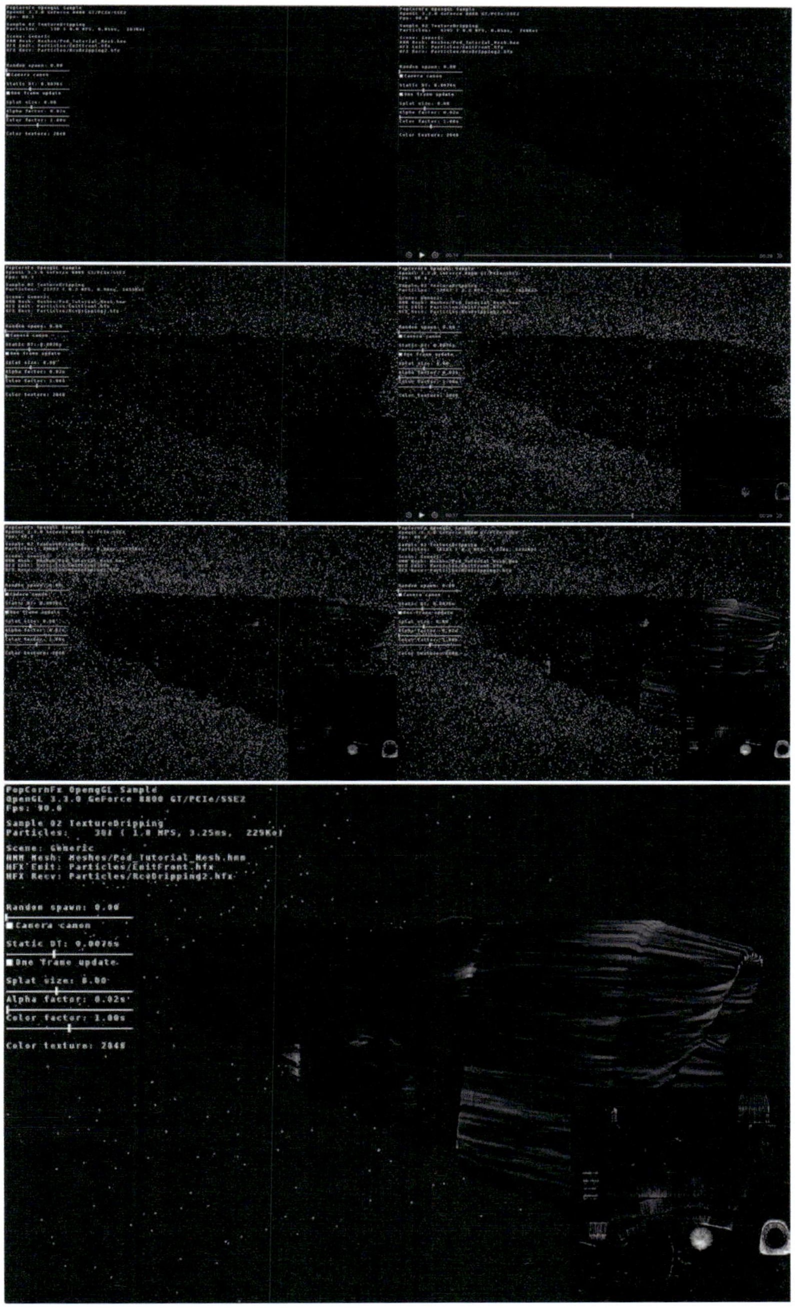

Figure 29.4: This same prototype (see figure 29.3) in action on another 3D object (a pod inspired by the Star Wars universe), receiving a very large number of particles, here simulating a more global effect of air penetration and the accumulation of drips and dirt, as seen in the photos in figure 29.2. Here again, once the particles come into contact with the surface of the pod, they adopt a different behavior and leave traces (in white, here) which we can see accumulating, in particular at the front of the reactors, as would happen in 'real life.' These results were incredibly encouraging.

29.2 A new product

The decision to begin development of a new product resulted in a lot of internal questions and confusion. In particular, we needed a dedicated team, to give the product the freedom to evolve in an agile and unconstrained way, and to avoid disrupting the development of Substance Designer. Designer was doing very well, and we didn't want to slow down its progress.

And so we created a team, and gave this new ambitious project to Clément Jacob, and to recent arrivals such as Stéphane Guy and Alexandre Chassany (see Chapter 22), with the overall vision of the product largely defined by Jérémie Noguer. Christophe Soum was also involved in the generation engine, as he'd have to integrate Substance Engine, in order to use parametric textures previously created in Substance Designer as a sort of 'parametric ink.' This was the beginning of an ecosystem of products that fed into one another (here, specifically from Substance Designer to Substance Painter), which would ultimately prove very successful.[5]

5: Years later I wrote an internal article outlining the concept we can see here, the difference between 'left-brain artists' and 'right-brain artists.' With Substance Designer, we were catering to LB-artists; with Substance Painter, we had RB-artists in mind. Many of these texture artists hadn't really connected with Substance Designer, even if they could clearly see the power of it—but they'd been waiting for a tool like Substance Painter.

Figure 29.5: Clément Jacob shows off his artistic talents; these are the results of the first tests in real-time 3D painting in Substance Painter.

In retrospect...

It should be noted here that Stéphane Guy pushed for a new 'agile' approach to development while working on Substance Painter. This was a small revolution in Allegorithmic, one accomplished without conflict or noise, as we'd never worked in this way. Essentially, the idea is that the reality of software development means that it makes little sense to try to predict the medium- and long-term development cycle of a tool; rather, it's more practical to divide this development into small increments of time with clear, defined objectives, negotiated upstream with all concerned parties. This approach is tempting on paper, even though it creates a lot of stress for sales and marketing teams, who are unable to anticipate what's coming. I personally had a very hard time getting used to this approach, yet I observed Stéphane implement this system with such intelligence and patience that I couldn't help but give way: it really did work, and Stéphane and his team inspired a major cultural change within Allegorithmic which is still in effect today.

Figure 29.6: The closed user group badge, for a very special event organized for GDC 2013, in March in San Francisco. We'd prepared a little surprise for our guests (see figure 29.7).

29.3 (We have seen) the future of texturing...

The first prototypes developed in 2012 were very promising and throughout the entire development cycle of the tool, once we'd taken the decision to launch a new product, we tried to raise suspense within our community, from time to time revealing a few images or videos of prototypes. We reached an important step in the process when, at GDC 2013 in San Francisco, we organized a special presentation for several guests from the world of texturing, and particularly from video games. This was our 'exclusive user group'; we wanted to show them a few elements of our road map, and present a little surprise.

The surprise, of course, was our new product dedicated to 3D painting. But not just any kind of 3D painting: GPU-based, non-destructive,

Figure 29.7: The exclusive user group from a special event organized for GDC 2013, in March in San Francisco, where we showed prototypes of Substance Painter for the very first time.

multi-map, real-time 3D painting, possessing features that nobody else could offer, such as support for parametric textures from Substance Designer, and a never-before-seen technique for particle painting.

Our audience were surprised and excited, to put it mildly. Even though we were showing them something that wasn't very advanced (in reality, we showed them many of the prototypes developed the previous year, rather than the tool itself—our painting tool was still in development and wouldn't have created the 'wow' effect that we were looking for), its potential was obvious, and this presentation created buzz ambassadors for us, people who were incredibly respected in the video game industry, who would be able to say that they had seen 'the future of texturing.' We went so far as to print T-shirts with this slogan: *I have seen the future of texturing* (see figure 29.8), which we gave to our guests that night so they could wear them throughout the conference that began the next day!

Figure 29.8: Here, Jérémie Noguer had just received the T-shirts we were going to distribute during GDC 2013, during which we would reveal our ambition with the tool that would become Substance Painter. The T-shirt reads, "I have seen the future of texturing."

We reused the user group formula from San Francisco during SIGGRAPH, in July 2013 in Anaheim, south of Los Angeles, as we can see in figure 29.9. And we achieved the same success: the excitement from the 3D artists who saw the tool was palpable, and boded well for Substance Painter's official launch on the market.

For the rest of 2013 we continued to increase the anticipation by gradually releasing information on a new upcoming product. Then we displayed a countdown on our website, showing two brains, illustrating two approaches to working in 3D—the technical approach with the left brain (which would ultimately reveal a new version of Substance Designer, which would be released a few weeks later), and the right-brain artistic approach, here with the revelation that we had a second project in development: Substance Painter (see figure 29.10). On December 5, 2013, the countdown reached zero, and we revealed our announcements, as well as a teaser video in our own distinctive style, unlike many of the videos produced in the 3D industry. The announcement was a big success, and created a loud 'buzz.' And with this, our community began to eagerly await the release of Substance Painter.

Figure 29.9: The closed, very special user group for an event organized for SIGGRAPH 2013, in July in Anaheim. We used this event to continue generating a buzz around what was still a work in progress project: Substance Painter.

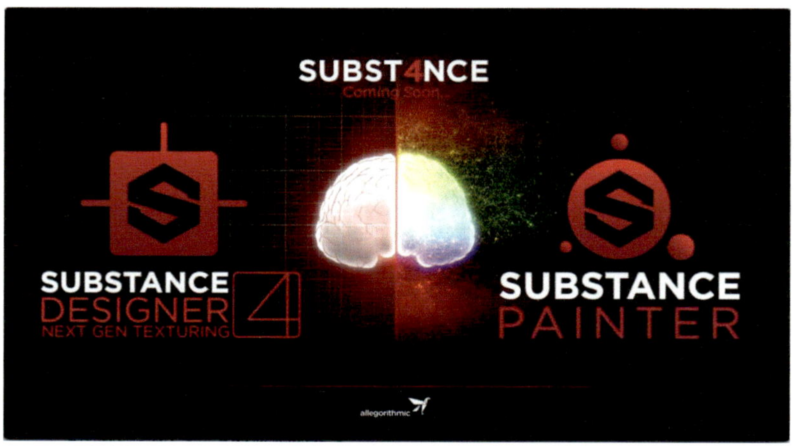

Figure 29.10: Teaser for the reveal of Substance Painter.

Launch Rocket

Continuing in the same spirit as before, so that we could generate a little more buzz around Substance Painter, we used an experimental service developed by a French company called Launch Rocket to gain more attention on the day of the product's release. The principle went like this: first, we asked followers of the Substance Twitter account for permission to let a bot send out a tweet on their behalf on release day (the bot would generate the text, but users could edit it as they liked)... Then, on release day, a large volume of tweets on the same subject would be posted simultaneously; with a bit of luck, the release of Substance Painter would start trending.[6] Many Substance followers were happy to play the game, and we received an excellent response from the operation, amplifying the positive noise around the release of the product.

6: These actions to generate buzz, coupled with using this type of communication service, was a significant step in the evolution of Allegorithmic's marketing activity. Up until this point we'd been very focused on B2B and our community; now we were venturing into the world of social media and modern marketing trends...

GDC 2014: the beta is finally launched

The public release date finally arrived, to coincide with GDC 2014 in San Francisco.[7] We first presented this version to the same user group that we'd assembled the previous year, slightly extended. This was not quite a version 1.0 because, objectively, we were not ready. And so we presented a beta version of the tool; it would remain this way for a few long months. But even though the tool was not yet 'final' we preferred to launch it in this state—it was nonetheless usable (though not for production, as we made sure to point out), and above all it was very 'fun.'

7: Prior to GDC, on March 6, 2014, we'd launched the beta video for Substance Painter [37].

We received feedback from the first users at once: the tool was fun, and it allowed them to really grasp the complex art of texturing—going so far as to make it the most 'fun' step within the whole process of creating an asset.

We launched the product, and it experienced great success, which would propel Allegorithmic forward for many years.

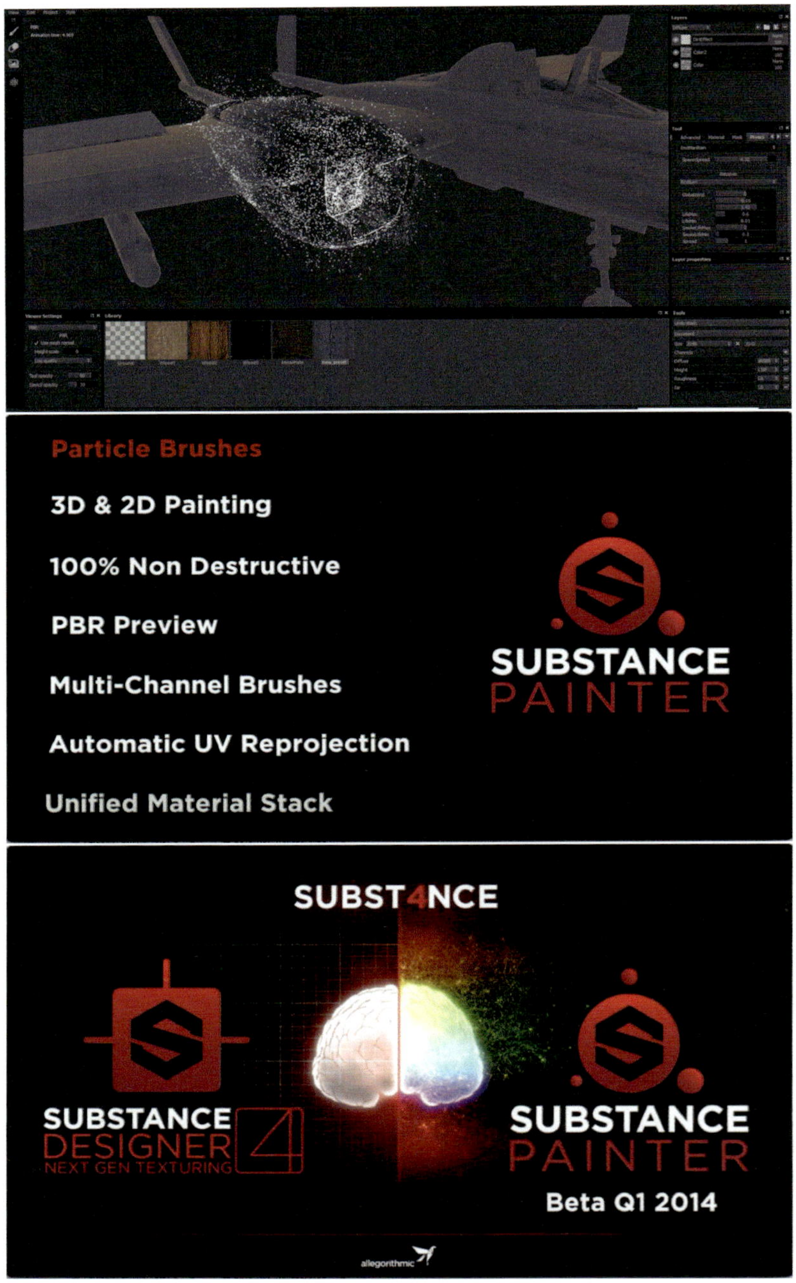

Figure 29.11: The 'reveal' video for Substance Painter, December 5, 2013. We announced a new product!

Figure 29.12: The team at GDC in San Francisco that year: Eric Batut, Alexis Khouri, Jérémie Noguer, Sébastien Deguy, and Wes McDermott, the day after our first presentation of what would become Substance Painter to a specially selected group.

Figure 29.13: Laurens Corijn giving a presentation for our closed user group at GDC 2014, in March in San Francisco. This was our first presentation of Substance Painter Beta, which we launched during the conference.

Figure 29.14: The start of pre-orders for Substance Painter on Steam, at the beginning of March 2014 (Clément Jacob programmed an Arduino which linked the sales counter on the platform to a monitor we placed in the room in which Substance Painter had been programmed). We felt it was a great start! Top, part of the team taking a photo in front of the counter. Sitting: Amandine Lorrai, Nathalie Delfour (behind the cardboard mask), Clément Jacob, and Stéphane Guy. Standing: Alexandre Chassany, Benoît Barbier, Christophe Soum, and Gaël Granier.

Figure 29.15: The Substance Painter development team celebrating its release on Steam at a bar in Clermont-Ferrand. Clément Jacob, Eric Batut, Alexandre Chassany, Stéphane Guy, Benoît Barbier.

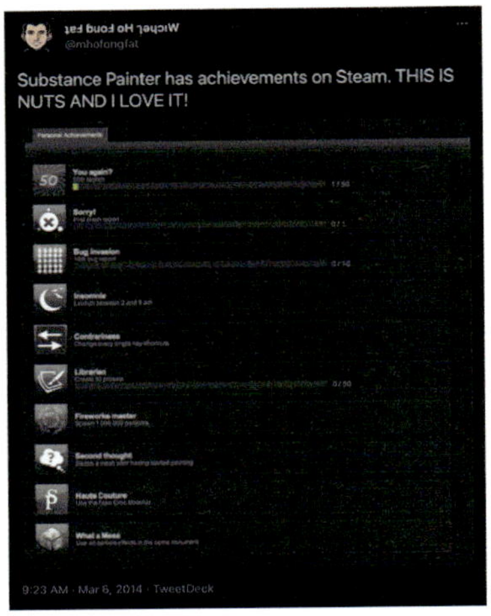

Figure 29.16: A user who appreciated the gamification of Substance Painter on Steam.

29.4 Substance Painter 1.0 and 1.3

Version 1.0 of the product was finally released in October 2014. Our website at the time was not the most robust, and we were anticipating, or rather hoping for, many visitors the day of the release. And so we decided to set up several servers which, we hoped, could support a large number of visitors. We remained on site the day of the release to monitor everything. The website held up fine, and everything went as we'd hoped. Sales of Substance Painter were off to a strong start.

The version that changed everything, and that confirmed the huge success of Substance Painter, was version 1.3, which we finally released in March 2015 during GDC. It contained in particular smart materials and bakers. These features established Substance Painter as the absolute reference tool for this new generation of texturing. The impact that this release at GDC had on the industry was notable (see Chapter 34), and its success would only grow from that moment on.

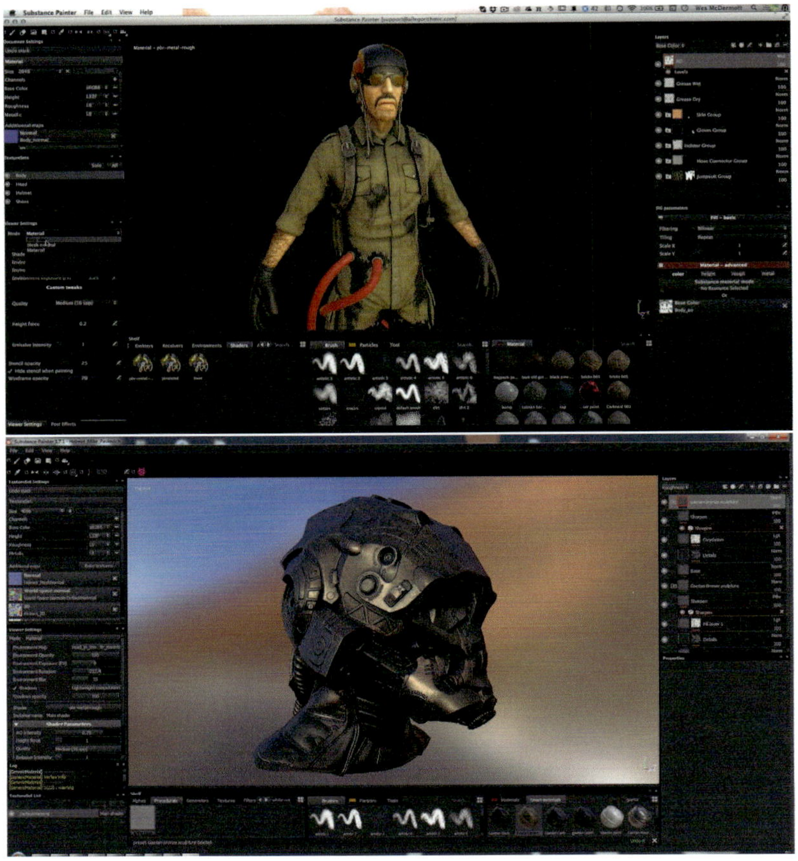

Figure 29.17: The user interface of Substance Painter 1.0 (top), with a preconfigured project made by Christophe Desse, and of Substance Painter 1.7.1 (below), showing a 3D model by Mike Pavlovich, textured by Gaëtan Lassagne.

30 Demos, games, and products

30.1 Hardware

2011 and 2012 were years very focused on hardware for Allegorithmic and, as seen in the previous sections, we at times tried to get closer to hardware creators by offering them joint demos that would take advantage of our technologies and their hardware components. Companies constantly try to anticipate coming technical developments. They simultaneously imagine developments and copy one another, the winner defining the standard of the moment.

And so giants like Intel, Img Tech, Qualcomm, AMD/ATI, ARM, NVIDIA and others, in partnership with key players like Microsoft and its DirectX graphics API, or the Khronos Group with standards like OpenGL, compete in terms of ingenuity, looking for any differentiator that would position them at the bleeding edge of the market.

In this context, the technologies developed by Allegorithmic presented interesting potential: procedural textures were demanding in terms of computing power, and the next generations of chips were looking for such applications. Whoever managed to demonstrate how games, for example, would look more beautiful when running on their latest product—thanks to this available computing power—would win.

Figure 30.1: A meeting with Samsung at the offices of the Ministry of Finance for tech developers like Allegorithmic, organized by Fleur Pellerin, at the time Secretary of State in charge of Digital Affairs. Samsung was looking for technologies that would make their phones stand out from the rest.

The stakes were colossal because in many cases the content would largely determine the renewal of machine parks (both laptops and desktop computers), and the more the difference between machines was visually distinctive, the higher the chance of a rapid renewal.

The team therefore spent a significant amount of time adapting Substance Engine on all platforms in development. This porting work, on hardware

DOI:10.1201/9781003534624-30

that was sometimes barely emulated,[1] and at best available in the form of a kit that required special consideration to ensure that it wouldn't fry our French electrical networks, was complex and frustrating: our teams had to work with work-in-progress (and therefore unreliable) hardware, with incomplete software libraries, while blindly debugging, even though the end goal of the process was high performance!

1: I remember a brief meeting with Dave Aronson in the NVIDIA parking lot; Dave who handed me an experimental graphics card in one of those thick, transparent plastic bags. I hid the card deep in my suitcase, leaving for San Francisco airport for my flight to Paris a few hours later. It was an incredible sensation for me, who'd grown up watching science-fiction films about bleeding edge technology, to see that NVIDIA considered Allegorithmic interesting enough for them to provide us with one of the rare prototypes of their upcoming hardware! With this card, the team in Clermont-Ferrand went on to optimize Substance Engine, and had a preview access to a number of tech innovations that NVIDIA would offer in the years to come. . .

Figure 30.2: Cyrille Damez and Christophe Soum visiting NVIDIA, in Santa Clara, California.

This type of partnership is double-edged. It can bring great visibility through co-marketing with the giants in question (and for a micro-company from Clermont-Ferrand, being singled out by a giant like Intel or NVIDIA is an extraordinary opportunity); conversely, however, the effort and investment required, generally monopolizing the more technical members of the team, can prove to be a huge distraction, which has very little chance of resulting in something concrete. . .

We tried this out (see the various demos in this chapter), ultimately with little success, for multiple reasons—from the lack of power (ultimately, our procedural textures were still very demanding) to a lack of adoption by our customers for procedural textures generated at runtime. But the effort wasn't wasted, as our tools emerged from this period more well-rounded, robust, and efficient. And while our textures weren't suitable for mobile phones or a games consoles like the Xbox 360, we were still able to render textures fluidly and interactively, while the 3D artist was working, rather than while a game engine was running, actively needing to calculate and display a texture. Procedural textures would eventually prove their value at this creative stage (see Chapter 27, for example).

We explored a range of demos, partnerships, and experiments with these key players throughout this period, as we'll see in the rest of the chapter.

30.2 The beginning of virtual reality

Brendan Iribe and Oculus

Brendan was CEO of Scaleform when I first met him. Scaleform offered middleware for creating Vector Graphics for video games, in particular for interface displays in games (allowing you to move through menus). Around ten years later, this product was used by almost all game developers, and the company enjoyed well-deserved success.

Always wearing a huge smile, Brendan was a friendly, brilliant, likeable man. He had the flair of a used car salesman, with the notable difference of being trustworthy.

In 2011, he sold Scaleform to Autodesk, the undisputed giant of 3D tools and middleware at the time. For this, he presented Autodesk with a slide deck demonstrating not only that Scaleform was essential for all game creation (a market that Autodesk intended to dominate), that the team was about to sign a huge commercial deal with Nintendo, and that the next version of Scaleform, which they were about to release, would include major innovations: announcing all of this, and releasing the product under the banner, would be a big win for the 3D giant.

Two months after the sale, Brendan left Autodesk. When I asked why, he told me that he wasn't suited to working in a company like Autodesk, and that the team was in good hands with its new leader, the CTO of the company who would now be the technical leader of Autodesk Scaleform.

It had taken 11 years for Brendan to carry out his first major operation. An entrepreneur and businessman at heart, he threw himself into his next project: Gaikai. This adventure would be shorter, and he'd ultimately take part in the company's sale to Sony just a few years later.

Then it was time for his next adventure, which would leave a profound, lasting mark on the world of technology, and the world in general. After letting Gaikai and Sony stand on their own two feet, he became CEO of a small company of virtual reality enthusiasts, which he helped create in 2012 with a certain Palmer Luckey, and Michael Antonov: Oculus.

He called me when he was in Paris a few months later. "Seb, I have to show you something!" I joined him in his hotel room, not far from my apartment in the fourth *arrondissement*, and there he showed me what looked like a ski mask covered in electronic chips, with a myriad of cables dangling from it which he plugged into one of his laptops. "Try this!" I then had the chance to test one of the very first prototypes of what would become the Oculus Rift, which would be released a few years later.

For the first time, I experienced virtual reality as I'd always dreamed it should be, and the sensation was utterly astounding. Despite the low resolution of the screens of the ski helmet / virtual reality headset that I was wearing, and the crudeness of the experience and the games that I tested out, I could nevertheless feel, deep in my gut, the power and infinite potential of virtual reality. Reading science-fiction authors or watching films about it does nothing to prepare one for the shock we feel once our brain is 'hacked' by stereoscopic images and sound which project us into imaginary universes. I'd discovered VR (virtual reality), and have been a fan of it ever since.

I ran into Brendan several times, at trade shows or when he took me to test-drive his Audi R8 (a rocket. . .), and each time it was a pleasure to discuss our respective entrepreneurial journeys. After a frantic race to be the first on the market, he would resell Oculus to Facebook in 2014, and would continue to drive the development of virtual reality. . . within a large company.

Figure 30.3: A valve at the entrance to the offices of Valve, in the Seattle area.

Valve and the future Vive

A few years later, in March 2014, I had the opportunity to test out one of the first Valve VR headsets in Seattle, while traveling back from GDC in San Francisco, before returning to Paris.

The future Vive was of such high quality, and everything that I experienced that day was so immersive, that I was literally overwhelmed by the encounter overall. This was the first time that I'd viscerally felt the potential of virtual reality.[2] Here we were, and there was no way back. People would immerse themselves body and soul in these virtual universes; they would live there, and die there.

I didn't know how long it would take for VR to establish itself, but the potential was dizzying, and Allegorithmic would enter this creative space several years later with demos for big players like IKEA and Hermès (see Chapter 35).

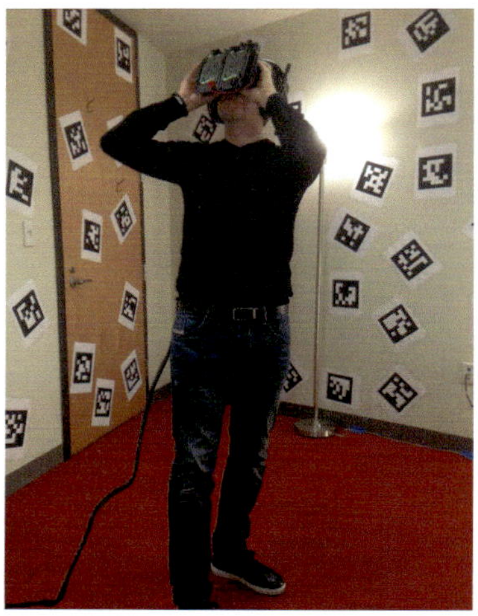

Figure 30.4: At the end of GDC 2014 in San Francisco, I was invited to make a detour to visit Valve, before returning to Paris, visiting the Seattle area so that I could test the future Vive. Aside from the birth of my first son, this was to date the most remarkable experience of my entire life. I was literally overwhelmed by the potential of the device, the first time a virtual reality headset had attained this level of sophistication. Everything I experienced in this headset was incredibly immersive. It was a real shock for me.

2: I wrote to Brendan to tell him that I'd just had the second-most-life-changing experience of my life!

30.3 Our technical demos

Faithful to our tradition of producing technical demos, and wanting, as mentioned, to get closer to the major players in global technology, we would go on to produce technical demos pushing machines to their limits, like those created by Futuremark with their annual benchmark demos 3DMark, demonstrating the power of a particular graphics processor or a particular SoC (System on Chip). We would therefore work with NVIDIA and Qualcomm to create our Windmill and Paleo Raft demos.

Windmill

The Windmill demo presented a windmill placed on a small floating island, a poetic 3D vision of a soothing and inspiring environment. The goal was, as in many of our demos, to show the evolution of textures, in this case as a magical tempest drew nearer. We produced a first PC version of the demo for the GDC Austin conference, in 2009 (under the direction of Gaëtan Lassagne), and we found an arrangement with NVIDIA to port the demo to their new SoC Tegra 3.

Figure 30.5: Jérémie Noguer and Alexis Khouri trying to connect the Tegra development kit from NVIDIA, before the demo at GDC 2013.

Figure 30.6: The tech demo Windmill on the SoC from NVIDIA, Tegra 3.

Paleo Raft

The Paleo Raft demo came out of the partnership we launched with Qualcomm to demonstrate the technical capabilities of their latest portable processor. We convinced them to create an infinite runner-type game, which we would produce in early 2013.

Beneath

In 2013, the Allegorithmic studio began what would perhaps be its last major independent demo. The idea was to build a real-time mini-game based on Unreal Engine, in Lovecraft's universe. The production was long and complex, but we managed to create a very beautiful demo, which made a strong impression when we presented it.

Figure 30.7: The tech demo Windmill on PC.

However, with this production we began to question whether it was interesting for us to invest more and more time in the creation of these technical demos. We would therefore start to approach things differently and Beneath would be one of the last 'pure Allego' productions.

And others...

During these years, we produced other demos, such as Atlantis, in 2014, with the studio Xpec (see [38]), or our work on the game ShadowGun, from MadFinger Games, on Tegra 3. But an idea had begun to take root—namely, if interest in technical demos was limited, the production of whole games might have a completely different return on investment...

Figure 30.8: A few images from the infinite runner-type mobile game "Paleo Raft," which we developed at the beginning of 2013 for Qualcomm, to demonstrate the graphical capacity of their new portable chipset.

Figure 30.9: The Beneath demo, which we developed at the beginning of 2013 using Unreal Engine.

Figure 30.10: The Beneath demo, which we developed at the beginning of 2013 using Unreal Engine.

Figure 30.11: The Beneath demo, which we developed at the beginning of 2013 using Unreal Engine.

30.4 Game production

One weekend in 2012, I began to do the math: I must have spent 60 euros recently on *CSR Racing*, a car racing game that I'd just installed on my iPad. It turned out that this game was developed by BossAlien and published by Natural Motion, a technology and middleware company from the video game world that we knew very well, which was developing a product dedicated to procedural animation. Some time before, its founder and CEO, the impressive Torsten Reil, had presented us with his product, which would prove to be very successful in video games. However, during a discussion, he'd revealed a wish to produce games himself, mentioning in particular an idea he'd had for a horse management game. Alexis and I hadn't paid too much attention to this detail, instead focusing on the technology.

Yet these words returned to me when I considered how addicted I'd become to *CSR Racing*, a game coming from Torsten and his team... I immediately contacted him on Skype, and told him that he owed me a beer, and that I'd like to know more about his approach. He answered me immediately, while traveling on a plane between London and San Francisco, and confirmed that he'd made a lot of money with this game,[3] which was the perfect realization of his vision at the time: a free2play game with extremely simple gameplay, with high-quality graphics, and in 3D. It was precisely what he'd told us previously: with this formula (already used successfully on his game *My Horse*, released in 2012), the game could stand out from the crowd and ride the free2play movement which was exploding on mobile.

3: I won't share the exact figure here; I'll just say that it was fortunate that I was sitting down when he told me how much the game generated just through micro-purchases every single day.

I was astonished to realize how much the revenue from this one game dwarfed the revenue that his company generated with Natural Motion technology, which they'd developed with such complexity over many years...

I convinced myself that we too could do the same thing, and I developed the idea of a game of knights using the same formula as *CSR Racing*.

Knights

If Natural Motion could do it, why not us? So I pushed hard for us to create *Knights*, our own CSR. Throughout 2012 we worked on this with Édouard Albert to develop the project, and managed to convince Joseph Mbayen (see Chapter 11), who'd made his fortune with his company that promoted apps on the iOS market store, to produce the game.

The teams worked hard until the game *Rival Knights*, produced by Gameloft, was released while we were in the middle of production. The concept was too similar to our game, and Joseph told me that they'd have to halt the production of *Knights*. We couldn't finance the rest of the development ourselves, so this was the end of production, and our dream of producing our own CSR...

Figure 30.12: Work session with Édouard Albert for our game project *Knights*.

Figure 30.13: Performance tests for the game *Knights*, in 2013.

Flight of the Condor

Drawing on our experience gained with all the demos produced in previous years, and games like *Paleo Raft* and, although aborted, *Knights*, we developed a game that our shareholder Cédric Littardi, who'd acquired the rights to adapt the intellectual property "The Mysterious Cities of Gold," wanted to produce (see Chapter 23).

We developed the game on a very tight schedule and under heavy constraints. It was released on iOS in 2013. Even though we were happy with the product, it wasn't a huge success. . .

In retrospect. . .

The mixed results of some of our technical demos, or even our setbacks with the game *Knights*, for example, made us realize that producing games was a different art from creating technological tools. While some companies manage to do both, Allegorithmic does not. We had to admit it: this was not our strong suit. This realization therefore pushed us to focus on the technology and tools, with which we were successful and which constituted the DNA of Allegorithmic. The decision was made, at the end of this period, to cease pure content production.

Figure 30.14: Some screenshots from the game *Flight of the Condor*, ("*Le Vol du Condor*," originally) based on the world of The Mysterious Cities of Gold, which we developed for iOS.

30.5 Our products

Substance Designer

This was a great time for Substance Designer. The tool, notably thanks to our strong partnership with Naughty Dog (see Chapter 27), was taking off and establishing itself in the world of 'AAA' video games as the tool of reference for procedural PBR[4] texture creation. The tool had established itself as the absolute reference for the creation of 'tileable' PBR textures, and evolved very quickly between 2011 and 2015, with the inclusion of some particularly key stages, such as the first version of the software which integrated a major feature: 'bakers.' Bakers are functions that automatically calculate textures or masks from a 3D object provided as input. For example, it's possible to calculate maps like 'ambient occlusion,' 'curvature,' position in space, and so on. These maps are then used as input for a Substance Designer graph; like this, it's for example possible to correctly identify the edges of a metallic object, and correctly position wear and tear in these areas specifically. These bakers are particularly important in order to adapt the 'pure' textures that Substance Designer could produce, and uniquely personalize them to a given 3D model.

4: See Chapter 26 for more details on PBR, or physically based rendering.

Substance Designer 2.2 was released in March 2012 (for GDC), with a first version of the bakers. The addition of this feature had a profound impact on the workflows of 3D artists and would finally make it possible for the tool to enter usage in game development studios. With this release of Substance Designer 2.2, we started to see Facebook comments appear for the first time when we made an announcement! This was a huge step for us, the beginning of the creation of a community...

Notably, these bakers crashed the application just a few hours before its official release... It was Cyrille who debugged the app, and the teams, including Nicolas Liatti, who tested it out in real time. Everything was fixed in the final minutes and we could finally launch the product!

Substance Designer 3.0 was released just a few months later, in August 2012. It included a 'batching' tool, which allowed users to generate a large number of textures using a command, rather than having to do everything by hand, as well as a painting tool for bitmap masks. We'd launched pre-orders for the tool in June and were pleased with the interest it received, as well as the revenue generated. As is often the case in the company's history, we finished the launch video, email, and product webpage late at night, right before release...

Substance Designer 4.0 was released on November 27, 2013, and it was the first version that embraced PBR, and which integrated the idea of a 'material graph.' This was the version that would really cause us to take off, thanks in particular to the work with our gaming 'muse,' Naughty Dog (see Chapter 27). But the launch was painful, as Nicolas Liatti recalled; at that time he was living in Shanghai and, when he came to spend a week in France to follow the post-launch with the teams, he received this SMS, just as the plane was about to take off, and lose all network contact: "Nico, we have a problem with the launch... " Upon arrival, he found he'd received hundreds of emails requesting support from people who'd paid for the software, then found they couldn't download it. (Nicolas practically comprised our entire support team at that time!). We were finally able to resolve the problem during the day, and Nicolas got to work responding to hundreds of people one by one to apologize, and tell them that the problem was now resolved. Shortly after, Substance Designer 4 was reviewed in 3D Artist, in February 2014, receiving an excellent 8/10!

Substance Designer 5.0 was released in February 2015. It introduced new nodes in Substance Engine, integrating the fifth version of Substance Engine here, as well as in all our integrations within third-party products. In a month, between February 2015 and March 2015, we released Substance Designer 5.0, Substance Database 2.0, Substance Painter 1.3 (integrating smart materials and bakers), and launched Substance Live (see below).

The Great Elders of Substance Designer

It was during this period, between 2011 and 2015, that those that I like to call the 'Great Elders' of Substance Designer came into being: the first users, technical artists who pushed the tool to its limits and worked hand in hand with the developers on the team to make it the tool that would become a reference in its field. Three artists in particular stood out: Nicolas Wirrmann, Gilles Fleury, and Gaëtan Lassagne, who were considered by everyone, and in particular in the small, very selective environment of new-generation procedural texturing that Substance Designer had brought to the fore, as the artists who had pushed the tool the furthest, inspiring the next generation of great artists who would then take over in turn to inspire the world of 3D and create the school of 'Substance Designer Artist': the Grand Masters of Substance Designer (see Chapter 43).

Bitmap2Material

Version 2.0 of B2M was released in December 2012, thanks in particular to the tireless work of Gilles Fleury, who improved its algorithm;[5] it could now produce more convincing results, sometimes at the price of more complexity in its manipulation. At the same time, we added 12 grunge maps directly in B2M, which could be mixed directly with the captured material, to add richness. In March 2013, a review of B2M in 3D Artist lead to a stellar 9/10!

5: Gilles has an impressive ability to develop complex algorithms, using Substance Designer as a 'canvas,' without technical training. He can 'see' a Substance Designer graph for any given task. The success of B2M is in large part due to Gilles.

Version 3.0, the first to generate PBR materials, was released almost two years later, in September 2014.

30.6 Substance Live, and rent-to-own

In March 2015, we launched our first 'rent-to-own' offer. We didn't invent this business model; it originally stemmed from the automotive world. But it had never yet been used in the world of 3D software, as far as we knew.

The world of software in general had in recent years made a shift toward 'SaaS,' Software as a Service, which offered access to software according to a subscription model, with a monthly or annual payment, and which in return allowed users to continuously obtain the latest versions of the tools in question. For software publishers, it was a way to transform a 'hit and miss' business into a business with recurring revenue, which ensured better financial visibility and took the pressure off developers, since it was no longer necessary to condense everything (sometimes by artificially retaining features longer than necessary) into a single release and hoping that it would prove sufficiently impressive to encourage users to pay for an upgrade. Investors loved this business model, which established itself very quickly everywhere, for very understandable reasons of recurring revenue (at that time, Adobe was a perfect example of successful transformation toward SaaS, with an exponentially growing market valuation, and a similarly exponential number of users). Finally, independent teams and graphic designers generally liked this payment method, which often allowed access to much more value for a very modest cost, with payments spread out over time. Freelancers and hobbyists were less impressed with the SaaS model, typically preferring to have more control over their set of tools and their expenses, and 3D (in this case) probably wasn't their main source of income.

Considering all of these points, we came around to the idea of rent-to-own: a model which allowed users to pay monthly for access to Substance software (Substance Painter, Substance Designer, B2M, for $19.90 per month) then, if they wished, to acquire a perpetual version after 18 months of continuous subscription (the latest version released). And so, Allegorithmic had the advantage of subscriptions, which gave us a constant income and relaxed certain production constraints, while users had a choice of payment method and the certainty of being able to continue using the tools even in the event of unanticipated expenses elsewhere, and the inability to pay monthly for licenses (or even if they simply decided not to do any 3D for a little while).

So as not to distance ourselves from professionals, however, we also introduced another idea—which was kind of inspired by taxes… We established three levels of licenses, one for the 'Indies' at $19.90, then a more expensive license for 'Pros,' and a third for 'Enterprises' (price to be determined). The way we segmented these types of users was based, as with taxes, on the income generated by the licensee in question. If the income from using our tools was less than 100K dollars per year, then we classed this user as an 'Indie.' If income from 3D was between 100K dollars and 1 million dollars, we were into 'Pro' territory. Anything beyond this required an 'Enterprise' license, we decided.[6] In this way, we made our tools very accessible, at a price that was as fair as possible.

6: How did we verify this? Factually, we had no way of checking! We depended on users to respect our approach. Only in very rare cases would we impose a specific type of license on a licensee—if, for instance, a CAC 40 business wanted to acquire an Indie license.

This model was an immediate success, and strengthened the trust we received from our users—particularly with independents, who rightly saw this as our desire to make our tools as accessible as possible to everybody, including the many non-professionals and enthusiasts in the world of 3D, keeping in mind that 3D wasn't their primary source of revenue.

It's worth mentioning too that we developed this offer super-quickly, within three months. In the tradition of agile development (here applied to all parts of our company, as we had to accept monthly payments, set everything up with accounting, etc.), the first version was an 'MVP' (Minimum Viable Product, the simplest functioning version of a product) which allowed us to test things out with the market. The offer then evolved greatly in the following years, and quickly represented 90% of our revenue, as well giving us the feeling that we were treating our users, our investors, and our internal teams well.

In retrospect...

Our move to rent-to-own was a turning point in the development of Allegorithmic, as our original solution, which combined the advantages of SaaS with a fair approach to the range of pricing to be paid depending on user income, would prove to be a winning solution for the entire 3D ecosystem, and would create a strong connection between Allegorithmic and its users. Many 3D software publishers, particularly smaller organizations that could easily accommodate this model, would regularly follow our approach over the following years.

Substance B2M

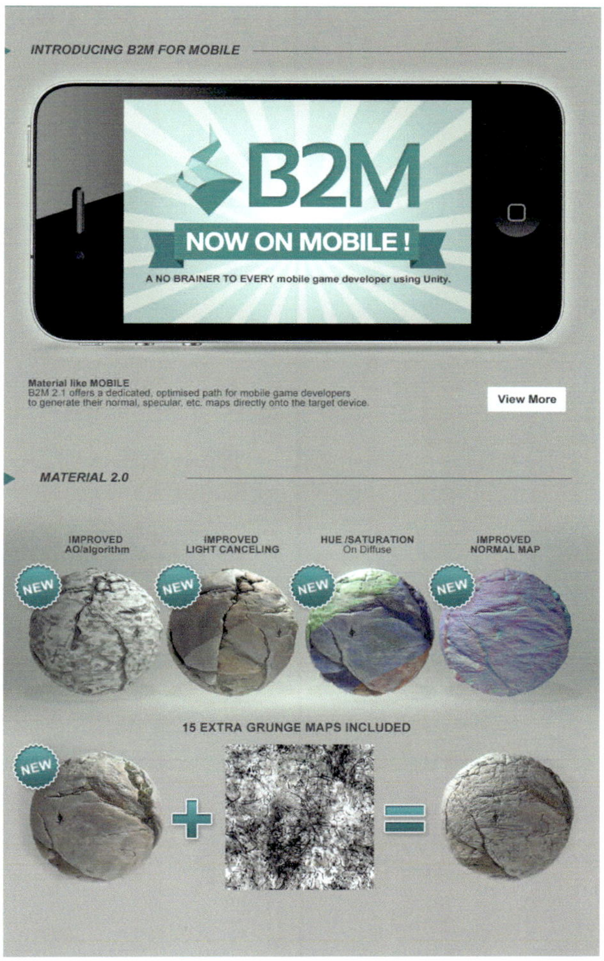

Contests 31

To motivate our community to test our tools and show off their own know-how, we came up with the idea of a contest. We needed to find the right balance so the contest wouldn't take too long and wouldn't be a way for us to exploit the free labor of 3D artists participating. We found a formula that worked,[1] as well as some generous prizes (like high-end hardware such as graphical tablets and GPUs, perpetual Substance licenses, and even a trip to LA, all expenses covered, to meet the team there), so we launched our first contest in 2014, titled "Battle of the Titans."

1: Contrary to the majority of contests organized in a similar way, we didn't possess any reproduction rights to the participants' creations and needed to ask for their permission, at times with a fee, if we wanted to use an image as part of our communications.

31.1 Battle of the Titans

This first contest, in 2014, was for a company of our size very successful, as it brought together a large number of participants and, above all, the quality of creations was impressive (see figures 31.1 and 31.3). It also allowed us to get to know incredible artists like Sylvain Castelanelli, Vincent Gradt, and Eddie Muñoz.

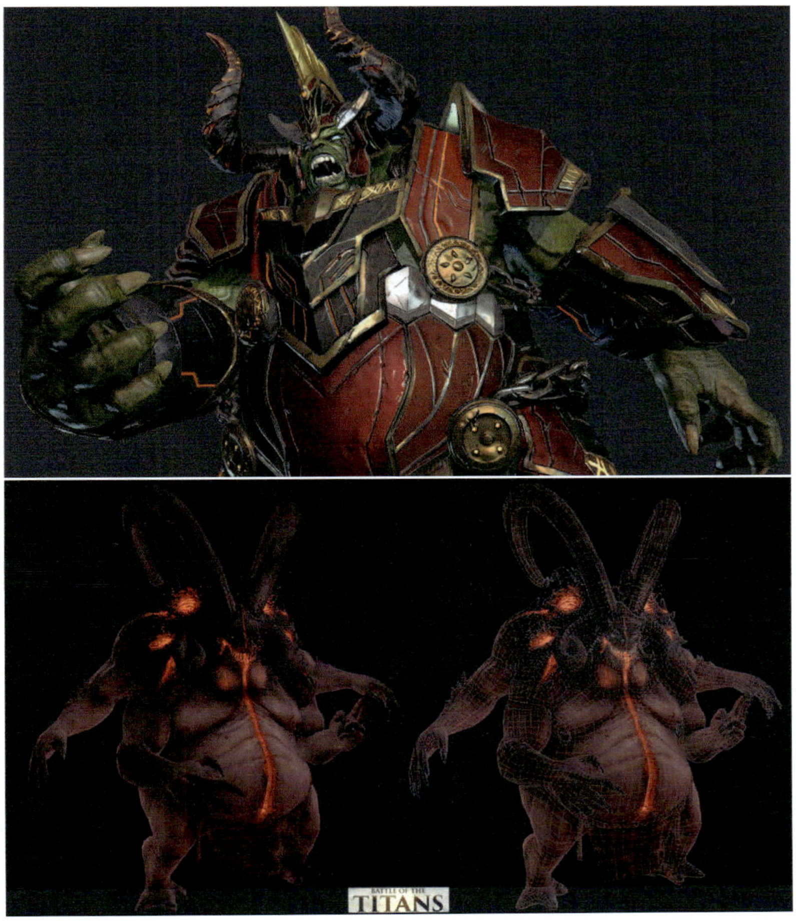

Figure 31.1: A few images from our texturing contest "Battle of the Titans."

The winner of the contest was Nicolas Garilhe with "Unchained Titan."

DOI:10.1201/9781003534624-31

Figure 31.2: A few images from our texturing contest "Battle of the Titans."

Figure 31.3: A few images from our texturing contest "Battle of the Titans."

Figure 31.4: The winner of the "Battle of the Titans" contest, Nicolas Garilhe with "Unchained Titan."

31.2 The Throne Room

Encouraged by the success of the Titans contest, we wanted to launch another competition a short time later, in 2015, in partnership with the website Polycount [39], a reference in the technical domain of 3D art. This time around we decided to launch an environment creation contest, a style of art well suited to our tools, and a use of Substance Designer that we saw a lot, particularly in the domain of video games.

Figure 31.5: The contest "The Throne Room" was launched at the beginning of 2015, in partnership with the website Polycount, a reference in the technical domain of 3D art.

We agreed on the theme of "The Throne Room" and managed to find some high-quality prizes, which attracted a significant number of participants and allowed us to witness the creation of some truly inspired 3D artwork, as can be seen in the following images.

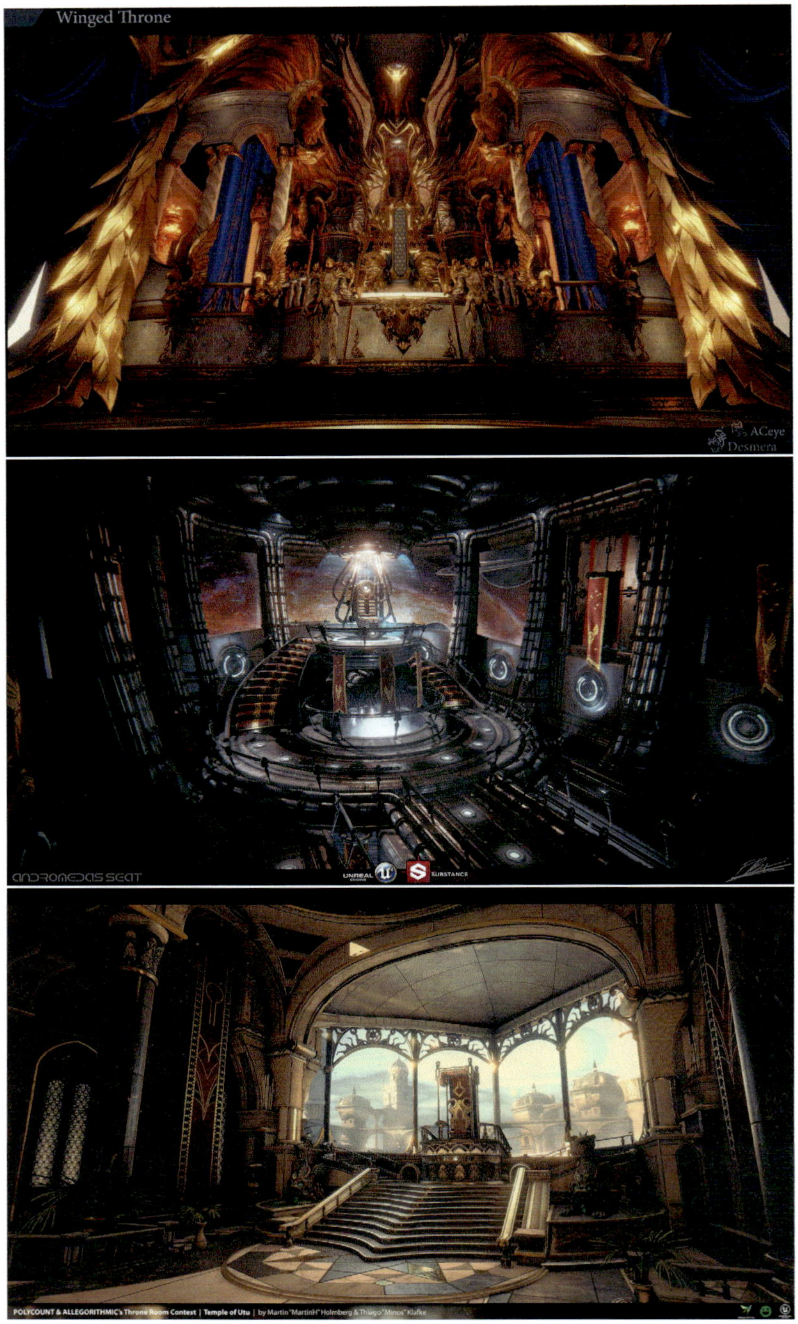

Figure 31.6: Winners of the contest The Throne Room, at the beginning of 2015. The artists are ACeye and Desmera, followed by Noscope, MartinH, and Minos.

Conferences and commercial prospection

32

The explosion of interest for our tools was very rewarding, and conducive to ongoing prospection, whether by attending trade shows, trips all over the planet to areas rich in studios, or through in-person or online training. During this period, we were constantly on the road, giving demo after demo, setting up and subsequently taking down stand after stand, at every conference that seemed interesting for Substance, and visiting game developers all over the world, who opened their doors to us with greater pleasure than ever. It was a very intense period, but our efforts were paying off, and we could sense the excitement among the developers we met: the time of doubt and infinite questions about what we would present to them was behind us. Now the questions were more practical ("How should I go about integrating the tools into my pipeline? How much does a license cost?") and more technical ("How do I ensure that the roughness maps produced by the artists are physically correct? How can I optimize my Substance Designer graphs?").

Figure 32.1: On the left, my collection of badges (around 170). Each of them represents at least one, or more often several, days at a conference, meetings, discussions, answering questions, parties, trips (often far away, by plane), jet lag, short nights, and accumulated fatigue. This collection is perhaps the best illustration of the stamina needed to successfully advance a project... On the right, a typical scene of my return from my trips (here coming back from GDC 2017 in San Francisco: I'm greeted by my partner and my two little guys at the airport. It's a powerful moment each time, which has been repeated regularly for years, after each conference and road trip.

32.1 Conferences

During these 5 years, between 2011 and 2015, we took part in many conferences—in the US of course, but also in Europe and Asia: in China, Korea, and Japan in particular. These industry meetings, such as GDC and SIGGRAPH (see Chapters 25 and 13, for instance), mark crucial steps in the development of companies like Allegorithmic. Professional conferences allowed us, after having rented a space at exorbitant prices,[1] to send a dedicated team, who were responsible for all the marketing material prepared for the occasion, to present to visitors the latest news about our products, and our content. Such conferences dictate the rhythm for product releases, and it was quite typical that, for any given feature in development, we'd give ourselves the objective of releasing it, 'in the

1: The cost of conferences is an eternal source of debate: is the expense justified in terms of business impact generated? The link between this expense and commercial success is difficult to measure, and so the question is always relevant, and CFOs and budget managers must return to it at regular intervals...

DOI:10.1201/9781003534624-32

version of Substance Painter that we'll present at GDC next March,' as it would be 'perfect for this audience,' and was going to 'generate a lot of noise'... This imposed cadence encouraged us to follow the sustained tempo of the industry, moving neither too quickly nor too slowly.

These conferences also allowed us to take the pulse of the industry. Seeing a company release a product, or make an alliance with another; hearing the way a company talks about current trends, or accidentally mention a piece of confidential information; watching a company push forward too carelessly, or seeing it raise money with this or that investor, or hearing it announce its acquisition, so that it joins this group, and so on, and so forth... These are the vital pieces of information that become apparent at conferences—information that induces movement all across the industry, as companies rethink their strategies and reposition themselves, sometimes quite urgently.[2] After months of working in the shadows, the whole industry steps out into the light at these conferences, for all to see.

2: For instance, I once asked the entire Allegorithmic team present at a GDC to meet at 10:00pm in the lobby of the Handlery Hotel in San Francisco, where we were staying, to discuss the potential implications of a new material layering technique I'd just heard about from a few key people at the show, which had the potential to partly make texture production obsolete by moving material creation into shaders—which could be very dangerous for our product line and the future of our company, as we didn't have any tools dedicated to shaders. Discussing this existential threat couldn't wait—we needed to consider this in real time, to adapt to visitors who would ask us about this the next day.

Figure 32.2: A colorful costume party by Blizzard during GDC 2014. From left to right: Josh Coyne, Jérémie Noguer (wearing a hat), Alexandre Bagard, Christophe Soum, Eric Batut (wearing a hat), Sylvain Paris, Wes McDermott.

Figure 32.3: Our stand at Unite, August 2012 in Amsterdam, with Jérémie Noguer.

Figure 32.4: Our presence at Korea Game Conference, in October 2012. With Nicolas Liatti and Christian Kim.

The work of representing the company was intense and tiring, but it was fundamental to our success, especially because it allowed us to create strong connections between the human beings present during the event. Such connections might be those between the representatives of different companies, during numerous meetings which are organized by email weeks in advance—or even during the event, while wandering from stand to stand, or during the numerous parties organized by the big names in the industry.[3] These connections are particularly useful in business, as interactions like these allow people to develop respect and trust for one another, and sometimes even friendships with various members of the industry. These significant figures in the market, who we see every year at conferences,[4] are present because they share our passion for this field. At times the human connection can even be strong with competitors. And sometimes these semi-professional, semi-personal connections created over years of meeting up can play a role much, much later. The 3D world is small, and the same pool of people can rotate and

3: Tickets for which are sometimes rare and expensive. A good example can be seen in figure 32.2.

4: There are quite a few members of the 3D community in France that I see more often during SIGGRAPH in California, on the far side of the world, than I do in Paris.

Figure 32.5: Our stand at Unite China, in April 2013. With Wang Cong and Gilles Fleury.

end up in key positions as the years pass.

And conferences create and reinforce very special connections between members of the Allegorithmic team who are present in the same place at the same time. The marketing team will be present, of course; they'll take care of communication, and of the smooth running of the event. They'll make sure the stand is assembled on time, and ensure the availability of materials to distribute, such as T-shirts,[5] brochures, and many other things (the marketing team is usually exhausted at the end of an event). The sales team will also be here; they'll try to develop, and sometimes close, commercial opportunities with customers, often accompanied by technical artists who will give product demos, whether in small groups or at the stand, to an audience of passers-by. And developers will also be there, to hear users talk about a product, and to answer their many technical questions, as well as attending the many dedicated technical talks in order to expand their knowledge.

5: A real cult of T-shirts collectors exists in the technical and creative world. At conferences, it's typically very easy for a collector to pick up T-shirts bearing the logo of a particular company or product. . . Allegorithmic's first logo-bearing T-shirt was a big step for us; see Section 9.4.

Strong attachments were created during these trips, while we were together continuously, sharing hotel rooms and meals, parties, and problems, sitting beside one another on plane seats or in rental cars, feeling the stress before presentations, and many other experiences unique to this context. This continuity of presence and connection was, in my opinion, one of the fundamental components of entering a state that allowed us to ask the right questions about our work, put our fingers on the truth, and decide potential solutions for the evolution of the company. These interactions and first indications, this continuum of reflection and presence at the heart of the flow, these hidden elements and intersections are components of an incredible power that no Zoom meeting can ever recreate. So too are the repeated trips and jet lags, the events behind closed doors, the rituals,[6] the parties, again and again, and the short nights that are absolutely exhausting, but so crucial.

6: For instance, for our team dinner the day before GDC begins, once our team from all over the world has met up in San Francisco, we have a ritual of going to Mel's Drive In on Mission Street, across from Metreon in San Francisco.

Figure 32.6: Our little stand at GDC, in March 2013. With Alexis Khouri and Wes McDermott.

Figure 32.7: Cyrille Damez in good company during SIGGRAPH 2013, then with Jérémie Noguer and Alexis Khouri.

Figure 32.8: Meizi Yan and Nicolas Liatti in good company during ChinaJoy 2013.

Figure 32.9: GDC 2014, San Francisco. Our stand, which was overwhelmed throughout the entire conference!

Figure 32.10: Presentation by Meizi Yan during Unite China 2014.

Figure 32.11: Presentation by Wes McDermott during Unite 2014, in Seattle.

Figure 32.12: March 2013. It's in this car, during the trips between San Francisco and Los Angeles, before and especially after GDC, that some of the most important strategic decisions in Allegorithmic's history have taken place. The pattern was often the same: articulation of what we'd just experienced at the conference, and digesting the fundamental information we'd acquired concerning major changes in the industry, then an argument on one subject or another, then lapsing into silence... After this, a hesitant resumption of communication some time later, once the tension had died down. And it's in this last phase, together in this enclosed space, that the strongest ideas and decisions were expressed, choices that would change the direction of the company as a whole, marking the major inflection points in the curves of Allegorithmic's life. Numerous times, the destiny of the company was played out during these few hours of travel, between Jérémie Noguer, Alexis Khouri, at times Nicolas Liatti, and myself.

Figure 32.13: Team dinner after GDC 2014, in San Francisco. From left to right: Christophe Soum, Eric Batut, Jérémie Noguer, Alexis Khouri, Thomas Bidaux, Wes McDermott (who, as per tradition, systematically tells us highly improbable, very funny stories during this dinner, often from his childhood in the American midwest), Sébastien Deguy, Josh Coyne, Alexandre Bagard, Sylvain Paris, and Laurens Corijn.

32.2 Commercial visits and training

During this period the commercial teams multiplied their visits and presentations. The members of our sales teams formed duos with the technical artists available in the region. Working without constraints in terms of the training they provided or the region where they operated, some duos were particularly hard at work, accumulating miles and hotel stays together—notably, Alexis Khouri and Jérémie Noguer in North America, Nicolas Liatti and Gilles Fleury in Asia, and even myself and Nicolas Wirrmann in Europe.

Figure 32.14: Visiting Pixar, in January 2013.

Figure 32.15: Commercial presentation in London in November 2013. Nicolas Wirrmann poses in front of a London post box, which he reproduced and textured with the help of Substance Designer.

Figure 32.16: Visiting the premises of Gnomon School of VFX, in Hollywood. The premises were also home to the company Pixologic: here we see Jaime Labelle next to Alexis, and a life-sized Avatar character.

Figure 32.17: Presentation at the development studio DICE, in Stockholm, in March 2014. Cyrille Damez, Laurens Corijn, and Nicolas Wirrmann gather around our host on that occasion, while taking a break on the rooftop terrace of their incredible office.

Figure 32.18: Presentation by Gilles Fleury to the studio Virtuos, in June 2014.

Figure 32.19: Presentation by Christophe Desse, from Naughty Dog, during his trip to Japan in November 2014. We were lucky to have Christophe join us during this trip, as he was able to bring an astonishing credibility to our offer and our commercial push.

Figure 32.20: Presentation at UC Santa Cruz, by Jérémie Noguer, in April 2014.

32.3 Meetups

Demos and Knacki balls

The website meetup.com changed a lot of things for meetings and other encounters between enthusiasts of all kinds. Just as people we starting to talk about our tools, we took the opportunity to create a series of meetups dedicated to Substance in a number of cities (Paris, London, then in California; Paris was by far the most active as being based in France ourselves we could really follow up with attendees afterward).

Each city offered a different type of public: while in Paris the rooms were mostly filled with students who wanted to learn more about the new tools on the market, in London the audience was much smaller, but essentially composed of professionals.

Figure 32.21: Meetup in London, in February 2014. We see Nicolas Wirrmann giving a demo of Substance Designer, and of what would become Substance Painter, to a dozen people present. Contrary to Parisian meetups which mostly attracted students, this one, our first in London, was of interest to professionals, such as Lee Devonald, who later joined Quixel and Rocksteady. We gave our demos in a small room that was part of a London club, with an ever-present deafening background noise.

In Paris in 2014 we began our 'Demos and Knacki balls' evenings, in the school Isart Digital, at Bastille. They were an opportunity for the school's 3D students to meet and connect, but they were also open to anybody else who was interested in the subject, which would prove to be quite important in establishing a relationship with the larger 3D community, many members of whom we'd meet around a drink during these evenings. Significantly, during one of these meetings I met somebody who would play an important role in Allegorithmic's development.

Anthony Salvi

I met Anthony Salvi during one of the Substance Meetups, which we held within the 3D school LISAA, at the foot of the Tour Montparnasse in Paris, whose director at the time was Renaud Jungmann.[7] At the end of our presentation, Anthony asked me a unique question which would become a running joke at Allegorithmic: "What about color management?" At the time, absolutely nothing in our tools addressed color management, and I admitted my ignorance on the subject; game developers didn't talk

7: It was Renaud who, a few years earlier, had given me the idea for the name 'FX-Maps' about this, but Anthony already knew that the subject would become fundamental for us once we ventured out of this one specific field.

Figure 32.22: Meetup organized at the LISAA school, in Paris, in October 2014. We see Nicolas Wirrmann giving a demo of Substance Designer and Substance Painter, to a group composed mostly of students. However in the second row we can see Anthony Salvi (in a blue shirt). We first met during this meetup. Anthony asked about color management support; my reply was, "Excuse me?" He joined us sometime later, and color management would become part of our tools a few years after that.

We spoke again at the end of the event. Anthony was truly passionate about images, and his career amazed me: though he wasn't an engineer, he'd done some pretty heavy IT work, both in hardware and in software, and he'd also been a digital assistant to some well-known photographers, while also being interested in 3D and mastering advanced tools like Houdini and Unreal Engine. He believed the future of imaging lay in the advance of real-time techniques, and saw a bright future for the Substance tools because of this. Though the Substance tools had come from the world of video games, Anthony anticipated that they would soon prove interesting for customers far beyond this universe.

His words made an impact on me, and an idea began to occur: we should bring our tools to new domains, outside of video games. Anthony was a specialist in these other domains, and our future discussions involving Jérôme Derel confirmed this. Anthony was particularly talented, and I asked him to join us some time later.[8]

8: When I texted him to confirm that we'd like him to join Allegorithmic, he replied that he couldn't call me right away as he was on a set, photographing Natalie Portman. . .

New markets | 33

33.1 Beyond video games

At the start of 2015, the company was going well. We anticipated growing success in the video game domain, and since becoming profitable in 2013, we'd been trying to find our next sources of growth. According to the principles of bringing innovation to a market, brilliantly presented by Geoffrey Moore in his work *Crossing the Chasm*,[1] it was possible, after successfully penetrating a 'niche' market and having obtained measurable success in that universe, to consider investing in new markets, with the same tools, or tools that were very similar. If we were to believe the theory laid out in the book, these new markets would react very quickly, if they had any technological interest in innovative tools.

1: See [33]. More generally, many books, articles, and other concepts have helped the successful development of Allegorithmic. And although no single work can provide an absolute response to all the questions that emerge during the life of a company, which is by definition infinitely complex, they still gave me, and many other members of the company, tangible elements and tools, developing poorly defined hunches on paper, and imbuing them with a scientific, or at least sufficiently rigorous, foundation. I cite here just a few of them, which had a particularly important role: [40], [41], [42], [43], [44], and [45].

We chose to test out this theory, and starting in 2014 launched our first explorations into areas that we'd identified as potential new markets: architecture, product design, and fashion. Interest from these markets seemed to be present, driven by their interest in techniques coming from video games. On paper, our technology accelerated design cycles; real-time rendering made it possible to carry out numerous design iterations very rapidly, essentially making more conventional approaches to the high-quality visualization of images—which were expensive and time-consuming—obsolete. Our tools had begun to establish their presence in the world of video games; we were pleased, and more than a little reassured, to see that this growing influence helped us outside this specific universe, as well. Geoffrey Moore appeared to have been correct.

We were encouraged by our initial success, but we didn't know these new markets, and so we decided to hire the right people to drive this new initiative. We ultimately recruited Jérôme Derel, who came from Dassault Systèmes, who'd been telling us for some time that we needed to push our tools into these new areas. Jérôme was an absolute visionary, capable of describing and then producing in incredible detail technological objects that fused engineering and technical art. We also hired Anthony Salvi, whom I had met a little while earlier (see Chapter 32), and who had made such a strong impression on Jérôme and myself that we'd wanted to bring him onto the team as soon as possible.

This was also the beginning for Allegorithmic's Paris office, within a Regus office space on rue d'Amsterdam (see figure 28.3).

33.2 François Cottin

Now we needed someone who could direct this new initiative. For this, we thought of someone that Alexis and I had known for some time (since ESSEC, for Alexis): François Cottin.

François had a fairly unusual background, having gone to business school (ESSEC), thinking upon leaving to take over a Parisian theater

DOI:10.1201/9781003534624-33

(this ultimately didn't happen), and then going on to carry out innovation on a large scale for the major French telecommunications company Orange, as well as managing some patents; after this he worked in strategic counseling in a big company (Boston Consulting Group), then created his own company, selling luxury computers, named Cottin Paris.[2] The company ultimately didn't take off as anticipated, and relationships with its shareholders and partners became strained to breaking point. And so François shut down his company at the end of 2014.

2: François asked me around 2013 to be part of his board of directors, which I accepted with great pleasure.

It was shortly after this that he called me to tell me that he was interested in Allegorithmic, particularly in its new potential chapter targeting these new markets, which we'd discussed from time to time when we'd met up, sometimes walking beside the river, not far from his shop at Quai des Orfèvres. He wanted to leave his former project behind him, and get back to work right away. François has an exceptional capacity for resilience which allows him to focus on the positive aspects of any experience, sometimes to the point of the autosuggestion technique developed by Émile Coué. He wasn't familiar with the 3D world specifically, but he knew well the more industrial sector that we had little experience of. His profile made him the perfect person to direct Allegorithmic's new adventures, and we brought him on board in January 2015.

Figure 33.1: François Cottin confirms the interest in Substance in the world of product design.

The first mission lasted around 6 months, and it involved contacting the industries concerned and determining the most mature sectors that needed our technologies, but above all determining if we could target these markets with our existing products, or whether we had to adapt our tools, or develop new tools. Internally, we had a range of opinions and, even though the final answer was quite nuanced, the initial investigation phase by François and the team confirmed that we should push forward with our tools as they were, with Substance Designer taking the lead. François joined us permanently at the end of this first phase and would play a very important part in Allegorithmic's development over the years, ultimately becoming Managing Director during the last few years of Allegorithmic's independence.

34 Summary of progress up to mid-2015, and conclusion of this period

34.1 A golden age

This period, between 2011 and 2015, constitutes without a doubt the golden age of Allegorithmic. It was our most exciting period, comprising the greatest technological pivots and the beginnings of commercial success, as our revenue was still growing exponentially (see figure 34.1). This was also the period during which we became profitable, in 2013, which profoundly changed our dynamic and provided our investors and partners with confidence—those in the field of 3D and video games as well as the institutions in the Clermont-Ferrand region that had been following our progress for many years, and could now breathe more easily.

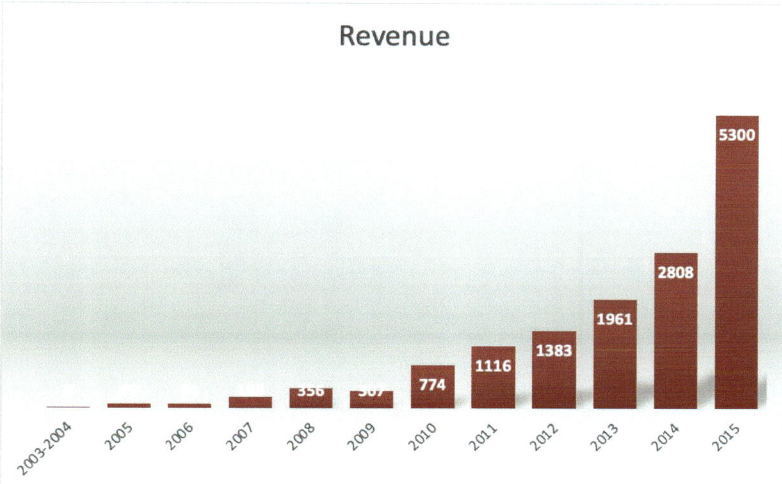

Figure 34.1: Allegorithmic's revenue, between 2003 and 2015. These were years of explosion with the 2015 revenue standing at 5.3 million euros, almost twice the revenue of 2014. Our products were selling better, and the Substance suite was establishing itself as the new default standard in the world of video game development, particularly with our apps Substance Designer and Substance Painter. 2013 was our first profitable year! This was a major milestone in the life of Allegorithmic, 10 years after its creation...

At the beginning of the 2010s, and for the five years that followed, we saw how the market turned toward a new rendering paradigm, PBR (see Chapter 26), and transformed this into an opportunity for our long-standing product Substance Designer, which adapted very easily to these new techniques and provided an immediate solution to the constraints associated with texturing. On paper, at least, the path before us was clear, but it would still take several years of joint work with Naughty Dog, the legendary game developer, who trusted us and who was betting on our nascent product and our small team of little French people from the other side of the world (see Chapter 27). Getting as close as possible to this 'alpha-site,' stretching from Los Angeles to Shanghai, with detached teams dedicated to the success of this deployment, we managed to shape a tool which would establish itself in the following years as a reference in game development in particular, and 3D in general: Substance Designer was really born at this moment.

It was also during this period, and while Substance Designer was still in full development and not yet adapted to PBR, that we decided to take a big risk, both technologically and in terms of marketing, with

DOI:10.1201/9781003534624-34

the development of another totally independent tool: Substance Painter was born almost at the same time as the first real version of Substance Designer—we took a big risk, which would ultimately pay off. This was perhaps Allegorithmic's greatest leap, in several ways: in the development of its initial idea and the first prototypes; in the decision, very early on, to make it a separate product (a somewhat crazy marketing gamble, but one which would pay off in a big way, and pave the way for our approach to distinguishing technical and non-technical artists); in its technical execution; and in its launch and positioning on the market, with the benefit of the introduction of a new business model, rent-to-own (see Chapter 30)... At the end of these 5 years, we had two products and one business model in line with market demand, the pillars of our development on which we would rely to build the future.

Figure 34.2: The team in December 2015. On this photo: Damient Climent, Gaëtan Lassagne, Alexandre Bagard, Antoine Gonzalez, Benoît Barbier, Stéphane Guy, Felipe Restrepo, Jean-François El Hajjar, Benjamin Maréchal, Christophe Soum, Fabrice Piquet, Jérémy Bouny, Robin Faury, Daniel Lachal, Rosalie Martin, Nathalie Delfour, Laëtitia Boully, Damien Bousseau, Loic Anquetil, Sylvain Paris, Alexandre Chassany, Camille Masson, Victor Lucquin, Eric Batut, Gaël Cathelin, Anthony Salvi, Damien Letournel, Clément Jacob, Xavier Courbouleix, Frédéric Kohler, Nicolas Wirrmann, Denis Fondras, Amandine Lorrai, Jérémy Matichard, Jérôme Derel, and François Cottin.

The team grew throughout these years (see figure 34.2), and it was a very outward-looking period, during which we built a unique relationship with the community of 3D artists, via meetups in Europe, presence at as many conferences as possible, tours and demos in studios all over the world (see Chapter 32), and increasingly successful competitions (see Chapter 31). I like to believe that this growing trust, this mutual willingness to listen to one another between Allegorithmic and the community of artists using the Substance tools was one basis of the commercial success that we would go on to establish.

Finally, at the end of this period, we started taking an interest in what was happening outside the world of video games, not in special effects for cinema and television, but rather in the domains of product design, architecture, and advertising. The arrival of François Cottin and a few other key people, in particular in Paris where we were opening our third site (see Chapter 28), allowed us to confirm growing interest and a potential for exploiting our technologies and products in the areas that we called 'new markets' (see Chapter 33).

It was finally at the end of this period, as if to mark a milestone, that an event significantly positioned us for the next step in our adventure. I recount it here:

34.2 Our main competitor gives up the fight

It was the last day of GDC 2015, in March in San Francisco. The doors had just closed to the public. The founders of our fiercest competitor had sent us an email that morning asking for a meeting; we gathered with them in our small stand. And here they told us that they felt we'd achieved tremendous success with Substance Painter. The tool represented what they would have liked to accomplish themselves, their tools still being some steps behind ours. . . They thought we'd been particularly fast, and developed the tool of their dreams. After a few minutes of discussion, they floated the idea of us buying them out, so that we could join forces.

This was a big surprise for us. In recent years, these competitors had been among the most talented members of the industry. Despite having products that, I think it's fair to say, were visibly below ours in technical terms, their teams were very much in tune with the needs of the market and were masterful in communicating around their products. Their efforts had inspired within us a lot of both envy and respect.

They were about to release new tools that seemed even more advanced than ours and that, in principle, worried us. Joining up could indeed be particularly interesting, resulting in a partnership that could achieve great things. The only potentially difficult element in the equation concerned a cultural fit: our teams had been in fierce competition for years, perhaps with no small amount of resentment. It was possible, even probable, that combining teams would produce sparks. . . And then, there was the simple question of feasibility: did we have the means to make such a deal, and were they really ready to go forward with it?

After some brief discussions on due diligence and internal conflicts within the company in question, however, and before even knowing for sure if we could have found a solution to the complicated equation of buying a competitor, discussions halted. We would therefore remain independent, and continue to be competitors.

And yet this episode clearly illustrates the important stage that we were passing through in our development: we were no longer the little team stepping into the field, the small structure from the far end of the world appreciated by everyone. We now had our hands on a growing market, and we were seeing competitors emerging ready to fight. Allegorithmic, during this period from 2011 and 2015, was able to take a strong position in the niche field of video game texturing and game development, with the implication that this was a position that inspired both admirations and enmity.

allegorithmic

WHO'S WHO
November 2015

CLERMONT-FERRAND
31 rue Gonod 63000 Clermont-Ferrand FRANCE

LOÏC ANQUETIL
3D Artist

BENOÎT BARBIER
Senior Software Engineer
Substance Painter/Designer

ÉRIC BATUT
Lead Software Engineer
Substance Engine

LAËTITIA BOULLY
Administrative Assistant

JÉRÉMY BOUNY
Software Engineer
Substance Painter

GAËL CATHELIN
Software Engineer
Substance Painter

ALEXANDRE CHASSANY
Senior Software Engineer
Substance Painter

CYRILLE DAMEZ
Chief Technical Officer

ROBIN FAURY
Intern

DENIS FONDRAS
Network Administrator

ANTOINE GONZALEZ
Senior Software Engineer
Integrations

STÉPHANE GUY
Lead Software Engineer
Substance Painter

CLÉMENT JACOB
Senior Software Engineer
Substance Painter/Share

DANIEL LACHAL
Software Engineer
Substance Designer

GAËTAN LASSAGNE
Senior Product Manager
Substance Database

AMANDINE LORRAI
Management Assistant

BENJAMIN MARÉCHAL
Senior Graphic Designer

SYLVAIN PARIS
Lead Software Engineer
Substance Designer

FABRICE PIQUET
Product Specialist
Substance Painter

NATHALIE POUGHON
Financial, HR and Administrative Manager

CHRISTOPHE SOUM
Lead Software Architect

NICOLAS WIRRMANN
Senior Product Manager
Substance Designer

PARIS
87 rue Taitbout 75009 Paris FRANCE

ALEXANDRE BAGARD
Sales and Marketing Manager

DAMIEN BOUSSEAU
3D Artist

FRANÇOIS COTTIN
Chief Marketing Officer
Secretary-General

XAVIER COURBOULEIX
Chief Financial Officer

SÉBASTIEN DEGUY
Chief Executive Officer
President and Founder

JÉRÔME DEREL
Chief Product Officer

JEAN-FRANÇOIS EL HAJJAR
Lead Research Scientist

FRÉDÉRIC KOHLER
Business Development Director
Europe

VICTOR LUCQUIN
Intern

ROSALIE MARTIN
Senior Software Engineer

ANTHONY SALVI
Creative Director

LYON
Pôle Pixel Bâtiment M 26 rue Émile Decorps
69100 Villeurbanne FRANCE

DAMIEN LETOURNEL
Senior Software Engineer
Integrations

CAMILLE MASSON
Senior Software Engineer
Integrations

LOS ANGELES
1600 Main Street 90291 Venice, California UNITED STATES

JOSH COYNE
Lead Software Engineer
Integrations

ALEXIS KHOURI
Chief Sales Officer
Vice President

NICOLAS LIATTI
Chief Operating Officer

WES MCDERMOTT
Senior Community Manager

JÉRÉMIE NOGUER
Senior Product Manager
Substance Painter

TOKYO
JAPAN

IMMANUEL MARTIN
Business Development Manager
APAC and Western US

SHANGHAI
9/F Eco City, 1788 Nanjing West Road Jing'an District
200040 Shanghai CHINA

GILLES FLEURY
Technical Art Director

WANG CONG
3D Artist

YAN MEIZI
Community Manager

SEOUL
39-29 Samseong-dong, Gangnam-gu
135-090 Seoul SOUTH KOREA

CHRISTIAN KIM
Area Manager
Korea

INHO KIM
Community Manager

Part VIII

2015–2019

Structure and Culture 35

The whole period between 2015 to the very beginning of 2019 was marked by continuous growth, in terms of both revenue and number of users, but also in the size of our internal teams. In this, our development didn't quite correspond to the classic model of a startup, which can place an unreasonable emphasis on gaining users, without considering revenue as important in this initial phase of growth and market positioning. The investments necessary to support such an approach were then naturally uncorrelated from the resources generated by the activity alone. Since our last round of investment in 2011 (see Chapter 23), then since 2013, the first year when Allegorithmic was profitable, we were in a different situation to 'classic' startups: we could sustain our growth because we were profitable, and so we didn't need to raise funds, thanks in particular to the fact that our products seemed to be of interest, without any particular effort, for markets other than those we'd originally targeted (see Chapter 33).

Such company health imposed two things on us, however: anticipation and careful management of our finances,[1] as well as a company structure that would allow us to grow in good conditions. As we evolved significantly, we needed to set up functions dedicated to finance, legal, and human resources at Allegorithmic. And of course we continued to expand our sales team, and created teams dedicated to 'special projects' and 'Labs.'

1: Among other things, the famous 'Working Capital Requirement,' or 'WCR,' was a notion it took me years to understand, only becoming significant out of necessity... To give a much-simplified summary: the more successful a company becomes, the more it becomes necessary to have money available, in order to cover losses between, for instance, the start of a new product project and the time it actually goes on sale, and starts generating income.

We also opened new sites, both in France and abroad, in order to give teams means to work in the best conditions and develop the Allegorithmic culture wherever our company was present. In order to strengthen this culture, we wanted to push our 'Global Gathering' concept further, which had been close to our hearts since the creation of the company (see Chapters 17 then 40), to allow all employees, wherever they were, to meet up for a few days in the same place.

And this was the culture, or rather the values, that would constitute one of the particular areas of focus of this period, as we'll see in this section.

35.1 Structure of the support functions

Financial and administrative structure, the 'College'

Xavier Courbouleix

The financial and administrative management of the company was one of our first areas of transformation. The current structure had allowed us to develop without any problems until that point, but now we needed to bring in more people to manage the smooth running of the company and to develop a financial growth strategy which set up good conditions to reach the next stage of our journey. We needed an experienced CFO.[2]

2: A Chief Financial Officer.

DOI:10.1201/9781003534624-35

François Cottin proposed Xavier Courbouleix, who had been the CFO of a company that François had created a few years earlier (Cottin Paris, see Chapter 33), and whose background perfectly matched what we were looking for, as he had experience with companies of all sizes (in addition to his experience in Cottin Paris, he'd notably worked alongside Xavier Niel as his company launched their phone service 'Free,' which ultimately became a telecommunications giant in France). Our first meeting affirmed his enthusiasm for his financial functions, but also his apparent ease navigating through this universe we'd have to work within in a more connected way.

Xavier confessed to me later, as we were talking about his arrival, that he felt reassured and excited by what I'd expressed to him during our meeting. Allegorithmic was evolving within an ever-moving technical universe that he loved, with extremely solid foundations and a dynamic team. There was a lot to develop, and a lot of freedom in his mission. We reached an agreement quite quickly.

Xavier was very significant to the development of Allegorithmic following his arrival in 2015. When banks, investors, and other financial markets examined us all through that period, they found a company in perfect working order, without any financial flaws. A few years later, when Allegorithmic was ultimately acquired (see Chapter 42), the required due diligence failed to unearth even the slightest problem. Xavier was a pillar of support for us.

College

Xavier developed our financial activity over the years following his arrival, in close proximity to myself, and to a body that we created following the restructuration mentioned elsewhere: the College,[3] the team of directors, comprising Allegorithmic's CxOs: CEO (myself), CRO (*Chief Revenue Officer*, Alexis Khouri), CMO and General Secretary (*Chief Marketing Officer*, François Cottin), COO (*Chief Operating Officer*, Nicolas Liatti), CFO (Xavier Courbouleix), CPO (*Chief Product Officer*, Jérôme Derel), CSO (*Chief Science Officer*, Tamy Boubekeur), and CTO (*Chief Technical Officer*, Cyrille Damez).

3: More precisely, as French speakers, we named this body, *le Collège*. That can be translated in a few different ways—notably, it can refer to a secondary school or high school. Here, think of it more in the sense of an association: 'The College of Professors meets each week,' that sort of thing.

It was within this College, which would expand even further with the arrival of new directors, like Claire Reignier and Muriel Gellf (see below), that the biggest decisions for Allegorithmic would be taken in this final period of the company, following a lot of debate, but never any real major conflicts.

Structuring the management of human resources

Our growth was so significant that we had difficulty managing our hiring needs, and we were spending more and more time putting out job postings, seeking out talent, making shortlists, carrying out too many job interviews, negotiating contracts, welcoming new hires, and so on. We shared these tasks between everyone, from engineers to artists, managers, and myself—and I was very involved in the subject.[4] Recruitment was taking up more and more of our time. Moreover, making the right recruitment can be fundamental, making a real difference to a

4: Over time, I started spending less and less time on the subject of hiring, but still maintained an active part in the process. I would typically take part at the end of the cycle, when the candidate had been validated by all teams concerned, and I was particularly interested in the candidate's values (see later in this chapter), as well as their ambitions. I wanted to see if they were a good fit with Allegorithmic, and if we could provide them with an environment of professional development. It was very rare for me to block a cycle, but it occasionally happened, when there was an obvious misalignment on one of these critical considerations.

company—which we'd learned very early on, as I'd been lucky enough to bring Christophe Soum into the heart of the company from its very start (see Chapter 4). For all of these reasons, we decided we had to recruit a recruiter (sic).

And so we brought Claire Reignier into this critical position. Claire was highly recommended to us by a mutual acquaintance; she seemed ideal for the job because of her experience and her incredible (and sometimes even disturbing) ability to understand people. Even more importantly, she understood Allegorithmic, how it worked, and its values and culture, even though she didn't come from the world of technology.

Claire started her career at Allegorithmic as a recruiter, eventually becoming Director of Human Resources shortly before we joined Adobe (see Chapter 42). Claire was in charge of all the fundamental aspects of the lives of the people within the company, and had a major impact on the life and development of Allegorithmic, bringing people into the team who were incredibly talented and, notably, had a more diverse dimension that had previously been the case (in particular, the proportion of men to women). This had been missing in our structure and was a subject we felt it was important to work on. The growth of our structure and of Claire's team would open doors for us.

Structuring the legal functions

Our legal function also needed to evolve, and in particular to be internalized and structured to respond to the range of questions that came up on an increasingly regular basis. I had for many years taken charge of the majority of Allegorithmic's legal matters (see for example Chapter 22), but this had naturally reached a point where this setup was no longer feasible, and we needed to bring in somebody to head a dedicated team of specialists for this.

After a search in part assisted by Claire Reignier, this being one of her first big missions, we welcomed Muriel Gellf into the team, who'd just returned from expatriation in Montreal, where she'd been working as a legal director. Muriel did absolutely remarkable work for us, bringing a high level of professionalism, seriousness, and involvement that was particularly necessary, as well as rare personal qualities. She created a legal team from scratch, and took charge of all of the company's legal issues, some more urgent than others, for the years that followed. She also introduced us to Judith Raoul-Bardy, from the firm Gibson-Dunn, one of her acquaintances from her law studies, when we were in advanced discussions with Adobe (see Chapter 42).

Muriel joined the College soon after her arrival. With these 'support' teams in place for our production function, we were ready to expand further in good conditions, without worrying that the company might collapse under its own weight, or make existential errors.

35.2 Commercial prospection of new markets

Since the first half of 2015, and the positive, promising conclusion of our mission to explore new markets led by François Cottin, Jérôme Derel, and Anthony Salvi (see Chapter 33), our commercial prospection had accelerated, and our teams, masterfully led by Alexis Khouri, were traveling the world tirelessly. In addition to the world of video games, and that of visual effects and animation—our original target domains, which we knew well, and in which we were having great success—other areas became a significant source of development for Allegorithmic throughout this 2015-2019 period: architecture, to some degree, and product design in particular.

To complete the team, and to help the global initiative of development in all our markets, we brought the notable Frédéric Kohler on board at the end of 2015 (initially based in New York), then also welcomed Pierre Maheut at the start of 2016. Frédéric had previously worked as director of marketing at Roche Bobois, among other roles, and would play a major part in commercial development and sales for Allegorithmic. Pierre, for his part, was an immense fan of anything design-related, but in particular loved automotive design; he joined us after working at Dassault Systèmes, and brought his vision and energy to help us develop our positioning in these new domains. He also possessed a particular sensitivity that allowed him to anticipate needs and establish incredible connections with our partners and customers within these new markets.

Figure 35.1: Pierre Maheut, Frédéric Kohler, Marion Artolle, and Wes McDermott prospecting at Ferrari, Arch Motorcycle, a motorcycle creation company owned in part by Keanu Reeves, Coca-Cola, and Casio (accompanied by Born Digital, our software distributor in Japan).

Throughout this whole 2015-2019 period, this special team of Frédéric Kohler and Pierre Maheut, at times accompanied by François Cottin and some demo artists such as Guillaume Meyer, Jérémie Noguer, and a few others, set out to meet the key figures of this new wave of development for our company.

35.3 'Labs' and research

Our product teams were focused on producing, as efficiently as possible, reliable, high-performance software tools that met the growing needs of users. And yet, in parallel with this activity, we started to think about the idea of dedicating a separate space to projects of a more experimental nature. Many articles and books[5] discussed the need to have new ideas and see how they play out, operating somewhat separately from the heart of the machine, the production teams. However, this space, whose goal was sometimes very close to the goals of the product teams, operated with one significant constraint removed: it could[6] fail.

5: For example, see [46], which I consider a small masterpiece of its genre.

6: And had to. . .

We therefore launched several incarnations of a 'Labs' function during this period, under the direction of Davide Pesare, and a 'Research' space called AllegoRI, a joint lab with a public laboratory, Télécom Paris, under the direction of Tamy Boubekeur. The two would eventually merge and Tamy would lead the joint 'Labs.'

Figure 35.2: A VR version of Substance Painter, developed by the Labs, presented at GDC 2015. We see Fabrice Piquet on the right of the image.

Labs members[7] were in some cases permanent, but the majority would temporarily pass through to propose a new idea, ultimately integrating it into the production cycles of products.

7: The team members joining the Labs included: Davide Pesare, François Beaune, Rosalie Martin, Nicolas Brack, Jean-François El Hajjar, Andréa Machizaud, Romain Rouffet, Gaël Cathelin, Christophe Darphin, Samuel Bourasseau, Anthony Salvi, Jérôme Derel, Arthur Roullier, Luc Chamerlat, Pierre Déjoué, Pierre Gueth, Artem Bishev, and Mathieu Sanchez.

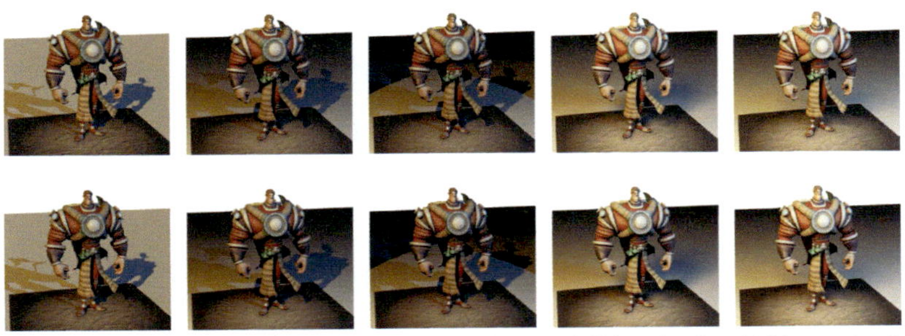

(a) Directional	(b) Point	(c) Spotl (45°)	(d) Disk area ($\rho = 2$)	(e) Sphere area ($r = 4$)
$I_1 = 2, I_2 = 1$	$I_1 = 200, I_2 = 100$	$I_1 = 200, I_2 = 100$	$\mathbf{L}_{e1} = 30, \mathbf{L}_{e2} = 15$	$\mathbf{L}_{e1} = 8, \mathbf{L}_{e2} = 4$

Figure 35.3: Illustration of 'Enriched Light Sources' (ELS), which shows how our unique lighting model allowed us to interpolate and extrapolate existing models. This technique was developed inside the Labs and was the subject of several patents.

A great deal of value emerged from the Labs, taking the form of scientific papers (25 scientific publications, 8 of these for SIGGRAPH), patents (16!), features that would end up integrated within our tools, and even new projects in and of themselves. Here, I'm thinking of the 'delighter,' and the 'normal2height' by Jean-François El Hajjar, or a VR version of Substance Painter (see figure 35.2), 'Sharp Tessellation,' 'Enriched Light Sources' (see figure 35.3), 'Structure,' Anorigami, Captis (with HP), a hardware and software device to capture materials, or even 'MaterIA,' a material generator using machine learning.

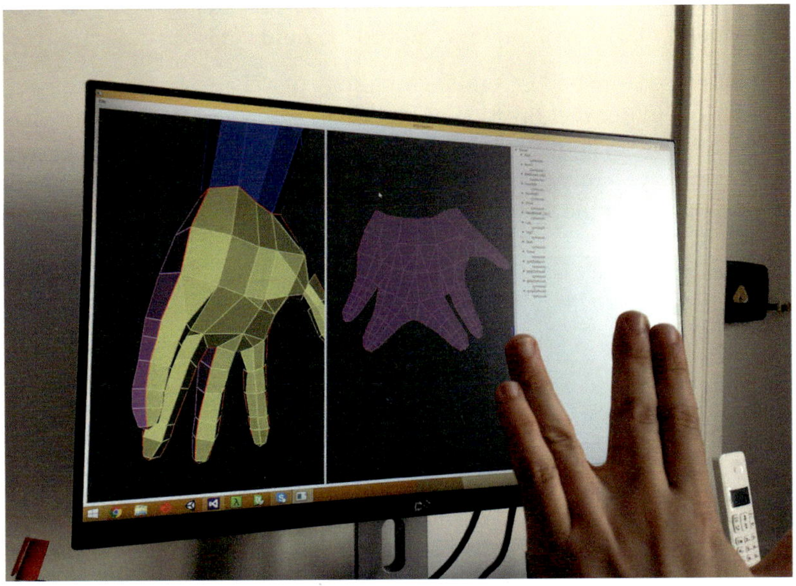

Figure 35.4: The beginnings of Anorigami, a 'UV unfolding' technique, by Jean-François El Hajjar.

35.4 Special projects

We regularly felt the need for a mixed team detached from the constraints of pure production. We were frequently approached by key figures in the 3D market, or in markets interested in 3D, who were looking for partners like Allegorithmic to guide them in this field. These included companies like IKEA, represented by the brilliant, demanding, and very human Martin Enthed (who was justifiably Jérôme Derel's biggest fan), who were interested in our know-how in terms of digital matters; we ultimately developed an important partnership with IKEA over several years, leading to the creation of a virtual reality experience for them. We developed another virtual reality experience for Hermès, using our expertise to best render the brand's exceptional materials (see figure 35.9).

The Special Projects team was born from these needs, and Jérôme Derel, Anthony Salvi, and Pierre Maheut were the key drivers within this team we'd created, that never stopped evolving.

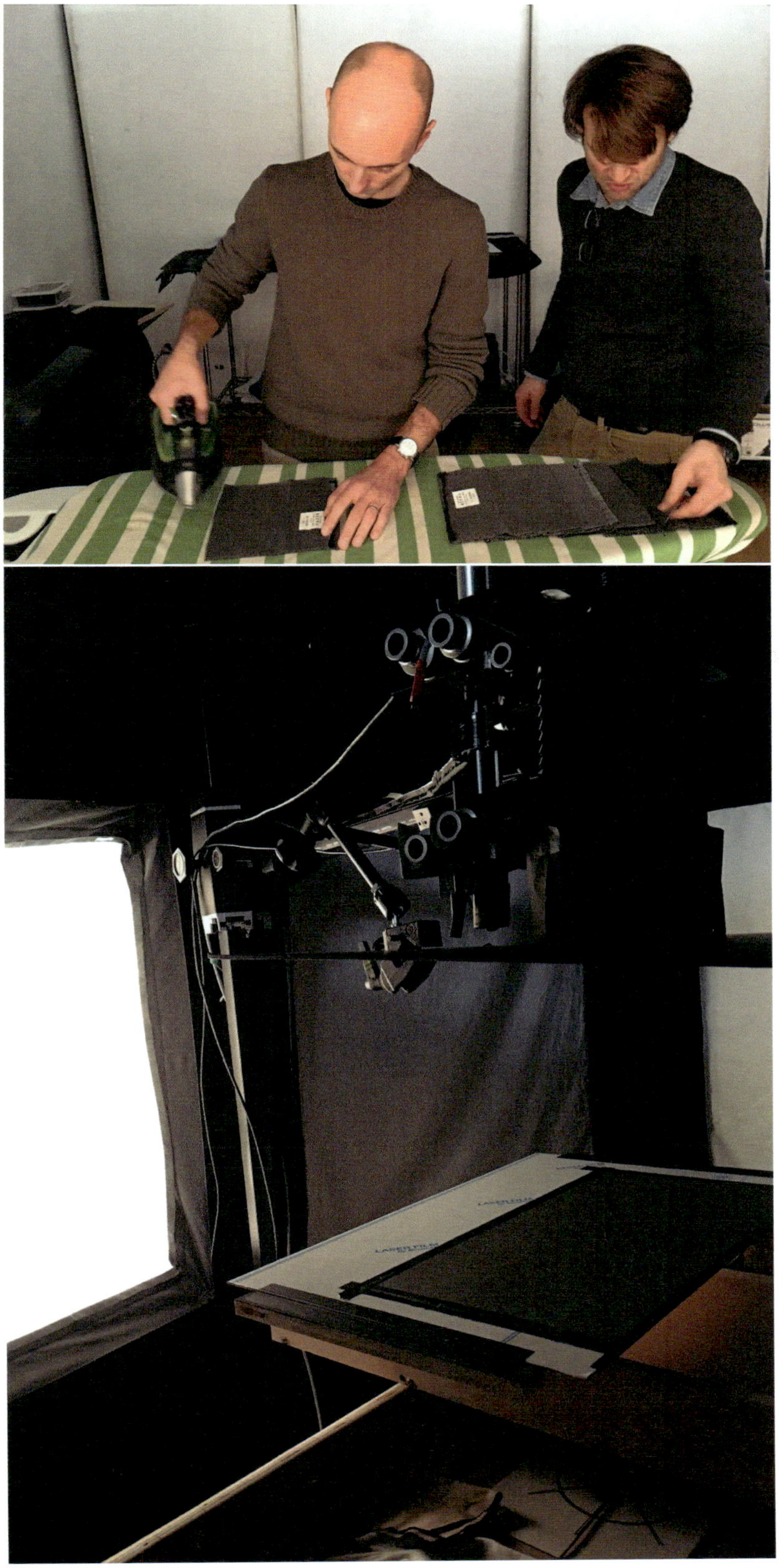

Figure 35.5: A material capture system, and preparation of materials, by François Cottin and Frédéric Kohler.

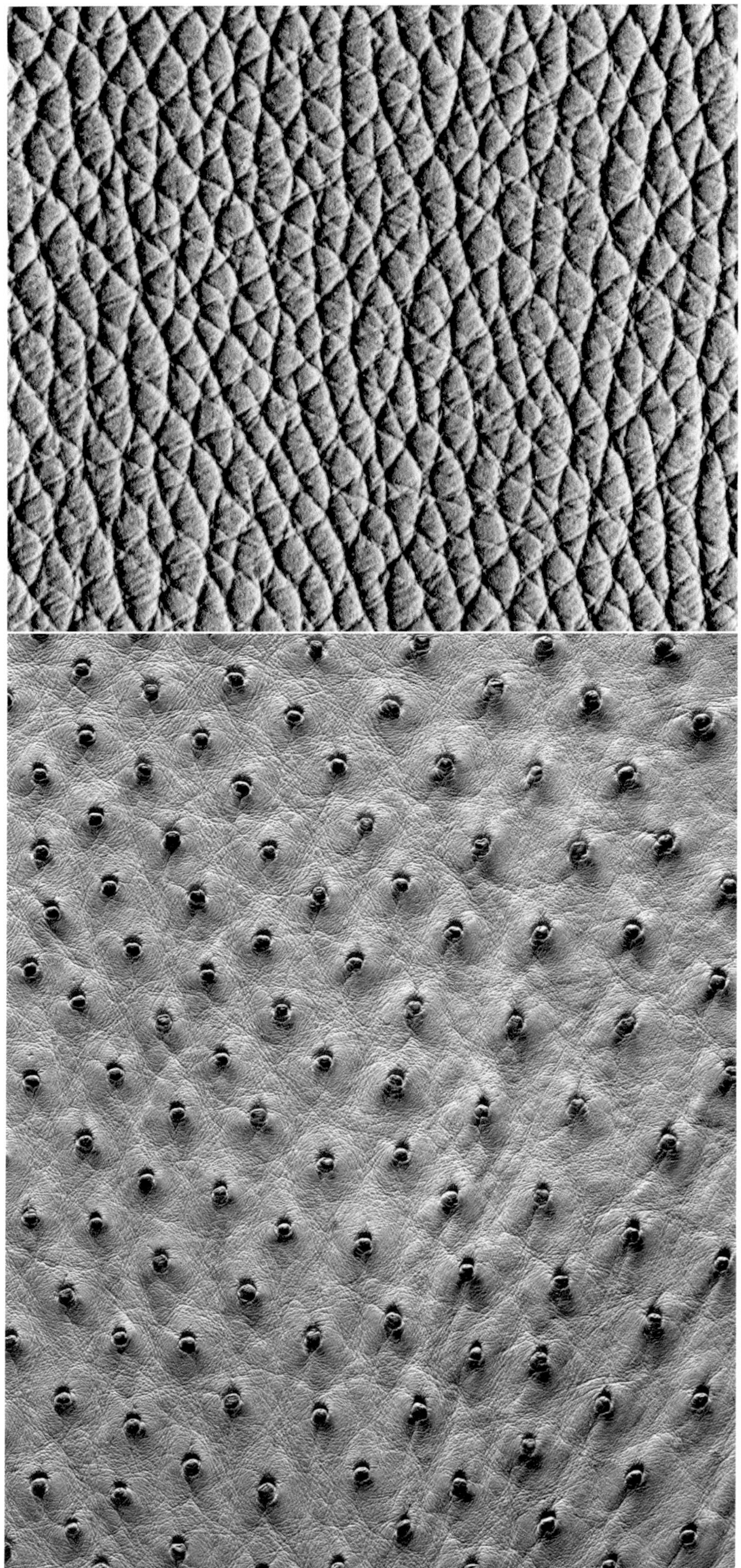

Figure 35.6: Two captured skin materials.

Figure 35.7: A 'homemade' material capture system set up by the Special Projects team—here we see Anthony Salvi (at the back) and Romain Rouffet.

Figure 35.8: Experiments in virtual reality by Jérôme Derel and Frédéric Kohler, in 2016.

Figure 35.9: Virtual reality experiments for Hermès, by Jérôme Derel, Anthony Salvi, and François Cottin, in June 2015. This is the very first HTC Vive headset.

35.5 Valère Lucquin

After discussing the Special Projects team, it's only appropriate to talk about another person who would play a special, very major part in the development of Allegorithmic: Valère Lucquin. Valère joined us when things had started to settle into place for the company, in the second half of the 2010s. He'd finished his studies in a notable Parisian business school (ESCP), and then worked for a time at Dassault Systèmes; now, he wanted to join a developing team in the technological domain that was nonetheless much smaller than the French software giant. He'd learned about Allegorithmic through, among others, his brother Victor, who'd done his PhD thesis with us under the co-direction of Tamy Boubekeur and myself.

Valère immediately made a strong impression on everybody. Particularly brilliant and enthusiastic, we sensed in him an incredible potential for development, a great capacity for work, and simply an endearing human being who would establish himself as one of the most appreciated people in the company. We needed, and I especially needed, somebody like Valère, who could play a strategic support role in the College, via in-depth market analyses, ideas for improving our way of operating and our marketing and commercial actions, and a day-to-day implementation of all these thousand and one little things that make a company run.

Valère quickly became indispensable, a pillar of the company who was respected and listened to by all of Allegorithmic. He contributed significantly to the growth of the structure, but also greatly assisted the members of the College, and me in particular... Many of our discussions took place late in the evening, when I entered his office to ask him, "What do I need to know?" The extraordinary relevance of his answers, and the fundamental, unfiltered discussions that grew out of them, absolutely allowed Allegorithmic, and myself, to reach many new levels.

Figure 35.10: Valère Lucquin in the offices of our Parisian site at 9 rue de Milan.

35.6 Offices

New offices in Clermont-Ferrand

With our growing success, and with more and more people joining the company, our historic premises on rue Gonod in Clermont-Ferrand began to feel a little small, and so we started looking for a new site that could accommodate us. We wanted to stay in the city center rather than move out to one of the business parks around Clermont-Ferrand, and so, after a long and complex search carried out by Xavier Courbouleix, who became quite passionate about the subject, we began looking at the most modern building in Clermont-Ferrand's city center, in 'Centre Jaude 2,' at 3 avenue Julien. We rented out an entire floor in the part of the building dedicated to offices, and moved in. Moreover, we worked with an outstanding interior architect from the area, Philippe Tereygeol, who proposed a fantastic way of organizing our space (see figures 35.12, 35.13 and 35.14).

We realized soon after moving in that, even in this new building, we would shortly find ourselves over capacity;[8] nonetheless, the teams

8: We ultimately rented a second office a little further away on place de Jaude, and divided the teams between these two sites, which was sadly far from ideal. . .

Figure 35.11: August 2016:François Cottin, clearly very inspired, while visiting our future offices in Clermont-Ferrand, at place de Jaude.

felt good in that building, and we remained there until the end of the adventure.

In Paris, we move three times

Growing exponentially, and supported by an investment from Adobe (see Chapter 39), we moved our Paris office three times during this period, as it was easier to recruit here than on our other sites.

We'd previously used the services of Regus, once again driven by Xavier Courbouleix, but now we wanted to move into our own premises. First, we invested in a big apartment at 87 rue Taitbout, in September 2015, which we loved. It was the beginning of a real team feeling in Paris, with enough critical mass for the site to develop. The office at rue Taitbout was full of activity and good humor (see figures 35.15 and 35.16).

But our offices at rue Taitbout started to feel cramped quite quickly, and so in April 2017, we started searching for new, bigger premises. We were

Figure 35.12: Our office at Jaude 2, in Clermont-Ferrand, in 2017.

Figure 35.13: Stand-up meetings of the Substance Designer team (top) and the Painter team (bottom), in the office at 'Centre Jaude 2,' in Clermont-Ferrand, in 2017.

looking for something that we knew would be quite temporary, while we continued looking for a longer-term site to move into, some time later. For now, we moved to 24 rue de Clichy, in a beautiful, typically Parisian,

Figure 35.14: A technical presentation by David Cœurjolly, researcher at CNRS, the French National Centre for Scientific Research, in the large break room of our new offices in Clermont-Ferrand.

Figure 35.15: The Paris team at our office at 87 rue Taitbout, full of excitement on Valentine's Day 2017, gathered around the central island in the meeting room that had been transformed into an office. Here we see Pierre Bosset, Jérôme Derel, Arthur Walter, Claudia Vance, Alexandre Bagard (from behind), François Cottin, Charles Brégeon and Marion Marchive.

Figure 35.16: The Paris team gathered in a large room in our office at rue Taitbout, during one of our '360' meetings (we can see the Clermont-Ferrand team on the screen).

extensively renovated apartment (see figures 35.18 and 35.17). The place allowed us to grow, but it was a little dark, and its general layout didn't do much to encourage interaction between teams.

Figure 35.17: A tradition, on this day in July 2017: Guillaume Polaillon, who managed the Allegorithmic account at NVIDIA from Paris, brought us (excellent) macarons during one of his many, welcome visits (here in July 2017, he is on the right of the photo, next to Pierre Maheut) at our office at 24 rue de Clichy. Guillaume followed our progress for many years, and was certainly the best partnership facilitator that I've met in the industry. He was an exceptional person, and an exceptional professional, and we were lucky to work with him.

Figure 35.18: Filming at 24 rue de Clichy, in my office.

Finally, during summer 2018, we invested in a mansion house at 9 rue de Milan, not far from Saint-Lazare train station. The building was magnificent, and very Parisian; we decorated it, and even organized the space and flow of people, in a similar vein to that of our new Clermont-Ferrand office (see above). We even hired artists to paint murals in the big staircase between the floors of the building.

The result was splendid, and we spent some extraordinary moments in that place, which we filled with a lot of effort and innovation, and also with good times, parties, and celebrations (see figures 35.19, 35.20, 35.21 and 35.22). And also food. Lots of food.

New premises in Lyon, at Grand Hôtel-Dieu

The Lyon team was also growing very well. By now, Xavier Courbouleix had made a habit of driving the search for new offices; now, as we began the search for larger premises, Xavier again took the reins. Up until this point, we'd been based in a coworking site not far from the Pardieu train station. Ideally, we now wanted to find premises as close to the city center as possible, as we'd done in Clermont-Ferrand and Paris, and decorate and organize them in a similar way, using our layout in Clermont-Ferrand as a reference.

We had the extraordinary opportunity to rent two floors, as well as an attic space, of the newly renovated Grand Hôtel Dieu, just a few steps away from Place Bellecour, right in the center of Lyon. The premises were sublime and the team could settle in and develop its own culture. Here too food played a unifying role, and the office was soon full of good humor (see figures 35.23 and 35.24).

Figure 35.19: The Paris office at 9 rue de Milan.

Figure 35.20: The Paris office, at 9 rue de Milan, with various teams. The ground floor areas were the center of life where we would see each other all the time. I usually worked in the kitchen in the morning, to connect with everyone. These connections, and the serendipity that we established, were fundamental for a company focusing on innovation, like Allegorithmic. Our working premises were therefore vital.

Allegorithmic Canada, in Montreal

Our delegation in Montreal consisted of just three people, so we subleased a part of the offices of our friends at the company Artstation (see figure 35.25), which allowed us to limit our investment while remaining close to the universe that drove us, and a team that we greatly appreciated.

Allegorithmic Korea develops

In South Korea, we had the continuous local presence of Christian Kim, and now Inho Kim; in addition to this, our visits to Korea became more frequent, and Allegorithmic's attachment to Seoul and to the country

Figure 35.21: The Paris office, at 9 rue de Milan, and board games, ping pong, PlayStation 4—whether in VR or not—and lots and lots of FIFA.

overall grew stronger and stronger (see figures 35.27, 35.28, 35.29 and 35.30).

Christian went so far as to develop the 'Korean Substance Academy,' which opened in March 2017 (as we can see in figure 35.26).

Figure 35.22: The Paris office, at 9 rue de Milan—what incredible food! Top, Thomas Jequece, then descending, Vincent Gault, who brought jamón ibérico from Barcelona, Feten Hammad preparing her famous couscous, Stéphanie Carret and Mikaël Quéric preparing fries, and Émilie Kowalski, who is helping herself to some crumble.

Figure 35.23: The Lyon office is here, within the new Grand Hôtel Dieu complex, in the center of Lyon.

Figure 35.24: The Lyon office, within the new Grand Hôtel Dieu complex, in the heart of Lyon. Guillaume Domaigne tests the latest technological innovations.

Figure 35.25: Allegorithmic Canada (officially called 'Les Logiciels Allegorithmic') occupying part of the Artstation office, in Montreal. From left to right: Casimir Perez, Quentin Clauss, Alexandre Bagard and me.

Figure 35.26: The Korean Substance Academy in Seoul, at the start of 2017. And a surprise visit to the academy in 2018.

Figure 35.27: Commercial prospection in Korea in 2015, with Alexis Khouri and Wes McDermott in 2015.

Figure 35.28: Substance Seminar with the association of VR in Korea, with Christian Kim, in 2016.

Figure 35.29: The group of Substance Experts in Seoul, April 2017.

Figure 35.30: Visiting the offices of Blue-Hole, the developer of PUBG, in Seoul, in 2018, with Christian Kim and Josh Lynch.

35.7 A precursor of the Global Gathering, Auvergne, 2015

In summer 2015, on a day experiencing a heatwave, we decided to organize a special version of our traditional 'Corporate Meeting': in addition to bringing together as many employees as possible for a presentation lasting about two hours, we planned a full day of activities that would take the teams from Clermont-Ferrand, Lyon, Paris, and other places (for those who could make the trip), out into the countryside of Auvergne. The program included a little work, but above all: quad bikes, water guns, and electric scooters.

With this slightly schoolyard atmosphere of fun, we came away at the end of the day with a few injuries among us,[9] but we'd accomplished the goal we'd had in mind: we'd all spent time together, and we'd mixed moments of serious reflection with fun times, and this was always good for the team cohesion, especially when our team was spread out across several sites. This day out was the precursor for our future 'Global Gatherings' (see Chapter 40), which would play a very important role in defining the Allegorithmic culture.

9: Sometimes I think back to how this day might have gone very differently, and tremble. . .

Figure 35.31: A few photos from the 'pre-global gathering' which we organized in summer 2015, during a heatwave. Throughout the day, in a slightly schoolyard atmosphere of fun, we tried our best to avoid major injuries during some very physical activities... Here we see Alexandre Chassany, and Xavier Courbouleix (who had just joined us as CFO).

35.8 Culture

When a company grows, it necessarily goes through phases of transformation. These changes are inevitable, but some may be undesirable. In Allegorithmic's case, the transition from a few people to dozens, spread across several sites, in countries with sometimes different cultures, can have the unwanted consequence of widening the distance between team members. Here, 'culture' is a keyword to keep in mind; throughout the life of the company, and particularly during this period of strong growth, we tried to preserve the 'Allegorithmic culture' that we were so proud of, which had carried us so far, and to which we owed a part of our success.

I spoke at length with Émilie Duquenne on this subject. Emilie is one of my best friends, an expert in the domain of human resources[10] and a personal coach (the type that is very competent and useful). Émilie made me realize that cultures and rituals can vary completely depending on different personalities and places of activity—but that a shared base of values was indispensable. She wisely advised me to write down the values of Allegorithmic. I did so, and soon saw precisely how useful it was to articulate these values—not merely as window dressing, but because they helped us with a lot of our decision making, on a day-to-day basis. Generosity, which was the first value on the list, was, for instance, the slight imbalance which, in the event of a difficult decision, would tip our choice to the side of generosity, rather than in another direction—too often the direction of soulless principles. In my opinion, in any case...

10: In April 2017 she was featured on the front cover of the magazine 'Management,' as Director of Recruitment for L'Oréal.

I include these values here, exactly as they were written on the Allegorithmic website:

Generosity, *in all its dimensions. Generosity at its core is what urges us to run the extra mile, to always treat our environment, community, ideas and people well and give more than expected. Generosity is fairness, amplified: while fairness is harmony, generosity is positive imbalance. Generosity is the 0.002% quantum fluctuation in the cosmic microwave background density that gravity* *amplified to cluster galaxies and create the world as we know it, in all its richness and life. Generosity is the beginning of all things.*

Passion *is the mother of all energy. Passion is the result of drive and of love, and Allegorithmic is all about love: love for innovation, love for our team and community, love for our tools and our field. Passion is mass, binding space and expressing itself as gravity. Passion is what makes us grow, thrive and innovate. Innovation and risk-taking are what propel us to the next level.*

Honesty. *Being honest with our clients and colleagues (openness to new ideas and various point of views), and being intellectually honest: admitting we do not know, admitting we were wrong, being able to change our minds in front of evidence without letting our egos, habits or culture obstruct the path. Honesty, agility and genuineness is what will keep us from hitting that iceberg.*

High Standard. *The vital fluid at Allegorithmic, infused in all and flowing relentlessly, we all thrive for the highest standards and, while embracing simplicity and efficiency, refuse unprofessional, dispassionate easiness. High standards is what makes us all refuse the status quo and progress in the mastery of our kung-fu.*

Freedom *for individuals to be singular and authentic. Freedom for teams to organize their own schedules, techniques and processes. Freedom to think outside of all the boxes. Freedom is what will make us as unpredictable as individual particles' paths like in the Double-slit experiment, yet be the building blocks of form and matter. Freedom with self-responsibility is what will make the Allegorithmic ship sustainable and autonomous.*

Our products 36

In the period between 2015 and 2019, the Substance ecosystem evolved very rapidly, introducing new products, services, content libraries, exchange platforms, and other certifications, which were all very complex when considered together. Figure 36.1 shows our offer and the branding associated with it, developed by Benjamin Maréchal and his team.

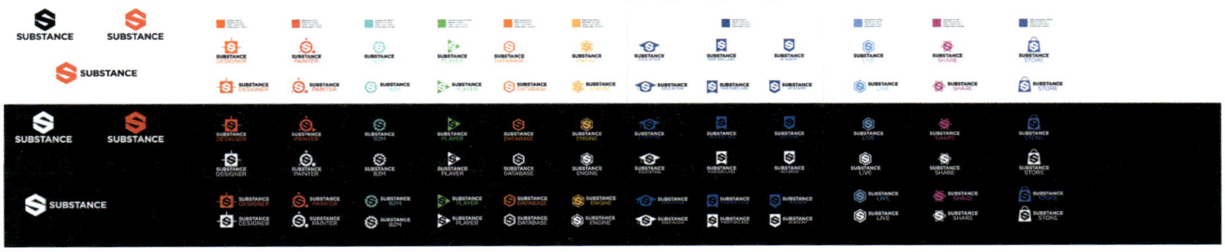

Figure 36.1: The ecosystem of Substance products and its branding, in 2016.

36.1 Substance Designer

The tool evolved quickly and profoundly

During this period, we released many versions of Substance Designer, with its development team, led by Sylvain Paris, producing new version after new version at an incredible pace. I'd personally anticipated a very large difference between the number of licenses sold of Substance Painter and Substance Designer (my estimate was a ratio of ten to one), but ultimately the difference, although present, was never so big: Substance Designer found its audience and established itself as a 'must have' in the world of serious 3D. The movement that we saw emerge in the first part of the 2010s grew throughout this whole period and the level of excellence reached by the users of the tool was simply extraordinary,[1] well beyond our wildest expectations.

1: Thanks in part to subgraphs, which allow each new user to easily benefit from the discoveries of 'previous generations.'

The Grand Masters of Substance Designer

We saw the growth of a school of technical artists specializing in tools, and a new profession: 'Substance Designer Artist'! And since the 'Great Elders of Substance Designer,' the very first artists who used the tool, while creating it (see Chapter 30), several 'Grand Masters' took over such an inspirational role during this period, from Brad Smith[47] to Josh Lynch[48], from Daniel Thiger[49] to Jonathan Benainous,[50] from Christophe Desse[51] to Rogelio Olguin,[52] or Javier Perez,[53] Emrecan Cubukcu,[54] Mark Foreman,[55] Pauline Boiteux,[56] and many more... These artists were not part of Allegorithmic, yet they were eager to adopt the tool, integrating it within their respective studios, in a complex production pipeline which proved its value. Their work inspired a whole

DOI:10.1201/9781003534624-36

generation of technical artists, who in turn found a privileged spot within the studios looking for these rare skill sets.

MDL and Genesis demo

Driven by, in particular, Jérôme Derel, Anthony Salvi, and Pierre Maheut, Substance Designer also evolved to reach beyond our usual fields of application within video games and visual effects, to address the world of product design. To accomplish this, it was sometimes necessary to emphasize certain functions, or even integrate new functions which were only necessary in this new framework. The tool in particular integrated a set of functions allowing the creation of materials in MDL ('Material Definition Language') format, a format defined by NVIDIA and for which Substance Designer became the first creative tool allowing such formats to be developed with a nodal graphical interface. For this, we created a new type of graph, an example of which we can see in figure 36.13.

In the context of these new markets, we also developed several demos that were more appropriate than our usual monsters or rusty, dented science-fiction vehicles. Two of these demos would play a particularly important role in our growing success with luxury brands and automobiles: a demo for Hyundai for their new luxury brand Genesis, where we used Substance Designer to make high-quality renders and material explorations, and a demo for Harley Davidson, in partnership with NVIDIA, which demonstrated specific features of MDL material generation combined with the sorts of classic textures that our tool was known for creating (imagine: drawing flames on the motorcycle's fuel tank!). See figures 36.12, 36.13, 36.14 and 36.15.

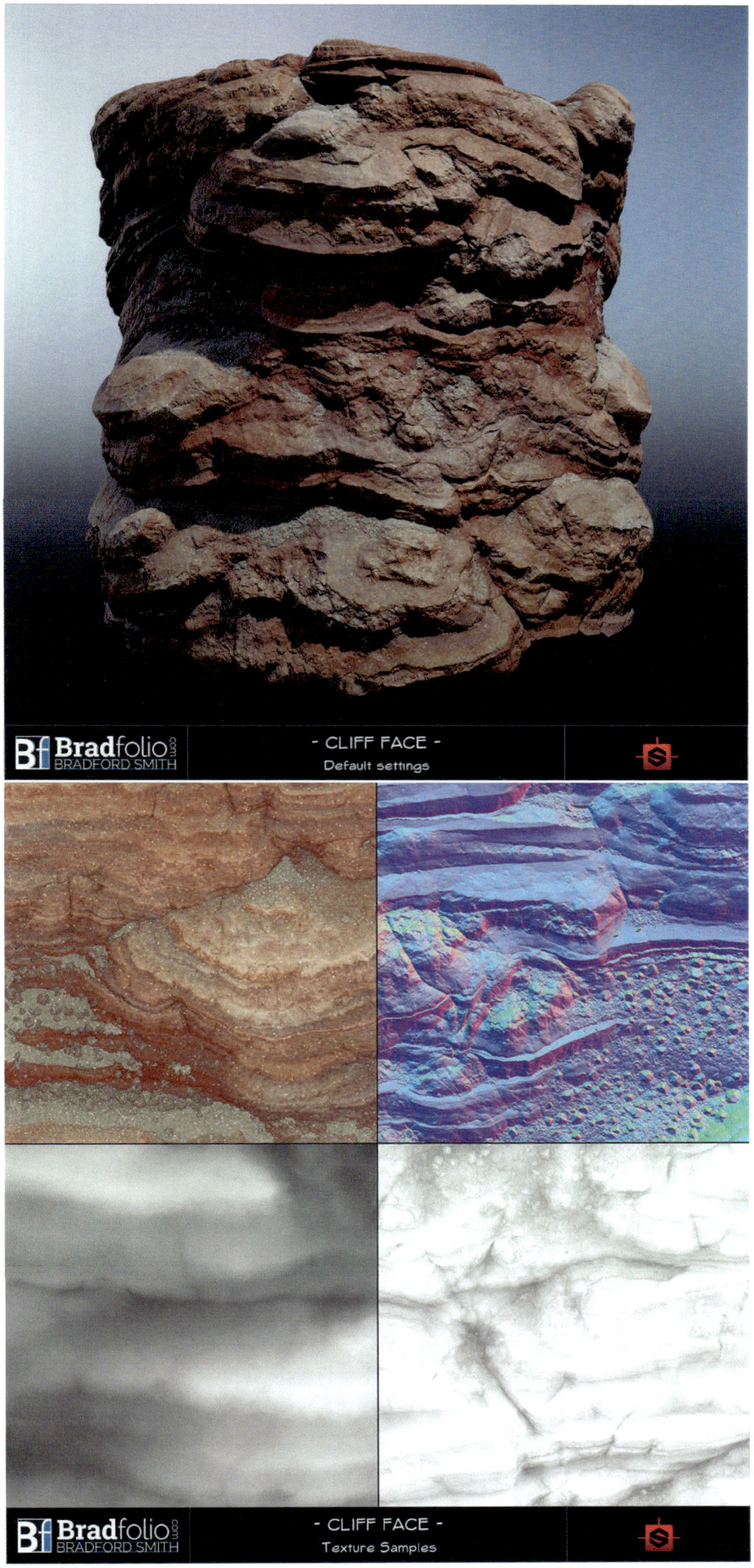

Figure 36.2: An iconic creation of a Grand Master of Substance Designer, Brad Smith, in 2015.

Figure 36.3: An iconic creation of a Grand Master of Substance Designer, Mark Foreman, in 2015. Mark demonstrates the value of a procedural approach, easily creating variations of the initial design for this rock material. At the bottom of the image, we can also see Mark's Substance Designer graph. During this period, 3D artists would share more and more images of their material composition graphs made in Substance Designer.

Figure 36.4: An iconic creation of a Grand Master of Substance Designer, Rogelio Olguin, in 2016.

Figure 36.5: An iconic creation of a Grand Master of Substance Designer, Jonathan Benainous, in 2017.

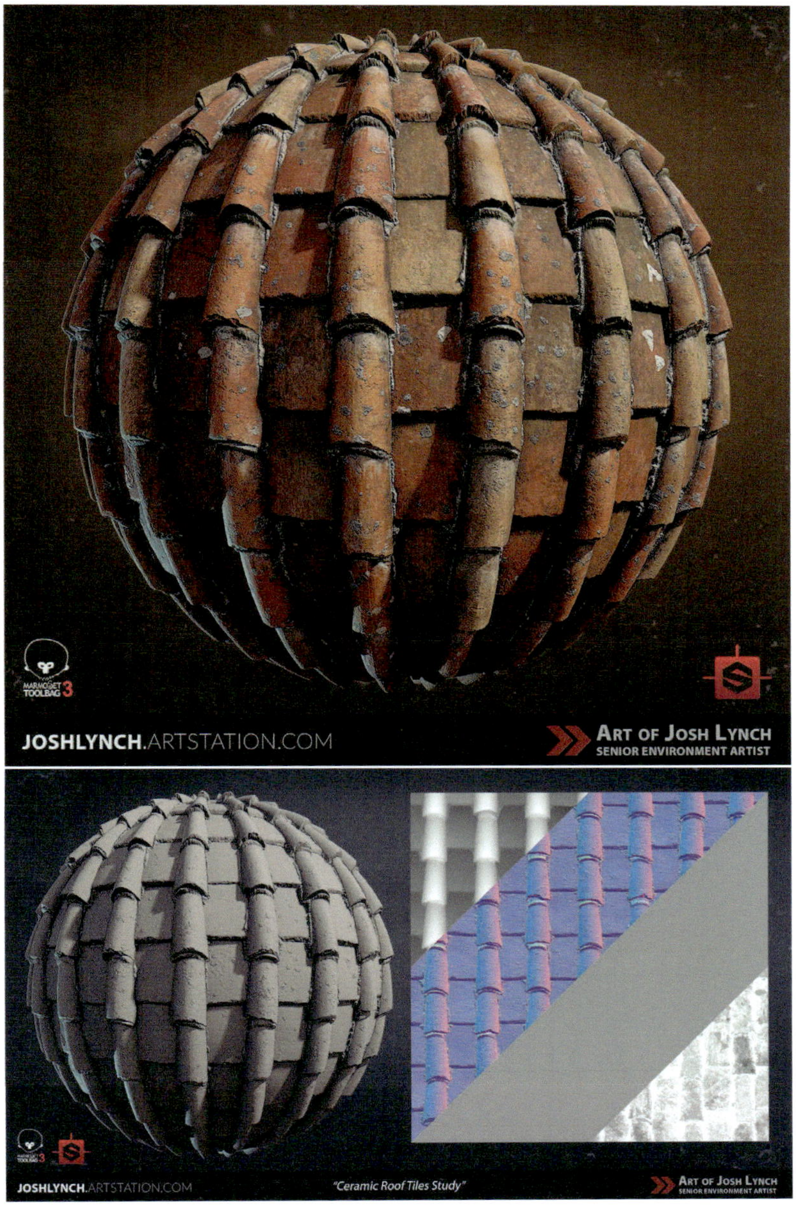

Figure 36.6: An iconic creation of a Grand Master of Substance Designer, a fully procedural digital material by Josh Lynch, in 2018.

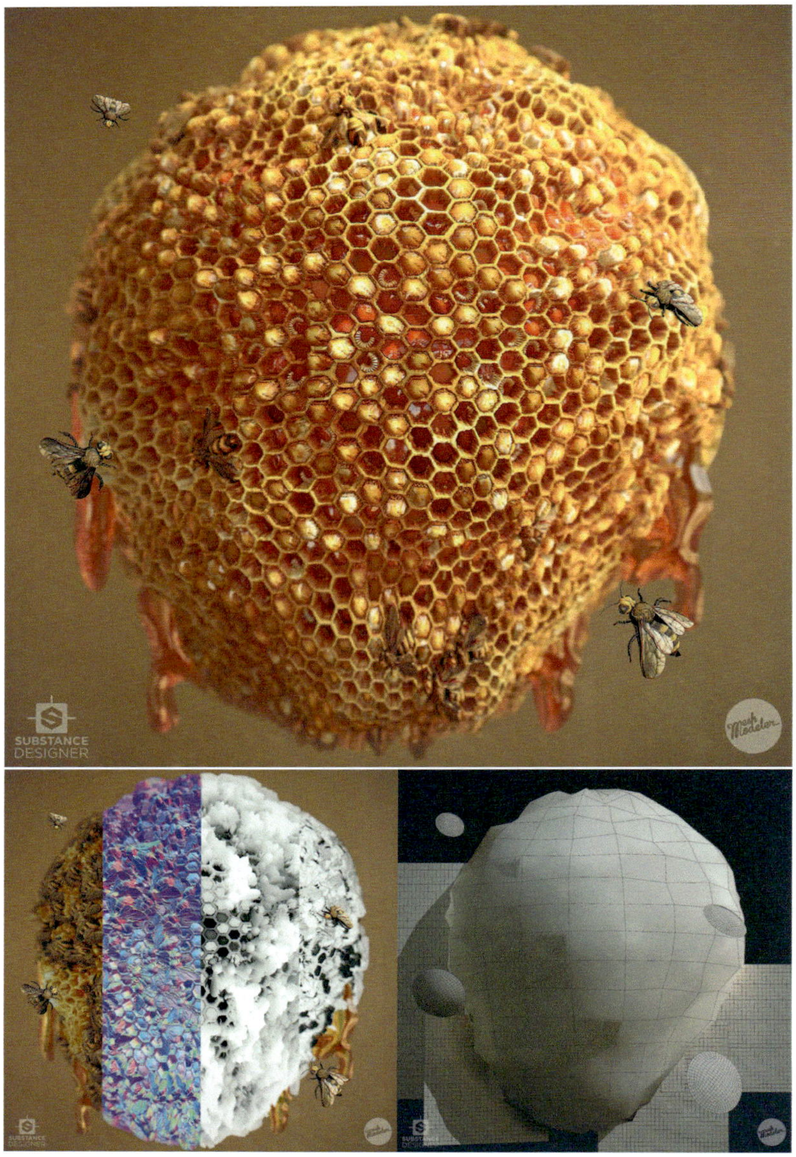

Figure 36.7: An iconic creation of a Grand Master of Substance Designer, Javier Perez, in 2018. Everything here is procedural, and we can see in the bottom right a very simple 3D model to which this material has been applied. All useful information here comes from the textures.

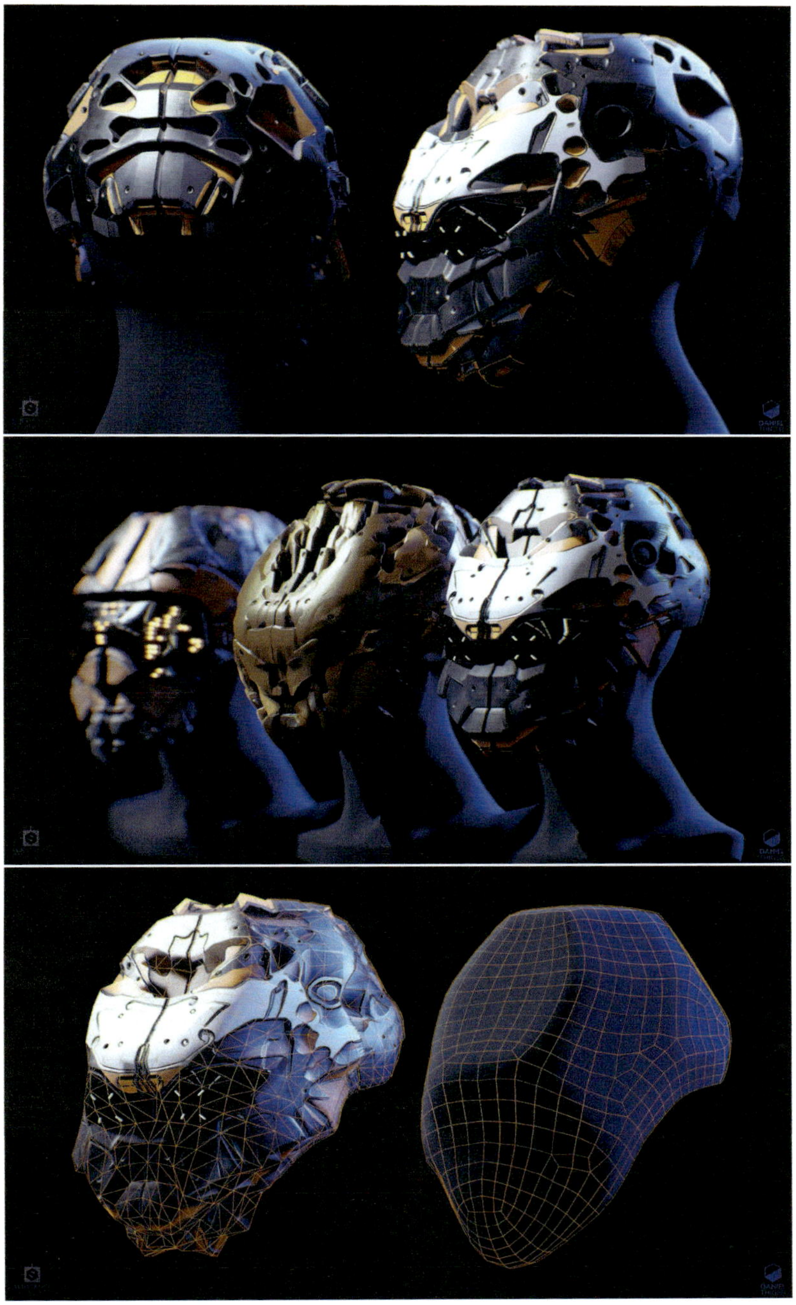

Figure 36.8: An iconic creation of a Grand Master of Substance Designer, Daniel Thiger, in 2019. Daniel demonstrates the value of a procedural approach, easily creating variations of his initial design of the helmet. We can also see, at the bottom, the 3D model to which the material is applied. All useful information here comes from the textures.

Figure 36.9: Splash Screens of Substance Designer 5.

Figure 36.10: Splash Screens of Substance Designer 6 and 7.

Figure 36.11: Splash Screens of Substance Designer 8.0 to 9.0, with an image by Nicolas Wirrmann (the racing car) and by Pauline Boiteux (the fabric). The last Splash Screen was the first from the Adobe era (see Chapter 42).

Figure 36.12: The Genesis demo, for Hyundai, created in Substance Designer, which supported MDL materials. Courtesy of Hyundai.

Figure 36.13: The Genesis demo, for Hyundai, created in Substance Designer, which supported MDL materials. Courtesy of Hyundai.

Figure 36.14: The Genesis demo, for Hyundai, April 2016. Created in Substance Designer. In this image, we see an example of the impact of the support of MDL materials: the 'clear coating' is visible here in the second image. Courtesy of Hyundai.

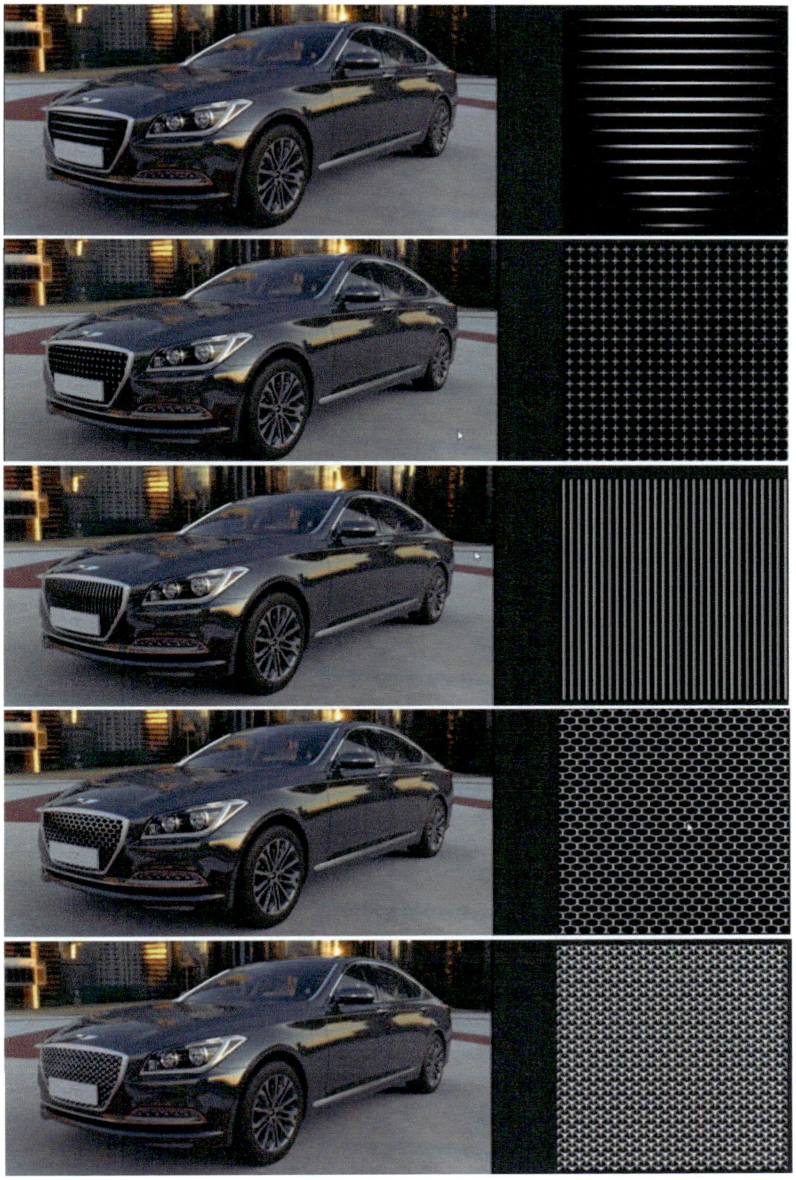

Figure 36.15: The Genesis demo, for Hyundai. Explorations of grille designs with Substance Designer. Courtesy of Hyundai.

36.2 Substance Painter

We released version 2.0 of Substance Painter for GDC in San Francisco, in March 2016.[2] The level of anticipation was very high in the 3D community and we were carrying out the launch[3] with a lot of excitement, and yet two things didn't go as planned. . .

2: It was during this edition that we were very lucky to have Naughty Dog participate in our demos and presentations: see Chapters 27 and 38.

3: For those present on site, we were launching the app from our hotel rooms on the morning of the opening of the trade show!

First of all, after long discussions, we'd decided to increase the price of the individual plan for our tool, and in particular of this major upgrade, from 75 dollars to 100 dollars. The community received this change particularly badly, making this clear on social media, specialized sites, and even when speaking to us face to face. After many more internal discussions, we reversed this pricing decision after only two days. Our community approved of this step back to our original price, and this willingness to listen to them would be remembered as a fundamental element in their appreciation of Allegorithmic,[4] because we'd publicly admitted to having made a mistake (particularly on how we'd managed this change), and because we corrected that mistake very quickly.

4: We can also view this as a tactical error, but it's an error that I remain proud to have made, because we acted out of generosity, one of our core values (see Chapter 35).

Figure 36.16: The Dude, a character illustrating the release of Substance Painter 2 in March 2016, which we commissioned from Cédric Séaut. Initially, the character bore a New York Yankees logo but we had to make a more neutral version, after a lawyer from MLB contacted us to remind us that we hadn't acquired the rights to use this image.

Then, to promote the launch we'd commissioned original artwork textured with Substance Painter, from Cédric Séaut, one of my former students at Puy-en-Velay (see Chapter 4), who had since become one of the most renowned artists in the world of 3D, particularly for his creations using the ZBrush sculpting software, and who had eagerly adopted Substance Painter for his own artwork. Cédric did remarkable technical work for us, which can be seen in figure 36.16, but there was a small problem: on the original version that we published, the character was wearing a cap bearing the logo of the New York Yankees, the famous baseball team. Yet a few weeks after the image was released, we received an email on behalf of MLB, Major League Baseball, asking us to remove the logo and original images from the internet, under penalty of prosecution, as we hadn't obtained usage rights (we initially believed this to be a fake, but it proved to be completely valid). Nor were they interested in allowing us to buy a license to use the logo from them, due to the somewhat unsavory nature of the character in the image. . . And so we were forced to change all of our launch images and videos, which had the effect of erasing all of our social metrics, such as the number of views of our original video, which had been very successful. This was at least a good learning experience for us. . .

Despite this chaotic start, the success of Substance Painter was confirmed, and in the following years, the tool would establish itself as a 'must have' in all video game production pipelines in particular, and beyond.

Figure 36.17: An iconic creation by one of the best Substance Painter artists: Zhelong Xu,[57] in 2015. This image launched an entire style, and Zhelong became an absolute master of 3D (in particular see Chapter 38).

Figure 36.18: An iconic creation by one of the best Substance Painter artists: Pablo Munoz Gomez, in 2016, which made the cover of the specialized magazine 3D Artist, presenting Substance Painter as a "tool changing the entire industry"!

Figure 36.19: A creation inspired by the film "Jurassic Park," by one of the best Substance Painter artists: Omar Taher, in 2017.

Figure 36.20: An iconic image by one of the best Substance Painter artists: Eider Astigarraga, in 2017. I used this image a lot for our various presentations and live streams, in particular to encourage developers and artists to join our team: 'Join us!'

Figure 36.21: An iconic creation by one of the best Substance Painter artists: Maria Panfilova, in 2018. Top, the final result. In the middle, the 'naked' 3D model without textures (made with ZBrush). Bottom, texture work by Maria in Substance Painter.

Figure 36.22: For the spring 2018 version of Substance Painter, we asked ultra-talented 3D artist Nikie Monteleone to make an original creation. The result, which proved to be an iconic image for Substance Painter, was this magnificent chameleon.

Figure 36.23: The Splash Screens of Substance Painter, the last image here is the first splash screen of the Adobe era (see Chapter 42).

36.3 Substance Alchemist

Substance Alchemist was the last major product developed during the Allegorithmic adventure. It was born out of two trains of thought that eventually converged.

First of all, we, and in particular Jérôme Derel, saw an immense opportunity for a material creation product that was less complex than Substance Designer, as well as a tool that could generate a library of digital materials, similar to Adobe Lightroom. Very familiar with the world of product design, Jérôme identified a need for customers to move away from physical design, requiring a lot of 'hard' steps (prototypes requiring a very long time to manufacture), to digital design. However, unlike in the world of video games, the level of 3D expertise skills in these industries far removed from entertainment tended to be quite low, and a tool like Substance Designer was too complex to be adopted on a large scale, beyond the few early adopters that we inevitably find in these structures.

At the same time, techniques allowing the capture of materials from photographs were increasingly becoming accessible and effective.[5]

5: We published an article[58] written by Anthony Salvi which would make a big impact in the industry, providing a method of capturing materials using a simple smartphone. This article was often cited as a reference by manufacturers and 3D specialists.

These two areas developed separately, converging after a while: by combining a tool allowing the simplified creation of materials as well as material capture, we had the potential for our next major tool to complete the Allegorithmic offer.

The first line of code for a 'simplified Substance Designer' was written in November 2016, with the arrival of Jérémy Levallois in the Lyon team. He tested out new technologies that could be useful to the product, and led to new 'black magic features,' as we called them, features so new and unexpected that they seemed to be sorcery. After an initial prototyping phase, production began in April 2017.

The first prototypes of the tool for capturing and processing material scans were developed sometime later, in October and November 2017 (Project "MatterMaker," which arose after months of discussions and training sessions involving many Post-its (see image 36.24).

Finally, the decision to combine the two projects came in December 2017. "Project Alchemist" was born, in the form that we would present for the first time with a video teaser at GDC 2018, in March, then in London, in June 2018, during a local Substance Days. We presented our first demo of the product with a blurred UI.

The private beta, with just over 25 people, was launched in July 2018, shortly before SIGGRAPH 2018 in Vancouver, during which we gave our first live demos at our stand. The beta, increasing from 25 people to 500, opened in November 2018 (see the launch video: [59]). These were the last months of refinement before the official launch to all our subscribers in March 2019, during GDC, once we'd become part of Adobe.

In retrospect...

With a slightly difficult birth, which was the result of a lot of going back and forth, Substance Alchemist had difficulty finding its place

Figure 36.24: Brainstorming sessions for Substance Alchemist (top, June 8, 2017; bottom, October 3, 2017), with the help of numerous Post-its. Here we can see Damien Letournel, Christophe Darphin, Rosalie Martin, Mikaël Quéric, Pierre Maheut, Jérôme Derel, Anthony Salvi, Nicolas Paulhac, Baptiste Manteau, François Cottin, Camille Masson, Valère Lucquin, Stéphane Moretti, and Jérémy Levallois.

within the ecosystem of Substance products, despite its new ideas and visibly passionate project leaders. The team was divided into its design and strategy side in Paris and its technical side in Lyon, and yet the precise responsibilities of each group were poorly defined (this was a fine example of ineffective management, for which I was in large part to blame. . .), which ultimately generated a lot of noise. For many months, the team was unable to align on a common vision, whether regarding the product itself or how it should be developed. These difficulties were felt in the product we delivered, and the reception from the community was very mixed. The fact that this was only available via subscription to our full offer didn't help to promote the product, and it gained little visibility. In the end, at least during the years that Allegorithmic worked on this project, errors accumulated and the product didn't manage to find its place in the market. And yet as I write this, Substance Alchemist, now known as Substance 3D Sampler and focusing on its aspects of material capture, processing,

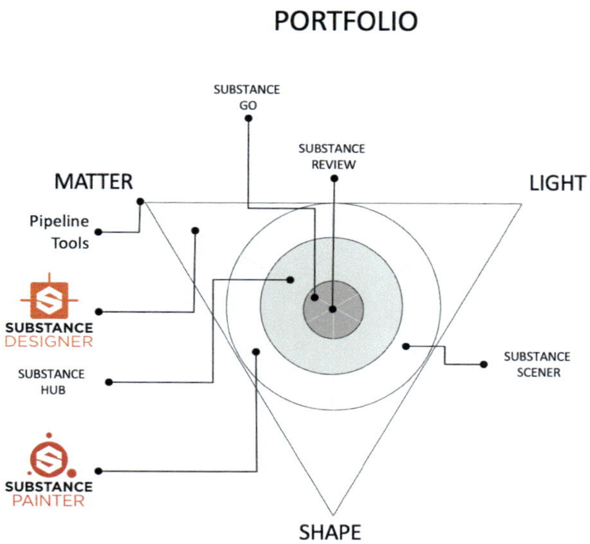

Figure 36.25: Design documents and searching for a graphic identity for Substance Alchemist.

and content creation (rather than the role of "MatterMaker" as a library manager, this new and refined focus allowing it to better position itself), is a product experiencing one of the strongest growths in our offer, and generating strong interest from many companies in the world of product design—the same companies that we identified as key targets years ago. . .

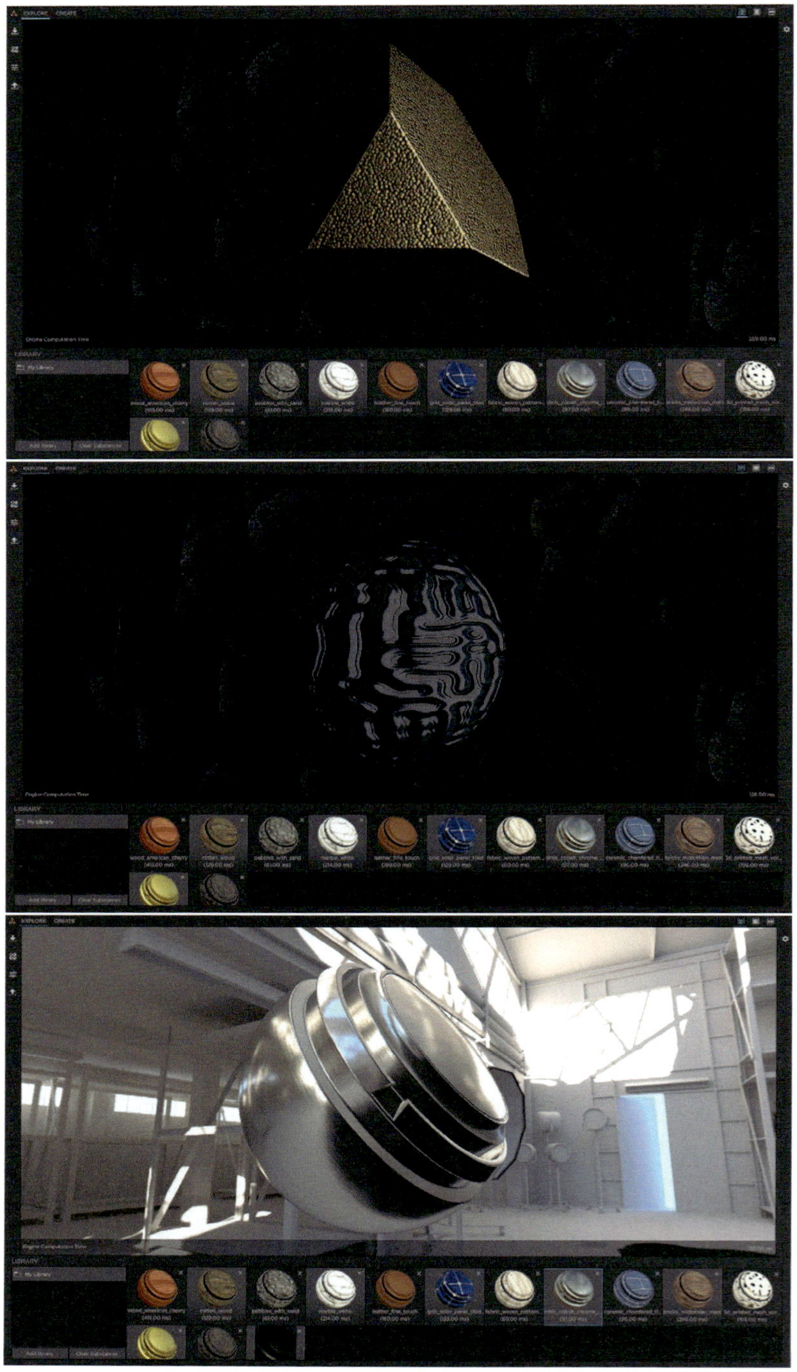

Figure 36.26: The first graphic interfaces of Substance Alchemist.

36.4 Substance Source

Substance Source evolved from Substance Database in November 2016. During that summer, shortly after launching the subscription model for our offers, we'd wondered how to provide consistent value to our subscription plan, going beyond software products alone, which tend to evolve in relatively infrequent, distinct steps. The constant provision of content provided an elegant solution, especially since the materials in the Substance Database were of extremely high quality and gave artists the possibility of working more quickly. Our competitors, in particular Quixel with their library Megascans, were also very popular with 3D artists. High-quality content therefore had a high perceived value.

Figure 36.27: Substance Source (we can see an example of its home page, at the top) came out in November 2016. For its release, we commissioned an image (below) from the Chinese 3D artist Zhelong Xu, an absolute master of 3D and Substance. We would go on to publish a book of his artwork (see Chapter 38).

We therefore decided to work harder on the content and highlight our library. We found a new, more inspiring name, (Substance Source), and we developed the platform in two months, from the start of September to the beginning of November. This was created by only four people (in Clermont-Ferrand, with Clément Jacob as lead): one person for front-end, one for back-end, one to create the content, and a product manager. It was a pure 'MVP' approach, much appreciated by enthusiasts of agile development.

Figure 36.28: Substance Source offered materials of outstanding quality, and at times we worked with guest artists, as we did here with Daniel Thiger, a world-class technical 3D artist, with a masterful knowledge of Substance Designer.

36.5 Substance Share

Substance Share was born from the desire to provide a place that, unlike Substance Source, we didn't control and that users could fill up and bring to life. In order to simplify maintenance and accounting management, as well as to avoid getting caught up in overly complex legal issues, we chose to authorize only free content provided by creators under a Creative Commons license.[6]

6: As I'd done during my best moments as Allegorithmic's legal representative, I suggested not bothering our legal team, and chose the Creative Commons license myself. I was wrong, of course, and we had to change the type of license some time later.

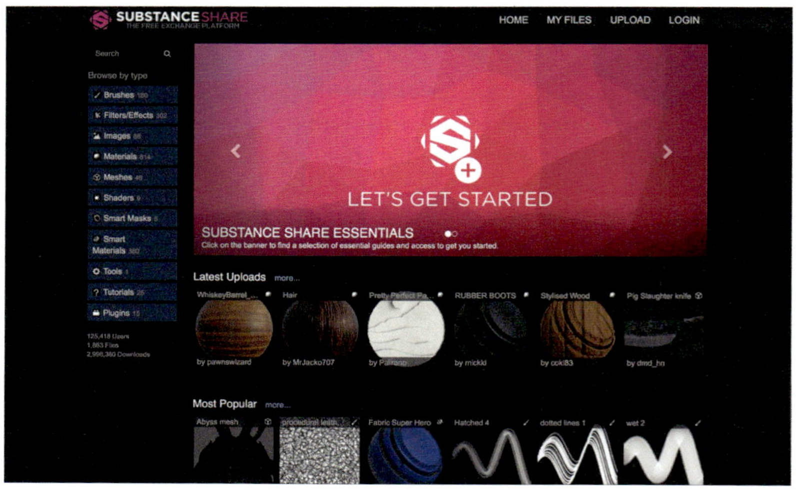

Figure 36.29: Substance Share was a platform for content exchange focused on Substance products, which we developed for our community. It was appreciated by our users.

The success of the platform was respectable, in terms of the number of assets uploaded. Moreover, its impact on our community was significant, as this was a 'safe' zone for exchange which found its place amongst our users, and fueled the Substance ecosystem.

The Meet MAT contest 37

37.1 Meet MAT

At the beginning of 2017, encouraged by the success of our previous contests and wishing this time around to highlight Substance Painter, which was rapidly gaining popularity and well-known through word of mouth, we decided to launch a new contest.

Pierre Maheut, who had been pushing for several years for the use of our tools in domains outside of entertainment (video games and special effects), pointed out a fundamental element of the multi-market approach which we would put in place during this time: when we visited creative studios, whether in the sectors of product design or video games, the artists we met all shared a passion for fictional universes, and they tended to decorate their offices in a similar way... Notably, we always saw figurines and other 'art toys' like those made by the appropriately named company Artoyz.

Pierre in particuar drew a link between the mascot Léo'z from Artoyz and the Peugeot Design Lab [60], both of which had made a strong impression on him: he saw that, starting from an object with a fixed design, an infinite number of decorations and designs could be added, each one more fascinating than the last, all transmitted solely by the way in which that object was painted. And so here was our idea: we'd launch a 3D painting contest with a fixed 3D object, which echoed Léo'z, and that had the potential to build the first bridges between our different target sectors, from video games to product design.

We now needed a 3D object to which we possessed the rights and which, if possible, could potentially become an icon for Allegorithmic and the Substance products...

Alongside Damien Lefauvre,[61] the team developed this little character whose head was a 'shader ball'[1] created by Jérôme Derel, Anthony Salvi, Mikaël Quéric, and Pierre Maheut, which could easily be found in places including Substance Painter, or Substance Share. This figure, which can be seen in figure 37.1 became our mascot! We named him MAT, which was both a common name and short for 'Material,' and we launched the "Meet MAT" contest, to present him to our community.

Figure 37.1: Here is MAT! Our new mascot, created by Damien Lefauvre, and the object of the painting contest "Meet MAT," which we launched in the first half of 2017. The head is a 'shader ball,' a classic object in the world of texturing.

1: A classic object from the universe of texturing, which is used to display digital materials and textures in an optimal way.

Wacom, NVIDIA, Artoyz, and Sketchfab were our contest sponsors this time around. We assembled a high-quality jury, with representatives from all of our target fields (video games, film, design, and architecture), and offered some extraordinary prizes. At last, we could launch the contest. To announce it, Damien Climent made a MAT inspired by Vespa, the famous scooter brand (see figure 37.2). The image was perfect, and seemed inspiring, and the response to the contest was incredible, and beyond anything we'd hoped for...

DOI:10.1201/9781003534624-37

Figure 37.2: Damien Climent from Allegorithmic made this version of MAT for the launch of the Meet MAT contest, mid-2017. The number 63 is of course a reference to the Puy-de-Dôme department, in the heart of France.

37.2 Our most successful contest ever!

To our immense surprise, we received over 1200 entries for the contest, of a quality and variety that was astounding! We were amazed and, to be honest, a little shocked. A few minutes of browsing through the entries was enough to understand how extraordinary the results were... but also to realize that a mountain of work lay before us to bring the contest to a successful conclusion. Choosing the winners, for instance, was not a simple task. We also had to rapidly review our prizes, requiring additional time which made participants impatient, as they were eagerly waiting for the contest results. Marion Marchive and Vincent Gault, among others, worked hard to pivot to these new requirements, and finalize the contest in the best possible conditions.

We ended up announcing the results several weeks later than initially communicated, and the winning entries proved to be phenomenal (see [62])! Here I include some entries, notably the top three positions of the 'general' category of the contest, and the winner for the student section: see figures 37.3, 37.4 and 37.5.

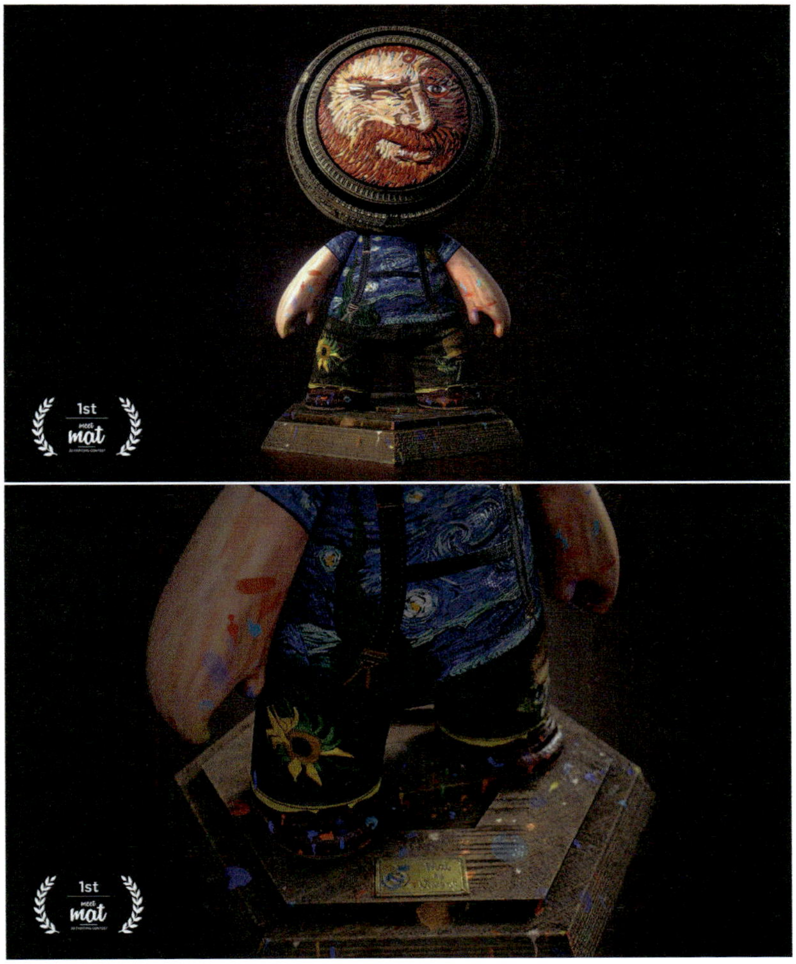

Figure 37.3: Gabriel D'Orazio (São Paulo, Brazil) took first place in the general category of the Meet MAT contest with "Mat by Vincent."

Figure 37.4: Liu Zinan and Andrii Mykhailov took second and third places in the general category of the Meet MAT contest. Rogelio Olguin and Rikki-Lynn Vitello took fourth and fifth.

We soon realized that we absolutely had to make a book with as many entries as we could and send a copy to each contestant. It would take us some time, but we ended up making [63], as can be seen in figure 37.7.

Even today, the Allegorithmic team is very proud of this contest and its success.

Figure 37.5: Guillaume Hecht (Nîmes, France) took first place in the student category of the Meet MAT contest with "The Substance Sheriff."

Figure 37.6: Some 18 months after its end, we were lucky enough to be visited by the two winners of the Meet MAT contest, in January 2019. I am next to Gabriel D'Orazio and Guillaume Hecht in this photo, taken in our offices at 9 rue de Milan (see Chapter 35).

Figure 37.7: The book and the 'Art Toy' (published by Artoyz) originating from the Meet MAT contest.

Conferences and Substance Days | 38

38.1 Substance Days

A step back: Unite 2009

I often think back to Unite 2009, a community event organized by the Unity team in San Francisco in October that year (see Chapter 24). The symbiosis and atmosphere at that event were remarkable; from what I could perceive of the connection between Unity, the company, and their users, the tone was positive and cheerful, and everyone was happy to be there. I could almost see the birth of a cult taking place—based around a love that users had for a tool, a company, a brand, and the people who had created all of this. And this love was mutual; it certainly radiated from the company's founders—but also from almost all the Unity employees that I had the chance to speak with. Some years later, David Helgason, one of the founders of Unity, invited me to his home after the legendary GDC in March 2015; over dinner, he told me that these Unite events were a fundamental element in Unity's success. These annual meetups between a company and its users had created a very strong bond in the Unity ecosystem.

And so, six years after this exceptional Unite event in 2009, and just as the beginning of Allegorithmic's success was confirmed, and our user base was growing, I considered whether we should also organize an event that would connect our users and Allegorithmic—our own version of Unite. The idea grew into what ultimately became "Substance Days."

Substance Days 2016, in Hollywood

In the middle of 2016 we launched what would become the first event entirely dedicated to the community of Substance users, the "Substance Days." The idea was similar to that of Unite: we would, over a few days, invite members of the Substance community, along with a few members of the Allegorithmic team, to a special place; we'd provide conferences highlighting the new features in our tools, and organize classes with specialists of the Substance tools, helping our users to learn new techniques; then, finally we'd simply socialize with our community members—we'd have a good time with our core users, and hope to build that same strong bond that I'd seen between Unity and its users, thanks to Unite in the late 2000s.

This first Substance Days took place at the end of July 2016 in Hollywood, in partnership with the legendary 3D school Gnomon, within their extraordinary premises, which were previously used as film studios, and now filled with inspirational sculptures and IT equipment. The event took place a few days before SIGGRAPH that year, which would be held in Anaheim, south of Hollywood. This meant that we could do the events

DOI:10.1201/9781003534624-38

one after the other with the same team, the majority of whom had come across from France, or from our local Los Angeles office.

The Substance Days were also a great opportunity for the teams to meet up, as well as a great source of pride as we could see the enthusiasm from our community of users close up. I think that the Substance Days had a fundamental place in the success that we experienced during this period between 2015 and 2019, and in the story of Allegorithmic overall.

Figure 38.1: The poster for the first Substance Days, in Hollywood, in July 2016, which took place in the premises of the legendary Gnomon School of VFX, and the background image of the title slide.

More Substance Days, all over the world

The first Substance Days in 2016 was so successful that we repeated the concept in the following years, in Japan, South Korea, and China, at times syncing them with conferences like SIGGRAPH or GDC, or with some other special occasion. The success of Substance Days continued to grow, producing rooms that were increasingly full, ever-longer queues, and stronger and stronger links between Allegorithmic and its customers.

The following photos illustrate some of these events, which took place between 2017 and 2018.

Figure 38.2: Keynote during Substance Days, in Hollywood, in July 2016.

Figure 38.3: The first Substance Days, in Hollywood, in July 2016, which took place within the premises of the legendary Gnomon School of VFX.

Figure 38.4: The first Substance Days, in Hollywood, in July 2016, which took place in the premises of the legendary Gnomon School of VFX. We put together an exhibition of the best 3D creations using Substance.

Figure 38.5: The room was packed for this first iteration of Substance Days in Tokyo, Japan, in April 2017. At the bottom: Alexis Khouri, Wes McDermott, and Mark Foreman, from CD Projekt Red, a legendary Polish studio, whom we'd invited to present his techniques with Substance Designer.

Figure 38.6: For this first edition of Substance Days in Seoul in 2017, the room was full once again. Christian Kim managed to assemble numerous 3D artists for a Saturday filled with presentations, including some by Inho Kim, our Korean demo artist.

Figure 38.7: Substance Days Seoul 2017.

Figure 38.8: Substance Days Shanghai, 2017. At the top, attendees crowd in to attend the day's presentations, notably by Zhelong Xu; Allegorithmic were so impressed by his work that we produced a book of his artwork—here, he is signing a copy of it (see figure 38.9). The room is full once again (500 places!); the presenters were Zhelong Xu, Gilles Fleury, Meizi Yan, and myself.

Figure 38.9: We were such fans of Chinese artist Zhelong Xu that we produced a book dedicated to his artwork, Yechawood.[64] We presented it for the first time during Substance Days Shanghai, mid-2017.

Figure 38.10: Substance Days at SIGGRAPH, Hollywood, July 2017.

Figure 38.11: Substance Days at SIGGRAPH, Hollywood, July 2017.

Figure 38.12: Substance Days at SIGGRAPH, Hollywood, July 2017.

Figure 38.13: Substance Days Seoul, 2018.

Figure 38.14: Wes McDermott and I gave the keynote for Substance Days at GDC, during the 2018 edition of the conference in San Francisco. The line to get into the conference was very long, and the room was packed.

Figure 38.15: Substance Days London, 2018. We announced the X-TAON on this occasion (see Chapter 41). At the bottom, the day's speakers.

Figure 38.16: Substance Days London, 2018.

Figure 38.17: Preparing Substance Days at SIGGRAPH, Vancouver, August 2018. Here we see Jérémie Noguer, Jérôme Derel, Pierre Maheut (standing) and Baptiste Manteau.

38.2 Various other conferences

In addition to the Substance Days, we of course continued to participate in numerous conferences, on all continents, to represent Allegorithmic and promote Substance products to local audiences. In April 2018 we expanded the team with the arrival of Vanessa Campinchi who, having organized concerts in Florida and managed events for a large French luxury group, would help us develop our presence at conferences such as Substance Days, and would develop the Allegorithmic Events team in a remarkable way. Vanessa is extraordinarily competent and enthusiastic, and would support us throughout the adventure, enabling us to carry out ever more successful events that were critical to the good development of a company and its employees.

The following images show some of our participations at major conferences, in particular GDC in San Francisco, which was our annual meeting with the video game development industry.

Figure 38.18: Presentation with Naughty Dog during GDC 2016. Sitting, Rogelio Olguin and Brad Smith. The bottom image shows how the room was filled in just a few minutes, before the session started.

During GDC 2016 in particular, we had the incredible opportunity to welcome several members of the Naughty Dog team as speakers, as they had used our tools on *Uncharted 4* (see Chapter 27). Their sessions attracted a huge number of people, both to our stand and during the various talks we'd organized (see figures 38.18 and 38.19).

Figure 38.19: Presentation with Naughty Dog during GDC 2016. We can see Christophe Desse, Brad Smith, and Glauco Longhi, who is signing an autograph.

Figure 38.20: A program of our busy schedule of presentations during GDC 2016.

The following images give an overview of some of our numerous participations in conferences and other events, particularly in the gaming world, but also in other sectors.

Figure 38.21: Our little stand for the FMX 2016 conference, in Stuttgart. We can see Alexandre Bagard, François Cottin (from behind), and Anthony Salvi.

Figure 38.22: Our presentations were always a great success at the stand during GDC 2017. Here we see, for example, Jérémie Noguer and Josh Lynch.

Figure 38.23: Fabrice Piquet on the premises for GDC 2018, in San Francisco.

Figure 38.24: Vanessa Campinchi at our little stand during Adobe MAX 2018, in October in Los Angeles.

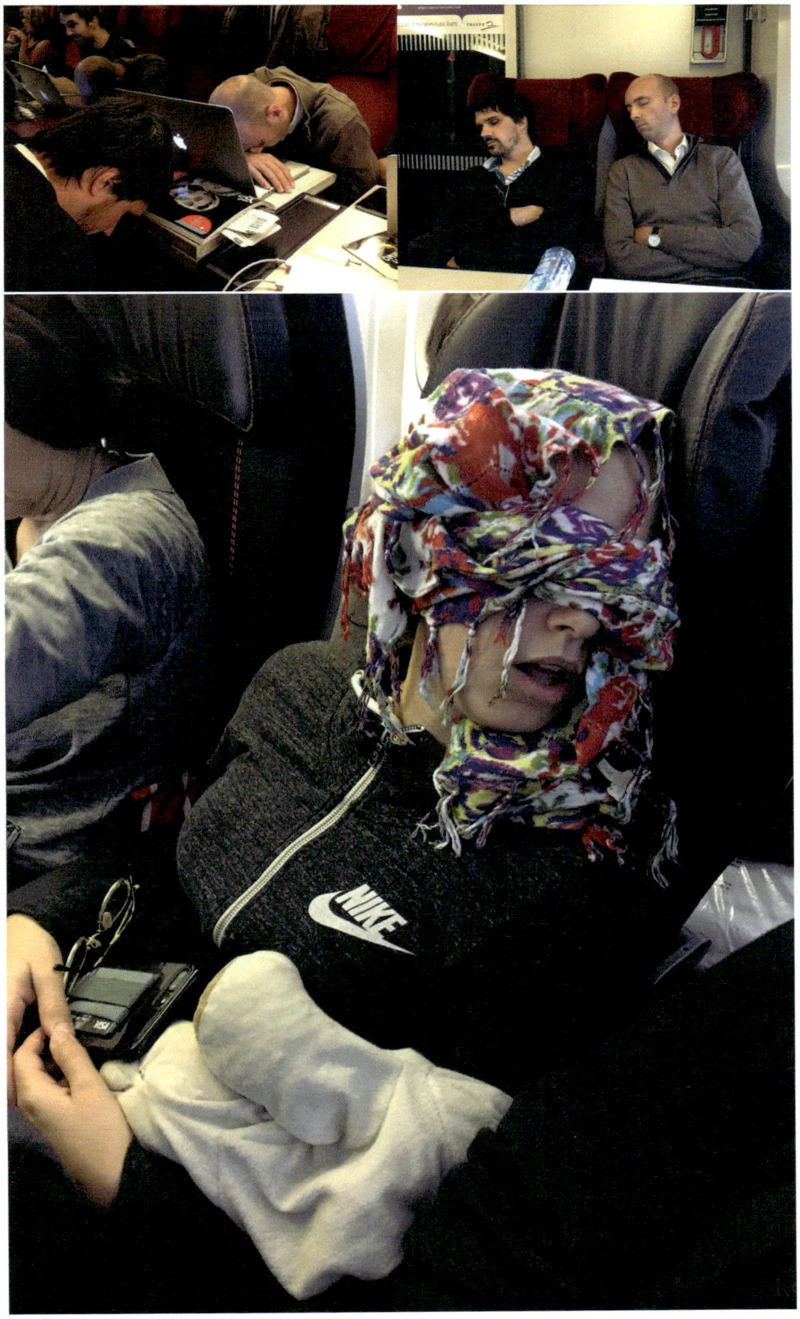

Figure 38.25: Incessant travel is tiring for everyone, as we can see in these images with François Cottin, Damien Letournel, and Marion Artolle.

39 Investment by Adobe, in 2017

39.1 The last hours before the signature

"I'm going to leave the room, your phone's going to ring, and I won't know about this call."

I was at the Paris office of a business law firm that Allegorithmic had been working with for a few months. I was alone with the lawyer for Dassault Systèmes, and we were waiting in a side room while the staff prepared numerous, voluminous documents to sign in order to finalize a major change of ownership for Allegorithmic, which would see Adobe enter the company's capital in place of Dassault Systèmes and Sofimac. We'd been working hard on this project for months, and were now just a few hours away from its culmination, which would allow Allegorithmic to enter a new development cycle with Adobe, the most prominent publisher of 2D creative tools who, with this move toward 3D via an investment in Allegorithmic, was sending a strong signal to the industry.

After speaking these words, the lawyer left the room.

A few minutes earlier, I'd told him that the previous evening I'd noticed a clause in one of the annex documents that I hadn't paid much attention to previously, one that could potentially put Dassault Systèmes at risk for the few months following the finalization of the change in shareholder. The risk was limited in duration and would only arise in very specific circumstances, even if I decided not to protect them. However, now that I'd spotted this clause, I couldn't in good conscience remain quiet about it. Dassault Systèmes were my current investors and, even if this would cease to be the case in a few hours, I owed them this prudence. I knew, however, that this small discovery risked restarting negotiations, potentially for months, or even derailing the entire operation if we didn't find common ground between all parties involved, who were already exhausted by months of tense negotiations.

My phone rang.

I answered. It was the financial and strategy representative of Dassault Systèmes responsible for overseeing the investment in Allegorithmic. We'd worked together, sometimes in a quite intense way, for several years.

"I'm glad to see that you raised the problem with this clause," he said. "We'd seen it too. We feel that the risk there is real, even if it's low. But we trust you not to abandon us as soon as the papers are signed—the fact that you've raised this issue today is reassuring, in fact. So, with this in mind, we aren't planning to highlight this clause; we're comfortable accepting this risk, unless you want to take steps to address this yourself. If you do, I'll inform the representative that you've just been speaking with and, when he comes back into the room, he'll block the signature and ask that we find an agreement on this particular clause. Which could of course lead to several more weeks of negotiation. . . "

DOI:10.1201/9781003534624-39

I was speechless. We were at an inflection point, a Gordian knot. What would have happened if I hadn't reported the information? What would have happened if, during many years of working together, a form of mutual respect had not been established?[1]

After some long minutes of discussion and contemplation, I decided to remain silent on that point, and we could finally begin signing the necessary papers. That took a little time (see figure 39.1 to see the volume of the documents involved); when we were done, we opened a bottle of champagne and properly celebrated the arrival of Adobe into the capital of Allegorithmic, which also had the effect of acquiring some stock from the team, allowing them (and me) to carry out our first 'cash out' operation.[2] It was the end of a cycle of over 10 years, and the beginning of a new cycle with an investor who seemed particularly aligned with our objectives, and who was ready to support us in our ambitions.

1: I'm certainly naive enough to believe that this element of trust played a fundamental role in the success of this operation, and in the company more broadly: my team and I have always attached great importance to building a relationship of trust, over time, with our investors, but also with suppliers, customers, employees, and so on. This event, on this day, is one of the most concrete examples I can see of the consequences of such a level of shared trust.

2: The 'cash out' is an operation to sell some or all of the shares held in a company. The valuation of the company is divided by all the shares held by the shareholders, and a new entrant must pay the price of each share, to each shareholder, so that each of these shareholders can carry out their 'cash out' operation. Here, each employee had the option to choose how many shares they wanted to sell to Adobe, up to a maximum of 20% of the shares held.

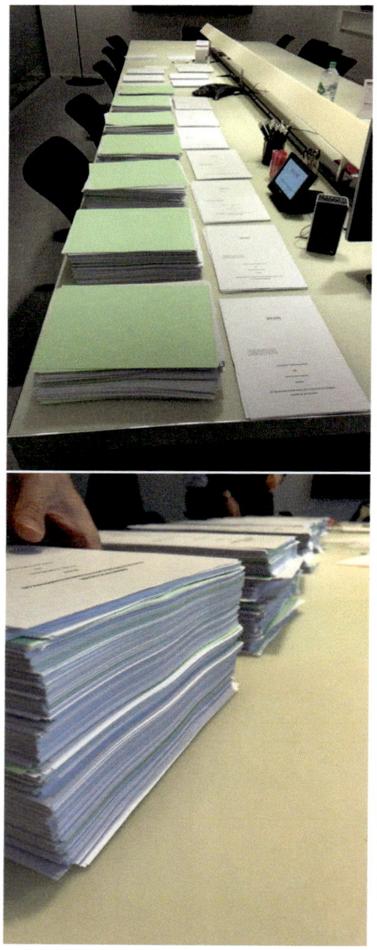

Figure 39.1: The very thick legal documents for the Adobe investment in Allegorithmic, in January 2017.

39.2 Return on investment

This capitalist operation took shape a little over a year before the signing. Our investor in venture capital, Sofimac (see Chapter 23), was coming to the end of their investment cycle, and had told us of they wanted to exit our capital, reminding us that it was our responsibility to find a buyer for their shares. When the value of a company has increased (and, here, everything suggested this was the case—Allegorithmic was progressing well), it's very natural for an institutional investor like Sofimac to try to seek capital gains in relation to its initial investment (the goal of any investment company, by definition). I hadn't realized, however, that it was the responsibility of the company (and so my responsibility, to a large extent) to lead the process. This was a very cumbersome process that could break my focus on other matters for months.

Moreover, as the primary objective of venture capital funding was to maximize return on investment, Sofimac was naturally pushing us to organize a real search of the market, to find the best possible offer. In our case, our best chances were with the major companies in the sector,[3] who would not only be able to appreciate the current state of the company—its turnover, its evolution, and consequently its overall financial valuation—but who would also be tempted by a premium price associated with 'goodwill,' this value that can be placed on intangible assets and on promises not yet fulfilled, an additional facet of a company's valuation that an analysis based on cash flow is unable to produce, but which some experienced potential buyers can nonetheless perceive. In short, this sense of goodwill was a very practical tool[4] that would allow us to return to the fundamental principle of sales: a party wanting to sell meeting with a party wanting to buy, and the two ultimately settling on a price that suits both.[5]

Sofimac strongly encouraged us to work with an investment banker, whose job was to find and negotiate the best offer for their clients. Investment bankers are generally paid on success, via a percentage of the sale price, which means they're very motivated to find the best price possible, even though their commission percentage generally drops with valuation levels. The metric for determining the 'best offer' is therefore very simple for a banker, yet here we had one of the first major concerns with this approach: this metric, the sale price, is not necessarily the principle focus of the company's founders, or other investors. In my specific case, for instance, I didn't want to bring in just anyone as an investor, and I was adamant about an investor bringing something beyond simple money to Allegorithmic, even if they were willing to pay the highest sale price according to the purely financial metric. Our current shareholder Dassault Systèmes had a different concern—they didn't want to see one of their competitors enter Allegorithmic's capital, regardless of sale price offered... This situation highlighted the misalignment of interests between Sofimac and the other shareholders in Allegorithmic, as well as its founders, employees, and myself; it would prove to be a very understandable and almost inevitable, but also very real, source of tension.

3: Some companies involved in 3D kept a keen eye on our progress, due to the success of our products...

4: And one that is entirely valid and legal, the 'goodwill' box being identified in the legal accounting documents.

5: Some call this negotiation phase 'haggling,' no different to what you might see at a market stall. Conceptually, that's actually pretty close.

39.3 Investment banking, and a complex equation

After meeting with several investment bankers, we became interested in a banker based in place de Paris, whose partner in charge of our file knew the 3D sector a little better than most of the others we'd spoken to. So we began the long, tedious task of explaining our activity,[6] and then the long, tedious task of modeling financial objectives for the next five to eight years, so that we could use Discounted Cash Flow (or DCF) models, and arrive at a sufficiently appealing valuation for the company,[7] followed by the long, tedious task of creating a 'deck' presenting the company, then the long, tedious task of contacting potential buyers, and then the long, tedious task of visiting various potential buyers and presenting our proposal, and so on.

In our specific case, we stopped quite early while preparing our proposal, as we (and the investment bankers) could see that the number of potential buyers was very small, and that we therefore didn't need to search very widely, or even visit potential buyers. I could actually just pick up my phone and call the directors of the companies in question, as I knew all of them personally. Here, I realized that in our particular case the help of an investment banker for a sale of shares operation wasn't really required.[8]

The work so far and the discussion with the investment banker had only confirmed that the equation was complex: only buyout of the company as a whole (not just an investment) by a major company in the sector would lead to maximum valuation thanks to goodwill. But this wasn't what I, nor the rest of the company's employees and shareholders, was looking for: we were making progress, and the company still had a lot of development potential ahead; it therefore wasn't the right time for this. Dassault Systèmes, who had been investors in Allegorithmic for almost 10 years and who possessed the 'ROFR' (Right Of First Refusal, see Chapter 18), were wary, and didn't want to see a competitor enter our capital with the significant number of shares that Sofimac were selling, nor did they want any competitors to attempt a complete buyout, in which case Dassault Systèmes would be tempted to trigger their ROFR. But Dassault Systèmes also knew that[9] I wasn't interested in joining their

6: Which was already complicated in itself, as our offers were technical and specialized, and it wasn't easy to define their value for a 'broader' audience in an elegant way. This extreme technicality alone dramatically reduced the number of our potential buyers, because all the companies able to understand our activity were already our partners and/or customers.

7: And here we had to find the subtle balance between what we could actually achieve in the future, with enough ambition for it to seem attractive, but not so much as to make it seem delusional, and harm our credibility. And here too there is a natural misalignment between the objective of the party selling their shares (to achieve as high a sale price as possible) and that of everybody who remains with the company—that is, the investors who retain their shares, as well as the company's employees and management team—who want the business to be successful *after* any changes in capital...

8: And so, during the next major change of investors, when we were selling the company at the beginning of 2019, we didn't work with an investment banker, and I managed the search for a buyer, and the negotiations, myself.

9: Didier Gaillot had directly asked me at the beginning of this process, "Would you be interested in joining Dassault Systèmes?" My answer was a clear "No."

company, and that triggering their ROFR could 'kill' the company once it was part of their group... There were many constraints that greatly limited our options.

39.4 Looking for investors, and the call from Adobe

The process began in spring 2016, and we contacted several companies and institutional investors to assess their interest in entering into the capital, or even acquiring the company entirely. After some weeks and months of discussion during which major figures in our sector expressed varying levels of interest, a software publisher in the 3D sector told us they were very interested. This wasn't a competitor of Dassault Systèmes, and so we began a cycle of deeper discussions and due diligence, and interest grew on both sides of the table. Although we were talking about total acquisition, the project proposed could nonetheless be interesting for my team and myself, as we'd clearly expressed our interest in continuing the adventure, advancing our products, and continuing to support our users, and to obtain more resources to carry this out than ever before. The only issue was that the valuation proposed by this publisher to acquire Allegorithmic was much too low. The publisher was limited in their means (they were not a big technological group), as well as by their owners, who had a purely financial outlook and were therefore not very inclined to place value on goodwill.

Then I received a phone call that would change everything. It was late, and I was hiding in the bathroom of my small Parisian apartment to take the call without waking our youngest child who was sleeping in the next room. From San Jose, California, John Leckrone told me that Adobe might be interested in taking a stake in Allegorithmic. He clarified that this would be an investment, not a buyout, as it was 'too early to talk about that.' Adobe didn't know much about 3D but was becoming more and more interested in the domain. It had recently acquired a small company in the field, Mixamo, created and managed by Stefano Corazza, whom I'd met numerous times at various conferences we'd both attended. Stefano was now leading a new 3D initiative at Adobe, which would become the Adobe Dimension software. Stefano had convinced several people at Adobe to not only take an interest in the 3D domain overall, which was already an accomplishment, but also in Allegorithmic specifically, as the company to acquire first if Adobe ultimately decided to fully enter this new creative space.

Hearing this, I immediately felt immense relief. Without fully knowing why, I had a feeling this option was the best for Allegorithmic. We were still of course very far from having a tangible offer on the table, and there was no guarantee that we'd ultimately finalize such an operation, but on paper this option had great potential to resolve the complicated equation created by the departure of Sofimac—a company that was able to place value on goodwill, and therefore provide a good valuation, and invest in a way that would allow me and my team to continue our adventure! Modulo one element: Dassault Systèmes might potentially view Adobe as a competitor. John and I discussed a potential solution: that Adobe should also buy the shares of Dassault Systèmes! That wouldn't be simple to organize at all, but it was potentially the only way to solve this complicated equation...

Alone in the bathroom of my apartment, I told him I was very interested in continuing to explore this possibility of an investment by Adobe. We agreed to speak again soon. Before progressing much further, Adobe, and all the others around the table, had to confirm their interest, or at least see the value of such an arrangement.

39.5 End of the cycle, and participation

The months that followed were particularly intense. We tried to find an agreement between Sofimac, Adobe, and Dassault Systèmes on a plan that suited everyone, and that also allowed Allegorithmic to position itself well for the future. It was a complex task, as everyone had their own interests, which at times didn't align with those of other parties. Everyone had come to the negotiation table with an army of lawyers, and with an investment banker right in the middle.

On the one hand, numerous discussions took place before Dassault Systèmes decided to sell their shares. After 10 years as investors, it was time for them to make a choice, and the group had lost interest overall in what we were doing some time before. I think that the conjuction of several factors had led to this. First, Dassault Systèmes hadn't succeeded in their mission to bring 3D to a wider audience than its traditional customers, who were often large industrial groups. The acquisition of Virtools in the late 2000s hadn't paid off, and instead Unity had managed to truly democratize the development of games and 3D experiences. The initial theory behind investing in Allegorithmic, in which our technology would help Dassault Systèmes develop its '3D for All' initiative, was becoming less and less relevant as Dassault Systèmes refocused on its core business. Moreover, our development, although constant, hadn't been fast enough for the group's liking, and we remained in their eyes a small, friendly side player, who addressed a video game market that didn't interest them. We were certainly not a future major player in 3D who would allow them to reach a new level in this field. Adobe's interest in buying out their shares and allowing Dassault Systèmes to exit the capital pushed the company to reach the end of their investment cycle. Once the conditions for a deal that suited them were met, Dassault Systèmes promised me they wouldn't use their ROFR, which had been in place since 2007. The sale of their shares and therefore the operation as a whole, had a chance of working.

Sofimac, on their side, wanted to maximize Allegorithmic's financial valuation, and after numerous complex discussions with Adobe, which lasted right up until a week before signing, we managed to arrive at a sufficiently significant amount which provided a good return on investment for the venture capital fund. Here too we could finally proceed.

On the side of management, we also put down on paper the basis of a collaboration plan with our future principal investor,[10] and the project completely aligned with our goals: Adobe would play an important role with strong participation on Allegorithmic's Board, but would

10: Once the investment was made, Adobe would own about 40% of the company's shares, becoming Allegorithmic's main shareholder.

not be in control. Notably, they could help us establish the move to a subscription-based model, a strategic change we'd been considering for some time. Adobe would have a ROFR, which we would limit over time. I felt comfortable with this structure; exhausted by this particularly difficult process of changing shareholders, I could nonetheless now see us entering a period of stability and construction of value, protected by a new investor and their ROFR that would discourage other interested parties. We would be able to concentrate on our products and our users, seek out new markets, and do the work we loved with generosity and passion, sheltered from the pressures of the 'outside world'...

Finally, I managed to negotiate that the shareholding change also result in a significant step for the current shareholding employees, who had received their BSPCE several years earlier (see Chapters 18 and 23), and the beginning of a new cycle with Adobe as investors. All of the current shareholders, including Sofimac and Dassault Systèmes, as well as the future shareholder Adobe, were aligned with and supported this idea. First, we'd allow our smaller shareholders and employees with BSPCE and other shares in Allegorithmic to sell up to 20% of their shares, allowing them (and me) to carry out a small 'cash flow' operation, which was a reflection of the common success provided by Adobe's interest and the valuation of our company. We also provided new BSPCE to all employees of our structure at the time of this operation (and kept a small number of BSPCE to distribute to employees who would join us over the next few months). Finally, we gave employees the possibility of investing in Allegorithmic, and placing part of their savings in the company's capital. A good third of our employees did so, which said a great deal about the interest of the team in what we did, and their confidence in our future. I was very touched by this show of trust.

We managed to put this complex mechanism in place after long and difficult—but fair—months of negotiations, and at the very beginning of 2017[11] we were finally ready to sign and start a new cycle.

11: I missed the deadline of mid-December 2016 that I'd set for myself, hoping that I'd be able to spend the end-of-the-year holidays in peace, without having to think about all of this...

39.6 The last few days before the signature

"You can't do this to me. Not now. You don't have the right."

It was very late on a Friday evening. After months of tough negotiations, all parties around the table were finally in agreement,[12] and we were technically ready to sign all the documents. We still needed a few days to finalize the drafts, print out the great slabs of documents, and prepare the rooms of the law office for the big day. We were aiming for the following Tuesday, January 24, 2017, to sign everything.

12: Often after phone calls in the middle of the night between John Leckrone and myself, so that we could reach an agreement between people who wanted this particular operation to end well, and for it to lead to a great mutual adventure afterward; each of us would follow these calls with instructions to our respective lawyers to accept this or that element, to unblock one point or another, and so on.

After a final busy day at the office, it was already dark outside. I gathered my things and began to walk from our office in the ninth *arrondissement* of Paris across to my home in the seventeenth. As I was leaving, I saw that my phone, which I hadn't looked at for a few hours, showed several missed calls from the same person, a long-time friend who was now part of a big American technology giant, working as head of a large division responsible for products and tools centered around 3D (I'll call him 'Byron' here). I called him back.

As he picked up, Byron said to me, "Seb, I understand that you're about to make a big move with Allegorithmic. You need to stop everything. We're interested in buying the company in its entirety, and if my sources are correct, I think we can do much better than your present offer. If you say "Yes," we'll come with a team this weekend to short-circuit the process and bring you in."

I answered immediately, without really thinking. "You can't do this to me now. I'm not even supposed to talk to you, because we're in the process of exclusive discussions and negotiations!"

I was of course shaken by what I'd just heard. I'd been counting on being able to spend a weekend resting, for the first time in a long time, happy to have finally found a solution that was acceptable for everyone, and exciting for the future. But it seemed I was in for an interesting night. . .

"Listen, thanks for your interest, but I can't do that to everybody else. And, anyway, why didn't you say this a few months ago, when we first contacted you about this?"

"It was a little too soon for us. But now we know more; we can see what you can bring to our group, and we're ready to move."

"You can't do this to me now. . . "

I asked him to wait a little while and, while I was still walking home through the streets of Paris, I called our lawyer (who answered at any time of the day or night). He was surprised, but also excited by the news. He confirmed that I wasn't supposed to discuss this with Byron at all, according to our exclusive discussion clause with Adobe, which ran right up until either the documents were signed, or Adobe withdrew from the process (if they happened to change their mind). But then our lawyer told me, ". . . But if you want to do this, give me the green light and I can set something up that will subtly spoil our relationship with Adobe. Sooner or later they'll cool off, and back out."

Again I was astonished. I spent a few minutes thinking about this by myself—I'd by now reached my apartment building, but I didn't want to continue my discussions at home for fear of disturbing my wife, or waking our two children. Then I told our lawyer that I didn't want to change anything—I'd made a commitment to Adobe. In any case, talking to Byron had given me the feeling that his company was particularly interested in our technology, and less focused on our products intended for 3D artists, our users. I also mentioned to our lawyer that I was conscious I was taking a risk by rejecting such an outstanding deal with a giant of the technology market—it was something that I might regret for the rest of my life. But, regardless, I told him I'd end the discussion with Byron, and I concluded our call.

Then I called Byron back, and told him what I'd decided. I thanked him as well, as it was no small thing to receive such interest from him and his company. Then I finally went upstairs and joined my family.[13]

13: Here again, that feeling of being 'in a movie' was very strong at this moment. There was no way now that I'd have a peaceful night, or a calm weekend. Now I was under even more pressure to make this investment operation a success—this choice of Adobe, and a risk, rather than the possibility of selling Allegorithmic immediately, potentially for an excellent price, which could provide security for my family forever, as well as marking a definite technological success for our company as a whole.

39.7 A new Board for a new cycle

The lawyer for Dassault Systèmes came back into the room once my call was completed. I confirmed to him that everything was in place for the signature. He said, "Great! let's go." We'd be able to open our bottles of champagne as planned, and move on to other things.

Once the operation was finalized, we could organize what would constitute Allegorithmic's new way of working, with a simplified capital structure free of investors who were tired out, with all employees invested, and a Board comprising Alexis Khouri and myself, as well as Stefano Corazza and John Leckrone from Adobe.

A new stage in the development of the company's structure, based on a very virtuous and benevolent collaboration, began.

Global Gatherings 40

40.1 Global Gathering, Auvergne, 2017

Now that we were experiencing a little success, and with the company growing all over the world, we decided to celebrate the occasion by organizing a Global Gathering for 2017, assembling absolutely every employee in the company in the same place for a week of work and fun, no matter where they were based in the world. This meant inviting the teams from Korea, China, Australia, Canada, Spain, the United States, and elsewhere... to Auvergne (the obvious choice). Nathalie Delfour organized a few days for us that would prove exceptional, in the mountains a few hours away from Clermont-Ferrand. Bus trips, work sessions, and presentations were combined with skiing, dog sledding, games of pool, and discussions around a drink... or a few drinks.

Figure 40.1: On the road to Global Gathering 2017, in Auvergne. Jérémie Noguer is visibly affected by jet lag, on the left. We can see Alexandre Bagard on the right.

DOI:10.1201/9781003534624-40

Figure 40.2: Alexis's presentation during the keynote of the Auvergne Global Gathering in 2017. He was ready to go hiking.

Figure 40.3: Working sessions and food during the Global Gathering 2017, in Auvergne.

Figure 40.4: An excursion with snowshoes and sled dogs during the Global Gathering 2017, in Auvergne. Visible here are: Alexandre Chassany, Xavier Courbouleix, Arthur Walter, Claudia Vance, Stéphane Guy (wearing a beanie), Daniel Lachal, and Quentin Couvidat.

Figure 40.5: Top: Arthur Walter, Wes McDermott, Jérémie Noguer, and Vincent Gault. Bottom, "Storytime with Wes." Wes McDermott is well known for telling extraordinary stories—often real adventures from his childhood.

40.2 Global Gathering, Lyon, 2018

The 2018 Global Gathering, again largely organized by Nathalie Delfour and her team, took place in Lyon at the start of summer. It was a form of consecration, 15 years since the creation of the company. Allegorithmic was doing particularly well, as we can see in figure 43.3 in Chapter 43, and one of our main areas of development was industrial design. We had exponential success in this domain, as can be seen in figure 43.4. We also had great ambitions for our future and wanted to share the news with the rest of the team, who took part in hectic working sessions, and equally wild evenings.

Figure 40.6: A few photos from the Global Gathering in Lyon, mid-2018.

This was also the moment for us to celebrate the opening of our new office in Lyon, and for the team to present me with a truly wonderful gift: a magnificent customized skateboard (which can be seen in figure 40.8), which I tried out right away. I took it to a nearby square in Lyon, and fell off it immediately, on my very first run. Nonetheless, I was happy to have shared these last 15 years with this wonderful team. The party was outstanding, and overall this Global Gathering will remain in some sense the culmination of the life of Allegorithmic, and of the efforts of everybody who had contributed to the adventure, up until that point.

Figure 40.7: In 2018, Allegorithmic celebrated turning 15 years old. Benjamin Maréchal and his team created the "Grey Shrikes" for this occasion.

Figure 40.8: The magnificent customized skateboard which the team (under the driving initiative of Benjamin Maréchal) gave me to celebrate 15 years of Allegorithmic, during the Global Gathering organized in Lyon in 2018. On the photo, on the left we can see Baptiste Manteau, and ; on the right, Amandine Lorrai, Benjamin Maréchal, and Xavier Courbouleix (far right).

X-TAON: the Allegorithmic concept car, and the contest 41

41.1 The X-TAON concept car

In our efforts to conquer 'new markets,' beyond the world of entertainment that we'd addressed for many years, we especially wanted to turn toward the automotive industry. Building on some success with cutting-edge manufacturers, we were refining our pitch and our demos to more directly address the auto designers that we met. As this industry was very secretive, we unfortunately couldn't show how one manufacturer used Substance in their pipeline to a competing manufacturer... Consequently, our demos were too theoretical and didn't present real use cases.

Then, in 2017, Pierre Maheut, a true automotive enthusiast, had a slightly crazy idea. "Why not develop our own concept car? This way, we'll be able to create a range of articles and demos based on this car that illustrate the benefit of our Substance tools in the conceptualization phase of a new vehicle—all without having to worry about any questions of IP!" It was a daring notion, and we let Pierre move forward with it. He was in contact with a few legends of the automotive design industry; he reached out, and attracted the curiosity of Takumi Yamamoto, who'd previously worked as an exterior automobile designer for Peugeot Citroën, then later for Polyphony Digital, the Japanese publisher of the Gran Turismo games,[1] as well as Frédéric Gasson, an automobile designer for Bugatti, Renault, and Toyota!

1: The choice of Takumi made a lot of sense for a Substance showcar, as he'd taken the exact opposite path to Allegorithmic: he'd started in industrial design, then moved into video games.

Figure 41.1: The very first concepts for the X-TAON, by Takumi Yamamoto, in our Paris offices in March 2018.

In December 2017, on the road between Las Vegas and Los Angeles while coming back from Autodesk University, Pierre and Frédéric Kohler finally managed to convince Alexis to finance the project, which required a not-insignificant sum. Soon after, back in Paris in January 2018, the project officially began. The team comprised Pierre Maheut, of course, and also Takumi Yamamoto, Frédéric Gasson, Arthur Coudert, Maxime Daguet, and Nicolas Paulhac.

We had to find a name for the car, and we soon agreed on X-TAON, in reference to the software with a graphical interface that I wrote during my thesis at the end of the 1990s (see Chapter 3). It was a name that seemed to suit a concept car, and which gave a subtle nod to the origins of Allegorithmic.

DOI:10.1201/9781003534624-41

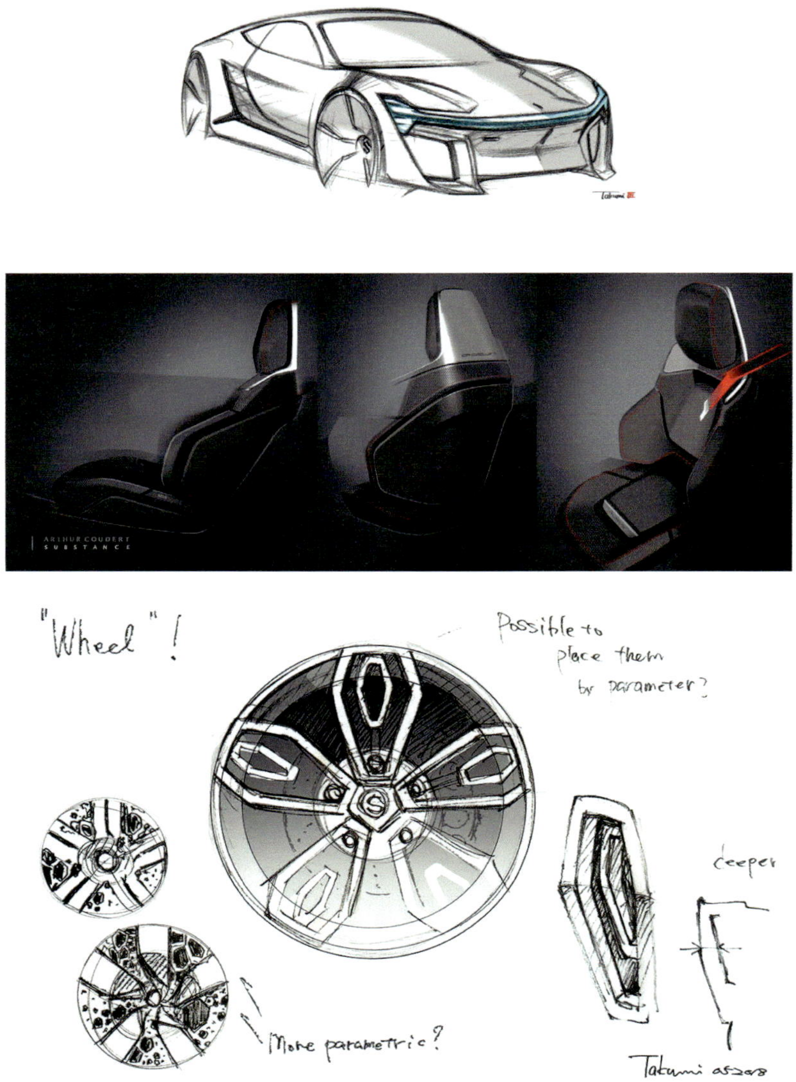

Figure 41.2: The first concepts for the X-TAON, by Takumi Yamamoto and Arthur Coudert.

The first concepts, signed by Takumi Yamamoto, arrived in February 2018, and the first 3D model was ready in May. We presented the final version of the concept car for the very first time on June 21, 2018, in London, during Substance Days London. This was the start of an unending use of the car in a wide range of demos, which focused on specific interior or exterior sections of the vehicle.

Figure 41.3: The model of the X-TAON in Autodesk Alias, by Frédéric Gasson, and a range of dedicated materials.

41.2 The artistic covering contest for the X-TAON

The car met with such success that it gave us an idea: we could use it as a creative 'canvas' for a customization contest! We officially launched the X-TAON Art Car Contest on November 27, 2018. The jury consisted of Jay Ward, Creative Director of the Pixar film *Cars*, Gabe Garcia, Forza Vehicle Art Director for the Forza games by Microsoft Studios, Pierre Maheut, Nicolas Paulhac, and myself.

We shared the model with our community on our Substance Share website, and we set the contest deadline for December 18, 2018. The results, announced on January 30, 2019, were once again exceptional, as can be seen in the following images (see the full article here: [65]).

The winners of the Pro category were Ispais Sedano, from Malta, in the first place, Guilherme Marconi, from Rio de Janeiro, Brazil, in second place, and JianYou Dong, from Hangzhou, China, in third place (see figure 41.4).

We could also now produce articles and demos non-stop thanks to this exceptional, unique asset: the Allegorithmic car! See in particular the outstanding work carried out by Onur Dursun[66] and Ronan Mahon [67].

Figure 41.4: The winners of the X-TAON contest: Ispais Sedano, from Malta, in first place, Guilherme Marconi, from Rio de Janeiro, Brazil, in second place, and JianYou Dong, from Hangzhou, China, in third place.

Figure 41.5: The X-TAON, portrayed by Ronan Mahon.

Figure 41.6: Details of the X-TAON, by Ronan Mahon.

42 Sale to Adobe

We were at cruising speed, two years after Adobe's investment in Allegorithmic (see Chapter 39). We were still progressing well, with an exponential growth in revenue, and in our number of users, and we were a 'cash flow positive' company (see Chapter 34). The whole team was enjoying the benefits of this period, and I very much appreciated this moment of relative stability, and the feeling of a job well done, and of being in the right place at the right time. We were absolutely not looking to raise funds, or even to sell the company. And so this was naturally the moment that we attracted external interest.

Between the stock market, investment funds, and major figures in the market, I'd stopped replying to the emails from VCs (Venture Capitalists) or the almost daily requests for contact that I was receiving on LinkedIn at the start of 2018. Things couldn't remain this way, however, particularly when a company that we knew well—I prefer to conceal its identity here; I'll call it 'Company X'—contacted me to say that they loved Allegorithmic's work, and suggested that we unite to write the future of 3D together. I'd heard this type of speech from several other companies in recent years, and I replied that we were enjoying our current stability, and had no wish to make any major changes. Company X insisted (a *lot*) that I hear them out, however, and after a few phone calls in which they explained their plans and their ambitions, I had to admit they were quite compelling...

Things accelerated quickly during GDC in San Francisco, a few weeks after this initial contact.

42.1 GDC, San Francisco, March 2018

"What figure should I put?"

Alexis and I had a meeting with the two main directors of Company X in one of their meeting rooms that formed part of their stand for GDC. The discussion had started a few minutes earlier, and now I saw their CEO start tapping something on his phone. Honestly, it seemed like something on his phone had distracted him, and he wasn't paying attention to us any more. That was when his colleague said, "I know my director pretty well, and right now he's writing an email offering to buy Allegorithmic." The CEO of Company X looked up from his phone and asked us, "What figure should I put? I have an email ready to go—I just need to know how much I should offer to buy out your company."

Trying to maintain a certain composure, we stated once again that we felt honored to attract such interest; we preferred not to give a figure right away, of course, but said that we'd go away and think about it. A few minutes later, somewhat stunned, we returned to our stand, feeling that we'd just experienced a strange moment that we'd never forget. From key moments like these, from these moments of truth, events tended to swing one way or another, their trajectory changed forever.

DOI:10.1201/9781003534624-42

As Alexis and I discreetly debriefed, I felt my phone vibrating in my hand, notifying me of a new email. It was from the CEO of Company X, proposing to buy Allegorithmic. He'd added some numbers to his message.

With a very simple, direct mail[1] from the CEO of Company X, we officially had an offer to buy out Allegorithmic from a serious, ambitious company. A company that we couldn't ignore, even though we weren't looking for this kind of proposal. The project he'd outlined was interesting—the team from Company X was very talented, and were experiencing enormous success. We felt great pride in having attracted the attention of such a team, to the point where they were seriously, and openly, considering the acquisition of Allegorithmic.

1: Which began like this, before going into detail on the proposition and the price offered: "Dear Sebastien, Company X would love to acquire Allegorithmic. . . "

I now had to tell Adobe, via Allegorithmic's Board, that we'd received this interest. Our statutes and our shareholders' agreement required me to do this, although the precise definition of interest in acquisition meant that I could have waited wait until I received a formal 'LOI'[2]—that is, a firm commitment for the interested company—before approaching the Board with the message. But the project and the team were so ambitious that Alexis and I knew that once the first email of interest had arrived, they were serious. The LOI wouldn't be far behind. I also wanted to give Adobe time to digest this information, prepare, and react with full knowledge of the facts, should we decide to continue discussions once the LOI was received.

2: The 'LOI,' or 'letter of intent,' is a letter that officially states an interest. It can be binding to a lesser or greater degree, depending on its format, but it is a first, official trace; in the case of statutes and a shareholder agreement such as those that governed Allegorithmic, presenting such a letter to the Board would require an official response from the members of the Board or company. An LOI would therefore represent an inflection point for Allegorithmic.

We spent the next few months in discussions back and forth between Company X and ourselves, as well as with Adobe and John Leckrone, who acknowledged their interest but took no firm action. John told us that Adobe didn't want to sell its shares, nor to speed up the discussions (it seemed Adobe was also happy with the cruising speed mentioned earlier, which had been working well until Company X complicated things), unless things became more serious than a discussion by email.

Alexis and I, and the few people with whom we could discuss the subject, also spent these months relentlessly questioning and second-guessing ourselves. Were we crazy not to consider such an offer? Was this the right time to sell, if an interesting project presented itself? What was the market saying? Should we be afraid of the economy slowing down? Were we sufficiently equipped for the continuation of Allegorithmic's development? Weren't we better off alone? Was this period of stability causing us to become complacent, when we should be pushing to accelerate things, whether with a big group, an institutional investor, or otherwise? And so on.

Then, as anticipated, events moved along and we had to consider such things in parallel with discussions on the subject, as often happens. On April 3 Company X approached us with a first draft of a letter of intent. And after several months of remote discussions, they invited Alexis and me to spend the day with them in July, to significantly advance the subject. This was an excellent opportunity for us to get to know them better and, in a way, to present our conditions should we agree to change Allegorithmic's current trajectory: Allegorithmic was doing especially well, and we weren't actively looking for investment—and so, nothing would push us to move for at least two years.

42.2 Semi-final of the World Cup, July 2018

When I arrived at the hotel, I checked in, then changed the channel on the large television set in the lobby—just in time to see the last 30 seconds of the semi-final of the football World Cup, France playing against Belgium. I'd been trying my best to follow the match from the moment we'd landed, and passed through customs and security at the airport; I'd been able to keep track of it in the car that Company X had sent to pick me up—and now, France had qualified for the final right before my eyes, and I could go up to my room doubly excited.

Alexis joined me a few hours later, arriving from Los Angeles, and we met up to prepare our visit to Company X, which would last all day and throughout the evening, to discuss the opportunity for Allegorithmic to join the company that had been trying to draw our interest since GDC, a few months earlier.

The charm offensive was launched, and the organization of the day was perfect. Once more we talked about the project, this time face to face; we discussed everybody's ambitions, and the various constraints and fears involved, especially on our side. The talks went well—though, once again, we didn't really have a compelling reason for Allegorithmic to make such a huge move at that time.

After a while that morning, the CEO of Company X joined us. He greeted us, sat down, and got a sense of the feeling in the room. And then, pulling the rug out from under his entire team, he tried to conclude discussions right away: "How about for this much?" he asked. . . [3] Everyone fell silent, waiting for our response. And of course, this significantly modified the equation. Nonetheless, we replied that we were of course honored by such interest in our company and our team, and that our shareholders would of course be delighted with such a valuation of our company—but that we also needed to understand what such a change would mean for our teams, our products, our customers, and ourselves.

3: He presented us with a figure that was much higher than anything we'd discussed until that point.

Honestly, I think it was at this moment, and then during the rest of the day and the evening, that the first cracks began to appear in the proposal: Company X didn't seem particularly interested in our current products, and seemed to think that a large sum would be sufficient to make us change our plans, without really giving much thought to what would come afterward.

42.3 Adobe Headquarters, San José, August 8, 2018

In the months preceding our visit to the headquarters of Company X, Adobe, despite adopting a position of waiting and observing (the company wanted to see whether Alexis and I would push this opportunity as far as presenting it to the Board as an interesting option for evolution), was also preparing to 'join the dance.' For a company like Adobe, and for its internal 'champions,'[4] this meant assembling a sufficient number of supporters and 'aligning' the organization. Our champions were in particular John Leckrone, Stefano Corazza (see Chapter 39), and Scott

4: The few people high enough in the company hierarchy and believing in the idea of acquisition firmly enough to develop the project, and defend it to decision-makers and key people with a view to a possible deal.

Belsky, the latter recently having joined Adobe as Chief Product Officer, with the goal of transforming and modernizing Creative Cloud. 3D was a domain that was almost untouched by Adobe, and Scott[5] wanted to change this.

5: Scott Belsky, first a brilliant student at Harvard, then an entrepreneur and author, had created the company Behance in November 2005, a website allowing digital artists to showcase their creations. The company had been acquired by Adobe in December 2012, with Scott becoming Vice President, Community at this time, a new position and a new mission for Adobe. Scott left to make investments in various funds a few years later, with great success, before being called back by Shantanu Narayen, Adobe's CEO, to take a position as Chief Product Officer. He was in charge of all of Creative Cloud in particular, with a mission to modernize the offer, as well as to invent products to ensure Adobe's success in the future. It was an extensive mission that Scott approached with overflowing, infectious enthusiasm.

We took a fundamental step at the beginning of August 2018, when Alexis and I visited Adobe's headquarters in San José, California. The building that wasn't particularly interesting on the outside—it could have housed a bank, or any other of generic activity—changed completely once you passed through its doors. It was filled with decorations and a general ambiance that encouraged creativity; it was in this setting that we met our hosts to seriously discuss the options before us. Adobe had been our major investor for a few years at this point, and possessed that particular right, the 'ROFR' (Right of First Refusal, see Chapter 39); they were therefore in a strong position, and could simply wait for Company X to move before reacting. All of our discussions around that time hinged on the fact that we wanted Adobe to finally clarify its intentions and its ambitions for Allegorithmic. It wouldn't have been ideal for us to agree to join Company X if Adobe then chose to activate its ROFR, and we were ultimately acquired by a group that had been forced to buy us out 'by default,' without any real ambition for us, and ending the bold plans we'd been discussing with Company X. In such a case, everyone would lose.

And so with this visit we wanted to discover what Adobe's intentions were for Allegorithmic, and to firmly ask that, if they weren't ready to take a step forward and launch into 3D with us, that they graciously let us leave.[6]

6: Alexis and I were well aware of the difficulty of this task.

The day of meetings confirmed that the internal alignment, mentioned earlier, was in place, and accelerating. This was reassuring. If Alexis and I were somewhat frustrated by the pace of this alignment, we appreciated the depth and seriousness of Adobe's approach. Unlike what we'd seen with Company X (which was certainly smaller and less 'processed'), the time taken for this alignment was proportional to a thorough analysis of this opportunity, and discussions essentially revolved around what would come afterward—that is, what would happen once an acquisition was made, what would happen with our products, the commercial operations we could set up, how we'd take care of our customers, and so on. This talk was refreshing; unusually, and because Alexis's flight back to Los Angeles had been canceled, we both returned to our hotel feeling good about Adobe's plans for Allegorithmic. Although we hadn't received a firm position from Adobe, we understood the reasons behind this, and that this was merely a matter of time, rather than because of a lack of interest.

Late that evening, I received a message from John alerting me to a last-minute opportunity: the CEO of Adobe, Shantanu Narayen, wanted to meet with us the next morning at 9:00am! This was an interesting twist, which suggested that things were becoming more concrete on Adobe's side—and if the company's CEO wanted to meet with us, that was a good sign. John confirmed that Shantanu had been hearing about us often, and had become curious; he'd then learned that we were here, and decided he wanted to meet.[7]

7: On my side, all I could think about was, "I don't have any clean shirts left for the meeting." Alexis saved me by ironing one of the shirts I'd barely worn (see figure 42.1), which I then reused for my meeting with Shantanu.

Shantanu Narayen had formerly been a part of Silicon Graphics;[8] we'd learn later that this meeting with him proved crucial to the internal decision-making processes within Adobe. Here he gained enough trust in Allegorithmic, but most importantly in Alexis and me, to give the green light to the continuation of negotiations, and for Adobe to provide an official commitment to the acquisition of Allegorithmic.

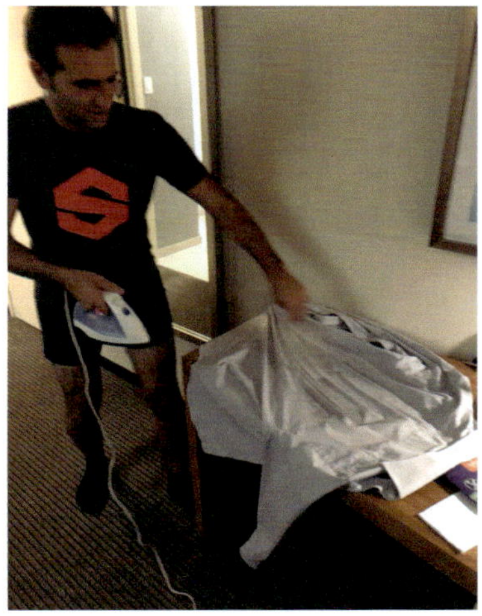

Figure 42.1: Alexis helped me out by ironing one of my shirts, in preparation for an unexpected meeting with the CEO of Adobe. We had to stay an extra day to meet him, and I had nothing left to wear. I took this photo on August 8, 2018, for posterity...

8: A legendary company in the world of 3D, providing dedicated machines in the 1990s (see Chapter 4).

42.4 Club Med, Opio, August 2018

It wasn't really the relaxing vacation I'd hoped for. And I needed one... But I felt excited, and made many calls in between the family activities, and reading by the pool, particularly with John Leckrone, often late in the evening due to the time differences, amid the smells of grilled prawns, and the sounds of other vacationers enjoying the all-you-can-eat buffet, listening to the music that got louder and louder as the minutes passed. I saw Laëtitia and our children not too far away, enjoying their summer evening; I waved hello to them, then pointed to my phone's headphones in my ears, as if to say, "I'm still busy, don't wait for me!"

I was also frustrated, as on Adobe's side the situation was progressing much too slowly for my liking. Despite the unanticipated recent meeting with Shantanu, no firm decision had yet been made. John suggested to me that the idea still had to spread a little more widely. Adobe wasn't in the 3D sector, and changing course took a while. Still, the fact that we'd received such interest from Company X was pushing Adobe to take an official position, and make a decision.

Finally, during one of these late-evening calls with John, he confirmed that Adobe wanted to get into the game. They were preparing an 'A2N,' an 'Approval to Negotiate,' an internal term designating an official document signed by the company's executives, which allowed the M&A (Mergers and Acquisitions) team to begin negotiations to buy a company.

And so here we were.

42.5 Paris, end of summer, then autumn 2018

The weeks following my return from 'vacation' were intense, between my day-to-day work for Allegorithmic and serious consideration of the big question: to sell, or not? And if so, to whom—to Adobe, or to Company X?

The approach of Company X over the last few months had pushed us to reconsider our vision of the macro-economic situation and of the little world of 3D in this environment. Its interest in Allegorithmic, its approach to us, and its ambition overall had proven one thing: in the years to come there would be significant movement in this universe—acquisitions, investments, and concentrations, which would redefine the landscape of the 3D sector that we currently knew.[9] The 3D market was heating up fast, and the period of stability that I mentioned earlier had only been an illusion. I'd become particularly complacent because of our own success—we'd essentially fallen asleep on our laurels (largely due to the extreme fatigue following the complicated process of changing

9: The future proved us right, with *hundreds* of acquisitions taking place in the 3D domain between 2019 and 2022; this kind of activity was wholly unprecedented in the sector...

shareholders, see Chapter 39), and ignored many warning signs of these fundamental changes in the industry.

Instead of enjoying our comfortable situation, we had to take action, and invest.

Several paths were available, including seeking investment from venture capitalists, entering the stock exchange, and getting closer to big, industrial players. Everything seemed positive if we wanted to raise funds or publicly sell shares, but we were wary of this due to some examples we'd witnessed—notably when the investment funds The Carlyle Group, and then HgCapital, had acquired the The Foundry, a highly respected company and a leader in software dedicated to special effects. We needed the same type of investment that The Foundry had received from these funds, with the same requirements for return on investment and above all quality of management, and we'd seen The Foundry transition from the innovation that characterized them to optimization of their bottom line, through savings and synergies, rather than by looking for new areas of growth.[10] Our own experience with institutional funds, whose metrics were entirely financial, was a reason for our lukewarm interest in significant funding from pure financiers. Fatigue was also mixed in with this feeling, and in the end it was an option that seemed much less attractive than anything we'd so far discussed with Adobe, or with Company X.

10: The CEO of The Foundry had told me, while I was visiting the company in London, that their driver of growth for the year was shifting to an aggressive fight against piracy... Honestly, the plan didn't strike me as a great idea...

Finally, after again considering the pros and the cons of such a move, and taking into account the options available, we made our decision: join Adobe. There were many reasons for this, but in the end it all came back to a deep certainty, a gut feeling that this where the sequel, Book 2 in the saga of Allegorithic, must be written. All the analyses in the world couldn't replace this feeling, because, in a case like this—which is defined by a choice of destination and a view of future projects, rather than a dry sale which halts a project, and whose metric of success is purely financial—a leap into the unknown is required, the success of which can only be measured *afterward*.

Now we had to obtain a slightly firmer commitment from Adobe. This finally arrived on September 2, in the form of an LOI (Letter Of Intent) which made the company's intentions clear. I could now formalize this path, which required that I first notify Company X that Allegorithmic had entered an exclusive discussion phase with Adobe.

I'd kept my contact at Company X waiting for a few days, even though he'd been becoming increasingly insistent. Now I sent him a mail with this new information. He called me shortly afterward and, after I explained the situation, he said that they, "wouldn't make the decision easy for us." He promised us wonders, after that, despite my repeated requests to no longer contact me on this subject. And in the exchanges that followed, one thing became clear: they weren't really interested in our products, but in our pool of engineers, and our knowledge and skills. They were even willing to make an arrangement that would see our team join Company X while Adobe acquired the Substance products! For me, this absolutely settled things, and reassured me that joining Adobe was the right choice for us, even if we were potentially turning down a higher offer in purely financial terms...

And so a new period of intense work and negotiations began, often late in the evening, with our current shareholders and Adobe, in order to reach an agreement[11] that was interesting for everyone. In particular, we managed to set up an operation which would be financially life-changing for *all* Allegorithmic employees, regardless of their length of employment, their level in the company, or their possession or lack of BSPCE. I was particularly proud of what we managed to achieve on this point.

11: I won't detail the legal discussions and other ups and downs of this phase here but, just as there had been many twists around the time of Adobe's investment a few years earlier (see Chapter 39), there were plenty here too. Perhaps not quite at the same level, but significant nonetheless. . .

The weeks went by. Many discussions took place, and Scott Belsky made a key visit to Paris, to our office, where he confirmed that he wanted to create a strong 3D division, as we'd envisioned. We were given guarantees that we'd be able to steer our ship as we wished, including what would happen to our team once integrated—and so, at last, we began to converge on a global agreement.

In terms of timing, I'd naively hoped to be able to finalize the documents before the end-of-year holidays. But, ultimately, everything was finished in January.

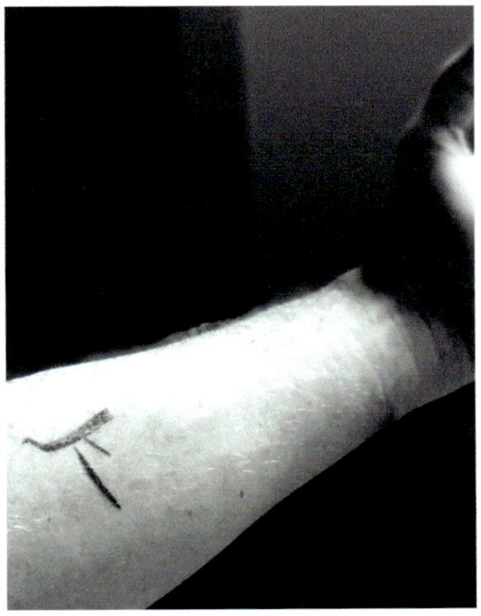

Figure 42.2: As discussions with Adobe seemed to be coming together, and without having planned it out in advance, one day I walked into a tattoo shop near our office and had the original Allegorithmic logo tattooed on my left arm. In my skin, forever. . .

42.6 Making the announcement to the teams

I had to find the right words.

I chose to announce our acquisition by Adobe two weeks before the official signing, scheduled for Wednesday, January 23, 2019 (a signing followed by a public announcement).

This was kind of a risk, as the information was highy confidential, and the final documents hadn't yet been signed. But I couldn't just surprise the teams, and tell them the news the same day it was made public. So I traveled to Clermont-Ferrand, to be with the team members who'd been part of Allegorithmic the longest, and I took over one of our regular '360' meetings[12] one Wednesday, to announce that after 16 years of official existence, Allegorithmic would join the Adobe group to form a new division dedicated to 3D. We would no longer be independent, but we had a mission before us.

12: A meeting lasting around 15 minutes, every Wednesday, that brought together all the teams of Allegorithmic, who would each present, in turn, what they were working on at that moment.

I explained the reasons for my choice, and what it would mean for us as a team, as well as for our products and customers. I provided context and tried to convey the ambition behind the operation. The idea that Adobe would come to us, a little company from Clermont-Ferrand, to build and manage a new division dedicated to 3D within this graphics software giant—a giant in every way, even—was simply extraordinary!

And finally, I spoke about an alignment of planets: we were being offered a fantastic project fueled by extraordinary ambition, inside a healthy company that treated its employees and its products well—the only tech company in our domain whose DNA involved producing creative, 'agnostic' software (that is, neither targeting nor excluding a particular market). In my opinion, it was also the right time to do this, just as major movements in the world of 3D were starting to take place.

I also tried to be reassuring, and to provide some elements of answers to the initial questions that were asked at the end of my presentation. Because there would of course be changes, and adaptation was necessary.

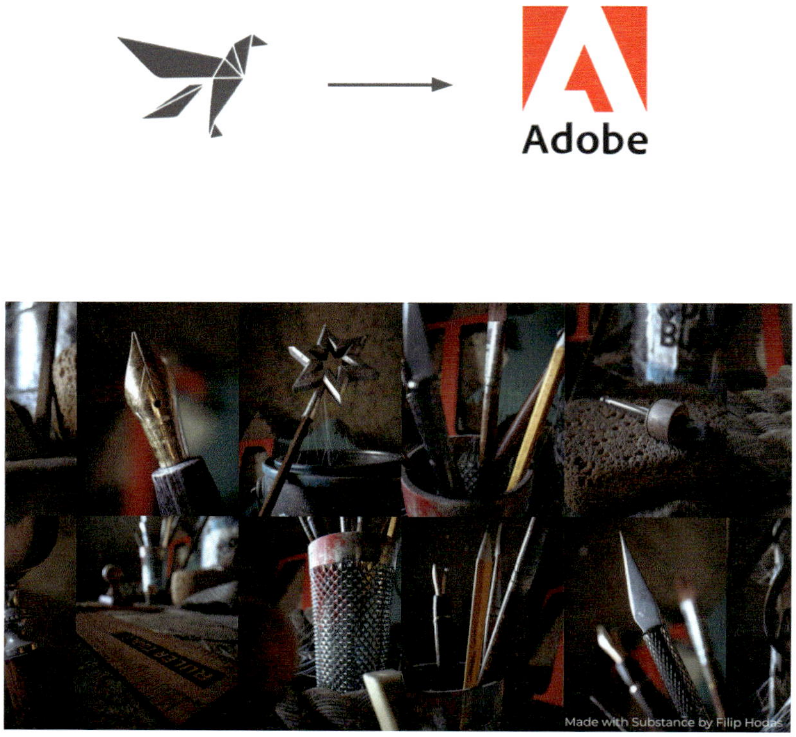

Figure 42.3: The first slide (top) that I presented to Allegorithmic employees, at the beginning of January 2019. Allegorithmic was joining Adobe. The second slide (bottom) is an image which summarized our ambition: we can see the classic tools of Adobe Photoshop depicted in 3D.

Finally, we set up a way for employees to ask questions anonymously, if needed.

Two weeks later, we joined Adobe.

42.7 Signature and public announcement, January 23, 2019

The day of the signing. It was Wednesday, January 23, 2019. A large part of the Allegorithmic teams (at least, those in France and the rest of Europe) was in Paris, and many representatives from Adobe had joined us to finalize the signing of the documents, followed by the official public announcement, and to welcome us within Adobe the following day, with a special evening at Adobe's rented premises in a Regus in Paris.[13]

13: I'll skim over this evening, which wasn't exactly glorious, and set a slightly sour tone for our first few days at Adobe. . .

The signing took place at the office of the legal firm Gibson-Dunn, who we'd been working with for some time by this point, in close collaboration with Judith Raoul-Bardy, who did a remarkable job throughout, finalizing the operation. There weren't many people around this early in the morning, and croissants and some champagne helped us to mark the occasion, while waiting for the rest of the day's events.

Once the signing was official, we returned to our office on rue de Milan, in Paris's ninth *arrondissement* to coordinate the public announcement. First I had to send out a lot of personalized emails to some people in the

Figure 42.4: A few photos from the signature of the official documents of the sale of Allegorithmic to Adobe, January 23, 2019. Here we can see Alexis Khouri, François Cottin, Xavier Courbouleix, and Muriel Gellf, representing Allegorithmic, Stefano Corazza, John Leckrone, and Victoria Shaw from Adobe, Judith Raoul-Bardy, who we had the pleasure of working with from the legal firm Gibson-Dunn, representing us, and Ludovic Robert, from BNP Paribas.

industry, so that they learned the news that we were joining Adobe from me, rather than from a press release. This information was important enough to change the dynamic of the 3D industry, as confirmed by the reply I received almost immediately from Tim Sweeney, CEO of Epic.

```
Hi Sebastien,
That's really big industry-changing news!
Congratulations!
Tim
```

Then we had to send out the press release dedicated to the acquisition, and monitor questions and reactions from the industry. All hands were on deck, and the atmosphere was charged, somewhere between excitement, disappointment at reactions from some members of our community, and above all permeated with the feeling of having accomplished something important, and perhaps turning a page on something that was so dear to us all.

We organized a party on our premises that evening, in that space that had become a continuum between work and celebration—which was somewhat indicative of our mixture of contradictory feelings; regardless, we were all happy to be together to mark this occasion. John Leckrone, who was wearing a Substance T-Shirt for the event, mixed in well with the teams, and told me later that what most struck him about the evening was that it hadn't been a moment of triumph—some great cry of victory—but rather a celebration of the remarkable work we'd accomplished together, which had granted us the opportunity to begin writing this new volume in the life of Allegorithmic. And that we were all happy to continue this story together...

At the same time I published a personal blog post on the platform Medium,[68] in which I allowed myself to express a personal sentiment at this moment in Allegorithmic's life: I felt much like Peter Jackson (keeping everything in perspective, of course), the New Zealand director who'd made a name for himself directing low-budget gory horror films in his native country, who was then asked to direct the Lord of the Rings, within a major Hollywood production setting; Allegorithmic, in turn, had started out from Clermont-Ferrand, creating niche software dedicated to texturing—and now we found ourselves with an offer to make a new generation of 3D tools, within the worldwide giant Adobe! This was our 'Peter Jackson moment'. . .

The reaction of our community to the announcement grew in the days following Wednesday, January 23, and it's fair to say that the community members were neither quiet nor unanimous in their views. While we received an incredible number of congratulations, often face to face, a sizeable number were also very vocal about their fears and disappointment,[14] often very aggressively.[15] On the Saturday following the announcement, I felt very personally affected by these criticisms, and I wrote a long email to the team where I noted that if we were able to tune out much of the noise, we could take note of the justified fears from our community which had been expressed at times clumsily: the members of our community had already experienced acquisitions of other beloved companies in the past, and feared that we would take advantage of our position to raise our prices, and stop providing free licences for students, and stop innovating; they were worried that we'd use only one business model (subscription, forgetting about perpetual licences), and that we'd abandon the Linux platform—essentially, that we would lose our soul within the big machine, now that our life had changed in this way.

14: We received a wave of unfiltered, extreme messages from social platforms such as Twitter.

15: This minority of animosity was the work of a few extreme individuals, and lasted for many months. We reasoned that people didn't like to see something they loved change; even so, this aggression was disturbing, particularly when it was outrageously unfounded and gratuitous, and aimed at specific team members. . . In any case, these messages gradually died down as we continued to release products, and uphold promises.

I told my team that we had to listen to these fears. We shouldn't let the unfounded criticisms discourage us, but rather we should use them as a tool. It was up to us to prove that we'd made the right choice, and that we'd continue evolving in the right direction.[16] We'd made this choice so that we could write the second volume in the tale of Allegorithmic, and that was exactly what we would do.

16: It's worth noting that as I write these lines, 4 years after the sale, we've kept every one of our commitments: we lowered rather than raised our prices, we still provide free licences for students, and we're innovating more than ever, with regular, major product releases, as well as adding new products to our range. We still have perpetual licences for our products, including for those that weren't yet available in our Allegorithmic days, and we still have Linux licences. We still have just as much passion for our work, and we fully intend to push things further than ever before.

42.8 A new home

The following weeks and months were entirely dedicated to our integration within the Adobe group, leading up to the internal announcement by Shantanu Narayen on March 15, 2019, to all of Adobe: Welcome Allegorithmic!

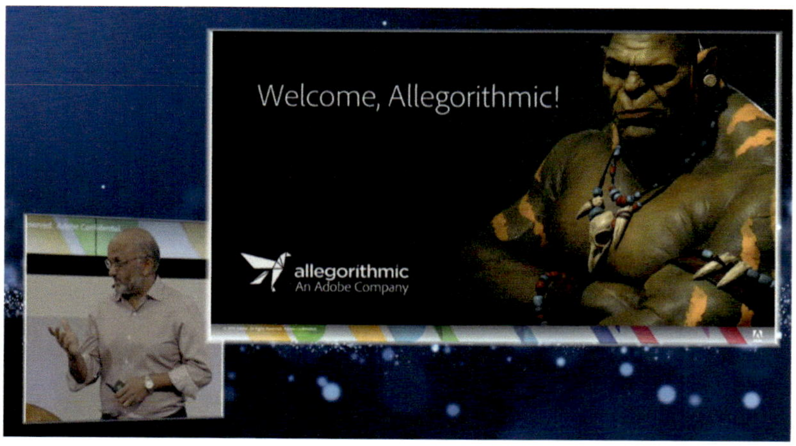

Figure 42.5: The internal announcement of Adobe's acquisition of Allegorithmic, by Shantanu Narayen, March 15, 2019. The announcement was made during an All-Hands, a virtual quarterly meeting for all Adobe employees.

43 Summary of progress up to the beginning of 2019, and conclusion of this period

The period from 2015 to the very beginning of 2019 was marked by great contrasts, from moments of relative calm, driven by a feeling of continuity and exhilarating progression, to moments of great change, of rapid evolution in the size of teams (see figures 43.1 and 43.2), with the challenges that this growth imposed on us (see Chapter 35), and even changes in shareholders, always a complex and exhausting event. We sometimes failed to get the timing of these changes quite right (see in particular Chapter 39).[1]

1: I admit sometimes navigating between relative boredom (during which everything was going smoothly, and I found myself impressed by the remarkable efficiency of the 'Allegorithmic machine,' but in which my work didn't completely fulfill my natural need for activity. . .) and periods of high-intensity stress, with 'moments of truth' that we typically only see a few of them in a lifetime (see Chapters 39 and 42 in particular).

Figure 43.1: By the end of 2018, Allegorithmic had around 140 employees scattered over several continents.

Figure 43.2: Mid-2018, the whole Allegorithmic team, during our Global Gathering in Lyon. There were 120 of us at that time. 20 more would join us in the coming 6 months.

In retrospect, however, I consider this period as the age of consecration for Allegorithmic and for its flagship products Substance Designer and Substance Painter (see Chapter 36 concerning the evolution of products, and for several competitions that each had a major impact, see chapters 37 and 41). Substance Painter in particular propelled the exponential development of the company, attracting customers and gaining recognition across a range of industries—game development,

DOI:10.1201/9781003534624-43

cinema, and the 'new markets' that we'd been seeking for several years, by then (see Chapter 33). With this tool, we'd successfully gambled on developing an entirely new software tool while the success of our first tool, Substance Designer, was not yet completely established, and while the need within our target industries had not yet been clearly articulated. The timing of definition and development, then the perfect execution of the teams, permitted us this incredible acceleration. Substance Painter, despite its young age, established itself during this period as a standard for 3D painting, particularly in the world of game development.

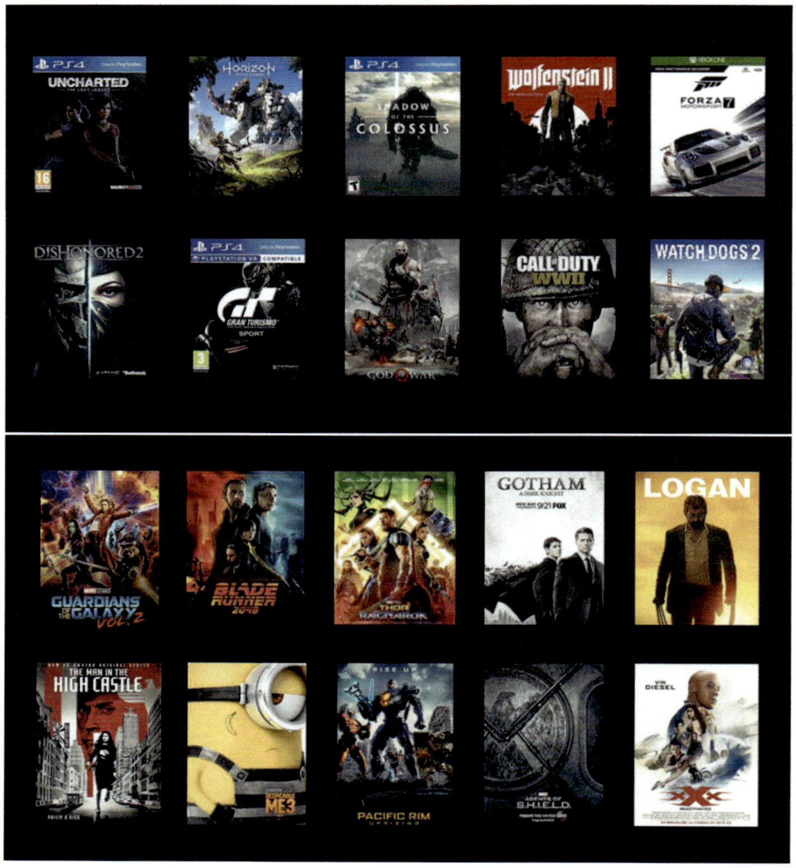

Figure 43.3: Top, some of the numerous games created with the help of Substance. At the end of this period, around 95% of 'AAA'-level games were created using our tools. Bottom, some films whose special effects were created with the help of Substance. Several won an Oscar for Best Special Effects, firmly establishing our tools in this universe as well.

Substance Designer in turn had established itself as the absolute reference for digital material creation everywhere it was used, and a new job had emerged: Substance Designer Artist! The 'Grand Masters' of Substance Designer (see Chapter 36) marked this period, actively participating in the redefinition of the texture creation pipeline. I also considered these creations of procedural materials using Substance Designer as part of a new artistic movement in its own right: it had its Grand Masters, and therefore its disciples, its creations of a new artistic type, its own methods and techniques, even its own dedicated hashtags...[2] It was with immense pride that all the members of Allegorithmic witnessed that, as had happened with the *Camera Obscura* in its time,[45] for instance, a tool that we'd created from scratch had allowed artists to breach new ground and have a profound impact on the world of digital art. Here again, things had come full circle.

2: We owe the hashtag #balls to the mischievous and particularly endearing Josh Lynch.

Building on our momentum and driven by both our own wishes and the needs that we identified in the market, we also launched the development

Figure 43.4: The evolution of our 'footprint' in the world of industrial design and architecture was exponential, as can be seen on these three lists of clients, between 2016 and 2018.

of numerous other projects, from Substance Source to Substance Alchemist, and even Substance Share, completing an ecosystem of products and services that was highly specialized around textures and materials, our niche of excellence—and a niche that we'd sufficiently expanded to make it a market in and of itself, one that hadn't existed a few years previously.

The success of the products then translated, thanks to the incredible work of our sales and marketing teams, and supported by our values and the strong structure that we quickly imposed on ourselves (see Chapter 35), into very good turnover growth (as we can see in figure 43.5, which I felt was the result of real recognition, both from users[3] and the industry at

3: I've always considered that this is one of the strongest indications of real success, essentially when a user 'votes' for you through the purchase of a license. The fact of paying, of purchasing a product, demonstrates in a tangible way that we'd created something that our customers appreciated, and considered sufficiently useful.

large wanting to work with us. We did this more and more via unique partnerships, brought about and brilliantly managed by our Special Projects team (see Chapter 35).

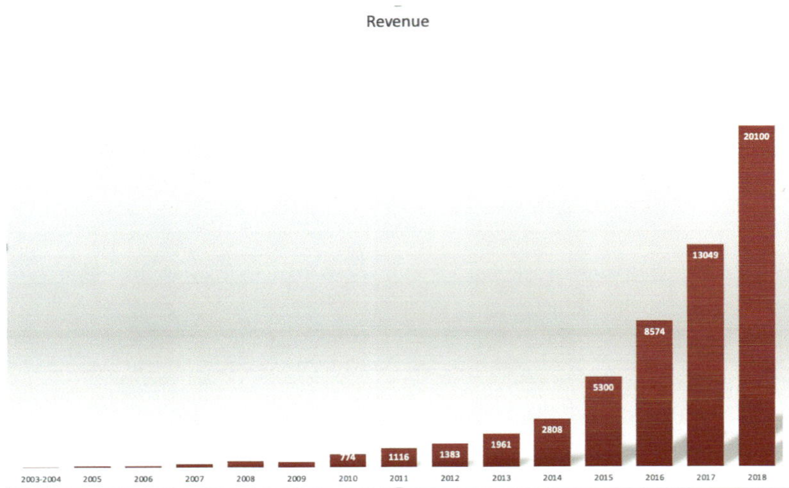

Figure 43.5: Allegorithmic's revenue, between 2003 and 2018. The exponential curve is established, and we reached a turnover of 20 million euros at the end of 2018.

Our size was becoming significant, and our success easily demonstrable;[4] a result of this was that we were not only working with significant companies in our own industry, but that we were being noticed by investors, stock markets, and local institutions (see figures 43.7 and 43.8). Allegorithmic was becoming both a local and national source of pride.

4: What could be more beautiful and meaningful than a game like *Uncharted 4* or a film like *Blade Runner 2049* to highlight the impact of our tools (see figure 43.3 which lists some of the major productions which used Substance tools in their development, and figure 43.4 which shows the evolution of our client portfolio in 'new markets' in just a few years)?

Two major events marked the end of the period. The first was an investment by Adobe in 2017 (see Chapter 39), and then, of course, the sale of Allegorithmic to Adobe in January 2019. This event clearly defined the end of one period and the start of another, this time within a creative software giant, which gave us the means to shape our destiny, allowing us to create an ambitious division centered on 3D within the group (see Chapter 42). This was the end of one period, and start of a new adventure. . .

Figure 43.6: My face on the cover of a specialized magazine, 3D Artist, in August 2017. It was the success of Allegorithmic and the Substance products that allowed us to be recognized by the 3D industry overall.

Figure 43.7: Allegorithmic was recognized by Business France in 2016, and was chosen as an ambassador company for France Créative (*"Creative France"*). Other laureates included Hélène Darroze, Philippe Starck, and the mathematician Cédric Villani. Being part of this panel was a huge compliment! The title chosen for Allegorithmic was "Créative Pigments" (with the accent on the 'e') and the accompanying image was created by Gaëtan Lassagne. The ceremony took place in London, and the award was presented by Muriel Pénicaud (center), president of Business France, who later became France's Minister of the Economy. I saw the posters for this event at St Pancras station in London as I was getting of the Eurostar; the surprise and pride I felt was remarkable.

Figure 43.8: For the 2018 edition of the Clermont-Ferrand International Short Film Festival, we made the decision to create a new prize alongside our friends at Sauve Qui Peut le Court Métrage, the association that organizes the event. The award was the *Prix des Effets Visuels Allegorithmic*, or "the Allegorithmic Visual Effects Award," in the festival's "Lab Competition." We have always been close to the event (several members of the team eagerly and passionately take part in the festival every year; Christophe Soum was even a member of the jury for the Lab Competition), and wanted to help the festival which had played an important role for Allegorithmic (for example, see margin note 6 in Chapter 10). Working from an idea by Nathalie Delfour, we worked with the artist Cathy Coureau to make a special 3D print of our MAT mascot, to create a unique, magnificent work of art. On the right, on February 2, 2018 Damien Climent presents the prize to the winner, an artist by the name of Rosto (who has sadly left us, since. . .) for the film *Reruns*.

Part IX

Conclusion and Postface(s)

Conclusion

Here, I begin to realize how foolish it was to try to define a 'formula for success'...[1]

Because, as I write this book's conclusion and reread the previous chapters, I realize how off the mark I was! Well, yes, we put in a lot of work at first—we can see this just by flipping through the many pages of this book, or even by counting the scars that remain. And of course, we had the talent, the intuition, the imagination, and a great ability of execution, which allowed us to produce major software which had a profound impact on the domain we were targeting, and the users we had dreamt of helping and supporting in their creative endeavors. And of course, luck was... decisive,[2] in particular during the moment when the industry pivoted toward PBR, which we were positioned to take advantage of (see Chapter 26). But what came out of this whole adventure, what remains and what in the end makes it either work or not is written between the lines in every chapter:[3] the real secret is resistance, stamina, resilience, grit. Never give up, always return without halting the attack, no matter what state you are in, or the outcome of previous attempts. Return again and again, try again and again. Then, and only then, the formula I've previously defined can come to life, and have an effect...

1: See note 4, in the margin of the Introduction to this book, in which I made an attempt to give a formula:

$$Success = Work \times Talent \times Luck.$$

2: Thanks to Valérie Buisson who suggested the French equivalent of this word, 'déterminant,' to me, as it related to determinism and the existential question that I'd asked myself (see Chapter 1) after the accident I'd experienced some time before that set me on the path that would lead me to create Allegorithmic.

3: And pointed out by many of my friends and members of Allegorithmic, such as Frédéric Kohler.

Because yes, this adventure is one of trials and errors, of failed attempts and changes of direction, of a journey of resilience, between the birth of the Allegorithmic project, the day after I defended my thesis on December 21, 2001, and 17 years later, the punctuation of an adventure that is protean in nature, but always driven by the same passion.

At first, an incubation period, between 2002 and mid-2003, during which the project was defined, the name Allegorithmic found and chosen, with its unique logo (see Chapter 6), during which the first Business Plan was drafted, which was wrong from the moment its last line was written, but which pushed us to ask the right questions and allowed us to define a direction, desires, and above all, needs. Human needs in particular, the need for partners, and for the backbones of teams, people like Christophe Soum, whom I noticed while he was still a student and thanks to whom I could start out in confidence, as he possessed immense talent and we were impatient to see what we could create together.

Then came the launch period, between 2003 and 2007, the first years of the company that we'd finally created, the first interactions with the 3D industry that we were so passionate about, the search for our first clients and our first product, which would take several forms before solidifying. It was a period of relentless development, a largely fruitless search for Product Market Fit, yet one marked by some fundamental successes, in particular with ProFX and the game *RoboBlitz* (see Chapter 13). During this whole period, our products were still embryonic, but our technology was intriguing and our team impressive. Our first clients didn't buy a solution, but a promise, and the contracts we had signed were above all contracts of trust.

Following that, the period between 2007 and 2011 was a difficult period for Allegorithmic. It was the weak point of the adventure, the moment of severe financial difficulties, and the need for help and institutional support. The world itself was impacted by a major financial crisis, and the task to search for investors was largely in vain: who would bet on a company from Clermont-Ferrand that hadn't yet generated any revenue, promoting a complex technology, some deep tech before it had even became an investment category as such, and that sold everything for export at the time of the biggest international crisis since the beginning of the previous century? Even here, the trust acquired during the previous period allowed us to find one of our first investors in the form of Dassault Systèmes, and in Pascal Daloz, a mentor for me. This strategic investor, one of the most widespread software publishers in the world, allowed us not only to accelerate our development but to complete the next round of investments more easily, because of its support and respectability.

The next period, between 2011 and 2015, marked a distinct contrast with this difficult time and would represent Allegorithmic's golden age, where our sales exploded and brought us major success in the world of video games, thanks to the cumulative effect of the time we'd had to refine our technology over the first phases of Allegorithmic's life, and to the giant pivot of the video game industry toward physically based rendering (PBR, see Chapter 26), which suddenly positioned us at the center of new technological needs for PBR texture production, and the trust (once again the trust. . .) granted to us by Naughty Dog, with whom we finished developing Substance Designer (see Chapter 27), which would fulfill the needs of the industry on a larger scale and establish itself as an absolute reference within development studios. During this period, Substance Designer became a must-have which we sold with exponential success, notably thanks to the drive of Alexis Khouri, who took Allegorithmic from a technological company to a real publisher of successful graphics software. This period also saw us take our biggest risk since the conception of the company—at the moment when Substance Designer was just beginning to achieve commercial success, we decided to develop *another product*, Substance Painter! This, simultaneously a success of vision, execution and time-to-market, would ultimately take over from the success of Substance Designer and would establish itself in turn as an absolute reference, because of its technical innovations and because it made certain parts of 3D work *fun*, something that hadn't previously been seen, particularly in the world of texturing.

The period from 2015 to the beginning of 2019, finally, marked a sort of consecration for Allegorithmic. A period during which our products continued to achieve great success within our core market areas, such as video games, but also began to establish themselves elsewhere, in the sectors of special effects and even product design. The company expanded greatly while still maintaining its fundamental principles, namely sound management and profitability, which allowed us to exist without too much debt, and to move forward with our own plans. Allegorithmic and the Substance products were establishing themselves everywhere, without conflict, providing additional value while respecting our users and developing all the while a company culture to which we were all attached (see Chapter 35).

This is, summarized very briefly and I hope *with substance*, Allegorithmic's journey over these 17 years, on this adventure that represents a point of absolute pride for me. From the first minute of dream and inspiration in December 2001 to a company full of life and tangible success by the end of 2018. From the very first ideas written down on scrap paper (with the name "Allegorithmic" hastily scribbled somewhere) to X-TAON, the Allegorithmic car. From our first fundamental contacts, Sébastien Rubens and Albert Benassi to the 140 employees at the moment of creation of the 3D division at Adobe.

This conclusion and this book will never be enough, as the truth, perhaps the most essential truth, is also present in everything I have not written. All these long periods, these non-events, these moments of calm, these initial indications, these questions, these failures, these small wins, these immense joys and other existential concerns, resolved immediately or left hanging on indefinitely, ultimately consumed by the immune system of the giant organism that is the company and the market. . . It is within all of this too that we can see the story of Allegorithmic. And all of this was written not only here and now by me alone, but over 17 years at the time of writing, in over 140 different places, by all of us who built everything, together.

Postface 1

At the start of 2023, twenty years after the official creation of the company, what better way for things to come full circle than with this Technical Achievement Award, that the Academy of Motion Picture Arts and Sciences[1] decided to present to Christophe Soum, Sylvain Paris, Nicolas Wirrmann and myself,[2] for the development of the 'Substance system,' and the software Substance Designer [69].

Figure 43.9: The 95th Oscars ceremony took place on February 24, 2023. Image courtesy of AMPAS.

This award, which is given each year to a few people after long investigative work carried out by specialized Academy committees, recognized the significant impact that Substance Designer and Substance Engine have had in the production of a large number of films,[71] over many years, enabling legendary special effects companies like ILM, Framestore, DNEG, and even major animation studios like Pixar and Disney, to produce ever more advanced visual effects and 3D animated films. Substance Designer, for example, was used by these companies in the creation of visual masterpieces such as *Star Wars: The Rise of Skywalker*,[72] *Dune*, *Blade Runner 2049*,[73] *Pacific Rim*, *Alita: Battle Angel*,[74] *Frozen 2*,[75] *Abominable*, *Encanto*, *Lightyear*, and many more.

A striking example is *Star Wars: The Rise of Skywalker*, for which ILM used the power of Substance Designer and Substance Engine to create all the textures of the iconic scene in which Rey, the film's heroine, visits the remains of the Death Star, crashed on a planet after its destruction. The wreckage is gigantic, and only a procedural tool like Substance Designer, accompanied by the Substance Automation Toolkit[3] could make it possible to create the huge number of textures necessary to represent the scene, all the while permitting studios to maintain a maximum level of artistic control.

The satisfaction, shared by everyone within the team, of seeing our tools help create the most striking visual effects of recent years, was in itself immense. Coupled with that, the knowledge that all of our work was now officially recognized by the Academy as having significantly shaped the field of cinema throughout so many years was simply extraordinary.

From a personal point of view, obtaining such recognition from the Academy represented, of course, a notable achievement. Cinema has always been a passion for me; as mentioned elsewhere, I even tried to join a film directing school before starting my doctoral thesis (see Chapter 2). I have always been fascinated by visual effects (see for example Chapter 10), and I had perceived, while still teaching, that my work could potentially bring something to the major tools of the time, in particular Softimage 3D (see Chapter 4), which led me to create Allegorithmic shortly thereafter... My primary objective with this company was from the beginning to develop and sell tools for 3D artists which produced digital images to support the unbridled imagination of the directors whom I have always admired (see Chapter 5).

And so with this award, I truly came full circle, and I feel that I can close this book on Allegorithmic—which I hope has been enjoyable to read—on this magnificent note which is shared with all the team. And

1: Responsible in particular for awarding the Oscars that we all know (for best director, best actor, etc.), but also, and this is less well known, the various 'Sci-Tech Awards' awarded to those people recognized by this same Academy as having significantly impacted the art and science of cinema over a significant period of time. The Sci-Tech Awards focus on scientific contributions to the world of cinema.

2: I should immediately clarify that, although the Academy stipulates that only a very limited number of people can actually receive the award, this award is obviously shared by the entire Allegorithmic team, because it validates the impact of the Substance Designer tool and the Substance procedural texturing ecosystem (whose cornerstone is Substance Engine) as a whole, throughout their years of existence. The number of people who have been involved in the conception, design, implementation, and then the marketing and sales of the tool (and beyond, all the support functions that make up a company) is much broader than just the four people named here.

3: Which encapsulates Substance Engine.

Figure 43.10: February 24, 2023, Christophe Soum, Sylvain Paris, Nicolas Wirrmann and I received a Scientific and Technical Award, granted by the Academy of Motion Picture Arts and Sciences, for Substance Designer. The video of the Award ceremony can be seen here: [70]. Images courtesy of AMPAS.

as head of this team, I feel it's fair to say that our work together has been well . . . *directed*.

Postface 2

Throughout this book, we've witnessed how Substance Painter has cemented its place as a vital tool in the production pipelines of video games, extending its influence into the realms of VFX and animation. With deep pride and a sense of fulfillment, I share this incredible news while finishing the work on the English translation of this book, originally witten in French: at the end of October 2024, Allegorithmic is set to be honored once again—this time with a prestigious Engineering, Science and Technology Emmy Award for Substance Painter [76].

Figure 43.11: Substance Painter is awarded a Engineering, Science and Technology Emmy Award! Bottom: at the ceremony in Los Angeles, October 23, 2024. From left to right: François Cottin, Alexandre Chassany, Jérémie Noguer, Cédric Marchessoux, myself and Alexis Khouri.

This accolade, in time for the 10 years anniversary of Substance Painter, is a powerful recognition of the remarkable impact the tool has had on the visual effects in numerous TV series over the past decade. The list of productions that have embraced Substance Painter is extensive, including titles like Game of Thrones (VFX by Scanline VFX), The Expanse (VFX by Spin VFX), Halo (VFX by Pixomondo and MPC), The Man Who Fell To Earth (VFX by Cinesite VFX), The Wheel Of Time (VFX by Cinesite VFX), Star Trek Discovery (VFX by Pixomondo), Love, Death and Robots (VFX by Blur Studios), among many, many more...

This recognition transcends mere technical achievement; it is a tribute to the countless hours of dedication, passion, and innovation by the Allegorithmic team. From its early experimental days to becoming a cornerstone in the workflows of leading VFX studios around the globe, the journey of Substance Painter—and Allegorithmic itself—has been marked by creativity, determination, and a profound influence on the world of digital art. The Engineering, Science and Technology Emmy Award is not just a milestone; it is a celebration of a collective vision realized, driven by a deep love for digital creation.

A heartfelt thank you to the Television Academy for this incredible honor. To the Allegorithmic team—thank you, again and again, for your relentless hard work and unwavering commitment. And to the community of 3D artists who inspire us daily—thank you for being our constant source of motivation and inspiration.

References

References, in citation order.

[1] Wikipedia. *Demoscene*. https://en.wikipedia.org/wiki/Demoscene (cit. on p. 6).

[2] Mentasm. *Gonzo*. http://janeway.exotica.org.uk/author.php?id=9545 (cit. on p. 6).

[3] J.P. Delahaye. *Jeux mathématiques et mathématiques des jeux*. Bibliothèque Pour la science. ISBN: 9782842450106. Belin / Pour la science, 1998 (cit. on p. 6).

[4] Sébastien Deguy. *Read My Lips (Part 1: Propaganda)*. https://youtu.be/IZnaWH_x3ls (cit. on p. 8).

[5] Sébastien Deguy. *Read My Lips (Part 2: Tarzagandawombat)*. https://youtu.be/G4BEcSNWV-U (cit. on p. 8).

[6] Sébastien Deguy. *Attack Of The Giant Oyster*. https://youtu.be/_FmQrHsp1Nw (cit. on p. 8).

[7] Sébastien Deguy. *Flying Oyster Circus*. https://youtu.be/zhXMA8J4ZlY (cit. on p. 8).

[8] Sébastien Deguy. *Oyster Invasion*. https://youtu.be/wk9xjZv35lk (cit. on p. 8).

[9] Sébastien Deguy and Albert Benassi. "A Flexible Noise Model For Designing Maps". In: *6th International Fall Workshop on Vision, Modeling, and Visualization, VMV 2001, Stuttgart, Germany, November 21-23, 2001*. Ed. by Thomas Ertl et al. Aka GmbH, 2001, pp. 299–308 (cit. on p. 18).

[10] Sébastien Deguy and Albert Benassi. "La cartothèque de Babel, un modèle de milieux complexes pour la génération de cartes de déformation". In: *14èmes Journées de l'AFIG, 2001, Limoges, France, November 28-30, 2001*. AFIG, 2001, pp. 199–213 (cit. on pp. 18, 25, 26).

[11] Wikipedia. *Serial Experiment Lain*. https://en.wikipedia.org/wiki/Serial_Experiments_Lain (cit. on p. 22).

[12] Simon Gibson and Paul E. Debevec, eds. *Proceedings of the 13th Eurographics Workshop on Rendering Techniques, Pisa, Italy, June 26-28, 2002*. Vol. 28. ACM International Conference Proceeding Series. ISBN: 1-58113-534-3. Eurographics Association, 2002 (cit. on p. 43).

[13] Wikipedia. *Displacement Mapping*. https://en.wikipedia.org/wiki/Displacement_mapping (cit. on p. 63).

[14] Wikipedia. *Bump Mapping*. https://en.wikipedia.org/wiki/Bump_mapping (cit. on p. 63).

[15] Wikipedia. *Autodesk 3DS Max*. https://en.wikipedia.org/wiki/Autodesk_3ds_Max (cit. on p. 67).

[16] Wikipedia. *Shader*. https://en.wikipedia.org/wiki/Shader (cit. on p. 73).

[17] Pierre Hénon. *Une histoire française de l'animation numérique*. ISBN: 978-2-905710-96-3. 2018 (cit. on p. 77).

[18] Wikipedia. *Gonzo*. https://en.wikipedia.org/wiki/Gonzo_(company) (cit. on p. 82).

[19] Wikipedia. *Machinima*. https://en.wikipedia.org/wiki/Machinima (cit. on p. 91).

[20] Luxology Allegorithmic. *Luxology imageSynth plugin for Photoshop*. https://www.ephotozine.com/article/luxology-imagesynth-plugin-for-photoshop-3369 (cit. on p. 94).

[21] Wikipedia. *Dave Taylor*. https://en.wikipedia.org/wiki/Dave_Taylor_(game_programmer) (cit. on p. 95).

[22] Wikipedia. *RoboBlitz*. https://en.m.wikipedia.org/wiki/RoboBlitz (cit. on p. 97).

[23] Allegorithmic. *Bathroom Tech Demo (Part 1)*. https://youtu.be/tOnbHMwCgd4 (cit. on p. 109).

[24] Allegorithmic. *Bathroom Tech Demo (Part 2)*. https://youtu.be/xlG5597nhR8 (cit. on p. 109).

[25] Allegorithmic. *Bayou Tech Demo*. https://youtu.be/rCpwAokxgSk (cit. on p. 112).

[26] 3DVF. *HUGH – Court-métrage ESMA*. https://3dvf.com/redaction/dossier-54-hugh-court-metrage-esma-html/3/ (cit. on p. 135).

[27] Chris Anderson. *The long tail: why the future of business is selling less of more*. ISBN: 9781401309664 1401309666. New York: Hyperion, 2008 (cit. on p. 146).

[28] Eric Caoili. *Acony Using ProFX For Free-To-Play MMO Parabellum*. https://www.gamasutra.com/view/news/112275/Acony_Using_ProFX_For_FreeToPlay_MMO_Parabellum.php (cit. on p. 151).

[29] GamesIndustry International. *Substance Redux - New texture-squashing tool unveiled at GDC*. https://www.gamesindustry.biz/amp/substance-redux-new-texture-squashing-tool-unveiled-at-gdc (cit. on p. 151).

[30] Wikipedia. *Visual Programming Language*. https://en.wikipedia.org/wiki/Visual_programming_language (cit. on p. 159).

[31] Allegorithmic. *Namacius Tech Demo*. https://youtu.be/pNtqp_4if5g (cit. on p. 167).

[32] Allegorithmic. *Namacius Tech Demo Making Of*. https://youtu.be/_Bm-8wqF5Kw (cit. on p. 167).

[33] Geoffrey A. Moore. *Crossing The Chasm : Marketing and Selling Technology Project*. ISBN: 9780061795862, 0061795860. HarperCollins, 2009 (cit. on pp. 185, 285).

[34] NoLife. *Cédric Littardi*. https://youtu.be/dyT1dUVrhrc (cit. on p. 192).

[35] Naty Hoffman. *Crafting Physically Motivated Shading Models for Game Development*. https://renderwonk.com/publications/s2010-shading-course/hoffman/s2010_physically_based_shading_hoffman_b.pdf. 2010 (cit. on p. 205).

[36] Ubisoft. *Assassin's Ceed Unity Art Dump*. https://polycount.com/discussion/144111/art-dump-assassins-creed-unity/p1 (cit. on p. 206).

[37] Allegorithmic. *Substance Painter Launch*. https://youtu.be/GChCFtm_Hts (cit. on p. 239).

[38] Xpec Allegorithmic. *Atlantis Tech Demo*. https://youtu.be/gpkhZzE8GPo (cit. on p. 250).

[39] Polycount. *Polycount - The Throne Room Contest*. https://polycount.com/categories/allegorithmics-the-throne-room (cit. on p. 267).

[40] Tom Rath. *Strength Finder 2.0*. ISBN: 978-1-59562-015-6. Gallup Press, 2007 (cit. on p. 285).

[41] Daniel H. Pink. *Drive: the surprising truth about what motivates us*. ISBN: 9781847678881 1847678882. Edinburgh: Canongate, 2010 (cit. on p. 285).

[42] A. McAfee and E. Brynjolfsson. *Machine, Platform, Crowd: Harnessing Our Digital Future*. LLCN: 2017016682. W.W. Norton, 2017 (cit. on p. 285).

[43] Clayton M. Christensen, Michael Raynor, and Rory McDonald. "What Is Disruptive Innovation?" In: Harvard Business Review 93.12 (2015), pp. 44–53 (cit. on p. 285).

[44] Kevin Werbach and Dan Hunter. *For The win: How Game Thinking Can Revolutionize Your Business*. ISBN: 9781613630235, 1613630239. Wharton Digital Press, 2012 (cit. on p. 285).

[45] David Hockney. *Secret Knowledge: Rediscovering the Lost Techniques of the Old Masters*. ISBN: 9780500286388, 0500286388. Thames and Hudson, 2006 (cit. on pp. 285, 408).

[46] Gordon MacKenzie. *Orbiting the Giant Hairball: A Corporate Fool's Guide to Surviving with Grace*. ISBN: 978-0670879830. Viking, 1998 (cit. on p. 297).

[47] Bradford Smith. *Brad Smith's portfolio*. https://bradfolio.artstation.com/ (cit. on p. 321).

[48] Joshua Lynch. *Josh Lynch's portfolio*. https://joshlynch.artstation.com/ (cit. on p. 321).

[49] Daniel Thiger. *Daniel Thiger's portfolio*. https://dete.artstation.com/ (cit. on p. 321).

[50] Jonathan Benainous. *Jonathan Benainous's portfolio*. https://jonathan_benainous.artstation.com/ (cit. on p. 321).

[51] Christophe Desse. *Christophe Desse's portfolio*. https://christophe-desse.artstation.com/ (cit. on p. 321).

[52] Rogelio Olguin. *Rogelio Olguin's portfolio*. https://rogelio.artstation.com/ (cit. on p. 321).

[53] Javier Perez. *Javier Perez's portfolio*. https://meshmodeler.com/ (cit. on p. 321).

[54] Emrecan Cubukcu. *Emrecan Cubukcu's portfolio.* https://emrecancubukcu.artstation.com/ (cit. on p. 321).

[55] Mark Foreman. *MarkForeman's portfolio.* https://oggyart.artstation.com/ (cit. on p. 321).

[56] Pauline Boiteux. *Pauline Boiteux's portfolio.* https://jappluz.artstation.com/ (cit. on p. 321).

[57] Zhelong Xu. *Zhelong Xu's portfolio.* https://www.artstation.com/zhelong (cit. on p. 337).

[58] Anthony Salvi. *Your smartphone is a material scanner.* https://substance3d.adobe.com/tutorials/courses/Your-smartphone-is-a-material-scanner. 2016 (cit. on p. 343).

[59] Allegorithmic. *Substance Alchemist Launch.* https://www.youtube.com/watch?v=x8zE8hvP23I (cit. on p. 343).

[60] Artoyz. *Léo'z.* https://artoyz.com/en/collections/leo-z (cit. on p. 349).

[61] Damien Lefauve. *La mascotte Meet MAT, par Damien Lefauvre.* https://damienlevaufre.artstation.com/projects/r4A4G (cit. on p. 349).

[62] Allegorithmic. *The Meet MAT 3D Painting Contest Winners Are.* https://store.substance3d.com/blog/meet-mat-3d-painting-contest-and-winners-are. 2017 (cit. on p. 350).

[63] Allegorithmic. *Meet MAT: The Art Book of the 3D Painting Contest.* ISBN: 978-2490071036. 2019. 350 pp. (cit. on p. 351).

[64] Allegorithmic. *Yechawood: The Art of Zhelong Xu.* ISBN: 978-2490071029. 2019. 204 pp. (cit. on p. 362).

[65] Allegorithmic. *X-TAON Art Car Contest: The Winners Are.* https://substance3d.adobe.com/magazine/x-taon-art-car-texturing-contest-and-winners-are/. 2019 (cit. on p. 393).

[66] Allegorithmic and Onur Dursun. *Onur Dursun Reinvents The X-TAON Showcar.* https://substance3d.adobe.com/magazine/onur-dursun-reinvents-the-x-taon-showcar/. 2019 (cit. on p. 393).

[67] Allegorithmic and Ronan Mahon. *Onur Dursun Reinvents The X-TAON Showcar.* https://substance3d.adobe.com/magazine/onur-dursun-reinvents-the-x-taon-showcar/. 2019 (cit. on p. 393).

[68] Sébastien Deguy. *My Peter Jackson Moment.* https://medium.com/@sebastien.deguy/https-medium-com-sebastien-deguy-my-peter-jackson-moment-7dd64ba1d1f1. 2019 (cit. on p. 405).

[69] Academy of Motion Pictures Art and Science. *8 Scientific And Technical Achievements To Be Honored With Academy Awards®.* https://press.oscars.org/news/8-scientific-and-technical-achievements-be-honored-academy-awardsr (cit. on p. 419).

[70] Academy of Motion Pictures Art and Science. *2023 Sci-Tech Awards: Sébastien Deguy, Christophe Soum, Sylvain Paris and Nicolas Wirrmann.* https://youtu.be/CdszmAGgpXs (cit. on p. 420).

[71] Adobe. *8 Scientific And Technical Achievements To Be Honored With Academy Awards®.* https://blog.adobe.com/en/publish/2023/02/24/academy-award-recognizes-substance-3d-for-transforming-movie-visual-effect-animation (cit. on p. 419).

[72] Allegorithmic. *Star Wars: Episode IX – ILM uses the Force of Substance.* https://substance3d.adobe.com/magazine/star-wars-episode-ix-ilm-uses-the-force-of-substance/ (cit. on p. 419).

[73] Allegorithmic. *Blade Runner 2049's Oscar-winning Texturing Workflow at Framestore.* https://substance3d.adobe.com/magazine/blade-runner-2049s-oscar-winning-texturing-workflow-at-framestore/ (cit. on p. 419).

[74] Allegorithmic. *Alita: Battle Angel – Texturing a Cyberpunk Future with DNEG Vancouver and Mumbai.* https://substance3d.adobe.com/magazine/alita-battle-angel-texturing-cyberpunk-future-dneg-vancouver-and-mumbai/ (cit. on p. 419).

[75] Allegorithmic. *The Highly Stylized World of Frozen 2.* https://substance3d.adobe.com/magazine/the-highly-stylized-world-of-frozen-2/ (cit. on p. 419).

[76] Television Academy's Engineering Emmy Awards Committee. *Engineering, Science and Technology Emmy Awards.* https://www.emmys.com/awards/emmys/engineering-emmys (cit. on p. 421).

Index

For Product Safety Concerns and Information please contact our EU representative GPSR@taylorandfrancis.com Taylor & Francis Verlag GmbH, Kaufingerstraße 24, 80331 München, Germany